# THE CHALLENGE OF THE LEFT OPPOSITION
## (1928–29)

# THE CHALLENGE OF THE
# LEFT OPPOSITION
# (1928–29)

by Leon Trotsky

**PATHFINDER**

New York    London    Montreal    Sydney

Edited with an introduction by Naomi Allen

Copyright © 1981 by Pathfinder Press

ISBN 0-87348-616-1 paper; ISBN 0-87348-615-3 cloth
Library of Congress Catalog Card Number 75-2714

Manufactured in the United States of America

First edition, 1981
Third printing, 1998

## Pathfinder

410 West Street, New York, NY 10014, U.S.A.
Fax: (212) 727-0150 • CompuServe: 73321,414
Internet: pathfinder@igc.apc.org

PATHFINDER DISTRIBUTORS AROUND THE WORLD:
Australia (and Asia and the Pacific):
    Pathfinder, 19 Terry St., Surry Hills, Sydney, N.S.W. 2010
    Postal address: P.O. Box K879, Haymarket, N.S.W. 1240
Canada:
    Pathfinder, 851 Bloor St. West, Toronto, ON, M6G 1M3
Iceland:
    Pathfinder, Klapparstíg 26, 2d floor, 101 Reykjavík
    Postal address: P. Box 233, 121 Reykjavík
New Zealand:
    Pathfinder, La Gonda Arcade, 203 Karangahape Road, Auckland
    Postal address: P.O. Box 8730, Auckland
Sweden:
    Pathfinder, Vikingagatan 10, S-113 42, Stockholm
United Kingdom (and Europe, Africa except South Africa, and Middle East):
    Pathfinder, 47 The Cut, London, SE1 8LL
United States (and Caribbean, Latin America, and South Africa):
    Pathfinder, 410 West Street, New York, NY 10014

# CONTENTS

*Note About the Author*                                             9
*Preface*                                                          11
*Introduction*                                                     15

Appeal of the Deportees                                            29
Problems of the International Opposition (Two Letters)             38
The International Factor                                            46
To a Few Exiled Friends                                            50
'Pravda' Sounds the Alarm                                          54
A Pair of Sancho Panzas                                            60
Pyatakov: A Politically Finished Man                               64
Our Correspondents                                                 67
The Relation of Criticism to Support                               70
Letter to Ryazanov                                                 72
We Cannot Follow a Short-Range Policy                              75
Conditions in Alma-Ata                                             82
The General Outline of My Work                                     85
The Opposition's Errors—Real and Alleged                           87
Preobrazhensky's Proposal                                         101
Portrait of a Capitulator                                         104
The Methods of Leadership                                         109
Rumors from Moscow                                                120
A Crudely Empirical Turn                                          127
Declaration to the Sixth Comintern Congress                      132
What to Expect from the Sixth Congress                           151
Radek's Theses                                                    157
The July Plenum and the Right Danger                             166
The Conflicts Are Still Ahead                                    176
The Law of Zigzags Remains in Force                              179
Who Is Leading the Comintern Today?                              182
Remarks After the Sixth Congress                                 212
Max Eastman: A Friend of the October Revolution                  221
A Heart-to-Heart Talk with a Well-meaning Party Member           225
The Sixth Congress and the Opposition's Tasks                    250
No Political Concessions to Conciliationist Moods                265
Analogies with Thermidor                                         268
The Danger of Bonapartism and the Opposition's Role              270
How to Criticize the Centrists                                   286
An Ultraleft Caricature of Stalin                                290
Our Differences with the Democratic Centralists                  292
Crisis in the Right-Center Bloc                                  301
On the Topics of the Day                                         336

Too Conciliatory a Line?                                          344
Marxism and the Relation Between
   Proletarian and Peasant Revolution                           347
What Is the 'Smychka'?                                            352
Reply to an Ultimatum                                            361
Reply to Two Conciliators                                        367
Protest Against Deportation                                      373
Message on Arriving in Constantinople                            375


*Appendix A: Bukharin-Kamenev Meeting*                           377
*Appendix B: Philosophical Tendencies of Bureaucratism*          389
*Appendix C: Summary of Charges Against Trotsky*                 410
*Glossary*                                                       411
*Further Reading*                                                427
*Index*                                                          429

LEON TROTSKY was born Lev Davidovich Bronstein in 1879 in the Ukraine. His first arrest for revolutionary activity was in 1898. He was exiled to Siberia, but escaped to collaborate with Lenin on *Iskra* in London in 1902. He broke with Lenin the following year at the time of the split between Bolsheviks and Mensheviks, was briefly aligned with the Mensheviks, but in 1904 broke with them and began a decade-long effort to reunite the Russian Social Democratic Labor Party. During the 1905 revolution he was the leader of the St. Petersburg Soviet and developed his theory of permanent revolution. He was again exiled to Siberia and again escaped. He was part of the tiny minority in the socialist movement who refused to support their governments in World War I. When the February revolution broke out in 1917 he was in New York, but he arrived back in Russia in May, joined the Bolshevik Party, was elected to its Central Committee, and in October was the leader of the Petrograd Soviet and the chief organizer of the Bolshevik insurrection. As the first commissar of foreign affairs, he headed the Soviet delegation to negotiate a peace with Germany at Brest-Litovsk. As commissar of war (1918-25) he created the Red Army and led it to victory through three years of civil war and imperialist intervention. He was a member of the Politburo of the Russian Communist Party from its formation until 1926, and of the Executive Committee of the Communist International from 1920 to 1927. He formed the Left Opposition in 1923 to fight for the preservation of Leninist internationalism and proletarian democracy. Defeated by the Stalin faction, he was expelled from the party in 1927, exiled first to Alma-Ata in 1928 and then to Turkey in 1929. In 1933 he abandoned his efforts to reform the Communist International and called for the creation of a new International. He viewed his work on behalf of the Fourth International, founded in 1938, as the most important work of his life. In his final exile he was hounded from country to country by both the Stalinists and the fascists. He lived in Turkey until 1933, France until 1935, Norway until 1936, and Mexico until his death in August 1940 at the hands of a Stalinist assassin.

# PREFACE

This is the third and final volume of Leon Trotsky's writings devoted to the Soviet Left Opposition in the years 1923-29. The first volume (1923-25) covered the beginnings of the Stalin-Zinoviev-Kamenev bloc (the "triumvirate") and the formation of the Left Opposition in the All-Union Communist Party (AUCP), following the defeat of the 1923 German revolution; the Opposition's support of Lenin's proposals to restore workers' democracy within the party and state, to promote rapid industrialization and economic planning, stem the growth of bureaucratism, and counter Stalin's self-serving perversion of party history and distortion of Lenin's views.

The second volume (1926-27), which began after the break-up of the triumvirate, opened with the formation of the United Opposition between Trotsky's Left Opposition and the Leningrad Opposition of Grigory Zinoviev and Leon Kamenev. By this time the economic situation had become critical, due largely to policies of the Political Bureau (Politburo) that favored the wealthy peasants over the poor peasants and urban and rural workers. The defeats of a developing prerevolutionary situation in Britain and an actual revolution in China had vindicated the Opposition's criticisms of the Comintern's international policy for all who cared to see. Thus, in addition to the issues of party democracy and the rate of industrialization, the Opposition used the lessons of the Anglo-Russian Committee and the Chinese revolution to show how Joseph Stalin and his allies and supporters in the leadership were overturning the Leninist policy of proletarian internationalism under cover of the "theory" of "socialism in one country." By the end of 1927 the United Opposition bloc had been expelled from the party and had split, the Zinovievist leaders capitulating to Stalin and the Trotskyists, maintaining their opposition to bureaucratism, about to be deported to exile colonies throughout Siberia and Central Asia.

Most of the contents of the present volume were written by Trotsky in Alma-Ata, Kazakhstan, where he arrived on January 25, 1928, accompanied by his wife, Natalya Ivanovna, and their

11

elder son, Leon Sedov (Lyova). Their younger son, Sergei (Seryozha), joined them for a short visit in the spring. This year was marked by a "left turn" by Stalin. In response to a new crisis in grain deliveries, the Politburo authorized "extraordinary measures"—requisitioning reminiscent of war communism—to collect grain from the peasants. There were new capitulations by sections of the Opposition who mistook Stalin's "left turn" for a genuine proletarian course; a controversy within the Opposition over Trotsky's proposal to give "critical support" to every bona fide progressive move by Stalin; the beginnings of a split between the party's center, led by Stalin, and its right wing, led by Nikolai Bukharin, and a campaign of phony "self-criticism" and scape-goat trials designed to discredit and undermine Bukharin's supporters. The Sixth World Congress of the Comintern, held in the summer, initiated the "third period" policies that were to hobble the Communist movement for six years. Within the exile colonies, the debate with the Democratic Centralist current over Thermidor and the need for a second party continued; and there was renewed debate within the Opposition over the validity of Trotsky's theory of permanent revolution, and discussion of the possibility of a bloc with the Bukharinist right wing to restore inner-party democracy.

These lively political exchanges were abruptly halted when Trotsky was declared guilty of counterrevolutionary activities and forcibly deported to Turkey. All of his published writings from then until his murder in 1940 by a Stalinist agent in Mexico, and much that was never published during his lifetime, are in the *Writings of Leon Trotsky (1929-40),* a twelve-volume series with a two-part supplement, and in several other volumes arranged by theme (see "Books and Pamphlets by Leon Trotsky" at the end of this volume).

Shortly after arriving in Alma-Ata, Trotsky initiated a correspondence, which became enormous, with Oppositionists in exile colonies throughout the Soviet Union. That correspondence forms the backbone of this volume. Many of his letters were intended to be circulated from hand to hand. These so-called "circular letters," which were often sent out in multiple copies and which frequently reached dozens of Oppositionists, served as discussion articles or position statements for the exiles. They may have been cloaked in letter form to evade or lighten the heavy-handed postal censorship inflicted upon the Opposition. In later years, Trotsky was apparently considering a collection of these letters for publication; and at some time before he sold his archives to

Harvard University in 1940 he went through the 1928 correspondence and selected some, which he numbered "AA" (Alma-Ata) 1-46, for possible publication. The choices for the present volume are based in part on his selection.

Trotsky's major work of the year 1928 was his book-length "Criticism of the Draft Program of the Communist International," prepared for the Sixth World Congress of the Comintern, which met in Moscow in July-September 1928. That and his long letter to the congress, entitled "What Now?" are not included here because they are in print in *The Third International After Lenin* (New York: Pathfinder, 1972), in a translation by John G. Wright. A list of other writings of this period and a glossary are in the back of this book.

Only about one-fifth of the contents of this volume have been published before in English, mostly by Trotsky's cothinkers in the United States. They were published in newspapers or magazines of the 1920s, 30s, or 40s and, with the exception of two short items, none has been in print for decades.

An editorial note preceding each selection explains its source and gives other information about the events mentioned in it. All translations from French have been checked against the Russian original for accuracy and stylistic consistency. Translations that were already in English in *The Militant, Fourth International,* or *New International* have likewise been checked and partly revised against the original Russian. Wherever possible, we have replaced Trotsky's citations of Russian texts with references to the standard English translation: in the case of Lenin, all references are to the English edition of his *Collected Works* (Moscow: Progress, 1960-69). Stalin's *Works* (Moscow: Foreign Languages, 1952-55) have also been used.

Of great help in compiling this volume was Louis Sinclair's *Leon Trotsky: A Bibliography* (Hoover Institution Press, 1972). This project could not have been successful without the kind permission of the Harvard College Library and the Library of Social History to examine, translate, and publish material in their collections.

The Editors

# INTRODUCTION

The year 1928 marked an important turning point in the factional struggle within the USSR that would be an important determinant of the future course of that country and of the world working class movement for years to come. The second volume in this series ended on the eve of Stalin's deportations of Left Oppositionists, after the United Oppostion bloc had been expelled from the AUCP and had disintegrated. The Zinovievists recanted their Oppositional views while the Trotskyists reaffirmed theirs.

In 1926-27 the Left Opposition actively sought to arouse the proletarian core of the party in an effort to turn the party's policy back onto Leninist tracks. In 1928 it was forced into a different role. Although its voice was heard among the party's members (Trotsky said the Opposition was more a part of the party than the Zinovievist capitulators—at least the Oppositionists could speak their minds), the Opposition turned its major efforts to theoretical clarification and education within its own ranks. What was needed was to preserve a cadre that would be politically fit to step in when new opportunities arose.

In the beginning of 1928, immediately after the Fifteenth Congress of the AUCP, hundreds of Oppositionists were arrested, framed up on the charge of counterrevolutionary activity under Article 58 of the penal code, and banished to remote corners of the USSR. For the most part, they were scattered as far as possible from each other and from the major centers of European Russia. An unknown number of Oppositionists maintained an underground existence in the cities, not yet victims of the repression but unable to speak out openly; they circulated leaflets and manifestos. In Moscow they even ran an underground printshop for a time.

The exiled Oppositionists were men and women from all areas of party and Soviet life. Many of them had borne the heaviest responsibilities during the revolution, the civil war, and the work of socialist construction in the years that followed. Freed from these responsibilities as well as from the rigors of the faction fights of the previous years, the exiled Oppositionists sought to use their enforced idleness to educate themselves, to clarify theoretical and political questions, and in some cases to begin works of scholarship that they had not had time for in the past. In addition to closely following the life of the party and the Comintern and writing theses and position statements on the major events of the day, many of these men and women began important studies: Karl Radek started a biography of Lenin, Khristian Rakovsky wrote a biography of Saint Simon and a study of utopian socialism, and Yevgeny Preobrazhensky wrote on the economics of the Soviet Union and of medieval Europe. Trotsky began a study of the postwar decade—its international politics, economic developments, technological changes, etc., as well as a volume of memoirs. And the Oppositionists engaged in a voluminous correspondence with each other on the events of the day, both to help clarify the issues and to cut across the isolation of exile life.

Stalin hoped that by dispersing and silencing the Left Opposition he would have a free hand to maneuver with the right wing in the party—the Bukharin-Rykov tendency. The program of this grouping, Trotsky pointed out, reflected the pressures of the domestic and international bourgeoisie upon the party and the state. But the deterioration of the economy and the growth of capitalism in the countryside, stimulated by several years of erroneous economic policy and extension of the New Economic Policy (NEP), changed Stalin's agenda. The urgent need of workers in the cities for grain and the resistance by the rich peasants (kulaks) to selling it at state-fixed prices deepened class antagonisms that were reflected in a rift between the Stalinists and the Bukharinists over immediate economic policy. The major battle in 1928 developed between the right wing and the Stalinists, who were pushed into a "left turn" by the economic crisis and pressure from the working class.

Trotsky considered Stalin's grouping to be bureaucratic centrist because as a petty-bourgeois caste of administrators and bureaucrats it had no independent program. Wavering and balancing between the positions of the proletarian left and the bourgeois-pressured right, its chief concern was to maintain its monopoly of political power. In 1927 Trotsky repeatedly stressed that the right and the center were united by nothing except their common hostility to the Opposition and that removal of the Opposition would inevitably lead to a new conflict and to a split between the erstwhile allies. His analysis of this battle as it evolved in 1928 and of its implications for the Soviet workers' state makes up part of the contents of the present volume.

During the winter of 1927-28, grain supplies to the cities continued to decrease. Bukharin more than any other party leader had been identified with the agricultural policy of the years 1924-28, a distortion of NEP (adopted in 1921 under Lenin). The Bukharin policy encouraged capitalist farmers, who exploited wage-labor, to get richer through the unhindered action of free market forces. It promoted industrialization only to the extent that it could be supported without undermining the growing profits of the kulaks. This policy of "industrialization at a snail's pace" led to a permanent "goods famine," or shortage of industrial commodities, which in turn led the kulaks to refuse to sell their grain for currency that could buy them little.

It was the grain crisis that drove the wedge between right and center and compelled a confrontation. By early 1928, despite the steady increase in the amount of cultivated land and three excellent harvests, the state grain reserves were dangerously low. The lines outside the bakeries grew longer. State grain collectors in the countryside were met by riots and sometimes beaten and even killed. The rich peasants demanded a sharp rise in the price of grain and refused to sell it at the prices fixed by the state. Throughout the fall and winter, the amount of grain collected each month remained at about 50 percent of the previous year's collections.

On January 6 the Politburo issued secret instructions to party organizations to begin applying Article 107 of the penal code, which stipulated that stocks of grain should be confiscated from peasants who withheld grain. On February 15, *Pravda* carried an editorial acknowledging the growth of the kulaks' influence and wealth, attributing the grain crisis to the lag in industry and the scarcity of industrial goods. (The Opposition had been pilloried for presenting a similar view only weeks before.) The Politburo used the editorial to exhort party organizations to move more resolutely against peasants who refused to sell grain at the prices fixed by the state, including use of compulsory "loans" from recalcitrant kulaks.

It would be more than seven months before the Bukharinists would issue what amounted to a public manifesto of their differences, in the form of Bukharin's "Notes of an Economist" (*Pravda,* September 30). Its main contention was that industrialization was outstripping agriculture and that agriculture must be allowed to catch up if the shortages of grain and industrial commodities were to be remedied; the rate of industrialization must not be increased but should be geared to the development of agriculture. In the intervening months, the Politburo, to which Bukharin and his cothinkers Rykov and Tomsky belonged, assiduously denied the existence of disagreements among its members; Bukharin himself was drafted repeatedly to denounce the "right deviation" and to deny that it existed in the party leadership.

In the first weeks of 1928, all the major party leaders except Bukharin toured the countryside as part of the campaign to collect grain. And collected it was, frequently by brutal police measures that in some ways foreshadowed the forced collectivization campaign of the following year.

In his analytical memorandum "At a New Stage," written immediately after the expulsion and break-up of the Opposition bloc at the Fifteenth Congress in December 1927, Trotsky had summed up the relationship of forces in the party as follows: "The Opposition's plan has been rejected; the Stalin group has no plan at all; the right is afraid for the moment of making its real intentions clear—that's how the economic leadership looks at the present moment. The most likely thing is that in the event of a further aggravation of the economic situation, the line taken by the right, which was foreseen quite correctly in the Platform of the Opposition, will triumph" (*Challenge of the Left Opposition [1926-27]* [New York: Pathfinder, 1980], p. 499).

Nevertheless, the Fifteenth Congress inaugurated a turn not to the right but to the left, at least on paper. While it expelled the Opposition from the party and denounced its Platform, the Stalin faction adopted sections of the Platform. The Fifteenth Congress called for an offensive against the kulak, emphasis on collectivization of agriculture, increased capital investments in industry, and more economic planning.

In a letter to fellow-Oppositionist Aleksandr Beloborodov, Trotsky explained why he had been mistaken in anticipating the direction of the party turn. "It turned out that the next shift was to the left. This means that we ourselves greatly underestimated the good, strong wedge we had driven in. Yes, it was precisely our wedge that has made it impossible at this particular time to seek a way out of the contradictions on the *right* path. By itself this is a very great achievement, if only a temporary one, for time is an important factor in politics" ("The Opposition's Errors—Real and Alleged," May 23, 1928, in this volume).

Stalin's maneuver to the left had several purposes: to cope with the grain crisis by taking a tough stand against the kulaks who controlled most of the marketable grain; to stem the growing restiveness of the working class, which was expressed in a wave of strikes throughout the country; and to disarm the party by appearing to adopt important parts of the Opposition's program. He thus pulled the rug from under the Bukharinist right wing, while simultaneously sowing confusion and demoralization in the Left Opposition, which was still reeling from the expulsions and deportations of the fall and winter.

Trotsky called for a policy of critical support to Stalin's left turn. By this he meant that the Opposition should endorse every genuine step the Stalinists took that advanced the interests of the working class; but should criticize the repression of revolutionists and the brutal methods used against the peasants. (The massive violence and disruption of forced collectivization, during the period 1929-32, had nothing in common with the Opposition's program, which always stressed that collectivization had to be voluntary and based on the peasants' recognition that it was in their own interest, and that the Soviet government should also give economic aid to small private farming.)

Because so much of the "left turn" was purely verbal, and the little that was genuine was produced under the whip of Opposition criticism, Trotsky argued that the depth and significance of the left course depended largely on the response of the Opposition and its success in mobilizing the proletarian ranks of the party. Therefore the Opposition must maintain its criticisms, press the Stalinists to move from words to actions, and continue to warn against the danger of capitalist counterrevolution if the right-wing program triumphed. It should courageously point to the class struggle road to resolving the crises wracking the party, the country, and the Comintern.

As Stalin had hoped, his maneuver to the left created a crisis in the Opposition. One section, the conciliators, was inclined to give up the Opposition struggle and petition for readmission to the party to help carry out the new line. This group included those who were tired of the fight and ready to seize any pretext to give their capitulation the appearance of ideological reconciliation; but it also included some who simply didn't understand the opportunist and temporary character of Stalin's maneuver and mistakenly took it for good coin. Among the leading Opposition-ists who responded in this way to Stalin's left course were Preobrazhensky and Radek. Another current in the Opposition, the so-called intransigents, was shocked at the notion of endorsing any action of the Stalin group. They included Lev Sosnovsky and Boris Eltsin.

Trotsky had to argue against the sectarianism of the intransigents while trying to counteract the opportunism or gullibility of the conciliators. This task was complicated by the existence of the Democratic Centralist group, which had been part of the United Opposition in 1926 but had been expelled from it for calling for a new party. They had been exiled at the same time as the Trotskyists and conducted polemics with them. Their leaders, Timofei Sapronov and Vladimir Smirnov, argued that the party was a corpse and a new party had to be formed. They rejected support to any of Stalin's measures; refused to distinguish between the center (Stalin) and the right (Rykov-Bukharin); and believed the Stalin regime represented the victorious Thermidor (capitalist restoration). They criticized Trotsky for supporting the progressive policy shifts included in the "left turn" and had some influence on the "intransigent" wing of the Opposition.

Exile conditions created additional problems. The postal authorities interfered with the exiles' correspondence, permitting some letters to go through and stopping others, even those dealing only with family matters. The censorship was not indiscriminate: by manipulating the correspondence in this way, the authorities were able to govern which ideas reached the exiles, thus disrupting and disorienting the Opposition. In the autumn of 1928, they clamped down altogether, imposing a postal blockade on Trotsky, allowing only those letters to reach him that counseled capitulation or spoke of demoralization.

How the Opposition coped with these difficulties was indicated in Trotsky's memorial article to his son Leon (Lyova) Sedov, written ten years later (February 20, 1938).

"Commissioned by the Moscow Opposition center, Comrade X, very devoted and reliable, acquired a carriage and three horses and worked as an independent coachman between Alma-Ata and the city of Frunze (Pishpek), at that time the terminus of the railroad. It was his task to convey the secret Moscow mail to us every two weeks and to carry our letters and manuscripts back to Frunze, where a Moscow messenger awaited him. Sometimes special couriers also arrived from Moscow. To meet with them was no simple matter. We were lodged in a house surrounded on all sides by the institutions of the GPU and the quarters of its agents. Outside connections were handled entirely by Leon. He would leave the house late on a rainy night or when the snow fell heavily, or, evading the vigilance of the spies, he would hide himself during the day in the library to meet the courier in a public bath or among the thick weeds on the outskirts of the town, or in the oriental marketplace where the Kirgiz crowded with their horses, donkeys, and wares. Each time he returned excited and happy, with a conquering gleam in his eyes and the precious booty under his clothing. And so for a year's time he eluded all enemies. . . .

"The ideological life of the Opposition seethed like a cauldron at the time. It was the year of the Sixth World Congress of the Communist International. The Moscow packets arrived with scores of letters, articles, theses, from comrades known and unknown. During the first few months, before the sharp change in the conduct of the GPU, we even received a great many letters by the official mail services from different places of exile. . . .

"Between April and October we received approximately 1,000 political letters and documents and about 700 telegrams. In this same period we sent out 550 telegrams and not fewer than 800 political letters, including a number of substantial works, such as the *Criticism of the Draft Program of the Communist International* and others" (*Writings of Leon Trotsky [1937-38]*, pp. 168-69).

(One comment should be made on the reference here to "800 political letters" that were "sent out." This figure probably includes letters by Leon Sedov and by others that were copied and forwarded from Alma-Ata, as well as multiple copies of the same or similar letters by Trotsky sent to different addresses. In Trotsky's archives at Harvard there are, for the Alma-Ata period, about 150 political letters by Trotsky himself. All the most important ones are included in the present volume.)

These and other adversities cost the Opposition some of its members. The leaders of the Leningrad Opposition, Zinoviev and Kamenev, had capitulated with their closest followers at the time of the Fifteenth Congress in December 1927. However, their capitulation did not open the doors of the party to them. They were not permitted to write or speak about their ideas and were given humiliating assignments in the State Bank or Central Union of Consumer Cooperative Societies (Centrosoyuz). Trotsky wrote that Zinoviev's departure had freed the Opposition's hands to criticize the mistakes of the Fifth Congress of the Comintern (1924) and of the party leadership during the period that Zinoviev and Kamenev, with Stalin, had been in the leadership.

Many of Zinoviev's followers did not imitate his capitulation but instead went into exile with the Trotskyists. Some of these, like Georgi Safarov, Voja Vujović, and Ilya Vardin, did capitulate early in 1928 and were readmitted to the party, but many others remained with the Opposition. In the early spring, news reached Trotsky that some leaders of the old 1923 Opposition, Yuri Pyatakov, Vladimir Antonov-Ovseenko, and Nikolai Krestinsky, had also capitulated to Stalin. Despite defections, the Opposition maintained a precarious existence in the cities, and in the autumn Trotsky received reports of stepped-up Opposition activity in Moscow and the appearance of its leaflets pasted up in the city. This coincided with the beginnings of a further crackdown on the Opposition: the postal blockade, the arrests of hundreds of Oppositionists in Leningrad, Kiev, and Moscow, and finally Trotsky's arrest and deportation to Turkey.

In 1928 the Stalinists finally recognized that the stabilization of capitalism was ending. (Earlier they had resisted recognizing that after the defeat of the German revolution in late 1923 a temporary stabilization of world capitalism had set in; they recognized that only in 1926, at a time when the situation was actually starting to change.) 1928 was the last year of relative economic prosperity in the capitalist world before the onset of the Great Depression decade that led into World War II.

Until 1928, the Comintern, which had adopted many programmatic documents on specific questions, had never officially adopted a program, although it had considered drafts in 1922 and 1924. A new draft, written mainly by Bukharin and based on the revisionist theory that socialism could be established in one country, was submitted to the Sixth Congress, which met in Moscow July 17 to September 1, 1928.

To the coming crisis of capitalism, the Stalinists reacted with their theory of the "third period." Briefly, this was to be the period of cataclysmic and decisive revolutionary upheaval in the capitalist countries (as distinguished from the "first" period of revolutionary upsurges following World War I and the "second" period of stabilization and lull). Foisted upon the Comintern, this ultraleft theory meant that foreign Communist parties had to refuse to seek united action with Social Democrats and other working class currents. The Stalinists attacked these currents as the main enemy of the workers' movement and as "social fascists." They proposed setting up "Red" or "dual" trade unions under Communist leadership, and called on every section of the International to expel and eradicate all traces of ideological opposition in their ranks, the main danger being "right deviationists." With the exception of a minor functionary who served as scapegoat (Moshe Frumkin), the "right deviationists" remained anonymous until the spring of 1929, when Stalin publicly identified Bukharin, Rykov, and Tomsky as the leaders of such a faction in the AUCP.

The "third period" had its official debut at the ninth plenum of the Comintern Executive Committee (ECCI) in February 1928, where it complemented the "left turn" Stalin had inaugurated in the Soviet Union. To avoid an assessment of the recent disastrous defeat in China and the anti-Leninist policies that were responsible for it, the Stalinists simply denied that a defeat had taken place—proclaiming a course toward immediate armed insurrection, calling for the formation of Chinese soviets, and rejecting the struggle for democratic demands.

Although Bukharin was designated the only Soviet party spokesman at the Sixth Congress, Stalin actively undermined his authority by sponsoring no fewer than twenty amendments to Bukharin's theses and by conducting a whispering campaign in the corridors spreading rumors about Bukharin's sympathy for the right wing. This would be the last time Bukharin would appear at a Comintern podium representing the Soviet party. It was the end of his nominal control of Comintern affairs. It was also the beginning of the end for his supporters in Communist parties around the world.

Trotsky took advantage of the opportunity the congress afforded to produce a major critical evaluation of the Stalin-Bukharin leadership of the Comintern and the AUCP, which he entitled "The Draft Program of the Communist International—A Criticism of Fundamentals." His formal appeal to the congress for reinstatement of the expelled Left Oppositionists, entitled "What Now?" was devoted "mainly to problems of the crisis in the AUCP," and also to a brief characterization of "the conditions and methods of work of the Comintern." It was never shown to delegates at the congress, but a censored version of his criticism of the draft program was circulated to delegates in the program commission. There it was read by, among others, James P. Cannon of the American CP and Maurice Spector of the Canadian CP. In Cannon's words, "We let the caucus meetings and the congress go to the devil while we read and studied this document. . . . We made a compact there and then . . . that we would come back home and begin a struggle under the banner of Trotskyism" (*History of American Trotskyism* [New York: Pathfinder, 1974], pp. 49-50). Trotsky wouldn't find out until he arrived in Turkey the following year that his document had laid the basis for the formation of the American Left Opposition.

Trotsky also used the congress as an opportunity to raise three practical demands, which he reiterated frequently in his writings in this volume: (1) for democratic preparations so there could be an authoritative Sixteenth Congress of the AUCP; (2) for the immediate publication of all of Lenin's articles, speeches, and letters that had been hidden from the party; (3) for a reduction of the party's budget to one-twentieth of its present size, because the present budget was a basis of bureaucratic corruption.

The Comintern congress approved Bukharin's new draft program and issued resolutions on the national and colonial question, the danger of war, and the internal situation in the AUCP, endorsing the decision of the Fifteenth Congress of the AUCP (December 1927) and the ninth ECCI (February 1928) on the expulsion of the Soviet Opposition from the party.

Shortly before the Sixth Comintern Congress new developments occurred in the Opposition, which would culminate a year later in a new wave of capitulations. Radek—who had earlier been on the extreme left of the Opposition, who had announced that Thermidor was accomplished and the Opposition should form a new party, and who had called for unity with the Democratic Centralists on that basis—had been unprepared for the "left course" of the Stalinists and their sharp measures against the kulaks. His response was to greet the "left course" as a genuine turn in the fundamental policy line and character of the party leadership; to play down the Opposition's differences with the centrists; and to use Stalinist arguments against Trotsky's theory of permanent revolution (in effect an attack on the entire Bolshevik-Leninist view of proletarian internationalism) as a way of separating himself from the Opposition. The occasion for Radek's attack on the theory of permanent revolution was the ultraleft pronouncement on China by the ninth plenum of the ECCI, meeting in February 1928. Preobrazhensky also greeted this development with a critique of permanent revolution. Up until this time, Trotsky had not answered the attacks on "Trotskyism" or the theory of permanent revolution, which were first raised by the Zinoviev-Bukharin-Stalin faction in 1924. Instead he had argued that this was a smokescreen to cover their own abandonment of Leninism and proletarian internationalism under the cover of supporting the "theory" of socialism in one country. But in light of the experience of the Chinese revolution, Trotsky reluctantly decided to answer the charges against the theory of permanent revolution by replying to Radek and Preobrazhensky. (Trotsky's polemic with Preobrazhensky is in *Leon Trotsky on China* [New York: Monad Press, 1976], pp. 276-90; some of his polemic with Radek is in the present volume and the rest is in *The Permanent Revolution* [New York: Pathfinder, 1967].

The Sixth Congress provided another opportunity for the conciliators to make a move, and they did: Radek, Smilga, and Preobrazhensky addressed separate statements of a conciliatory tone to the congress. Radek eventually withdrew his under pressure from the Oppositionists, who had reacted indignantly; but all the signs of an impending split within the Opposition were present.

Despite the appearance of unity at the Sixth Comintern Congress, the Stalin-Bukharin bloc had already come to an end in the summer of 1928, when, after a brief reversal at the July CC plenum, Stalin resumed his left zigzag and Bukharin began looking around desperately for new sources of support. After helping Stalin to work the Opposition over for four years, Bukharin appealed to the Left Opposition through Kamenev, with whom he had secret meetings in July 1928, to make a bloc against Stalin. Trotsky replied frankly, in "A Heart-to-Heart Talk with a Well-meaning Party Member," in this volume, that on the major questions of industrial policy and political course there was no basis for a bloc; but that he was ready to join hands with the Bukharinists to restore inner-party democracy so that the party would have the opportunity to air and resolve its differences. This reply provoked some bewilderment among Oppositionists who ruled out the possibility of any principled bloc with the right wing. Trotsky tried to ease this resistance ("On the Topics of the Day," in this volume); but it quickly became apparent that the right wing, led by Rykov, Bukharin, and Tomsky, had no interest in a common front to restore party democracy.

Despite all the Stalinists' claims that the Opposition was crushed, they were faced at the end of 1928 with the fact that the Opposition continued to have an impact on party politics.

In deporting the Oppositionists the Stalinists had hoped to silence them and utterly destroy their influence in the party. By the end of 1928 it became apparent that this effort had not been successful enough. In 1929 Stalin did not feel strong enough to simply frame up and murder the Opposition. Nevertheless, he was able to push through the Politburo a motion to exile Trotsky abroad, hoping to cut him off more completely from the Soviet

Opposition. Almost exactly one year after he arrived in Alma-Ata, Trotsky was forcibly deported to Turkey, where he would live four and a hulf years before moving on to France, Norway, and Mexico.

Within the Soviet Union, the relatively benign restrictions applied to the Left Opposition in 1928 soon gave way to more brutal and systematic victimization. Special prisons (isolators) were used to confine Oppositionists under the worst imaginable conditions. Later they were also moved into labor camps. Some of the experiences of Oppositionists in the camps and isolators in the thirties are related in *Samizdat: Voices of the Soviet Opposition,* edited by George Saunders (New York: Monad Press, 1974).

In 1929 the Opposition suffered a wave of capitulations: in July, Radek, Preobrazhensky, and Ivar Smilga led this group, whose waverings may be detected even in the present volume. In October they were followed by another group led by I. N. Smirnov, followed by Sergei Mrachkovsky and Aleksandr Beloborodov. The main body of the Opposition was now led by Trotsky's old friend and cothinker, Khristian Rakovsky, who, along with Lev Sosnovsky, held out despite terrible conditions until 1934. Driven to wipe out every vestige of dissent, Stalin staged three big frame-up trials between 1936 and 1938, in the course of which he eliminated tens of thousands of Old Bolsheviks, both Right and Left Oppositionists, even those who had abjectly capitulated several times and been readmitted to the party. Despite the many forms of pressure brought to bear on them, unknown numbers of Oppositionists refused to capitulate to Stalin and vanished for good into the camps or dungeons of the GPU.

Trotsky made use of the last twelve years of his life, spent beyond the borders of the USSR, to organize the Opposition on an international scale. The Russian journal documenting these efforts was the magazıne he published abroad, *Biulleten Oppozitsii* (Bulletin of the Opposition), recently reprinted in four volumes (New York: Monad Press, 1973). Until 1933, the International Left Opposition considered itself a faction of the Comintern. The turning point came when the German CP allowed Hitler to come to power without a fight. The shock waves from this disaster were felt throughout the international labor movement, but they did not stimulate so much as a discussion in the Comintern over the sectarian policy that had led to this defeat. Trotsky and his cothinkers concluded that with this reaction the Comintern could no longer be considered a potentially revolutionary organization, and that it was necessary to build a new, revolutionary, International and new Leninist parties. The Fourth International was finally founded in 1938. In 1940 a GPU assassin murdered Trotsky in Mexico under Stalin's orders.

Naomi Allen

March 1981

# APPEAL OF THE DEPORTEES

## January 1928

*NOTE: Meeting in December 1927, the Fifteenth Party Congress had approved the wholesale expulsion of Left Oppositionists, which continued after the congress as well. The expulsions were in most cases followed by orders deporting the Oppositionists to distant and isolated corners of the USSR. By exiling the Oppositionists, and especially their leaders, the Stalinists hoped to put an end to the Opposition as a political force: widely scattered, they would find communication among themselves difficult and influence on the party almost impossible. The Stalinists hoped thus to demoralize the weaker elements and effectively disorganize the Opposition as a whole.*

*But the Oppositionists continued to try to maintain organizational links with each other and with the party. Their first organized act, after the deportation orders had been served, was to appeal their expulsions to the Comintern, which had de jure authority to rule on such matters. They applied for this purpose to the presidium of the Comintern Executive Committee (ECCI), which would meet in February and approve their expulsion. Long before the meeting of the ECCI, however, the signers of the appeal were on their way to their places of exile.*

*From* Contre le courant, *February 11, 1928. Translated from the French for this volume by Jeff White; checked against the Russian original by George Saunders. Points 1 and 12, which were missing from the French version, were translated from the Russian by L. Hall and Marilyn Vogt, by permission of the Harvard College Library. Point 9 was published in* Leon Trotsky on China, *p. 275. Excerpts from the appeal were in* The Real Situation in Russia, *pp. 354-57.*

We, the undersigned, expelled from the ranks of the All-Union Communist Party before the Fifteenth Party Congress or by a resolution of that congress, felt it necessary to appeal our expulsion in due course to the highest body of the world Communist movement, that is, to the Sixth Congress of the Communist International. However, at the orders of the GPU (or in part by a resolution of the party's Central Committee) we, Old Bolshevik party militants, are being exiled to the remotest parts of the Soviet Union, without the presentation of any accusation against us, for the sole purpose of preventing our communication with Moscow and the other working class centers, and, as a consequence, with the Sixth World Congress. We consider it necessary, therefore, on the eve of our enforced departure to distant parts of the Union, to address this declaration to the presidium of the Executive Committee of the Communist International, with the request that the presidium make our declaration known to the central committees of all the Communist parties.

1. The GPU is banishing us on the basis of Article 58 of the Criminal Code, i.e., for "propaganda or agitation calling for the overthrow, undermining, or weakening of Soviet power or for the commission of individual counterrevolutionary acts."

With calm disdain, we reject the attempt to subsume under this article dozens of Bolshevik-Leninists who did a great deal to establish, defend, and consolidate Soviet power in the past and who in the future as well will devote all their strength to defending the dictatorship of the proletariat.

2. This banishment of veteran militants by administrative order of the GPU is only a new link in the chain of events that are shaking the Soviet Communist Party. These events will have immense historical significance for years to come. The present disagreements are among the most important in the history of the international revolutionary movement. What is involved, in fact, is the issue of how to preserve the dictatorship of the proletariat that was won in 1917. Yet the struggle in the Soviet Communist Party has gone on behind the backs of the Communist International, without its participation, and even without its knowledge. The most important documents of the Opposition, dedicated to the major problems of our era, are still unknown to the International. Always the Communist parties are presented with accomplished facts, and they merely rubber-stamp decisions that have already been made. We maintain that such a dangerous situation grows out of the radically wrong regime within the AUCP and the whole Communist International.

3. The exceptional harshness of the struggle within the party recently which led to our expulsion from it (and now our exile, without any additional reasons being given) is the result of

nothing other than our desire to make our views known to the party and the International. Under Lenin such a desire by a minority was considered quite normal and to be expected. During that period, discussions were held on the basis of the publication and full examination of all the documents concerning the questions in dispute. Without such a system the Communist International cannot become what it must be. The international proletariat still has ahead of it the struggle for power against the very powerful bourgeoisie. This struggle presupposes that the Communist parties will have strong leadership, enjoying moral authority and capable of acting on its own. Such leadership can be created only over a period of years, by selecting the staunchest, most self-reliant, most consistent, and most courageous representatives of the proletarian vanguard. Not even the most conscientious functionaries can replace revolutionary leaders. The victory of the proletarian revolution in Europe and in the whole world depends, in large measure, on the solution of the problem of revolutionary leadership. The internal regime of the Communist International at present prevents the selection and training of such a leadership. This is most strikingly evident in the completely passive attitude of the foreign Communist parties toward the internal processes of the AUCP, with whose fate the destiny of the Communist International is intimately linked.

4. We Oppositionists have broken the norms of party life. Why? Because we have been deprived of the opportunity to exercise our normal rights as party members. In order to bring our point of view to the attention of the [Fifteenth Party] Congress, we were forced to make unauthorized use of a state-owned printshop. In order to refute before the working class the misrepresentation of our position, and in particular the vile slander concerning our alleged ties with a "Wrangel officer" and with the counterrevolution in general, we raised picket signs at the tenth anniversary demonstration bearing the following slogans:

"Let us turn our fire against the right: against the kulaks, NEPmen, and bureaucrats."

"Carry out Lenin's last Testament."

"For real democracy in the party."

These undeniably Bolshevik slogans were declared not only hostile to the party, but counterrevolutionary. We openly warn you that *in the future there will be attempts to invent so-called links between the Opposition and the organizations of the White Guards and the Mensheviks,* although we, of all tendencies, are the farthest removed from them.

No grounds were given by us for such an amalgam, but none were necessary—just as none were needed for our banishment.

5. In the declaration addressed to the Fifteenth Congress, signed by comrades Smilga, Muralov, Rakovsky, and Radek, we announced that we would abide by the decisions of the Fifteenth Congress, and that we were ready to cease factional work [see *Challenge of the Left Opposition (1926-27),* p. 486]. In spite of this, we have been expelled and are being exiled *because of our opinions.* Above all, however, we have stated—and we repeat here—that we cannot renounce our opinions, which we expressed in our theses and in our Platform, since the whole course of events is confirming their correctness.

6. The theory of building socialism in one country inevitably leads to separating the fate of the Soviet Union from that of the international proletarian revolution as a whole. To pose the question in this way is to undermine the very foundations of the theory and politics of proletarian internationalism. Our struggle against this thoroughly anti-Marxist theory, which was invented in 1925—that is, our struggle for the fundamental interests of the Communist International—is what has led to our expulsion from the party and our official exile.

7. The revision of Marxism and Leninism on the fundamental question of the international character of the proletarian revolution derives from the fact that the period since 1923 has been marked by very severe defeats for the international proletarian revolution (Bulgaria and Germany in 1923, Estonia in 1924, England in 1926, China and Austria in 1927). These defeats in themselves made possible what has been called the stabilization of capitalism, since they temporarily consolidated the position of the world bourgeoisie; because of the latter's renewed pressure on the USSR, these defeats slowed the pace of the construction of socialism; they reinforced the positions of our domestic bourgeoisie; they gave it the opportunity to strengthen its ties with many elements in the Soviet state apparatus; they increased the pressure of this apparatus on that of the party; and they led to the weakening of the left wing of our party. During these same years, Social Democracy enjoyed a temporary renaissance in Europe, accompanied by a weakening of the Communist parties, and a strengthening of the right wing within these parties. The Opposition in the Soviet CP, as its left, proletarian wing, suffered defeats at the same time as the positions of the world proletarian revolution became weaker.

8. While the parties of the Comintern have not yet had a

chance to correctly evaluate the true historical significance of the Opposition, the world bourgeoisie, by contrast, has already passed unambiguous judgment on it. All of the more or less serious bourgeois newspapers of all countries consider the Left Opposition their mortal enemy, and see on the other hand the politics of the present ruling majority as a necessary transition for the USSR toward the "civilized"—i.e., capitalist—world.

We believe the presidium of the Comintern ought to collect the opinions expressed by the political leaders and the major publications of the bourgeoisie concerning the internal struggle in the Soviet CP, in order to let the Sixth Congress draw the necessary political conclusions on this most important question.

9. The outcome and the lessons of the Chinese revolution, a revolution that constitutes one of the greatest events in world history, have been kept in obscurity, barred from discussion, and have not been assimilated by the public opinion of the proletarian vanguard. In reality, the Central Committee of the AUCP has prohibited discussion of the questions related to the Chinese revolution. But without studying the mistakes that were committed—the classic mistakes of opportunism—it is impossible to imagine the future revolutionary preparation of the proletarian parties of Europe and Asia.

Aside from the question of knowing who was immediately responsible for the leadership of the December events in Canton, those events furnish a striking example of putschism during the ebb of the revolutionary wave. In a revolutionary period, a deviation toward opportunism is often the result of defeats, whose direct cause is to be found in an opportunist leadership. The Communist International cannot take a single new step forward without first drawing the lessons of the experience of the Canton uprising, in correlation with the course of the Chinese revolution as a whole. This is one of the main tasks of the Sixth World Congress. The repressive measures taken against the left wing will not only fail to correct the errors already made but, even more serious, they will teach nothing to anyone.

10. The most blatant and ominous contradiction in the politics of the AUCP and the Comintern as a whole is this: after four years of the process of stabilization leading to a reinforcement of the right-wing tendencies in the workers' movement, the fire continues to be directed, as before, *against the left wing*. During the past period, we have witnessed mistakes and monstrous opportunist deviations in the Communist parties of Germany, England, France, Poland, China, etc. . . . Meanwhile, the left

wing of the Comintern has been the object of a campaign of annihilation that still persists. It is incontestably true that at the present time the working masses of Europe are moving to the left politically, because of the contradictions inherent in the process of stabilization. It is difficult to predict the pace of this leftward movement or the forms it will take in the near future. But the continuing campaign against the left-wing elements paves the way for a new crisis of leadership when the revolutionary situation becomes critical, as we have seen in recent years in Bulgaria, Germany, England, Poland, China, etc. Can revolutionaries, Leninists, Bolsheviks be asked to remain silent in the face of such a perspective?

11. We do not think it necessary once again to refute the absolutely false statement that we deny the proletarian character of our state, the possibility of building socialism, or even the necessity of an unconditional defense of the proletarian dictatorship against its class enemies from within and without. That is not what the discussion is about. It is about how to assess the dangers that threaten the dictatorship of the proletariat, what methods to use to combat these dangers, and how to distinguish true friends from false and genuine enemies from imaginary ones.

We contend that in the last few years, influenced by both internal and international pressures, the relationship of forces in our country has changed in an unfavorable direction for the proletariat; that its influence in the economy and in the political, economic, and cultural life of the country has shrunk, rather than grown; we maintain that in this country the forces of Thermidorian reaction have been strengthened, and that to underestimate the dangers that result from that is to worsen those dangers to an extraordinary degree. The expulsion of the Opposition from the party is an unconscious but no less real service by the party apparatus to the nonproletarian classes, who seek to strengthen themselves at the expense of the working class. It is from this point of view that we judge our deportation, and we do not doubt that in the near future the world proletarian vanguard will make the same judgment on this question as we do.

12. The reprisals against Oppositionists coincide with the new sharpening of economic difficulties unprecedented in recent years. Shortages of industrial goods, the disruption of grain collections after three good harvests, the growing threat to the monetary system—all of this slows down the development of the productive forces, clearly weakens the socialist elements of the

economy, and prevents improvements in the living conditions of the proletariat and the rural poor.

Under conditions of a worsening situation with respect to consumer goods on the market, workers inevitably repulse attempts to revise the collective agreements in the direction of lowered wage rates.

The GPU declares that these colossal failures of the prevailing course are criminally attributable to the exiled Oppositionists, whose actual crime has been to predict repeatedly, over the past several years, that all the present difficulties would be the inevitable consequence of the incorrect economic course and to have, in a timely manner, demanded that the course be fundamentally changed.

13. The preparations for the Fifteenth Party congress—which was called after a two-year interval, in violation of the party statutes—were themselves a glaring and serious example of the growing violence of the apparatus, which relies more and more on repressive government measures. As for the congress itself, without consideration or debate it adopted a resolution calling for biennial congresses in the future.

In a country with a proletarian dictatorship, of which the Communist Party is the expression, it was necessary ten years after the October Revolution to take away the party's elementary right to check up at least once a year on the activities of its institutions and, above all, its Central Committee.

Even under the most unfavorable conditions created by the civil war and the famine, congresses were sometimes held twice a year, but never less than once a year. Then the party truly discussed and truly decided every question, never ceasing to be the master of its own fate. What powers now force us to regard congresses as necessary evils, that have to be kept to a minimum? These powers are not those of the proletariat. They are the result of bourgeois pressure brought to bear on the proletarian vanguard. This pressure led to the expulsion of the Opposition and the deportation of Old Bolsheviks to Siberia and other remote places.

14. We reject the charge that we aim to create a second party. We warn that the elements of a second party are in reality taking shape, behind the backs of the party's masses, especially its proletarian nucleus, wherever the degenerated elements of the party apparatus meet those of the state and the new property-owning class. The worst representatives of the bureaucracy, whether they are card-carrying party members or not, having

absolutely nothing in common with the aims and methods of the international proletarian revolution, are becoming ever more concentrated, thus creating points of support for a second party, which, in the course of its development, could become the left wing of the Thermidorian forces. The accusation that we, defenders of the historical line of Bolshevism, aim to create a second party serves unconsciously to cover up the underground work of historical forces that are hostile to the proletariat. We warn the Comintern of these processes. Sooner or later, they will become obvious to everyone. But every day lost makes resistance to these processes more difficult.

15. The Sixth Congress of the International should be prepared for as in Lenin's time: publish all the most important documents touching the questions under discussion; put a stop to the persecution of Communists guilty only of acting upon their rights as members of the party; raise in its full dimensions, in the discussion preceding the congress, the question of the situation within the Soviet CP, its regime, and its political line.

The debated questions cannot be solved by additional repressive measures. Such measures can play a great positive role when they supplement a correct political line and hasten the dissolution of reactionary groups. As Bolsheviks we fully understand the role of such measures of revolutionary repression; we used them many times against the bourgeoisie and their agents, the Social Revolutionaries and the Mensheviks.

Nor do we consider for one moment renouncing such measures against the enemies of the proletariat. But we remember clearly that repression by our enemies against the Bolsheviks remained ineffective. What is decisive, in the final analysis, is the correct political line.

To us, soldiers of the October Revolution and comrades-in-arms of Lenin, our deportation is the clearest expression of the changes in the relationship of class forces in this country, and of the leadership's drift toward opportunism. In spite of all this, we remain firmly convinced that the basis of Soviet power is still the proletariat. It is still possible, by means of a decisive change in the line of the leadership, by correcting the mistakes already made, by profound reforms, without new revolutionary upheavals, to straighten out and solidify the system of proletarian dictatorship. This possibility may become a reality if the Communist International intervenes decisively.

We appeal to all the Communist parties and to the Sixth Congress of the International, urgently demanding that they examine all these questions in the open and with the full participation of the party membership. The Testament of Lenin never sounded more prophetic than at this moment. Nobody knows how much time the course of historic events will leave us to correct the mistakes that have been made. Submitting to force, we are leaving our posts in the party and the soviets for a meaningless and futile exile. But in doing so we do not for one minute doubt that each and all of us will not only be needed by the party again, but will take our places in the fighting ranks in the great battles to come.

On the basis of all that has been said we urgently request the Sixth Congress of the Communist International to reinstate us in the party.

M. Alsky
A. Beloborodov
A. Ishchenko (candidate member, Profintern Executive Bureau)
L. Trotsky
K. Radek
Kh. Rakovsky
Ye. A. Preobrazhensky
I. N. Smirnov
L. Serebryakov
I. Smilga
L. Sosnovsky
N. Muralov
G. Valentinov
Nevelson-Man
V. Eltsin
V. Vaganyan
V. Malyuta
V. Kasparova
S. Kavtaradze
Vilensky (Sibiryakov)

# PROBLEMS OF THE INTERNATIONAL OPPOSITION (TWO LETTERS)

## January 1928

*NOTE: These letters are concerned mainly with helping the West European Opposition groups to get their bearings and develop a perspective after the expulsions and capitulations. They needed to demarcate themselves from the capitulators; adjust to the position of being factions of the official parties although they had been, or were being, expelled from them; and come to terms with the debates over a second party, "Trotskyism," and the class nature of the Soviet state. On an international scale, they considered themselves a faction of the Comintern and would not call for the formation of a new International until 1933 (see* Challenge *1926-27, p. 32).*

*In France, this process of ideological clarification was complicated by the proliferation of groups that more or less identified with the Russian Opposition. In addition to the Monatte-Rosmer group of revolutionary syndicalists (see* Challenge *1926-27, p. 203), and the Souvarine group, a group had been formed around Suzanne Girault and Albert Treint, and one around the periodical* Contre le courant *(Against the stream), which had received financial aid from the Russian Opposition through Pyatakov before its leaders were expelled from the CP at the end of 1927, and which Trotsky hoped would become the focus of a unification of the French Opposition. The "S." referred to in point 9 has not been identified.*

*In Germany, the leadership of the Opposition was in the hands of Zinovievists Arkady Maslow, Ruth Fischer, and Hugo Urbahns; in March 1928 a section of the German Opposition would found the Leninbund.*

*A Central Committee meeting of the Belgian CP held in late November 1927 adopted a resolution noting the explulsions of the Soviet Oppositionists and demanding that the ECCI vote a suspension of those measures and convene a world congress*

*immediately to judge the situation. The Belgian party congress in*
*March 1928 was stacked by the Stalinists, and the old leaders,*
*including Van Overstraeten, Hennaut, Lesoil, and others, were*
*ousted and expelled. They promptly set themselves up as a*
*separate organization in solidarity with the Soviet Opposition,*
*with publications in French and Flemish.*

*Translated from the Russian for this volume by Tom Twiss.*
*The GPU intercepted these letters and published them in* Pravda,
*January 15, 1928, evidently hoping that the sharp discussion of*
*Zinoviev and Kamenev's "treason" would embarrass the Opposi-*
*tion and further discredit Zinoviev and Kamenev. The second*
*letter is addressed to an unidentified "Pyotr" or "Peter." The*
*editors have tried to reconstruct a line in point 11 of the first*
*letter which was omitted from the* Pravda *version. In his May 26*
*letter to Yudin, Trotsky says that these two documents were*
*designed to correct the ultraleft line promoted by Safarov in*
*Berlin at a European Opposition conference.*

I

1. We must understand clearly that the breaking away of the
capitulators (Zinoviev and Kamenev) from the Opposition puts all
the members of the International Opposition to the test. The
question is, "With the Opposition in the AUCP or with the
capitulators?" This question must be faced squarely, and only in
this way, by every single Opposition group in Europe and every
single Oppositionist. We must break unconditionally with the
capitulators; we must dissociate ourselves openly from the vacil-
lating and the temporizing elements.

2. The treason of Zinoviev and Kamenev is a historical fact. We
must immediately draw from this fact all the necessary lessons
for the future.

3. The behavior of M. and R. [Maslow and Ruth Fischer] in this
regard seems ambiguous. M. actually shields Zinoviev and
Kamenev, contending that they are little worse than the others,
i.e., trying to erase the lines of demarcation between revolutionaries and capitulators. This actual support of the capitulators tries
to base itself on the first and second declarations of the left wing
[see *Challenge 1926-27*, pp. 473 and 481]. These two declarations
make really extraordinary concessions. But they are concessions
to Zinoviev and Kamenev. This was the last attempt to avoid a
split. (Some comrades in our own midst hoped it would be
possible to maintain unity at the price of concessions to Zinoviev

and Kamenev.) As soon as the break occurred, the Opposition issued the declaration of Smilga, Muralov, Rakovsky, and Radek to counterbalance the capitulators [Ibid., p. 486]. After that, to make no distinction between the Opposition and the capitulators implies nothing less than support to the capitulators.

4. The enclosed declaration of the leaders of the Opposition to the Executive Committee of the Comintern (ECCI) cannot leave any more room for doubts and vacillations. If even after this, M. lumps us together with Z. and K., we will have to treat M. as a conscious opponent.

5. We must distribute as widely as possible the declaration to the ECCI, along with the enclosed short biographies of the signers. We must confront every Opposition group with the question: Who is for it and who against? We must expose the masquerade by which some Oppositionists will try to join the capitulators under the pretext of combatting "Trotskyism."

6. We must now define our relation to Wedding, Pfalz, Suhl, etc., exactly along these lines. Now we must finally expose the charlatanism of the struggle against "Trotskyism" as a cover for opportunism (Stalin) and for centrist capitulation (Zinoviev).

7. We must apply the same criteria in regard to the French groupings. If Treint and Suzanne Girault are going to vacillate between capitulation and so-called Trotskyism, it will be necessary to leave them to their fate. In any case, we can go hand in hand with this group only if it clearly, precisely, and ruthlessly dissociates itself from the capitulators.

8. We can be sure that the *Contre le courant* group will go with us. If Treint and Girault also go with us, then pending unification, we must share all materials with both groups. If Treint and Girault are going to vacillate under the pretext of the struggle against "Trotskyism," then we must firmly bank on the *Contre le courant* group as the only group that truly holds our views. In that event the viable elements in the Treint and Girault group will come to us sooner or later.

9. In the event that the Treint-Girault group has a correct position, the merging of both groups is desirable as soon as possible. If this happens, from our point of view there can be no talk of a one-sided demand by the 1926 group that the 1923 group recognize its mistakes, as S. has proposed. It is extremely desirable to draw Rosmer into the work of the magazine *Contre le courant*.

10. A correct relation to Monatte's group is necessary. We must form a bloc with the revolutionary anarcho-syndicalists. The

criminally absurd struggle against "Trotskyism" (1923-24) re-pelled them from the party. We cannot mix ranks with the anarcho-syndicalists. But they are our allies, not our enemies.

11. We have not yet seen a single issue of the journal of Treint and Girault. Therefore we cannot comment on it. Please regular-ize the sending of all publications. We have not yet seen the latest publications [of Souvarine's group. Their differences] with us are serious, to judge by the first number of their bulletin. On a number of questions (especially the Anglo-Russian Committee) Souvarine took a fundamentally incorrect, rightist position. Souvarine's approach to the English workers' movement is often erroneous. Souvarine is inclined to replace a class analysis of politics with a psychological one. But he is a gifted historian and a revolutionary. We do not lose hope that his path will merge with ours for the greater gain of the French workers' movement.

12. It is necessary quickly to attain clarity regarding the Czechoslovakian Opposition. Here too it is better to have a smaller but tightly united leading group than a formless bloc with the right wing, staggering back and forth. Your report that N. [Neurath] is guided by selfish considerations more than by political ones (assuming you are not exaggerating) suggests that he and we are not traveling the same road. It is criminal to break without good reason from anyone, no matter who, but it is even more criminal to cling to individuals if even now, after the capitulation of Z. and K., they are still going to waver and equivocate.

13. Isn't it possible to get the Belgian Central Committee to publish our materials for the information of the [Belgian] party? As far as we know, this CC is vaguely inclined toward a "buffer" position. Isn't it possible to pressure the CC from below, finding a point of support there? It is necessary to pay special attention to Belgium, without, however, relying on the buffer CC, but trying to create for ourselves the necessary support from below. This task must be entrusted to our French cothinkers.

14. In Holland our documents were published earlier. How are things going now?

15. In conclusion, once again on the question: one or two parties? M. and R. think, evidently, that we are against a split in view of the specific conditions of the USSR. This is not true. We are opposed to a second party or a Fourth International—most intransigently opposed. Here we proceed from the interests of international Bolshevism. We also evaluate the specific condi-tions of the USSR from the international point of view. From the

point of view of the international working class as a whole the Opposition would put itself in the hopeless position of a sect if it allowed itself to move toward the position of a Fourth International, which would be counterposed in a hostile manner to everything connected with the USSR and the Comintern. The task is to win over the Comintern. The differences are sufficiently deep to justify the constitution of a left faction. But the faction is, in the present period, an instrument for influencing the Communist Party, i.e., its proletarian core.

## II.

1. What is the main task of the Opposition in the sections of the Comintern? To win over the Communist parties from within. Since the Communists were able to win over the majority in the German Independent Socialist Party and the French Socialist Party, there is no basis for thinking that given correct policies, the Opposition will not be able to win over the proletarian majority in the present-day Communist parties.

2. For an Opposition group to have a correct policy toward the Communist Party in its own country, it must have a correct attitude toward the Comintern, the AUCP(B), and the USSR. It is necessary to be fully aware of the specific contradictions and peculiarities of the present transitional situation and not to take something that is in process for something that has been completed.

3. To proceed from the view that Thermidor has been completed in the USSR is incorrect; that would mean to facilitate its completion. The class forces have not yet said their decisive word. The politics of the International Opposition must be directed, together with the Opposition in the AUCP, to preventing the further development of Thermidor and to winning back the positions the proletariat has lost.

4. The petty-bourgeois elements in the AUCP rule the party and the state, but they are obliged to base themselves on the working class and to oppose imperialism. They are heading toward concessions to the bourgeoisie. But a sharper onslaught by the bourgeoisie can create a decisive shift to the left in the party. No process has yet been completed.

5. Even with its present petty-bourgeois leadership, the USSR plays a revolutionary role on an international scale. The existence of the USSR was a source of nourishment for the Chinese revolution. The leadership of the AUCP doomed the Chinese revolu-

tion to defeat. We must hit at the leadership of the AUCP, without opposing ourselves to the USSR.

6. This also applies to the party, which has become more and more fused with the state, and to the Comintern. If the Opposition simply opposed itself to the USSR as a bourgeois state, and to the AUCP and the Comintern as petty-bourgeois parties, it would be transformed into a sect. We must wage a struggle to win over the AUCP and the Comintern.

7. This means for the present period: not a second party, but a faction, organized to the extent necessary to ensure the possibility of systematic influence on the party.

8. The considerations above, as well as the recent experience in Germany (Altona), argue against our presenting independent candidates. It is impermissible to break with the whole line over some problematic seats in parliament.

9. The creation of a "union of left Communists" is mistaken. The name of the Opposition is sufficiently popular and has an international character. The name "union" adds nothing, but could become a pseudonym for a second party.

There is considerable basis for thinking that the insufficient understanding of the need to fight to win the party from within comes from the same tendencies which formerly led to the rejection of the united-front policy and of work in the trade unions.

10. The question of an independent daily paper must be answered from the same point of view: such a paper can play an enormous role as a means of influencing the party independently and along with it, but secondarily, the nonparty masses. But an incorrectly conceived newspaper could quickly isolate the Opposition from the party workers and transform it into a sect.

11. The relation of M. and R. to the Opposition in the AUCP appears, on the basis of available evidence, to be based more on "maneuverist" than on principled considerations. The overall aim of M. and R. is to lower the authority of the Opposition as a whole. Their most immediate task is to bloc indirectly with the capitulators (Zinoviev, Kamenev), contending that others, too, are no better than they. Such a position gives M. the appearance of a strict and incorruptible judge, but in essence it is an alliance (a *smychka*) with the capitulators.

Without in any way straining relations unnecessarily, we must rebuff these maneuvers, explaining their hidden meaning (orally or by letter; but not in the press, except when absolutely necessary).

12. It is necessary to publish as widely as possible the declaration of the four (Smilga, Muralov, Rakovsky, and Radek) at the Fifteenth Congress and especially the declaration to the ECCI by those about to be exiled, explaining that this declaration comes from the leaders of the 1923 Opposition, plus Smilga, who has joined this group.

13. The struggle against so-called "Trotskyism" is the fishhook Stalin uses to haul in Zinoviev, and which Zinoviev uses on those to his "left" (Safarov et al.). So long as M., too, still hangs on this fishhook, he is compelled to whitewash the capitulators, asserting that they are little worse than others.

14. It is necessary to publish as widely as possible in various languages the letter to the Bureau of Party History devoted to the question of "Trotskyism" [in *The Stalin School of Falsification* (N.Y., 1972), p. 1].

15. The enclosed letters about Zinoviev's and Lashevich's admissions concerning "Trotskyism" (the letter of Trotsky, Pyatakov, Preobrazhensky, etc.) for the time being are not for publication, but it is necessary to use them for information [Ibid., p. 89].

16. The French publication *Contre le courant* gives a good impression. Unfortunately, we have received only two issues, by chance (1 and 4). We have not even received the platform of the French Opposition. The editorials are good. It is not entirely clear why the editors make the qualification that they are responsible only for the editorial. The editors can and must take responsibility for all articles. The publication of the faction must distinguish itself by complete ideological unanimity.

17. In connection with the considerations of principle developed above concerning the relation of the Opposition to the USSR, it is necessary to make several remarks about the article "The Return of Those Who Saw" (*Contre le courant,* December 19, 1927), and the other articles devoted to the internal situation in the USSR.

The lead article in no. 1 says, completely correctly, that "to unmask opportunist politics does not at all mean to serve the bourgeoisie." But it is extremely important to point out to the reader in each separate case the point of view from which we approach the internal situation of the USSR. The Communists of capitalist countries must always underline three points:

(a) Even with an opportunist leadership the Soviet state gives the workers and peasants immeasurably more than a bourgeois state would at the same level of development of the productive forces.

(b) The main cause of the very great internal difficulties in the USSR is the insufficient activity of the European proletariat and the insufficient combativity of the European Communist parties.

(c) European Social Democracy (Menshevism), which gloatingly plays up all information about the internal difficulties in the USSR, bears the main part of the responsibility for these difficulties.

\*      \*      \*

18. The congress of the Red International of Labor Unions will open March 15. We must immediately put this question at the center of our attention.

(a) Do everything possible to get Opposition delegates to the congress.

(b) Prepare positions of principle and practical proposals, based on the trade union experience of each country.

We must not lose even a minute, for there is very little time left.

19. We must also begin preparation now for the congress of the Comintern:

(a) We must prepare theses on all the questions on the agenda of the congress, so that together these theses will constitute the platform of the International Communist Left (Opposition).

(b) We must raise a broad campaign in connection with the excluded Oppositionists in the whole Comintern and in connection with conditions in the USSR.

(c) We must begin work to draft a program for the Comintern (Bukharin's [1922] program is a bad program of a national section of the Comintern, but not the program of a world Communist Party).

# THE INTERNATIONAL FACTOR

## February 1928

*NOTE: A letter to Ivan Nikitich Smirnov in Novo-Bayazet, written in the second week of February.*

*On January 27,* Pravda *published a letter from Zinoviev and Kamenev (referred to here as the "two musketeers"), reaffirming their separation from the Opposition and claiming that the differences with Trotsky hinged on the question of a "second party." Their slogan now was "Back to the party and back to the Comintern."*

*By permission of the Harvard College Library. Translated from the Russian for this volume by L. Hall and George Saunders.*

Dear Ivan Nikitich:

Today I received your postcard and sent you a telegram. Your letter is the first I have gotten here. Whether this is because the postal service takes a more attentive attitude toward the former commissar of posts and telegraph or for some other reason—I don't know. Immediately upon arrival here [January 25] I wrote you a postcard addressed to Zangezury. I also wrote to the other hermits whose addresses I know, but have had no answer yet. The mail is generally slow here too, and right now the February snowdrifts add to the problem. I have received answering telegrams from Rakovsky, Kasparova, Sosnovsky, and Muralov. They have all settled in, are in good spirits, and are working, Sosnovsky and Muralov in local planning agencies; as for Rakovsky, I don't know . . . I haven't received an answer to my telegram to Serebryakov, in Semipalatinsk. They haven't moved him somewhere else, have they? I haven't received an answer from Radek—"no address indicated." Apparently Radek has not yet visited his local telegraph office or perhaps he too has been sent somewhere else?

Your invitation to visit Novo-Bayazet is very tempting, but to accomplish that would involve some difficulties. The journey here was very fatiguing, and to top it all off, our traveling companions contrived to lose two of our suitcases, one with my most precious and necessary books . . . Going by the technical appearance of this letter, you might perhaps think that I had a secretary here but that is absolutely, *absolutely* not so. True, I have a typewriter, but the work on it has had to be organized on a new basis.

There is hunting and fishing here, so I can return your kind invitation. Although we will soon have lived here for three weeks, I have not yet gone hunting. The reasons for this are many, but the main reason, if you will, has been the high temperature which I have had and which never left me during the trip here. Natalya Ivanova and Lyova have had to make a lot of complaints, because we still have not been provided with living quarters. We are living in a hotel left over from Gogol's era.

You of course have read the two musketeers' letter to the editors. It would be hard to imagine a more pitiful and worthless little document. Now it turns out that the *Contre le courant* group is the farthest of all from Bolshevism. What kind of Bolshevism? The kind our two unfortunate musketeers preached until yesterday? Or the kind they attacked? Not a word about that, and no wonder. Their flattering, deceitful, fawning, and obscene document is based entirely on avoiding the most fundamental issues at the heart of the argument.

The international situation and the international revolutionary movement promise much that is new and important in the near future. *Pravda* is correct when it writes: "The period of a certain apathy and discouragement, which began after the 1923 defeat and which allowed German capital to strengthen its position, is beginning to pass away" (January 28, 1928). Nowadays this kind of statement, about the apathy and discouragement since late 1923, is repeated at every turn. Yet at one time, those who didn't understand the meaning and importance of the 1923 defeat accused those who predicted the inevitability of such a period of— liquidationism! Without an understanding of the *international* character of this period, it is impossible to understand our internal affairs properly. The 1923 defeat had a weaker effect on England than it did on the Continent, and a new upsurge began there in 1926, but was broken off by the defeat of that movement. The most profound effects of the 1923 defeat were felt, of course, in Germany itself, and—if you will—in our own country. *Pravda* is correct when it says that the apathy and discouragement are beginning to pass away in Germany. Unfortunately, I do not get German periodicals here, or the foreign press in general. And yet they must be followed more closely now than ever before, because the entire course of events is bringing the international questions more and more to the fore.

It is useful to go over in one's mind the old disputed questions in the light of the new events. Our evaluation of the European situation after the 1923 defeat was linked with the question of America's role in Europe. By now our view has already gained the strength of a prejudice—that to look at the fate of Europe without looking at the role of the United States is like trying to keep accounts without listing the owner's transactions. The so-called "normalization of Europe" was accomplished with American aid. On this basis Social Democracy revived, with its new religion (which now is already on its way out) of American democratic pacifism. The European proletarian vanguard would be stronger right now if it had foreseen this period of apathy and discouragement, Americanism and pacifism, etc., if it had not been instilled with the idea that such a prediction was "liquidationism." This was the fundamental error of the Fifth [Comintern] Congress. The mistakes of the Maslow-Ruth [Fischer] leadership already had a derivative character. People thought that the rungs of the ladder led up and not down and so they lifted their feet instead of stepping down. In such cases one inevitably bumps one's nose. The period of downturn, and the strengthening of Social Democracy within the German working class, lasted four years, according to *Pravda*. Only now is it "beginning to pass away." But we never predicted such a long period. The truth is that the period was prolonged because of an incorrect evaluation of our era in general and the incorrect strategic orientation resulting from that.

Right now America is much more the master of Europe than it was four years ago, when we first raised this question in theoretical terms. Too much steam has built up in the American boiler, however. Of course, the financial might of the United States and its monopoly organizations, makes "planning" and "regulation" possible to an unprecedented extent (for capitalism). This allows particular crises to be mitigated, postponing them, while the internal contradictions mount up. Apparently the situation in the United States has now reached the point of a general commercial-industrial crisis, a crisis of the economy as a whole. How deep, severe, or prolonged it will be is difficult to predict. But it's not at all difficult to predict that America will rectify matters for itself *at Europe's expense,* and that means, first and foremost, at England's expense. Already the

Anglo-American antagonism has emerged from the slightly masked forms of Anglo-American "cooperation." In the coming period this antagonism will be the axis of world politics. And for Europe this will mean everything except "democratic pacifism." The whole problem now is to evaluate this correctly, both the process as a whole and each successive stage in particular. In the coming years the international factor will dominate everything.

In India significant events seem to be in preparation. I must confess, however, that I know very little about India, much less even than I know about China, which is the main thing I'm working on now. Unfortunately, my books on India were in one of the lost suitcases. Right now, I am attempting to get a new package of books from Moscow. Unfortunately, all this involves quite a few difficulties, particularly in terms of wasted time.

As I understand it, what you mail to me goes through Baku and Krasnovodsk. If this is true, it may turn out that you and I are more like neighbors to each other than either of us is to Moscow. But all this remains to be tested out empirically.

# TO A FEW EXILED FRIENDS

## February 28, 1928

*NOTE: Trotsky used this "circular letter" to assess the bloc with Zinoviev and Kamenev ("the two ill-fated musketeers") in the light of their capitulation and to repeat that its most important feature—that it represented a bloc of the most advanced workers of Leningrad ("Petersburg") and Moscow—justified it fully. Despite their groveling, Zinoviev and Kamenev were being held at arm's length by the ruling circles, which followed publication of their letter with publication of a contemptuous critique by Maslow and Fischer.*

*Cut off from most forms of employment by his expulsion and exile, Trotsky was able to earn a living as a translator, thanks to the goodwill of David B. Ryazanov, the head of the Institute of Marx and Engels, who commissioned him to translate Marx's* Herr Vogt *and other works.*

*By permission of the Harvard College Library. Translated from the Russian for this volume by George Saunders. Parts of this letter appear in a slightly different form in Trotsky's auto-biography,* My Life, *p. 549.*

This is to report to you briefly about everything that has happened since we left Moscow. Probably you already know about the departure itself. We left from the Kazan Station in a special train (one locomotive, plus the car we were in). It quickly caught up with an express, which had been held up for about an hour and a half. Our car was attached to the express about forty-seven versts [thirty-one miles] from Moscow. Here we took leave of Franya Viktorovna Beloborodova and our younger son, Seryozha, who had accompanied us. We had nothing with us in the railroad car. As a result of endless telegrams all our things were finally sent along. Our things caught up with us only on the seventh or eighth day, when we were already in Pishpek (Frunze). It took so long to make the trip because of the snowdrifts. We went on from Pishpek by truck—and fairly froze along the way. We crossed the Kurdai pass in wagons, for about thirty versts [twenty miles]. Then onward in a car, sent from Alma-Ata to meet us. Our things came along behind, in a truck, our escorts contriving along the way to lose two suitcases containing the most necessary things. My books about China, India, etc., are gone.

We arrived in Alma-Ata late on the night of January 25, and were put in a hotel. In all good conscience I must admit that no bedbugs turned up. In general it was quite vile, living in the hotel. (I say this because "self-criticism" is now officially recognized as necessary.) In view of the forthcoming transfer of the Kazakhstan government to this place, all the houses here are "on the register" [i.e., reserved]. What is politely called "red tape" began to delay things. Only as a result of the telegrams that I sent to the most exalted personages in Moscow were we at last given our own quarters, after a three weeks' stay in the hotel. We had to buy some furniture, restore the ruined stove, and in general build up a home—though not on the state planning system. The effort is not finished to this day, for our worthy Soviet stove will not get hot. During the trip there came a renewed bout of fever, which has flared up now and again here too. In general, though, I feel quite satisfactory.

When the letter of the ill-fated two musketeers appeared in the papers, I recalled for the umpteenth time Sergei [Mrachkovsky]'s prophetic words, "We shouldn't bloc with either Joseph [Stalin] or Grigory [Zinoviev]. Joseph will deceive, and Grigory will sneak away." Sure enough, Grigory did sneak away. Nevertheless the bloc was justified insofar as it was a bloc between the advanced workers of Petersburg and Moscow. The pitiful musketeers apparently expected that after their pathetic and stupid letter, they would be pardoned. Not so. *Pravda* graciously published Maslow's rebuttal, which hit the nail right on the head. Despite the many other big minuses, there is at least one plus, that these imaginary numbers are retiring from the scene—presumably for good.

I am studing Asia a great deal now, its geography, economy, history, and so forth. Thus far I receive only two papers, *Pravda* and *Ekonomicheskaya Zhizn*. These I read with great diligence. I miss foreign papers terribly. I have already written to the necessary places asking to have such papers sent to me, even if they are not recent. In general the mails reach here after great delay and with extreme irregularity. First there was the snowdrift phase. Then it turned out that the horsedrawn mails between Pishpek and Alma-Ata were not properly organized. The local paper, the *Dzhetysu Iskra* (which comes out three times a week) promises that the postal irregularities will be overcome ("outlived") because negotiations with a new contractor have begun. In a word, "things will be set right."

The events in India call for exceptionally close attention. The economic basis for them seems to be the deep crisis in Indian industry, which expanded rapidly during the imperialist war but which now is forced to retreat under the pressure of foreign goods, Japanese in particular. This apparently has given broad sweep to the national-revolutionary movement. The role of the Indian Communist Party is extremely unclear. The newspapers have printed reports of the activities in various provinces of "workers' and peasants' parties." There is reason to be alarmed by the very name. The Kuomintang too was at one time declared to be a workers' and peasants' party. How can this turn out to be anything but a repeat performance?

The Anglo-American antagonism has finally come to the fore in all seriousness. This is now the fundamental factor in world politics and the world situation. Our newspapers, however, oversimplify when they represent the situation as if the Anglo-American antagonism, which is growing in intensity, must lead directly to war. One cannot doubt that there will be several more abrupt twists and turns in this process. For war would be too dangerous a thing for both sides. They will still make more than one effort to achieve agreement and peace. But taken in general, the process is developing by giant strides toward a bloody finale.

I am now translating Marx's *Herr Vogt* for the Institute of Marx and Engels. To refute some dozen slanders by Karl Vogt, Marx wrote a 200-page book, in small type, marshaling documents and the evidence of witnesses and analyzing direct proofs and circumstantial evidence . . . If we were to set about refuting the Stalinist slanders on the same scale, we would have to publish an encyclopedia of a thousand volumes.

It was only recently that they announced: "We have thoroughly smashed and destroyed the Opposition. Now, enough of polemics. Let's get down to practical constructive work." Instead, a new chapter of polemics has opened, and this time, in order not to repeat the stale old repertoire, they find it necessary to polemicize against the number of suitcases and boxes we traveled with (tripling their number for better effect) and against our hunting dog. My dear dog Maya doesn't even suspect that she has been drawn into high politics.

Incidentally, about the hunting. I came here with some inflated notions of the wealth and variety of the local game. In recent years, game has been slaughtered mercilessly. Of course there is still quite a bit of game, but one must travel dozens of versts to reach it. I haven't gone hunting even once so far. On one occasion Lyova went out on a trip of about twenty-five versts [seventeen miles], but without results (possibly because they slept past dawn that morning). In eight or ten days the spring flights will begin here. I will then take a trip to the River Ili (which flows into Lake Balkhash). Don't forget that I am living virtually in China. They say that many flocks of wild birds fly past there. Near Balkhash itself snow leopards and even tigers are found. With the latter I intend to sign a mutual nonaggression pact.

I already mentioned the slowness of mail deliveries. Muralov wrote me a letter on January 24. (He telegraphed me about it.) Today is February 27 and I still haven't received his letter. I have managed to exchange telegrams with nearly all our friends. Serebryakov is the only one from whom I haven't received an answer. No letters have come from anyone, except for one postcard, sent by Sibiryakov while en route to his place of exile.

Our quarters are in the middle part of the city, which is quite a bad area. In April or May we plan to move to the so-called orchards, that is, higher up in the mountains, where the climate is incomparably healthier. The weather here is already spring-like. Almost all the snow has melted (there was an unusually large amount this year).

# 'PRAVDA' SOUNDS THE ALARM

## March 5, 1928

*NOTE: A letter to Lev Sosnovsky in Barnaul. (Ivar Smilga was in Narym.)*

*Sosnovsky was one of the firmest of the deportees, a representative of the "intransigent" current, which rejected any conciliation with the Stalinists. In this letter Trotsky questions him about the attitudes of Vardin and Safarov, old friends of Sosnovsky and followers of Zinoviev who had refused to capitulate with Zinoviev and Kamenev, went into exile, but suffered from conciliationist moods and would in fact capitulate at the end of March. Trotsky refers again here to the letter, published in* Pravda, *of Zinoviev and Kamenev (the "knights of the rueful countenance"), attacking the Opposition's "Two Letters" intercepted by the Stalinists.*

*When Trotsky speaks of the elements that emerged in the party "who do not see classes in the village" and asks sardonically how it is that they did not adhere to the "Social Democratic deviation," he is referring to the tag the Stalinists had pinned on the Opposition for pointing to and warning against precisely these elements.*

*In this letter Trotsky uses an image that permeates his writings during this period: the right-wing "tail" that strikes at the centrist "head" of the body of state. He meant this as an admonition about the growing strength of the right wing—not only in the party but also in the country as a whole (the kulaks and other property-owning elements), and behind them the international bourgeoisie, which was waiting its chance—and the danger it presented to the dictatorship of the proletariat.*

*By permission of the Harvard College Library. Translated from the Russian for this volume by Marilyn Vogt.*

I received your letter three days ago; it took about twenty days to get here. This should be taken into account in future correspondence.

From your letter it undeniably follows that Barnaul is a far better place than Narym: Hurray for the wise ones who crossed out the word Narym on your travel orders and wrote in Barnaul.

I have already exchanged telegrams with Ishchenko and have written him a letter. I intend now to write to Vaganyan, having learned his address from your letter. You again mention Vardin and Safarov. Can't you let me know what kind of mood they're in and what impression the rather stupid and whining letter of the two "knights of the rueful countenance" made on them? Most remarkable is their argument about trade unionism. In the published document ["Problems of the International Opposition (Two Letters)"] we said that despite all the mistakes of the leadership—the miscalculations, the artificial slowing of the tempo of development, etc.—the Soviet government is doing immeasurably more for the working class than any bourgeois government could or would do, given the same general level of wealth of the country [see the second letter, point 17]. Our two philistines—pitching their voices by the official tuning fork—object that this is a narrow trade unionist criterion, that after all, the task of the Soviet government is not just to raise the material level, etc., etc., but also to build socialism.

Ah, what intelligent and clever individuals! How could we, nonbelievers in socialism, even dream of such wisdom? . . . If all the workers in the world believed that the criterion of the dictatorship of the proletariat was higher than narrow trade union criteria, we would have nothing to worry about. But the problem is that the bourgeoisie and Social Democracy scare the workers away from the dictatorship of the proletariat precisely by arguing that the dictatorship in itself leads to the impoverishment of the proletariat, citing the comparative living standards of the workers without regard to the development of the productive forces. It is in response to this basic argument of the Social Democratic scoundrels against the USSR and against the dictatorship of the proletariat in general that we assert: The workers of a bourgeois Russia, with productive forces at the same level, would never have had a living standard as high as they have now, despite all the mistakes, miscalculations, and departures from the correct line. And this is the argument that our repentant philistines call "trade unionist"!

Thank you for the newspaper clippings about the kulaks. They are very, very useful to me. Did you notice the editorial in *Pravda* February 15 on the grain collections? This editorial is truly remarkable. I quote: "Among a whole number of causes for the difficulties in grain collections, it is necessary to single out the following: The villages have expanded and enriched themselves. Above all, it is the kulak who has expanded and enriched himself. Three years of good harvests have not passed without leaving their mark."

This means that the obstacle to the grain collections, which means to the building of socialism as well, is the fact that "the villages have enriched themselves." And this because "three years of good harvests have not passed without leaving their mark," the article says instructively. Not without leaving their mark! One might think the author was talking about three earthquakes or about three plague epidemics. It turns out that "the increase in the income of the peasantry . . . given the relative lag in the supply of industrial goods, made it possible for the peasantry in general *and the kulak in particular,* to hoard grain." Further we read that although the kulak, that same kulak for which three epidemics of harvest have not passed without leaving their mark, although he is "not the principal hoarder of grain, nevertheless"—listen to this—"nevertheless he is the economic authority in the village"—why is this?—"has established a *smychka* with the urban speculator"—how did this happen?—"who pays higher prices for grain"—why is this?—and that "he (the kulak) has the possibility of drawing the middle peasant behind him" . . . Lord almighty, what kind of panic over the kulak is this? Why does this kulak "have the possibility of drawing the middle peasant behind him"? That is exactly how the article puts it. Why, you know, this is an antiparty document, not an editorial. As for the author, Barnaul would be too good for him. I would cross out Barnaul and write in Narym . . .

Further it says: "The line of our party in the village in a whole number of regions (???) has proven to be distorted." In which regions? What regions are exceptions? About this nothing is said, but to make up for it we learn that "the party organizations . . . have far from everywhere organized work with the village poor as yet." In a whole number of regions . . . far from everywhere . . . It would be good to be more precise about this geographically: then we could find out if we are talking about one-tenth or nine-tenths of the country. But the most striking passage comes further on:

"In our organizations, both in the party and elsewhere, certain elements alien to the party have emerged in the recent period who do not see classes in the village . . . and who attempt to conduct the work in such a way as to offend nobody in the village, to live in peace with the kulak, and in general to maintain popularity among 'all the layers' of the village." An amazing thing! Where did these elements "emerge" from when for four years the process of merciless "Bolshevization" of the party has been going on precisely over the question of the peasantry (1923-27)? And apparently these elements (it would be good if they were named by name) have not only "emerged" but have had such influence on policy that as a result, "the kulak is the economic authority in the village . . . and has the possibility of drawing the middle peasant behind him."

One more question remains: How is it that these "elements alien to the party"—further on they are called "degenerated elements," which means they did not "emerge" but *degenerated*— how is it that these alien, degenerated elements did not reveal themselves in connection with the most important questions of party life in recent years? How is it that they didn't adhere to the "Social Democratic deviation"? The fact that they are alien to the party and have degenerated was discovered somehow in passing in connection with the grain collections as a kind of surprise. Can one doubt that these alien elements and degenerated individuals were and are the most inveterate haters of the "Social Democratic deviation," and the most ardent supporters of the "building of socialism in our country?" We can expect more than a few surprises from them in the future. The grain collections are a big problem; but after all there are bigger problems: for example, war or revolution in Europe. If the kulaks have the possibility of drawing the middle peasants behind them, and if elements who more than anything else want to live in peace with the kulak have emerged, appeared, or degenerated in the party, then in the event of major upheavals, complications, or policy turns, this could have a very telling effect. It is *bound* to have. This is the same old tail which has struck at the head (as yet only gently) in connection with the grain collections. In the event of a war, this tail will try to replace the head, or in any case will present its own stiff terms. But those in Barnaul, Narym, Alma-Ata, etc., will unconditionally and without reservations defend that very "socialist construction" which they supposedly do not recognize.

In the way of practical measures, the kulak's "surplus grain" is being confiscated, with *Pravda* recommending that 24 percent of the confiscated grain be handed over "to the poor." This is a much harsher measure than a compulsory loan of 150 million poods [2.7 million tons] from the top 10 percent of peasant households [see "Platform of the Opposition" in *Challenge 1926-*

*27*, p. 337]. Yet the proposal for a compulsory loan and other, similar proposals were said to be a renunciation of NEP, a return to grain confiscations, war communism, etc. Having heard so many speeches like that, the tail is now striking at the head, and apparently the blows are not all that gentle, because the *Pravda* editorial says further:

"Talk that we are allegedly abolishing NEP (listen well!), introducing grain confiscations, dispossessing the kulaks, etc., is counterrevolutionary chatter, against which it is necessary to wage a decisive struggle." The author of the celebrated slogan "Enrich yourselves" [Bukharin] is clearly offended. . . .

Charges of wanting to go back to war communism are appropriate for literary "discussion" against the Social Democratic deviation, but when the kulak is squeezing your tail, then the matter is no longer literary and you even recall something from Marxism. Further on, there are even threats directed at the "counterrevolutionary blowhards who talk about the abolition of NEP," and there are demands for purging the party of "alien and infiltrated elements." (But they have just been striking out at alien elements—or weren't those the right ones?)

The light-minded author of the article imagines that the alien elements who have appeared, infiltrated, or degenerated in our midst can be dealt with by an editorial. No, the matter is more serious than that. But years of falsification of Marxism have created a whole generation which "wants to live in peace with all layers" (except the layer of ["Social Democratic"] deviators). Meanwhile, underneath this new generation, and the degenerated elements of the old, major shifts in the social order have taken place, [that is,] "three years of good harvests have not passed without leaving their mark." And an ever heavier tail has been formed, which is testing its strength: first against the "Social Democratic deviation," and then on the grain collections question; later on it will get around to the question of power in its full dimension. No, dear friend, there will still be need of us, even great need.

Our advantage is that we have correctly foreseen. Marx says in his *Civil War in France* that at the time of the Commune, the Proudhonists and Blanquists ended up being forced to do exactly the opposite of what they had advocated before the advent of the Commune. We are seeing the same kind of surprises now, not only in the case of the grain collections but also in the case of the Canton uprising. We were told that soviets are appropriate only for a socialist revolution and that in China what is going on is a struggle against feudalism. And what really happened? In Canton, a city that is far from China's main industrial center, the overthrow of the reactionary forces, even if it was episodic, placed power in the hands of the workers, and this power immediately took the form of soviets, and these soviets proclaimed not only the confiscation of the large landholdings (to the extent that they existed) but the nationalization of the large industrial and transport enterprises. "Skillfully was it written on paper" (or let us admit, not so skillfully), but in reality things have turned out quite the opposite. I had many arguments with Zinoviev on this subject, oral and in writing, early last autumn. It was with these in mind that he later spoke of "regurgitation." But events came along and tested things out!

But enough about the large questions. In spite of your proposal, we have not once gone to the movies. This is most likely explainable by the fact that there are three of us and one of you. Rakovsky is in Astrakhan, not in Krasnaya Yara.

# A PAIR OF SANCHO PANZAS

## March 10, 1928

*NOTE: A letter to I. N. Smirnov, one of the most authoritative Oppositionist leaders in exile. Trotsky uses the letter of Zinoviev and Kamenev ("the two brave knights who, through the bitter irony of fate, both turn out to be Sancho Panzas") as a springboard to a fuller discussion of their political characters and finds still another way of explaining the United Opposition bloc to those who retrospectively questioned it.*

*In paragraph 4, Trotsky writes about Zinoviev: "He then advanced the slogan of support to the Wuhan government 'insofar as.'" This is a reference to Stalin's position in March 1917, supporting the Provisional Government "insofar as" it fortified the steps of the revolution and followed a course of satisfying the demands of the working class and the revolutionary peasantry. Only after Lenin returned to Russia from exile did the Bolshevik Party accept the slogan of no support to the Provisional Government.*

*By permission of the Harvard College Library. Translated from the French and Russian for this volume by Duncan Williams and George Saunders.*

Dear Ivan Nikitich:

At last I received your letter from Novo-Bayazet. And here I thought the climate was tropical there, with bananas growing right up to the table, tame leopards in the garden, etc. Alas, alas. The pleasant-sounding appellation Novo-Bayazet turns out to be a cover name for a backwoods hole-in-the-wall.

What you write about the grain collections and forced loans from the peasantry sounds indisputable to me—a drastic effort to get out of the difficulties they blundered into with their eyes closed. I have written to Sosnovsky about this in some detail. I enclose a copy of my letter to him. . . .

Today there came from Moscow—as part of the first package of letters—the first reaction to the letter of the two knights, who through the bitter irony of fate *both* turn out to be Sancho Panzas. Politically it is as though they had merged into a single figure. One person has made a witty reference to Zinoviev's "epidermal leftism." This was meant to suggest that while Zinoviev totally lacks any serious baggage, as far as a capacity for generalized thinking goes, he makes up for it with an instinctive inclination, lodged in his epidermis, as it were, to twitch to the left on every new occasion. But it is the very "skin deep" quality of his leftism, similar to an itch, that makes him so limited. In cases where some solid *musculature* is needed to back up one's leftism, Zinoviev fades out. But what kind of serious historical action is possible without solid muscle?

That is why Zinoviev fades out every time his erstwhile leftism is tested in action. In July 1923 he wrote some high-flown theses, insubstantial as ever, about the German revolution and concluded with this proposal: "to mark the anniversary of the [German] revolution—November 9 (1918)—with an antifascist demonstration." He was organically opposed to having the question of armed insurrection posed pointblank ("setting the date"), although things were made easier for him by the fact that the revolution was happening in a far-off place, "many forests and fields away." He wrote some no less high-flown theses on the question of the General Strike in Britain, ending with the words: "It goes without saying that the Anglo-Russian Committee must be maintained in the future as well." As in the case of the German revolution, he surrendered only after a fight. His theses on the Chinese revolution—not only before Chiang's coup but after it as well—ended with the conclusion that the "Communist Party must, of course, remain within the Kuomintang." Here he would make no concessions, and the result was to render his position on the Chinese question valueless. He then advanced the slogan of support to the Wuhan government "insofar as . . ." In the fall of last year, when the counterrevolutionary role of the Kuomintang in all its shadings had become crystal clear, he continued to defend the slogan of the *bourgeois-democratic* revolution in China, viewing the slogan of the proletarian dictatorship as—"Trotskyism." (At my very first meeting with Kamenev in May 1917, in reply to my words that I had no differences with Lenin, I remember he said, "I should think not—in view of the April Theses . . ." Of course not only Kamenev but dozens of others, leaving the Lyadovs aside for the moment, considered Lenin's position "Trotskyist" and not Bolshevik at all . . .)

Zinoviev's position on the new stage of the Chinese revolution was not "accidental," as we can see. Zinoviev is aware of this Achilles' heel of his, and therefore all his left-sounding resolutions and articles are preceded by qualifications which allow him to jump back when he has to face action. His entire tactical concoction at the Fifth Comintern Congress, with its thoroughly ambiguous resolutions, was based on this approach. The special Zinovievist interpretation of party unity was the same kind of qualification, allowing him to jump back in case of need. As you surely remember quite well, we all had a very clear realization of this. But we added: this time it will be rather difficult for him to jump back, because this time it will mean jumping *down* into nothingness. As it turns out, however, even that didn't stop him.

As for Kamenev, the opposite is true. His inclinations were always instinctively *to the right,* toward restraint, conciliation, avoidance, etc. The prayer he feels most affinity for, of all churchly prayers, is the one that says, "Let this cup pass from me." But unlike Zinoviev, he has a certain theoretical schooling. True, the scraps or trimmings cut from Lenin float to the surface with too much fat on them; nevertheless, the Leninist content is not totally distorted. He understood sooner than Zinoviev the need to dissolve the Anglo-Russian Committee. He seemed to recognize the need for the Communist Party to withdraw from the Kuomintang, but held his tongue. I think that if he had not been in Italy, he would have understood better than Zinoviev that for China after May 1927 the formula of the democratic dictatorship of the proletariat and peasantry was just as obsolete as it had been for Russia after February 1917. In the present situation too Kamenev understands better and more clearly what "capitulation" means. But political nature has had its way. Zinoviev jumps back from his leftist conclusions. Kamenev fears he will end up the victim of his own rightward inclinations. But on important questions they converge along the same line. What can we call this line? Neither whoa nor giddy-ap.

I have told many comrades, and probably you too, the brief conversation I had with Vladimir Ilyich shortly after the October Revolution. I said something like this to him: "What surprises me is Zinoviev. As for Kamenev, I know him well enough to be able to predict where the revolutionary in him will end and the opportunist begin. Zinoviev I don't know personally at all, but from descriptions of him and a few of his speeches it seemed to me that he was a man who would be stopped by nothing and who feared nothing." To this V.I. [Vladimir Ilyich] replied: "He fears nothing when there's nothing to fear." With that the conversation ended.

Of course one can ask the "nasty" question: If all this was known in advance, how in the world could the bloc have been possible? But that is not a serious approach. The bloc was not a matter of personalities. In the case of the Anglo-Russian Committee, we were lectured: What counts is not the leaders but the masses. That approach of course is false and opportunist, because what is involved is not only the *masses* but also the political *line*. One cannot abandon the correct political line for the sake of being with the masses. But the struggle for the masses, given the correct political line, may include a bloc not only with the devil or the devil's grandmother but also with a pair of Sancho Panzas.

# PYATAKOV:
# A POLITICALLY FINISHED MAN

## March 17, 1928

*NOTE: A letter to A. G. Ishchenko in Kainsk. Pyatakov disavowed Opposition ideas and appealed for readmission to the party in a letter dated February 28 and published in* Pravda *the next day.*

*By permission of the Harvard College Library. Translated from the Russian for this volume by Ron Allen. Parts of this letter appear in* The Case of Leon Trotsky, *p. 118.*

Dear Aleksandr Gavrilovich:

I received your letter of March 2 yesterday, March 16. It's a new speed record. And here's the best evidence of that: your letter referred, "on the basis of *Pravda*," to Pyatakov's little letter of confession; yet we did not receive the issue of *Pravda* containing his letter until today. You speak of Pyatakov's deceitful and stupid document with indignation. I can fully understand that, but I must confess that I don't feel that way myself, because for a long time I have considered Pyatakov to be a politically finished man. In moments of frankness he told me more than once, with a tired and skeptical tone, that politics did not interest him and that he wanted to change his status to that of a "specialist." More than once I told him, half-jokingly, half-seriously, that if one fine morning, he awoke to find himself under a Bonaparte, he would still take his briefcase and head for the office, inventing on the way some miserable pseudo-Marxist "theory" to justify himself . . .

When you and I entered into sharp, but transitory, debate, what distressed me most was the fact that some comrades did not want to see, as it were, that Pyatakov is a political corpse who pretends to be alive and invents all sorts of slapdash sophisms to give himself the appearance of a revolutionary politician. Of course, some great European or worldwide revolutionary wave might bring even Pyatakov back to life; after all, they say Lazarus rose from the dead, although he already stank . . . In that event, Pyatakov, left to himself, would inevitably make *ultraleft* blunders. In short, Lenin was right again when he wrote that in a serious political matter Pyatakov cannot be relied upon [see Lenin's *Collected Works,* vol. 36, p. 595].

Of course, I do not mean to say that Pyatakov's defection, or Zinoviev's or Kamenev's, does not matter from the point of view of the development of Bolshevik ideas. I have never expressed such an opinion. Every individual who stands for anything represents a tiny counterweight, or even an entire pendulum, within the clockwork of the class struggle. I have had occasion to speak and debate with Pyatakov hundreds of times, in company as well as tête-à-tête. This alone testifies that I was in no way indifferent to the question of whether Pyatakov would be with us or against us. But it was precisely these numerous talks and debates that convinced me that Pyatakov's thinking, despite all his abilities, is absolutely devoid of dialectical force and that there is much more insolence than willpower in his character. For me it has long been clear that at the first test of a "split" this material would not hold.

It distresses me very much that you are obliged to devote such a substantial part of your time to pure office work. You are, after all, one of the youngest in our ranks and you very much ought to utilize the present suspension from real work for arming yourself theoretically. However, it's evident from your letter that you don't need this advice. What you need is free time, which is eaten up entirely at your office. How vexing it is! That your office is smoke-filled and stuffy is an additional outrage. If I were in your place, I would demand that the local Soviet executive committee, or party committee or Rabkrin [the Workers' and Peasants' Inspection], instead of jawing about rationalizing work processes in general, make the elementary improvement of forbidding smoking in workplaces during working hours.

I complained to you about not receiving foreign newspapers, and in your letter you responded to this. But just yesterday afternoon I began to receive a few foreign newspapers, first of all from Rakovsky in Astrakhan, but apparently also from Moscow. (I haven't yet gone through the past few days' mail properly; I have been absent for five days.)

You tease me with [stories about] the ducks, geese, and swans at Kainsk. Well, I just returned yesterday from a hunt for ducks, geese, and swans. I went hunting with my son for the first time since we came here. We went to the Ili River, about one hundred versts [sixty-six miles] from here. The hunting there was very good, although we went too soon; the migratory flights have barely begun. But the worst thing was the difficult physical conditions on the hunt. At Iliysk, seventy-three versts from here [forty-eight miles], there is still some sort of shrubbery, but beyond that stretches bare steppe, with saline soil in which only wormwood grows, or in flooded areas, reeds. Only Kirgiz inhabit these areas, the majority of them extremely poor. Our first night was spent, believe me, in the hut of the local representative of the Soviet meat-procurement agency Myasoprodukt. The hut was like a dungeon, with little windows barely above the ground and no furniture other than a felt mat. There were fourteen of us on a floor that was sixteen arshins square [thirty-seven square feet]. Right there in the room was the hearth on which muddy water was boiled for tea. The second night was spent in a Kirgiz *yurt,* even smaller in size, even dirtier, and even more confining. As a result I bagged only fourteen ducks in all, but to make up for it, I got a much larger quantity of insects. Nevertheless, I am planning to repeat the trip in a day or two, since the hunting season ends on April 1. But this time I will get a commitment from my companions to spend the night outdoors: it's immeasurably more pleasant.

# OUR CORRESPONDENTS

## April 12, 1928

*NOTE: A letter to Karl and Rebecca Griunshtein, in Cherdyn. This letter gives a summary of the far-flung residences of the deportees and some flavor of the conditions of their lives.*

*By permission of the Harvard College Library. Translated from the Russian for this volume by Julie Tihey and George Saunders.*

Dear Friends:

Your letter of March 24 was received today, April 12. This is a relatively acceptable length of time for mail delivery. Sometimes it's much worse. On the day I received the telegram from you, I sent you a postcard. I hope you received it. Your letter is especially good in that it gives a rather clear picture of your living conditions. Unfortunately it is not a very cheerful or comforting picture. I gather that obstacles are being placed in your way in regard to correspondence and in regard to fishing and hunting. If that is so, it is undoubtedly a case of local authorities acting on their own. It was the same for us here at first. But after protest telegrams were sent to Moscow the situation changed. I think that you must resolutely protest senseless interference of every kind.

The arrival of the mail is the high point of our day, just as it is for you in Cherdyn. During the first few weeks there was no mail at all. We sent postcards and telegrams to all the friends' addresses that we then knew. Your address was one of the last to reach us. Gradually we began to receive answers, at first by telegraph and then by mail. Rakovsky and Sosnovsky write most regularly of all. We have managed to exchange several letters with them already. Besides that Rakovsky sends me foreign newspapers from Astrakhan. I have begun to receive foreign newspapers from Moscow as well, along with books . . .

From I. N. Smirnov we have already had a letter from his place of residence, that is, Novo-Bayazet in Armenia. His hole-in-the-wall sounds as though it could compete with Cherdyn, although it is located at the other end of the map. From Serebryakov we have received only a postcard. He is working on the Turkestan-Siberia Railway and is well situated but complains of boredom. There was a card from Radek. He is reading and working a lot, complains of kidney trouble. (He did not write us about that himself; his wife did.) There was a letter from Beloborodov (from Ust-Kulom in the Komi autonomous region). In that exile colony it is hard to get candles and kerosene. Valentinov lives there too. There was a letter from Ishchenko from Kainsk, 37 Kraskov Street. He has a job there and complains that the extreme red tape robs him of all the time he wanted to spend on his own projects. Ishchenko wrote under the fresh impression of Pyatakov's extremely stupid letter [capitulating to Stalin], which aroused Ishchenko's great indignation. We received a very cheerful letter from Kasparova from Kurgan (109 Sovietskaya St.). It seems that Kasparova's son has also been exiled from Moscow, according to what they write to our son. Thus far there have been only two telegrams from Mrachkovsky (Veliky Ustyug, Kurochkin Street). In the second telegram received only a few day ago he complains of not receiving any letters from me, although I wrote the first letter to him back on February 28, that is more than a month ago. N. I. Muralov is working in a district planning office (town of Tara, 3 Fourier St.). We have received two letters from him. There was also a letter from Preobrazhensky from Uralsk (13 Nekrasov Square). Preobrazhensky is also doing government work, side by side with a former member of the Central Committee of the Right SRs—Timofeyev. He is doing a lot of theoretical work. Incidentally, right now he's in Moscow because he has had a son born there . . . I have written to Smilga in Narym several times and received a telegram from him and a group of comrades located in the same area, but no letter from there as yet (Kolpashevo postal district, Narym). There was also a telegram from Vrachev, in Vologda, and from Yushkin and Drozdov, in Andizhan. The telegram was sent while they were en route [to their place of exile]. Eltsin is in Ust-Vym (in the Komi region). Comrade Sermuks ended up there also. We received a telegram from him in the last few days. That seems to be all of the comrades with whom we have established, or are in the process of establishing, correspondence. With the exception of Moscow. Today at the same time your letter came we received a letter from Rakovsky. He's doing a lot of work in the provincial planning commission and a lot of literary work. He's working on the topic of Saint-Simonism for the Institute of Marx and Engels. In addition he's working on his own memoirs. That seems to be all the most important information that I can pass on to you briefly about our friends at this point.

I am working on the postwar decade. The long-term aim of this work is to draw the generalized lessons of the postwar international revolutionary struggle, based on an assessment of the main trends in postwar economics and politics. Part of the material I brought with me. My younger son will have to bring the rest of the books. We are expecting him to arrive here within the next few weeks. Besides that I'm translating Marx's pamphlet on Karl Vogt from German and I'm planning to translate a small book by the British utopian socialist Hodgkin for the Marx and Engels Institute's publishing house.

As for our domestic arrangements, they are fairly pleasant, especially in comparison with other friends. My health was fairly good until I caught cold recently. Now I have bronchitis in the wake of the grippe. But it seems I'm already on the mend. Things are not so well with Natalya Ivanovna. She has had a relapse of malaria, which is very widespread in this region. The sanitary conditions are terrible. The local doctor suspects that I too have malaria, not just the grippe. We have big hopes for the summer season when we can go up into the hills some eight versts [five miles] from the city, where there are orchards and summer houses (dachas)—more accurately, summer barracks. The climate there is incomparably better. It's cool there in the summer and the malaria hardly reaches that high. We can move to a summer house in early May.

I am enclosing a report on our hunting expeditions written for the hunting comrades Preobrazhensky and Muralov, and for the candidate hunter Rakovsky. The hunting season is now over. We have to wait until the first of August. In the meantime we are getting ready to fish. We will send timely reports on our successes or failures. I hope that you too will have the chance to put your hunting and fishing tools to work.

# THE RELATION OF CRITICISM
# TO SUPPORT

## Early May 1928

*NOTE: In this memorandum, which may be an excerpt from a longer piece, Trotsky makes use of an analogy between the Soviet state and the labor movement to help clarify the debate over whether the Opposition should give critical support to Stalin's "left turn."*

*By permission of the Harvard College Library. Translated for this volume from the Russian by Sonja Franeta.*

The question of [critical] support is more and more in need of theoretical discussion, because according to official doctrine, any criticism that accompanies support, by its very existence, cancels out that support and places the critic directly in the camp of counterrevolution. The question is presented in either-or fashion—either there is support without criticism or there is criticism, but from the other side of the barricades. Is this kind of approach correct?

Let's take the attitude of the Communist toward the present-day British working class movement and its organizations. Did we support the General Strike and the miners' strike? More energetically than anyone else. Did we criticize the leadership? Not enough by far. But that was our failing, not something to our credit. (I am speaking of the official line.) Is criticism compatible with support? One would think there would be no question here. In most cases criticism is the most important part of support.

One could argue that the General Council [of the British Trades Union Congress] is one thing and the leadership of our country another. But the only thing that follows from that is a difference in the kind of criticism, its depth or sharpness. That is a problem that must be considered substantively in each case. The crux of the matter is, however, that since 1923 two closely interrelated principles have become firmly rooted among us: (1) any criticism at all constitutes an "ism"—an "ism" of the right or of the left;

and (2) any criticism of the blunders or oversights, or especially of the wrong line, of the leadership helps the "bourgeoisie" and is therefore counterrevolutionary.

From this not very elaborate "doctrine" (which would more accurately be called nonsense) there follow, however, certain political consequences of enormous importance. At each particular stage the parties of the Comintern are being cut up into right and left parts, so that no room remains for any criticism. At the root of this practice lies the a priori assertion of the leadership's infallibility. Of course this "doctrine" would not last one day if the leadership were not linked with the state. The state, being in an economically backward country, faces its own particular dangers. These dangers give rise to shifts of position. The most important guarantee against retrogressive shifts is international class control. But in fact the opposite happens. Every new shift domestically results in the Comintern being cut in two along a new line.

The official rejoinder is that not every criticism is counterrevolutionary, only the kind infected with an "ism." Splendid. But let them show us a single case of criticism that would not be taken as an "ism," that would be accepted as valid. The history of the Comintern for the past four years and more shows no such instance.

# LETTER TO RYAZANOV

## May 1928

*NOTE: A letter to David B. Ryazanov, the director of the Institute of Marx and Engels.*

*In deportation, Trotsky was able to make a living as a translator and editor for the Institute of Marx and Engels. In addition to Marx's* Herr Vogt, *he was translating some writings of the British Utopian socialist Thomas Hodgkin and the nine-teenth-century economists David Ricardo, John Ramsey McCul-loch, and John Stuart Mill. This letter reveals with what serious-ness he applied himself to this literary work.*

*Evidently in answer to a query from Ryazanov, Trotsky reviews the history of his relations with the State Publishing House (Gosizdat), which had published fifteen volumes of Trotsky's* Collected Works *before it ceased publication in 1927 and began suppressing and destroying all of Trotsky's work as part of the struggle against the Opposition.*

*By permission of the Harvard College Library. Translated for this volume from the Russian by Michael Sosa.*

Dear David Borisovich:

First allow me to give an account of the state, which is still quite modest, of my work for the Institute. From *Herr Vogt* I have translated roughly three Russian printer's sheets. They still need revision, particularly the places where there are quotations in many languages. They tell me that you are not insisting upon this translation. In any case, it would be a pity if the part already translated went unused. I intend to revise it, therefore, and depending upon your answer, to send it to you. I am not refusing, however, to do a complete translation of the whole book, only please do not insist upon an exact date.

As far as Hodgkin goes, in another month and a half I will finish it. He has quotations from Ricardo, McCulloch, and Mill. The translation of them does not present any problems, but as I understand it, you are publishing or already have published Ricardo. Perhaps in the interests of maintaining a scholarly consistency for the publishing house, the wording of the quotations should follow the text of your edition. For this I would need to receive Ricardo.

Today I received volume one of the works of Marx and Engels. The edition creates, from only a surface glance so far, a genuinely magnificent impression. Today I will begin an attentive reading of the book. As I understand it, my task comes down to a purely literary polishing of the text, that is, to the replacing of unsuitable expressions with more suitable ones. Do I understand it correctly? Concerning those places where the very sense seems doubtful to me, not having the original at my disposal, I can only draw the attention of the editorial staff to them.

Those are all the questions I have connected with the work carried out for the Institute.

My son told me that you expressed interest in the question of my accounts and general relations with Gosizdat. On this account the matter stands as follows. Upon the initiative of Gosizdat, and after great insistence by Meshcheryakov and others, I agreed to the publication of a collection of my works. My secretariat was included in the agreement with Gosizdat on my behalf. According to the agreement Gosizdat was obliged to pay, under normal conditions, for the work of editors, authors of notes, typists, and others. Concerning myself, I refused any fee in order to try to keep down the price of the edition. This was stipulated in the agreement as a special point.

Gosizdat discontinued publication for political reasons, and not business ones. Long before the publication was discontinued, every measure was taken to ensure that subscription to the publication would be made quite difficult. Retail sales, it seems, were dropped entirely, etc., etc. In ceasing publication Gosizdat gave as its formal reason the fact that in the agreement, the overall size of the edition was to be 500 printer's sheets, while the edition had actually exceeded these limits. It is possible. But when the agreement was written, these 500 printer's sheets were in no sense limiting. It was simply necessary to project on paper an approximate number of volumes and the general cost of the edition. Work on the publication was constantly conducted in dependence upon the available material, and not on the approximate number of printer's sheets mentioned above. The best proof of this is that the most important volumes, to which both the editors of my works and the editorial board of Gosizdat attached more serious significance, remained unpublished to the end. More careful and detailed work was carried out on them. For example, the Comintern volume, in which it was necessary to place the numerous documents of the Comintern written by myself. The publication was suppressed under the false pretext cited above. Several volumes, which are totally prepared and supplied with notes, lie in my archive. Workers remained either unpaid or half paid. I am not able to give you an exact account, since Comrade Poznansky was in charge of this work. I recall that he said to me that representatives of Gosizdat privately cited their contradictory position. He said that the publication might bring Gosizdat a large profit, but that Gosizdat was compelled to follow a policy that would produce a deficit. However, a deficit is not financially advantageous to Gosizdat, etc., etc. However that may be, the role of Gosizdat in this matter, in regard both to myself and to my collaborators, has been, to say the least, unsavory.

In conclusion, allow me to thank you very, very much for the books sent by the Institute, and to express a modest hope for the continuation of this in the future. I am presenting the list of books received separately. The books arrived all right by registered book rate, although the first volume of Marx and Engels was somewhat battered on the way.

With best Marxist and Communist greetings,

L. Trotsky

P.S. Where would you like me to make my editorial comments on the Marx and Engels texts: in the margins of the book itself, or on a separate sheet with an indication of the page number? If you prefer the first way, then another copy of the works will be necessary, otherwise I will not have one of my own.

L.T.

# WE CANNOT FOLLOW
# A SHORT-RANGE POLICY

## May 9, 1928

*NOTE: Apparently a circular letter. A note in Trotsky's hand-writing at the top of the first page said, "So as not to hold things up, I am sending this along for the time being. I will answer your letter tomorrow or the day after."*

*In this letter Trotsky broaches the subject of the collective Opposition declaration to be submitted to the Sixth Comintern Congress in July. That declaration is in this volume. In February, the ninth plenum of the Executive Committee of the Comintern (ECCI) had been held. Here he assesses the Stalinists' left turn at that plenum, pointing out that it vindicates the Opposition's stand for party unity and against a new party. He defends and explains the tactic of critical support, pointing out that the left turn opened up "many more possibilities and opportunities" for the Opposition than it had had six months or a year earlier. And he points out that it is precisely because of the Opposition's uncompromising criticism that the centrists were unable to seek a way out of their troubles by turning to the right, which would have benefited the Ustryalovs. (Ustryalov was a member of the bourgeois Cadet party who fought on the White side in the civil war. After the victory of the Bolsheviks he went to work for the Soviet government as an economist because he believed it would inevitably be compelled to restore capitalism. The Left Opposi-tionists, following Lenin, often used Ustryalov as an example of the alien class forces favoring and working for the restoration of capitalism within the Soviet apparatus.)*

*By permission of the Harvard College Library. Translated from the Russian for this volume by L. Hall. A small part of this letter is in* The Case of Leon Trotsky, *p. 111.*

Dear Friend:

From here we cannot conduct a short-range policy, speaking out episodically on individual, even if vital, questions. A certain small advantage does result from the enormous "inconveniences" of our situation. That is, we can speak only in generalizations, about the situation as a whole. We must send a declaration to the Sixth Comintern Congress—collectively, insofar as that is possible—presenting our positions on current international and domestic policy.

The purpose of this declaration is to "say what is." There must not be any exaggerating, or any disregard of the present official attempts to get out of the quagmire. But also there cannot be any diplomatizing, lying, falsifying, or corrupt politicking in the spirit of Zinoviev-Kamenev-Pyatakov, no self-indulgently officious, thoroughly irresponsible Pontius Pilate–like washing of the hands, in the spirit of Krestinsky, and no Smerdyakov-like groveling in the spirit of Antonov-Ovseenko. Of course, there is no need for me to mention this. What we must speak is the truth, the whole truth, and nothing but the truth.

It is necessary to present the domestic questions from an international point of view. No domestic policy can be of any help without a correct and tenacious course toward the international proletarian revolution. In fact, a correct domestic policy is not even conceivable without a correct, well-thought-out international policy. We must squarely pose the question of all the disastrous mistakes made by the Comintern, beginning in 1923—Bulgaria, Germany, Estonia, England, and China. All the authority accumulated over several decades and reinforced by the October Revolution has been directed toward disrupting revolution. At first this was done only episodically, through thoughtlessness, short-sightedness, and superficial thinking, but more recently this has been done as part of a new system which elevates those three qualities to the level of "theory."

As long ago as 1851 Engels wrote: "If the revolutionary party lets decisive moments pass, without having its say, or if it intervenes and doesn't win, then it can be considered ruined for a certain length of time." In our case revolutionary moments have systematically been missed, and what is worse there have been "interventions" directed *against* the objective logic of revolutionary developments. The decisive moments that have been missed were in Germany and Bulgaria. Opportunist intervention that ran counter to the course of development took place in England and China. Adventuristic intervention that was opposed to the logic of development occurred in Estonia and Canton. I cite only the most outstanding examples. In this way, it is possible, as Engels expressed it, "to ruin the party for a certain length of time." Under the powerful impulses of the age of imperialism, the masses again move to the left and toward us. But when the situation reaches a decisive pitch, we opportunistically disrupt it; later on we try adventuristically to repair the irreparable. We end up, like the Danaids, eternally trying to fill a sieve with water.

Let me give just one illustration. It is very fresh and truly staggering. The Central Committee of the Chinese Communist Party—opposed to us—was declared to be irreproachable. Then suddenly it turned out to be Menshevik. It was deposed. A new, genuinely Bolshevik one was put in—and all this behind the scenes. After Canton comes a new surprise: the "irreproachable" Central Committee, in its second edition, turns out to be an advocate of "permanent revolution." Kaleidoscopic changes of leadership, without any proper kind of ideological life, without any critical assessment of experience, and without any continuity or revolutionary maturing process.

The question of a fully rounded discussion and theoretical elaboration of all aspects of the Chinese revolution is in no way less important than the evaluation of the present domestic economic turn. Once again, not even the "finest" domestic policy will bring victory if the revolution is disrupted by an erroneous international strategy and, most importantly, *if the International does not learn from its mistakes.* But the latter is not possible as long as the concealment of mistakes is made a matter of government prestige, backed up by the *resources of the state.* This is a life-and-death question for the international proletarian revolution.

Concerning the essence of the line in China. The slogan of a bourgeois-democratic coalition dictatorship of the proletariat and the peasantry has already become a reactionary slogan for China. This is far clearer and more apparent than it was for Russia after the February revolution. Tomorrow this slogan will inevitably become a new trap for the Chinese party and a screen for a new Kuomintang at a higher stage in the revolution's development.

The question of so-called workers' and peasants' parties in India, Japan, and so on, is no less important. These are all embryos of a new Kuomintang.

The decisions on domestic matters (in regard to the kulak, etc.) and the decisions of the recent ECCI represent an inconsistent and contradictory step; but all the same they are unquestionably a step in our direction, that is, toward the correct path. This must be stated plainly and distinctly. But, in the first place, we must

not overstate the size of this step. After the experiences we have
gone through, we must be more cautious than ever when a turn
comes, giving no unnecessary credit in advance. In the second
place, we must briefly explain the causes, the mechanics, and the
ideology behind this turn.

Why is this necessary? Because what is most important to us is
what stands out in the minds of the vanguard, or the vanguard of
the vanguard. It is not only *what you do,* but *how you conceive of
what you do.* Political empiricism (narrow pedantry, pragmatism)
is the mortal enemy of Bolshevism. No indulgence to empiricism.
No indulgence to epigonism, which strains at gnats but swallows
camels. (They have made the party, the country, and the whole
world repeat by rote what so-and-so said in 1904 about the
revolution and its permanence; meanwhile they slept through the
entire vast Chinese revolution of 1925-27; has there ever in
history been such pernicious epigonism?)

Why did the changes in our attitude toward the kulak in our
country, toward MacDonald and Purcell in England, toward
Blum in France, and toward the Kuomintang in China—all
happen to come so fortuitously at the same time? Where can we
look for the source of any objective need for this change? In
Shanghai? In London? In Paris? In these places the objective
necessity for doing away with opportunist policies was evident
long ago. Nevertheless . . . this necessity was felt in Moscow.
Who created it? Surely we did, as "the only conscious expression
of the unconscious process." If we had not been present, the
current economic difficulties would have resulted in an enormous
victory for the Ustryalovs.

Why were we crushed organizationally? We have already
answered that question. The defeat was the culmination of an
enormous shift in the worldwide balance of forces that took place
over the last several years, specifically from 1923 to 1928.

More than once in history the vanguard has, through its own
defeat, ensured the taking of a step forward or at least delayed a
retreat or a slide downward. Thus, the Paris Commune, aside
from its central importance as a landmark in the proletarian
struggle for power, ensured the establishment of the republic in
France. The Moscow insurrection in December 1905 ensured the
convocation of the state Duma. In different conditions, and in a
different sense, only because we paid a very heavy price but
succeeded in raising all the most important questions on a
nationwide and on a world scale, have the brakes been put on the
backsliding process and a serious step to the left been taken at

the present stage. All the less reason do we have to ignore this step or underestimate it.

We predicted that *the tail would strike at the head* and cause a realignment of forces (see in particular, the debate at the February 1927 Central Committee plenum).

And here, somehow, by accident, a trifle has been revealed: the state grain procurement is in the hands of those who want to live in peace with all classes. Where did these worthy builders of socialism in one country come from, and how did they acquire such strength? It is these elements that constitute the rightist, Ustryalovist tail (or more accurately, the party segment of this tail), which is hitting at the centrist head, trying to make it drop the leftist capers, which are not in the program. The tail will show itself further, for it has a powerful following within our country and, especially, beyond our borders, in the capitalist world. We are necessary to the party (to its proletarian-Bolshevik core) precisely in order to deal with this "tail."

*        *        *

On the other hand, the fact that a shift has taken place—that is, that it has proved to be possible within the AUCP and the Comintern and is *capable of becoming* (no more than that for now) the initial phase in a new course—this fact proves the correctness of another orientation of ours as well: that is, the unity of the party and the Comintern, the struggle for a Bolshevik line on the basis of *genuine* party-mindedness, the kind which is not afraid, whenever necessary, to place the essence of the matter higher than any form. In this we are correct against the second-party tendencies, both here and abroad.

I will not dwell on the theoretical (economic, class) evaluation of the indicated official shift. On the whole, what was said on this score by Comrade Preobrazhensky is correct. However, in this area I think we must emphasize as strongly as possible that the kulak question is not decided by groupings in the countryside or, in general, by rural politics. This issue is directly subordinate to the question of the commanding heights of our economy, above all, industry. Farsighted management of the state economy, including first and foremost its relation to peasant agriculture— that is the key question. Even in the capitalist system one large corporation may prosper, depending on its organization and management, while another is ruined. That giant corporation of corporations—the state economy—can also be ruined by shortsighted, unprincipled, uninspired management. Over and above the kulak question stands the question of industrialization (that's what Zinoviev didn't understand, not only in 1923, but also in 1927). And superseding both is the question of a correct leadership in the Comintern, and the training of cadres capable of overthrowing the world bourgeoisie.

Are we ready to support the present official turn? We are, unconditionally, and with all our forces and resources. Do we think that this turn increases the chances of reforming the party without great upheavals? We do. Are we ready to assist in precisely this process? We are, completely and to the utmost of our ability.

Charges that we broke the promise given at the Fifteenth Congress are rude and disloyal nonsense. We spoke honestly and sincerely of our willingness to renounce factional methods. In doing so we assumed with certainty that the above-mentioned tail would strike at the above-mentioned head and cause a change in the party, which would make it possible to defend a correct line without factional convulsions. But how can one speak of "nonfactionalism" when we have been expelled from the party? "Nonfactionalism" in this case is tantamount to renunciation of the party. Only a vile bureaucrat is capable of making such demands of a Bolshevik. Pyatakov thoughtfully explains to us that our position is "contradictory." That, you see, is why he has made his suicidal dive into the depths. It cannot be denied that for a drowned man, all contradictions disappear. But "the dead corpse of a drowned person," to use one of Chekhov's choice phrases, is hardly a fitting leader for a revolutionary struggle. The contradiction in our position is a living, historical contradiction, which can be overcome only through action, based on correct knowledge of the objective course of events.

In our letter to the Comintern, do we demand our reinstatement in the party? Absolutely. Do we promise to observe discipline and not form a faction? We do. Now, with the indicated official change of policy, one we helped bring about, we have many more possibilities and chances of keeping our promise than we had half a year or a year ago.

It goes without saying that the tone of the letter must be completely calm, so that the real state of affairs may be clearly seen; namely, that the epigones' policy of petty tyranny has not embittered us in the least—true politics knows no spite. We see higher and farther than that, and our very definite attitude toward narrow pedantry, opportunism, disloyalty, and treachery does not in the least obscure our attitude toward the historical Bolshevik Party and the historical tasks of the world working class.

# CONDITIONS IN ALMA-ATA

## May 16, 1928

*NOTE: Probably a circular letter. By permission of the Harvard College Library. Translated from the Russian for this volume by George Saunders.*

How are we getting along here? We have had to answer this question dozens of times already, for our "correspondents" are increasing in number very quickly. Nevertheless I recognize the total validity of the question, since I myself read with the greatest interest those letters in which comrades tell about themselves, about their being relocated, how they got settled, how they are getting along, and what work they are doing.

To report briefly: for about three weeks we lived in a hotel—after which we were given the opportunity to relocate to an apartment, which at first occupied half a house, but now comprises the entire house. This "house" however, consists of four rooms. By way of exception, the apartment has electricity. In view of the extremely feeble output of the local power plant, there is electricity only in government institutions and the homes of government employees. However, in view of the same feeble output and general worthlessness of the power plant, the electric current which is supposed to be functioning, according to the official schedule, roughly from 7 a.m. to 12 p.m. plays nasty tricks, going off for several minutes every now and then, sometimes for half an hour or more at a stretch. The apartment is left dark and its occupants begin calling out to one another: Should we light the candles and the kerosene lamp? Or wait for the electricity to come back on?

As for the availability of food, here too severe interruptions have been evident, especially when it comes to bread. Here it is, a month and a half already, that the city has been suffering shortages, especially a shortage of bread: terribly long waiting lines, extremely limited amounts of bread, and extremely poor quality. The price of a pood [32 lbs.] of wheat flour on the free market had remained constant at the level of ten rubles, but just in the last month it began going up and has reached twenty-five rubles. I must say, however, that personally, in this regard, we have been accorded every kind of preferential treatment. There was only one critical moment when it was completely impossible to get any bread. However, just before that happened, we quite unexpectedly received a package in the mail from Moscow, from P. S. Vinogradskaya, containing the very finest flour. From that we made our own bread, of the very highest quality.

There are very great difficulties here with meat also and with every kind of food in general. As far as manufactured goods go, what is sent here primarily are factory rejects, defective goods. In the bookstore I have not succeeded in finding a single book that I need. As it turns out, the library here is not short of books, at least not of old ones, but they are in total disorder, not catalogued but strewn about in chaotic heaps. I have access to them, however, and can choose any I need from them. It has very few new books published during the war or since the revolution, and absolutely no new foreign books. The number of periodicals received is also insignificant. All such things must therefore be obtained from outside.

As far as our so-called regimen is concerned, at first an excess of zeal was observed, which resulted in several very sharp conflicts. But now things have settled down, and I personally cannot complain in this regard.

The conception of Alma-Ata as a southern locality requires very substantial amendment. At any rate this year spring was very late, good days have been rare, interspersed with rainy and even snowy ones, with a last big snowfall coming at the end of April and damaging the cherry trees. This entire region, as is true of Central Asia in general, is a realm of horrifying dust, especially saline-soil dust. It is a region of malaria, and the presence of malaria in me is no longer subject to doubt. I swallow my quinine conscientiously every morning and this gives good results.

The city is laid out in terraces descending from the foothills to the plain. The farther down a section of the city is located, the more malarial it is. We live in the middle area and consequently have an average rate of malaria. In the summer it is almost impossible to live here because of the heat, the dust, and once again the malaria. At that time a migration goes on up into the "mountains," or more accurately the foothills, which here are called "the stopping places." Very extensive orchards are spread

out there and wooden "dachas" have been built, actually struc-
tures of a barracks type. During the summer period, houses are
also made simply of interwoven strips of lath which for some
reason here is called wickerwork. We too have secured for
ourselves a summer home.

At first we planned to move at the beginning of May, but now it
is already the sixteenth and we have not yet moved—both
because the summer house is unfurnished and because of the
rain, which has lowered the usual temperature greatly.

We subscribe to *Pravda, Izvestia,* and *Ekonomicheskaya Zhizn.*
Until recently the comrades have sent publications from Baku
and Tiflis. Sosnovsky frequently sends us very interesting clippings from Siberian and other newspapers. Foreign papers have
come from Moscow and above all from Comrade Rakovsky in
Astrakhan. Recently we have begun getting foreign newspapers
directly from abroad. I brought with me a certain number of
books for my work (alas, far fewer than was claimed in the
newspapers, which lied about the celebrated large number of
"boxes"). Our friends have sent books from Moscow. Some books
have also begun to come from abroad.

During this whole time I have been working mainly on China
and partly on India. I am still busy with the East primarily. But I
do not intend to limit myself to the East. I wish to draw some sort
of balance sheet on the postwar development of the world
economy, world politics, and the world revolutionary movement.
In my leisure hours I am writing memoirs, something Yevgeny
Preobrazhensky put me up to. Other than that, I am translating
some things for the Institute of Marx and Engels. And that it
seems is an ample reply to your question of how we are getting
along here.

# THE GENERAL OUTLINE
# OF MY WORK

## Mid-May 1928

*NOTE: A letter to Aleksandra L. Sokolovskaya, who recruited Trotsky to Marxism in the Ukrainian town of Nikolaev in 1897 and later married him while he was in prison awaiting Siberian exile. They had two daughters and later separated. Sokolovskaya, who had been an active member of the Opposition from 1923 on, was still living in Moscow. The Southern Russia Workers Union was the name of the organization Trotsky formed in 1897 in Nikolaev. The extensive research Trotsky did for his memoirs during 1928 was later incorporated into the first five chapters of his autobiography,* My Life.

*By permission of the Harvard College Library. Translated from the Russian by George Saunders.*

I received the memoirs by V. I. Vitte and am now reading them with interest. This book will surely prove to have things of use for me. That is because, in addition to my basic work—summing up world developments since the imperialist war—I am also working on my memoirs. Preobrazhensky put me up to that. I want to approach these memoirs in a broader way—that is, place them against the background of a certain epoch. I'm beginning from the "very beginning," from the countryside, followed by Odessa, later on Nikolaev, prison, exile, etc. The first part, which I have completed, culminates at Nikolaev—but before the Southern Russian Workers Union. I have dug the old periodicals, beginning with the 1870s, out of the library here. . . . I have made fairly wide use of these periodicals already and will make more excavations into them in the future. As auxiliary sources I'm now hunting up books of the most varied content, including for example, a guide to the cities of Odessa and Nikolaev, publications of the Kherson zemstvos and province zemstvos, memoirs by Narodniks and members of the People's Will, documents from the first phase of Russian Marxism, memoirs by officials, statistics on industrial development, especially in the south, and so on and so forth. . . . I absolutely do not intend to write a "scholarly work." But the main thing I want to do is provide—or more important, *preserve*—a sense of perspective, because the war and revolution have pushed aside the past, even pressed it back, so much that the young generation doesn't look for any long-term explanations of events. In particular this makes possible the most vulgar distortions of the prewar period.

This is the general outline of my work, which makes it both easier and more difficult to answer your question of exactly which books I need. I would give anything to have access to the Odessa newspapers of the period 1888-98 and the Nikolaev newspaper from 1895 to 1898. But it would seem that that is impossible unless some Odessa or Nikolaev comrade has kept a complete set from the old days, but that's hardly likely. . . . Of course I would conscientiously return anything sent to me to be read.

The second part of my memoirs will be on the Southern Russian Workers Union, prison in Nikolaev, Kherson, and Odessa, Butyrka prison in Moscow, the Alexandrov transit prison, Ust-Kut, and in general the whole period of Siberian exile. For the first part I have already written fairly extensive drafts. For the second part I haven't gotten down to work yet, but I have begun to collect material. Needless to say, on the second part your cooperation could have irreplaceable importance for me, both in the gathering of appropriate material and as far as personal reminiscences go. In particular I would like to go back over what we read in prison and exile, what books and issues concerned us, etc. I don't know if you've had occasion to write your memoirs touching on that period? It would be appropriate. They could of course be printed separately, but even in manuscript they could be of great help to me in my work. . . . It's hardly likely that one would find other such favorable conditions for writing one's memoirs as in blessed Alma-Ata. One condition: please do not buy any books for this work under any circumstances; just pick them up if a favorable occasion arises. As for the main work that I am doing, which I mentioned first, I will enclose here a brief report on what kinds of books I need. If you have appropriate books at hand, please send me a list of them without actually mailing the books, and then I'll write you which of them I would need. This way we would avoid duplicates being sent from different places. That's all, it would seem, as far as books go.

# THE OPPOSITION'S ERRORS—
# REAL AND ALLEGED

## May 23, 1928

*NOTE: A letter to Aleksandr Beloborodov in Ust-Kulom. Stalin's
"left turn" elicited a conciliatory tendency in some sections of the
Opposition. If Stalin could carry out important parts of the
Opposition's program in the countryside, then the Opposition
must have overestimated the degree of degeneration of the party
apparatus and the dangers of Thermidor. In this letter, Trotsky
demonstrates that the errors of the Opposition were exactly the
opposite: to preserve the bloc with elements that wavered and
hesitated, they had understated their position on many key issues
and failed to press their program as energetically as possible.
Then Trotsky turns to an explanation of what the left turn
represented and what should be the attitude of the Opposition
toward it, and discusses why he had erroneously anticipated a
turn to the right.*

*In March the authorities announced the uncovering of a
counterrevolutionary conspiracy in the mining town of Shakhty,
in the coal region of the Donets Basin (Donbass) in the Eastern
Ukraine. Fifty-five technical specialists and engineers in man-
agerial positions were arrested and accused of organized sabotage, corruption, and venality. A sensational trial followed in
May, with still more exposés later in the year.*

*This was a thinly veiled attack on the right wing, which was
most closely associated with the specialists and technicians. The
Bukharinist right wing in the party was responsible for management of the state apparatus (through Rykov) and for trade union
supervision of nonparty specialists and technicians (through
Tomsky).*

*This was the first of a series of "wreckers' trials" that were held
between 1928 and 1931. At first Trotsky viewed them simply as
scapegoat trials, in which the bureaucracy deliberately bared the
worst, most corrupt elements as a safety valve for public indigna-*

*tion and simultaneously as a way of striking out against the protectors of the bourgeois intelligentsia—the Bukharinist right wing. He also accepted the confessions of the accused as valid, a view he held until shortly before the first Moscow trial in 1936. In* Biulleten Oppozitsii *(Bulletin of the Opposition) no. 51, July-August 1936, he inserted the following note: "From the editors: The editors of the* Biulleten *must admit that in the period of the Menshevik trial [1931] they greatly underestimated the shamelessness of Stalinist justice and therefore took too seriously the confessions of the former Mensheviks" (*Writings of Leon Trotsky [1935-36], *pp. 552-53).*

*Trotsky's reference in point 6 to the Comintern draft program relates to the 1922 draft program, not the 1928 one, which was not yet public.*

*His argument against "parallel candidates" in point 13 (Oppositionists running against official party candidates in public elections) is simply an extension of the argument against a second party. Trotsky continued to urge Oppositionists abroad to act as factions of the official parties, rather than take organizational steps that would make them de facto separate parties. Nevertheless, a group of German Oppositionists expelled from the party established the Leninbund in March 1928, apparently over the objections of Ruth Fischer and Arkady Maslow, and fielded candidates in the Reichstag elections called for May 20. Radek sent a telegram disavowing any association with the Leninbund, and it was intercepted by the GPU and published in* Pravda *on May 4. Trotsky comments further on these issues in "The Methods of Leadership," June 2, 1928.*

*"The Master" was the way people in the party by now referred to Stalin. The Oppositionists, of course, used the term ironically.*

*The demonstration mentioned at the very end of point 13 is the tenth anniversary demonstration on November 7, 1927 (see* Challenge 1926-27, *pp. 263-66). When the Opposition formed its own contingents to take part in the demonstrations, they were savagely attacked by the Stalinist police. Zinoviev and Kamenev reacted to the savagery of the repression by retreating in the hope of avoiding further confrontations.*

*The Bleskov-Zatonsky case is described in "Preobrazhensky's Proposal," next in this volume.*

*Prince Svyatopolk-Mirsky, mentioned in the fifth paragraph from the end, was the minister in whose name the tsarist government carried out a half-hearted liberalization ("spring") at the end of 1904.*

*By permission of the Harvard College Library. Translated from the Russian by Tom Twiss.*

Dear Aleksandr Yegorovich:

Yesterday I received your letter of April 19 and it pleased me greatly. The letter contained much that was new to me. The voices talking about an overestimation of the backsliding absolutely have not reached my ears. The "letter" of which you speak is absolutely unknown to me. When I wrote my last letter (listing a number of points) I knew nothing about any voices referring to an overestimation of the backsliding. If there are such voices, we must give them the attention they deserve.

You write: "Most laughable of all is the woeful repentance that we overestimated the strength and speed of the backsliding. As though there exists in nature a yardstick by which one could measure the degree of backsliding and then, using the proper ratio, portion out the appropriate number of ounces of resistance to it. When and by whom was such a ratio ever established? As Bolsheviks, we were obliged to fight against the backsliding. And our estimation of it has been wholly confirmed in such areas as the grain collections, the goods famine, the sowing campaign, the Shakhty affair, China, the internal situation in the party, etc."

I subscribe completely to this general formulation of principle. But to supplement it I want to go back over the basic questions of the previous period very specifically to check on whether or not we did exaggerate the differences, go too far left, or overestimate the right deviation and the degree of backsliding.

1. *The miners' strike.* After the thwarting of the General Strike, it was completely clear that the miners' strike, as a protracted economic strike, had no prospects. Against the General Council, it was immediately necessary to take up the task of reviving the General Strike in as short a time as possible. In this spirit we wrote a short document predicting the inevitability of the defeat of a protracted, passively economic strike and the inevitability of the strengthening of the General Council by this. Pyatakov rebelled: "Is it conceivable to speak of the inevitability of defeat? . . . What will they say?" etc., etc. As if the question is decided by what they will say today, and not by what events will show tomorrow. But big concessions were made to Pyatakov along the lines of biological mimicry, that is, adapting to the coloration of the surroundings.

2. Closely connected with the first question was the slogan of dissolving the Anglo-Russian Committee. We raised this slogan a

little late, overcoming resistance. As in the first case, here too there was an underestimation of the disagreement and of the threatening results.

As a result of mistakes a gigantic movement produced insignificant political and organizational results: the General Council sits in its place and the Communist Party has hardly grown.

3. *China.* We publicly raised the slogan of the Communist Party's leaving the Kuomintang about two years later than was dictated by the entire situation and by the most vital interests of the Chinese proletariat and revolution. Even worse, there was a demonstrative renunciation of the slogan of leaving the Kuomintang in the Declaration of the Eighty-four [see *Challenge 1926-27,* p. 224]. This was in spite of the resolute (alas, not sufficiently so, but nevertheless, resolute) resistance by some of the signers of the declaration, including you and me. Here too there was a fear of what would be said and not of what events would show. Now only a blockhead or a renegade could fail to understand or could deny that the subordination of the Communist Party to the Kuomintang stood the Chinese revolution on its head. This means that here too was a mistake to the right and not to the left.

It was in the analysis of the experience and tendencies of the 1905 revolution that Bolshevism, Menshevism, the left wing of the German Social Democracy, etc., were formed. The analysis of the experience of the Chinese revolution has not less but more significance for the international proletariat.

4. Last fall we did not explain aloud that the experience of 1925-27 had already liquidated the slogan of the democratic dictatorship of the proletariat and peasantry for the Chinese revolution, and that in the future this slogan would lead either to a regurgitation of Kuomintangism or to adventures. This was quite clearly and precisely predicted. But even here we made concessions (completely impermissible ones) to those who underestimated the depth of the backsliding on the Chinese question.

5. To this day we have not come out decisively enough against the propagation of so-called worker-and-peasant parties in India, Japan, etc. We underestimated the full depths of the backsliding, expressed as early as 1924-25, in the illiterate slogan of "two-class workers' and peasants' parties for the East."

6. We did not raise the question of the Comintern program soon enough. In response to the theses we formulated on this question, Pyatakov objected: "It is not worthwhile to raise this. They will say we have even more programmatic differences. . . ." Yet Bukharin's draft is, at best, a left Social Democratic caricature of

a Communist program. Bukharin proceeds not from the world economy and its fundamental reciprocal relations (Europe-America-the East-the USSR) but from an abstract model of national capitalism. The adoption of this or a similar program now—after the experience of 1923 in Germany; after the events in Bulgaria and Estonia; after our discussions, in particular our discussions on America and Europe; after the experience of the English strikes; and especially after the Chinese revolution—would signify the ideological ruin of the Comintern, a precondition for its political and organizational ruin. We *underestimated* the importance of this question.

The allegation that Lenin "approved" Bukharin's program is a monstrous lie. Bukharin wanted his draft to be introduced in the name of the Politburo. At Lenin's initiative this was refused him, but he was allowed to introduce the draft in his own name as a starting point for discussion. Zinoviev told me that, after reading Bukharin's draft, V. I. said, "It could have been worse," or "I was afraid it would be worse," something of that sort. Bukharin was very interested in Lenin's opinion and kept asking Zinoviev about it. "I took a sin upon my soul then," Zinoviev told me, "by greatly softening Lenin's opinion."

7. To this day we haven't said even one-third of what we should have said on the basic questions of the policy of the Comintern and its regime. That is, again our sin was the exact opposite of an exaggeration of the differences or an overestimation of the backsliding.

8. But perhaps we overestimated the differences on *domestic* questions? Voices were heard to that effect (V. N. Yakovlev, Krestinsky, Antonov-Ovseenko, and others). They argued: "The domestic disagreements are not so great, but the party regime is intolerable." To this we answered: "(a) You are not inclined to evaluate the internal differences on the scale of world processes and world politics, but without that your evaluation becomes crudely empirical; you see little pieces but you don't see the way in which things are developing. (b) You doubly confuse things when you condemn the party regime, which you think has provided a correct political line [domestically]. For us the party regime has no independent significance—it only expresses everything else. That is why any experienced and serious politician must necessarily ask: 'If you think that a deep class shift in official policy has occurred, how do you explain the continuing "export" of people who are guilty only of having understood earlier and demanded a class shift earlier?'" The question here is

not at all one of justice, still less of "personal injury" (adults generally don't speak in such terms). No, this is a faultless gauge of how serious, well thought out, and deep is the shift that has occurred. Needless to say, the readings from this gauge are extremely disturbing.

9. In order to check whether or not we exaggerated the dangers or overestimated the backsliding, let us take up again the recent question of the grain collections. All questions of domestic politics intersect in this one question more than in any other.

On December 9, 1926, Bukharin spoke at the seventh plenum of the ECCI, supporting the charge of our Social Democratic deviation for the first time: "What was the most powerful argument that our Opposition used against the Central Committee of the party (I have in mind the fall of 1925)? They said then: the contradictions are growing monstrously, and the CC of the party fails to understand this. They said: the kulaks, in whose hands almost the entire grain surplus is concentrated, have organized a 'grain strike' against us. That is why grain is coming in so poorly. We all heard this. . . . Subsequently the same comrades took the floor to state: the kulak has entrenched himself still further; the danger has grown even greater. Comrades, if both the first and the second allegations were correct, we would have an even stronger 'kulak strike' against the proletariat this year. In reality . . . the figure for grain collections has already increased by 35 percent compared with last year's figures, which is an unquestionable success in the economic field. But according to the Opposition, everything should be to the contrary. The Opposition slanders us by stating that we are contributing to the growth of the kulaks, that we are continually making concessions, that we are helping the kulaks organize a grain strike; the actual results are proof of just the contrary" (Stenographic report, vol. II, p. 118). That's exactly what he said: "the contrary." Missing the mark completely. Our ill-fated theoretician finds evidence "to the contrary" in all questions without exception. And that is not his fault, or rather, not only his fault. In general the politics of retrogression cannot tolerate theoretical generalizations. But since Bukharin cannot live without this potion, he is obliged to proclaim at all funerals: "Carry [the coffin], but don't carry it too far."

Under pressure from those who were afraid to "overestimate," "exaggerate," or carry things too far, we spoke in muted tones at the seventh plenum. In any case, we did not reply to Bukharin's philosophy of grain collections. That is, we did not explain to him that one cannot judge all the basic tendencies of economic growth by conjunctural episodes, but that one must evaluate the conjunctural episodes in the light of basic processes.

10. But perhaps on this question we ran too far ahead, whereas others took account of the "peculiarity" of the new situation in good time? On this score we have the irrefutable and valuable testimony of Rykov. At a session of the Moscow Soviet on March 9, 1928, Rykov declared: "This campaign indubitably bears all the distinctive traits of shock-brigade work. If I were asked whether it would not have been better to manage in a more normal way, that is to say, without resorting to such a shock-brigade campaign, in order to overcome the crisis in grain collections, I would give the candid reply that it would have been better. We must recognize that *we have lost time, we were asleep at the beginning* of the difficulties in grain collection, *we failed to take a whole series of measures in time* which were necessary for a successful development of the grain collections campaign" (*Pravda,* March 11, 1928).

This testimony requires no comment.

11. In the document "At a New Stage," if you remember, we said: "The Stalinist pseudo-struggle against two parties conceals the formation of dual power in the country and the formation of a bourgeois party on the right wing of the AUCP, using its banner for camouflage" [see *Challenge 1926-27,* pp. 502-03].

At the February plenum of the ECCI Bukharin gave the following interpretation to those words: "Trotsky says: It is not we who are a second party; the AUCP is a second party. The AUCP has been degraded; we preserve the traditions; hence, we are the first party and the AUCP is the second. By these very words he admits the existence of two parties" (*Pravda,* February 17, 1928).

Thus, even in February of this year, Bukharin identified the interweaving of the bureaucrats and the new proprietors with the AUCP. Where we spoke of the germ of a second party, of the semi-Ustryalovist headquarters covered with the banner of the AUCP—thanks to the struggle against the left—Bukharin, as late as February of this year, replied: But, you see, this semi-Ustryalovist headquarters is in fact the AUCP. Moreover, in the grain collections crisis it is suddenly revealed that there are numerous and influential elements among us who do not recognize classes, or who want to realize the Martynovist theory of the bloc of four classes. For about two days they made a lot of noise about these elements. But somehow I have failed to notice that these elements, who control the grain collections not only in the center but also in the provinces, have been named by name, condemned, or anything like that. I am not even talking about the fact that not one of these elements has ended up at Ust-Kulom.

In any case we exaggerated nothing and overestimated nothing in regard to the grain collections or in regard to the semi-Ustryalovist headquarters forming under the cover of the AUCP, at the juncture of its right flank with the new proprietors.

12. Thus, politically, we were never guilty of exaggeration, overestimation, excessive deviation, or ultraleftism. On the contrary we made the opposite mistakes, yielding to weakness of character, indecisiveness, left-centrism, and demands for protective coloration. All this is demonstrated above, if such proof were needed at all. There is another question, however: Didn't we, perhaps, draw some *exaggerated organizational and tactical* conclusions from our political evaluations? Not in the slightest. The facts testify that we were not indulgent with those who tried, even in whispers, to declare the October Revolution liquidated, the party Thermidorian, the Soviet state bourgeois. We broke uncompromisingly with some excellent revolutionaries when they showed indications of taking a course toward a second party. (Incidentally, it is worth noting that Zinoviev himself opposed this break.) We accepted Zinoviev's "Lessons of the July Plenum" without closing our eyes to its wishy-washy character and the outright incorrectness of many formulations. We considered the basic idea of the theses—against two parties—indisputable, and that is precisely why we accepted them in spite of the isolated protests of comrades who, in this area, went too far to the "left." On the eve of and during the Fifteenth Congress, the urge for protective coloration totally overran us, on our right flank. This found expression in a number of declarations which were meaningless or actually wrong. We corrected this deviation with difficulty and with damage to the party.

13. In Europe also we carried out a resolute struggle against the line of two parties. In part, this was clearly expressed in the two letters published in *Pravda,* January 15, 1928. These were dedicated entirely to a concise substantiation of our course for the party and through the party. In connection with recent events I quote two paragraphs, the eighth and ninth, published without distortion:

"8. The considerations above, as well as the recent experience in Germany (Altona), argue against our presenting independent candidates. It is impermissible to break with the whole line over some problematic seats in parliament.

"9. The creation of a 'union of left Communists' is mistaken. The name of the Opposition is sufficiently popular and has an international character. The name 'union' adds nothing, but could become a pseudonym for a second party" [see "Problems of the International Opposition," January 1928, in this volume].

In connection with this it is necessary to explain the episode of Comrade Radek's recent telegram, published in *Pravda* with an editorial note on the fact that Trotsky refused to sign the telegram. In fact I answered Radek that sending the telegram seemed to me to be unnecessary and unsuitable, especially since our declaration *on this very question* had already been published both in *Pravda* and in *Rote Fahne*. Thus, if the official leadership wants to use our opinion in its interests against the advocates of parallel candidates, it has full opportunity to do so. It was especially incorrect to send a special telegram only about the German elections because, according to *Pravda,* Treint and others apparently ran parallel candidates in France as well. If the editors of *Pravda* had not played on Radek's opposition to me, they would have played on the fact that we are silent about the French elections, or about the very existence of the Leninbund, or a thousand and one other things. In a word, it was absolutely clear that if *Pravda* published our telegram, it would do so only in order to create further confusion. This was entirely confirmed. The conditions in which we are placed exclude the possibility of "episodic politics" for us. We don't even have enough information for isolated interventions. For example, to this day I don't really know whether Treint put forward his own candidacy. That is why, as I see it, Comrade Radek's telegram was a blunder— Lord knows exactly what kind, but a blunder nevertheless.

In connection with this, I recall a curious episode. Passing through Berlin [in 1927], Kamenev gave his blessing to the left for putting forward its own candidates. One of the Russian comrades wrote me an indignant letter about this, and, what's more, suggested that Kamenev was pushing the left down the road of parallel candidates so light-mindedly solely because he had decided beforehand to dissociate himself from them "with the maximum profit" at the first opportunity. At the time this hypothesis seemed unlikely and even cynical to me. But now . . .

14. Did we perhaps go too far tactically in the sense of the form in which we presented ideas? Krestinsky accused us of this. I answered him at that time in a detailed letter. (Krestinsky

appears there as X.) Krestinsky had no understanding of the essence of the disagreement, nor did Antonov-Ovseenko, of whom I wrote that in his position "helplessness and narrow-minded confusion find their most finished expression. It will be impossible to hold onto this position even for three months. The near future will show what path Ovseenko, who has forgotten how to think like a Marxist, will take to escape from narrow-minded confusion" (November 29, 1927).

The period of three months turned out to be fatal for Antonov-Ovseenko. May this serve, as they say in the copybooks, as a lesson and a warning.

But let us return to the question of "tactical excesses." We have never had any aim other than to present our views to the party. We used whatever methods the situation left available to us. As experience shows, we reached too few members of the party with too few of our views. If we are to blame for this, if it is not only the objective conditions that are to blame, our failing was that at certain moments some of us underestimated the differences and their dangers, and by our conduct gave people reason to think that it was a matter of secondary and episodic differences. In such cases the greatest mistake and the greatest danger is to let your pace be set by those who underestimate the differences, who do not see the direction in which processes are developing and therefore feel the need for protective coloration. By and large we correctly upheld the correct line. But as I have shown above, we have had isolated, and not insignificant, failures. And these were always failures to the right and not to the left. Tactically, we were able to make our way sucessfully until we would run up against a trap set by the "Master" in such matters. All our statements had a propagandistic and only a propagandistic character.

Sharpest was our action of November 7 [1927]. Sharpest was our slogan "turn the fire to the right, against the kulak, NEP-man, and bureaucrat," against the kulaks and NEPmen who are disrupting the grain collections and against the bureaucrats who have organized or slept through the Shakhty affair. On November 7 we encountered one more attempt by the "Master" to switch the inner-party struggle onto the track of civil war. We retreated in the face of this criminal scheme. Thus, the tactical zigzags followed from the entire situation, which was the result both of the conditions of the dictatorship in general and of its specific peculiarities in the period of retrogression.

The evening of November 7, after the demonstration, we called Zinoviev and urged him to return to Moscow so that we could raise the question of wrapping things up tactically. Zinoviev took the opportunity to answer by letter. A description of the events of November 7 in Leningrad was appended to the letter. And in the letter Zinoviev said: "The description is photographically exact. All information suggests that all these disgraceful things will bring great profit to our cause. We are worried about what happened to you. The *smychki* [clandestine meetings] are going well here. The change is big in our favor. We don't intend to leave here at present. . . ."

All this was written, I repeat, the evening or night of November 7. We repeated our demand for Zinoviev's immediate departure for Moscow. It is well known what happened on his arrival, twenty-four hours later.

\*     \*     \*

But enough of the past. I have only touched upon it to the degree that it is necessary for us now and in the immediate future. Whoever says that we "overestimated"; whoever says this not rashly, accidentally, or from impulsiveness (this sort of thing can happen with anyone) but deliberately and with conviction—that person will not hold to such a position even for three months . . .

Several comrades have put the question differently, namely: We did everything basically correctly, we came forward in good time and achieved a certain turn at the cost of great sacrifices when our predictions were confirmed by events. Now we must not miss this turn; we must recognize it and we must use it as a chance for a more normal and healthy resolution of party conflicts. In its general form I accept such a formulation entirely. It is only necessary to insert into this algebraic fomula more precise arithmetic quantities. But the crucial problem is that so far these arithmetic quantities are either completely unknown or nearly infinitesimal.

What is going on: a class turn or a bureaucratic maneuver? In my view such a formulation simplifies the question too much. With regard to "self-criticism," party democracy, Chinese soviets, etc., it is quite permissible to assume that there is a desire to escape from difficulties through maneuvers. But what about the grain collections, the waiting lines [in front of shops], the difficulties in foreign affairs, etc.? Of course it is clear to the authors of policy that a maneuver at the top will not bring in any grain. And yet it is necessary to get grain; generally speaking, this constitutes the precondition for all kinds of possible maneuvers in the future. It is here that the beginning of something far more significant than simply a maneuver at the top may emerge. The authors of policy are stuck in a situation where some deepgoing, serious turn is necessary. But because of their entire position and all their ingrained habits they would like to carry out this unavoidable turn—which incidentally is not yet very clear to them in the concrete forms it would take—they would like to carry it out by the methods of bureaucratic maneuver.

There can be no doubt (only a blockhead could doubt this now) that if all our previous work had not existed—our analyses, predictions, criticism, exposés, and ever newer predictions—a sharp turn to the right would have occurred under the pressure of the grain collections crisis. Sokolnikov firmly expected that when he dropped his differences. We also considered it likely. Thus, "At a New Stage" speaks of a rather imminent economic shift to the right under the pressure of aggravated difficulties. It turned out that the next shift was to the left. This means that we ourselves underestimated the good, strong wedge we had driven in. Yes, it was precisely our wedge that has made it impossible for them, at this particular time, to seek a way out of the contradictions on the *right* path. By itself this is a very great achievement, if only a temporary one, for time is an important factor in politics. It is not enough that a number of steps have been taken which, while remaining within the limits of a bureaucratic maneuver for the present, indicate a turn to the left. In order to assess this turn, just basic arithmetic quantities are not enough, for after all, what is involved here are classes, the interaction of the party apparatus with the state apparatus, and of the state apparatus with the various classes. It would be too rash to say that the sea has been set on fire just because the titmouse has promised to do it. Khristian Rakovsky, from whom we received a letter yesterday, very appropriately applies to this situation the English expression "wait and see."

True, a number of generalizations have been made in the press which seem to be directly plagiarized from our documents. But here too it is still entirely possible for them to sound the retreat, and oh, how loudly they could sound it! To think that the right is weak is to understand nothing. Opportunists are always weak by themselves within the framework of a mass proletarian party. They get their strength from other classes. In itself the right wing in our party represents the link onto which the new proprietors are holding, and through them, also the world bourgeoisie. If you break this link from the chain, by itself it is worth half a kopek. But in the present situation, the most powerful pressure of classes hostile to the proletariat is transmitted through this link. The rights are silent; they yield and retreat without a fight. They understand that within the framework of the party the proletarian core, even in its present condition, could crush them to bits in two seconds. They still cannot show their heads too openly. Besides, they understand the necessity of the maneuver to the left. Even Ustryalov has written to the specialists: "Let us allow the leadership some credit as it makes its maneuver to the left; without that the leadership cannot deal with the true foe."

For these elements, it is only a matter of a maneuver. They firmly count on the fact that a turn will not happen, that the attempt to make a turn will shatter aginst the resistance of the economic material (that is, the propertied elements) and that then, after the bankruptcy of the attempted turn, will come their, the right's, turn. In a letter I just received from Comrade Valentinov, he correctly raises this aspect of the process.

But if, for the right and for their nonparty bosses, the matter comes down simply to a maneuver as preparation for a turn to the right, then for the center and, following them, for wide circles of the party the matter is more complex. Here there are all shades—from bureaucratic tricksterism to a sincere desire to switch all policies onto the proletarian-revolutionary track. Here too it is necessary to wait and see how the component elements of the "turn" are defined as it takes its course. We have had a small example, but the clearest possible one, in the realm of "self-criticism." I have in mind the Bleskov-Zatonsky affair. Comrade Sosnovsky is widely popularizing this affair, seeing it as highly symptomatic. And this, it seems to me, is absolutely right. Is "self-criticism" just a maneuver? To be concerned with guesses on this account, that is, on the matter of intentions, is pointless. But the fact is that the machinist Bleskov took this matter seriously and even tempted the most innocent Zatonsky with the energy of his honest approach. Zatonsky went running off and used his influence to throw open wide the door of the [newspaper] *Kharkov Proletarian*. Moscow then gave the signal to close the door. Whether Zatonsky's nose or some other part of his venerable "worker-peasant" body will be hurt as a result of this affair, we cannot tell from here. But it is clear that a knot was coming untied, signifying the possibility that the maneuver would be changed into a turn—with very energetic help from below.

The same applies to the whole new "course" in its entirety. If we could use an analogy without fearing that the conjurers and swindlers would try to fabricate a Clemenceau thesis, we could say this: "Out of the 'spring' of Svyatopolk-Mirsky came the real spring of 1905. But it would be a worthless revolutionary who would try to grab the tail of the first bureaucratic swallow, thinking that it settled the problem of the spring." Of course, for us the question is not of revolution, but of reform in the party, and through it, in the state. But in the relationship between the elements indicated above [i.e., Bleskov and Zatonsky], there is an analogy. Taken all together, you see, there is material for a "Svyatopolk-Mirsky thesis."

What are the conclusions? Here I will quote from Comrade Valentinov's letter:

"Conclusion 1: More tenacity. Conclusion 2: As before, stick to long-range politics. Conclusion 3: Watch what is going on at the top, but even more attentively follow what is going on among the masses, for here is the source of strength for the defense of the revolution and for the resistance to Thermidor."

I drew the practical conclusions for *the days immediately ahead* in my previous letter, where I spoke of the appeal to the Sixth Congress of the Comintern.

However, it's time to close. My letter has already gone far beyond its originally intended limits.

# PREOBRAZHENSKY'S PROPOSAL

## May 24, 1928

*NOTE: A letter to Yevgeny Preobrazhensky in Uralsk. Next to Radek, he was the most prominent of the Opposition leaders to feel the seductive power of Stalin's left course. In April 1928 he sent Trotsky an essay entitled "The Left Course in the Country- side and Perspectives," in which he put great stock in Stalin's pronouncements and urged the Oppositionists to seek reconcilia- tion with the Stalin faction to enable them to help in carrying out the great tasks ahead. For this purpose, he proposed that the Opposition should ask official permission to call a conference of all its members to discuss the new situation and the Opposition's response. A tabulation Trotsky made in early July lists only four votes in favor of Preobrazhensky's theses, with 100 against.*

*In the version of the excerpt that is in* My Life *(pp. 551-52), Trotsky identifies the letter "filled with rotten moods" that he refers to in paragraph 1 as being "from Radek to Moscow." This letter is discussed more fully in "The Methods of Leadership," June 2, 1928.*

*In the French legislative elections referred to here, the French CP's voting strength had increased, although the number of its deputies elected had fallen.*

*By permission of the Harvard College Library. Translated from the Russian for this volume by George Saunders. This letter has been excerpted to avoid repetition.*

Dear Yevgeny Alekseyevich:

. . . After receiving your theses, I absolutely did not write a single word to anyone about them. I sent my proposal (or more accurately, my counterproposal) to you first. I don't know if you received it. I have asked everyone to whom I address letters to notify me by telegram of their receipt. Thus far I have not received a single telegram on this score. Three days ago I received from Kolpashevo the following telegram: "We emphatically reject Yevgeny's proposals and evaluation. Reply immediately. Smilga,

Alsky, Nechaev." Yesterday I received a telegram from Ust-Kulom: "We consider Yevgeny's proposals incorrect. Beloborodov." From Khristian Georgievich [Rakovsky] a letter came yesterday in which he expressed his attitude toward the "present moment" with the English phrase: "wait and see." Also yesterday I received letters from Beloborodov and Valentinov. They were both extremely upset over some letter that had been sent from the northeast to the west and that was filled with rotten moods. They are very hot under the collar. If they are conveying the contents of the letter accurately, then on this question I solidarize myself with them totally and completely and I don't recommend that anyone be indulgent to the impressionists.

Since my return from the hunting trip, that is, the last days of March, I have been sitting home without going out at all, with my pen in hand or nose in a book, roughly from seven or eight in the morning to ten at night. I am getting ready to take a break for a few days: Natalya Ivanovna, Seryozha, and I are going to Iliysk for some fishing on the Ili River. A report on this venture will be supplied to you in due time.

Do you understand what happened in the elections in France? So far I haven't been able to understand anything. *Pravda* has not even given the figures for the total number of voters, compared to the previous elections, so that it remains unknown whether the Communist percentage rose or fell. However, I intend to study this question in the foreign papers and then I'll write further. If you have any information on this point, or general observations, please let me know.

Are you up on the curious Bleskov-Zatonsky episode? Sosnovsky has sent clippings on this subject, along with highly interesting commentaries. Bleskov is a machinist in a Ukrainian factory, not a party member, who took "self-criticism" seriously and wrote Zatonsky a letter which a careful reading shows to be excerpted from a whole series of our documents. Zatonsky, by virtue of his inherent purity of soul and by virtue of a certain swelling of the head, did not grasp the essence of the matter or the "uniqueness" of the current moment. Owing to the abovementioned circumstances, that is, owing above all to swelling of the head, Zatonsky began ringing all the church bells without consulting the ultimate authorities [literally, without looking at the latest "saints' days" calendar]. He demanded that Bleskov's modest letter be printed in the pious newspaper *Kharkov Proletarian*. The editors, having decided that everything was being done according to the saints, carried out the request and accompanied Bleskov's letter with a minimum of officious bleating (just in case). But as soon as Zatonsky's word reached the sensitive ears of the editors of *Rabochaya Gazeta* (telephone number such-and-such) Zatonsky was immediately numbered among the belly-achers and skeptics. The point of this remarkable episode is that Zatonsky, who it seemed had passed through all the tests of fire and water, and through pipes of all possible diameters, admitted publicly, in the press, that Bleskov's letter was "remarkable," genuinely proletarian, deeply sincere, and deserving of full attention, etc., etc. But *Rabochaya Gazeta* found Zatonsky's letter to be a real-and-for-sure document of petty-bourgeois deviation. This kind of mix-up is produced by the extraordinary increase in the complexity and shifting directions of the administrative winds. Zatonsky is only the first victim of these increased complications. As for the Bleskovs, probably no small number of them have yet to make their appearance.

# PORTRAIT OF A CAPITULATOR

## May 26, 1928

*NOTE: Apparently a circular letter. In addition to Yudin, substantially the same letter was sent to Mikhail Okudzhava (excerpts from that are in* My Life, *pp. 552-53) and to Brover.*

*Many Oppositionists had been assigned to diplomatic posts abroad during the summer and fall of 1927, including Georgy Safarov, a former leader of the Communist League of Youth, who was assigned to Constantinople. He attended a conference of Oppositionists held in Berlin in November 1927, where he promoted an ultraleft line, which Trotsky calls "super-Detsist," from the abbreviation of the Russian words for Democratic Centralists. After he returned to Russia he capitulated to the Stalinists in a letter dated March 31, 1928. His explanation for why he was recanting—"Everything will now be carried out without us!"—was typical of the feelings of those Oppositionists who were inclined to capitulate as a result of the left course.*

*In May another series of scandals erupted, this time in Smolensk, in which leaders of the local party apparatus were accused of corruption and abuse of power. In accord with the much-touted campaign against the kulak, several functionaries were made scapegoats for the grain deliveries crisis of the late winter and early spring. Repercussions were felt for several months and hundreds of party members were expelled.*

*By permission of the Harvard College Library. Translated from the Russian for this volume by Tom Twiss.*

Dear Comrade Yudin:

I received your letter of May 11 yesterday, May 25: this is a very short time [for mail to take], really exceptional. Today I answered you with a telegram in which I promised to write. I am fulfilling that promise with this letter.

I read your letter with great interest, because it filled in the portrait of Safarov for me with the freshest possible strokes, still wet from the paintbrush, so to speak. Safarov is now ranting and raving against the foreign left, in the ranks of which there is now and will continue to be a great deal of confusion, exaggeration, deviation, and generally all sorts of small-group or study-circle nonsense: there are really not so many people there who can swim against the stream without being deflected from the fundamental course. But curiously, it was precisely Safarov who, when he was abroad last November, gave the foreign comrades a violent shove toward ultraleftism. Safarov arrived in Berlin from Constantinople during the period when our group was being crushed in Moscow. In his Berlin meetings Safarov proclaimed the coming of Thermidor. His formula was: "It is five minutes till twelve," that is, there were five minutes left before a full-scale coup d'état, and those five minutes had to be used to wage a frenzied campaign. A comrade arriving from Berlin told me how our closest friends there were astounded by the ultraleft, super-Detsist way in which Safarov presented matters. But since he was the most authoritative of the Russians there, the foreigners took the ultraleft charge from him. The two documents—instructions sent abroad—that were published in *Pravda* on January 15 were designed to correct the line dislocated by Safarov [see "Problems of the International Opposition (Two Letters)," January 1928].

Safarov arrived in Moscow from Berlin and immediately caught a train to our conference with Zinoviev and friends. After hearing the cautiously capitulatory speech of Zinoviev, Safarov pounced upon him in a rage. There was everything in Safarov's speech, not only "It is five minutes till twelve" (he repeated this formula after every five words) but also the direct accusation against Zinoviev that by his guarded raising of the question of the "regurgitations of Trotskyism" Zinoviev wanted to get back his party card. "I wouldn't want a party card on such terms," Safarov shouted desperately. On that point Naumov supported Safarov. Our crowd was quite pleased with Safarov's speech. But since I personally had had more than one chance to size him up, I warned the comrades: "Wait, he hasn't been worked over yet . . ." And sure enough, the next day you couldn't recognize him . . . [In Lenin's time,] whenever someone nominated Safarov for some kind of responsible assignment, Vladimir Ilyich would say: "Safarchik will go too far left, Safarchik will make a fool of himself." This was a kind of facetious saying of his. But with people who always like to go to the left, when they reach a certain age a change comes over them and they start going to the right just as blindly and one-sidedly as they formerly went to the left.

Safarov is a caricatured sub-type of the Bukharin type, which is enough of a caricature to begin with.

As to Safarov's political philosophy, as you yourself correctly point out, it isn't worth a damn. Essentially his whole orientation is to play on the economic and international difficulties, that is, the very kind of speculation which that crowd [i.e., the Zinoviev-ists] has so falsely accused us of since 1923 ("defeatism"). The opposition of the Stalinist center to the right wing was not invented by Safarov. We predicted that divisions could occur along this line to the extent that behind the centrist head there would be formed—not only in the party, and not so much in the party as outside of it—an Ustryalovist tail. We said that this tail would strike at the head and that this would give rise to major realignments in the party.

Without the preceding work of criticism and warnings, which have now been tested against the facts, the blow of the tail to the head—the grain collections, etc.—would have produced an inevitable shift to the right. We averted this at very great cost. For long? That is entirely unclear. The main difficulties, both foreign and domestic, are ahead. But here Safarov proposes that all hopes be placed in the "revolutionary character of our working class." That is a very serene view, it can't be denied. The revolutionary working class will exist by itself and the grain collections and much else will be managed by those who "do not see any classes"—by themselves. And Safarov will console himself with the revolutionary character of the working class and will see the main danger in the fact that Trotsky, while condemning the mistakes of Souvarine, does not consider him finally lost for communism. It is simply that he must somehow push himself away from his past. He is even willing to push away a straw [which a drowning man would normally be expected to grasp at]. But this willingness will in no way prevent him from drowning. Whether that will be a comfort to him or not is hard to say; probably not.

The present "new course," which we must follow very attentively, tries to solve the most important problems—problems we brought up much earlier and in a far more principled way—by using the old techniques and methods, which are quite obviously unsound. In order to carry out the new tasks it is first necessary to formulate them clearly and distinctly, ruthlessly condemning the old approach. Second, it is necessary to assure the selection of people who understand these new tasks and want to resolve them, not out of fear, but out of conviction. In *Pravda* of May 16 there is a very striking article by A. Yakovlev, "The Lessons of Smolensk." From this article I quote only one conclusion, printed in heavy type, which Yakovlev, one of the leaders of the CCC, has reached: "We must decisively change our attitude toward those party members and class-conscious workers who are aware of the abuses and keep quiet. . . ." You know, this one phrase is worth ten of the ultraleft and most radical platforms. To change—"to change"—*to change*—our attitude to those who know about the abuses and keep quiet. That is: until now they were praised and encouraged, but now they will be stigmatized. But who praised and encouraged them? And is it possible to believe that those who encouraged silence about scandalous practices, and encouraged it not accidentally but who obviously had an interest in it, will suddenly after Yakovlev's essay stop encouraging those who keep silent and begin to stigmatize and hound them? This is a serious answer to Safarov's fatalistic Menshevik reference to the immanent revolutionary character of the working class, given the existence of which it makes absolutely no difference whether silence about scandalous practices is encouraged or vilified.

Nevertheless, the new course will produce the most important consequences. Regardless of the wishes of the authors of the new course, it once again poses all the fundamental questions point-blank before the party ranks. Of course it is impossible to hope that the study of all these questions will go forward rapidly, but it will go forward.

We always thought, and said more than once (for example at the February plenum of 1927), that the process of backsliding cannot by any means be represented as an unbroken, descending line. After all, the backsliding process does not occur in a vacuum but in a class society with deep internal frictions. The basic party mass is not at all monolithic. To a large degree it simply represents political raw material. Processes of internal stratification and differentiation inevitably occur in it under the pressure of class impulses, both from the right and from the left. We are now entering a deeply critical period of the party's development. The critical events that have occurred recently and their consequences, which you and I are bearing, are only the overture to events to come. Just as an operatic overture prefigures the musical themes of the entire opera and gives them a sharp and compressed expression, so our political overture has only anticipated these melodies which will be developed fully in the future, that is, with the participation of the brasses, double basses, drums, and other instruments of serious class music. The course of events will confirm beyond all question that we are and remain correct, not only against the waverers and weather vanes—that is, the Zinovievs, Kamenevs, Pyatakovs, Antonov-Ovseenkos, and all the Smerdyakovs like Antonov-Ovseenko—but also against our dear friends to the "left," that is, the Democratic Centralists. Insofar, that is, as they were inclined to take the overture for the opera, to think that all the basic processes in the party and state were already concluded . . .

No, the party will still have need of us, and very great need at that. Don't be nervous that "everything will be done without us"; don't tear at yourself and others for nothing; study, wait, watch closely, and don't let your political line get covered with the rust of personal irritation at the slanderers and tricksters. This is how we must conduct ourselves. From your letter it is quite clear that you don't really need this advice.

# THE METHODS OF LEADERSHIP

## June 2, 1928

*NOTE: In this letter, Trotsky returns to the theme of the methods of leadership, citing with approval statements written by Rakovsky explaining the need for party democracy, and referring to Lenin's standards for party leadership (see* Lenin's Fight Against Stalinism, *New York: Pathfinder, 1975).*

*The results of the May 1928 elections in Germany were hailed in the Soviet press: The German CP increased the number of its deputies from forty-five to fifty-four, receiving 3,238,000 votes. The Social Democrats, who outvoted the Communists, participated in a coalition government with bourgeois parties, which was formed at the end of June. The Leninbund group of "left communists" received 80,000 votes and no deputies. The reference in paragraph 5 to the Communist Workers Party is to an ultraleft group that split in 1920 from the German Communist Party because of principled differences over participating in parliament and working in the trade unions; it was influenced by anarchosyndicalism. It began with tens of thousands of members but dwindled away within a short time.*

*The reference to Radek endorsing the ninth ECCI's resolution on China is accurate. This resolution charted a course in China toward armed insurrection and soviets—in the wake of the final crushing of the Canton Commune in December 1927—as a way of evading an assessment of the false course that had led to the defeat. In "A Wretched Document," written July 27, 1929 (in* Writings 1929, *p. 207), Trotsky says Radek was looking for reasons to capitulate when he endorsed the ECCI China resolution.*

*Trotsky refers to the February ECCI plenum's resolutions on France and Britain as "a muddled turn to the left" because the British and French CPs were instructed to adopt the slogan "Class against class" under the new theory of social-fascism. This represented a break from the earlier class collaborationism of both parties, but in an ultraleft, sectarian direction rejecting common action with other tendencies in the labor movement under the slogan that Social Democracy and fascism were the same.*

*In discussing the psychology of the capitulators, Trotsky refers to the Brest-Litovsk peace of 1918—a harsh treaty the Soviet government was forced to sign with Germany because of its weakness—as a metaphor the capitulators used in rationalizing their surrender to the bureaucracy. He also paraphrases Saltykov-Shchedrin, the nineteenth-century Russian satirical writer.*

*A "Fronde," by analogy with the rebellion of nobles against the king in seventeenth-century France, is an attempted palace coup that results only in the humiliation of the rebelling dignitaries and the strengthening of the central authority.*

*The Artemovsk case was another scapegoat scandal "exposed" in March 1928.*

*The month of June was dominated by Trotsky's work on his criticism of the draft program being prepared under Bukharin's supervision for the Sixth Comintern Congress, to be held the following month. The criticism, and a letter to the congress, "What Now?" are in English under the title* The Third International After Lenin *(New York: Pathfinder, 1970).*

*From* Fourth International, *July 1941, in a translation from the Russian by John G. Wright. Paragraphs 2-8, which were omitted from* Fourth International, *were translated from the Russian for this volume by Martin Koppel, by permission of the Library of Social History in New York.*

Dear Comrade:

I have recently received letters from many comrades, each complaining that there have been no replies from me. My son has been similarly accused. These charges are all due to "misunderstandings" in the post office. Not a single letter, not a single postcard, not one telegram has been received to which we did not reply either immediately, or, at the latest, on the very next day. There are many, many addresses to which we write without first waiting for a communication the moment news comes of the address of any new arrival [in exile]. Consequently, if any comrade receives no reply to his letter it simply means either that his letter did not reach us or that our reply did not reach his address. To characterize the condition of postal communications it is only necessary to state that I received yesterday, i.e., on June 1, a letter from my daughter in Moscow which she mailed on

March 20. The remarkable thing is that letters arrive quite promptly from certain points—for example, from Rakovsky in Astrakhan, Preobrazhensky in Uralsk, Sosnovsky in Barnaul. On the other hand, there are other points from which letters either do not arrive at all, or come after a great delay, and, furthermore, not all of them. Thus, for example, I have not received to this day a single letter from Comrade Radek. From Vrachev, the first letter, dated May 12, was delivered yesterday; yet he informs me that he has already written me two letters, both sent by registered mail, with a return receipt requested and prepaid. I did not receive these two letters. Comrade Vrachev is thus entitled to demand payment from the post office for the loss of registered mail. Other comrades should make systematic use of this method.

Almost all the letters received in the past few days deal with (a) the events in Germany, (b) the "left turn" here, (c) Radek's telegram in *Pravda,* and (d) the inevitable subject of my health.

Concerning the events in Germany, our newspapers are virtually my only basis for judging—in other words, a very shaky "basis" indeed. As for the elections in Germany (and in France), we will have to work on them in more detail, once we receive the relevant issues of foreign newpapers. The articles in our press about these events are, as usual, beneath all criticism. There is not a trace of a concrete Marxist analysis of the social and political movements in the country. It is replaced by agitational hackwork, whose preachings are forgotten the next day, not only by the readers but by the authors. What do the 80,000 votes that *Pravda* counts as "Trotskyist" represent? One thing at least is clear: that the elements closest to us, including Ruth Fischer and Maslow, did not put forward parallel candidates and did not support them. Their line on this question coincides with the "directives" which were printed in the January 15 issue of *Pravda.*

It was on these grounds that the split in the Leninbund itself occurred. Ruth and M. were against even organizing the Leninbund, as we were, but they remained in the minority and decided not to break but to try to paralyze the tendency toward a second party from within the Leninbund. The split, however, was inevitable for them over the question of parallel candidates. This is why the 80,000 votes are certainly not those of our cothinkers; evidently, these are the supporters of the ultraleft wing of the Leninbund and the ultralefts in general (Korsch, et al.). Our cothinkers called for a vote for the official party candidates and

acted correctly. But bureaucratic smugness is the only explanation for the fact that the *Pravda* editorial contemptuously shrugs
its shoulders over the 80,000 votes picked up by the ultralefts
(whom the falsifiers groundlessly term Trotskyists). Eighty thousand is a very large figure, if you keep in mind that only select
individuals could vote for such purely demonstrative candidacies:
i.e., cadre elements, not the masses.

In this parliamentary form we see before us a rebirth of
sectarian, semi-anarchistic tendencies, moreover on a very broad
scale, and this after the experience people went through in the so-
called Communist Workers Party. Anarchism has always been
and always will be the punishment for the sin of opportunism.
The leftward movement in the German working class is only
beginning. For the present the Social Democracy has gained from
it significantly more than the Communists. This shows that so
far there is a very amorphous and general movement to the left.
Its differentiation is inevitable.

A false policy can extraordinarily strengthen the group of
80,000. Isn't it a disgrace that under such conditions the liberal
Tryapichkin Kovrov is the one "informing" the Russian proletariat about the struggle of the German workers? This stupid and
slovenly character counts as a Trotskyist even the Suhlist Heim,
who sold himself to the Social Democracy. To the best of my
recollection, the Heim family was the local ruling dynasty that
dominated the Suhl organization both under the Social Democrats and under the CP. They went along with the Opposition
with the sole aim of not losing their long-held positions.

The split in the Leninbund is a cruel lesson for the German
left, which like the entire international left is still in very great
need of lessons. The fundamental political "disproportion" in
Europe consists in the disparity between the degree of maturity of
the proletarian vanguard and the maturity of the whole revolutionary situation. Of course, this "disproportion" also applies to
the entire [international] Opposition, which in essence is making
its first serious attempts at an independent analysis of the
situation, not simply saluting every new leader for the day. The
leading groups are being developed slowly, especially under the
present, totally exceptional circumstances. Hesitations, vacillations, desertions, splits will not be lacking in the period ahead,
both inside the official CPs and in those groups which at the
present stage have been forced out of their ranks. On this point
one must not have any illusions. People learn to walk only on
their own legs, and in the process they inevitably get themselves

plenty of bumps on the forehead, and on other places.

Radek's telegram in *Pravda* is the result of a certain extra impulsiveness, hardly more than that. Some comrades make reference to a letter of Radek's with which I am entirely unacquainted and in which he reportedly solidarizes with the resolution of the ECCI on the Chinese question. I believe there must be some misunderstanding here. While the resolutions on the English and French questions constitute a very oblique and muddled turn to the *left,* and by virtue of this represent the beginning of a movement in our direction, the resolution on the Chinese question is false from beginning to end and represents a direct continuation, development, and deepening of the policy of the bloc of four classes, the subordination of the Communist Party to the Kuomintang, speculations on the Left Kuomintang, with the inevitable supplement of such opportunist policy by something in the spirit of the Canton putsch. In my opinion this question is absolutely decisive for our entire international orientation. At issue is the guidance of a revolution in a land with 400 million people. The current resolution of the ECCI prepares for the destruction of the third Chinese revolution as inevitably as the pro-Kuomintang course assured the collapse of the second Chinese revolution of 1925-28. Moreover, there is the question of the revolution in India on the one hand, and the revolution in Japan on the other. It is necessary to think these questions through to the end.

So far as the "left course" is concerned, a part of its historical mission has already been fulfilled because it has aided in bringing about the natural evolution of the Zinoviev group. Safarov used to be in opposition to Zinoviev and Kamenev from the left. But this Safarov-leftism had only one historic design: to show the masters of the situation that he, Safarov, is ready to growl at and bite us far more decisively than are "opportunists" like Zinoviev and Kamenev. These are, as Saltykov used to say, the little people of the plaything industry; they wanted to play at the game of opposition, to amuse themselves with pranks on the apparatus of the dictatorship, and against their own will they were sucked into a great whirlpool. Small wonder that they now blow out bubbles of theory and hysterically thrash around with all their extremities, guided by the single desire: to remain on the surface, and, if possible, to prosper again.

They began by saying that it was necessary to accept a Brest-Litovsk peace, that is, to deceive the party. And by a stroke of luck, the left course suddenly turned up. "Look! Look!" say these little people of the plaything industry. "That's just what we said a long time ago." They did do a lot of talking but it was about something just the opposite, i.e., not about a left course but about a Brest peace, three months ago, at most six months ago. We have lost Pyatakov, Antonov-Ovseenko, Krestinsky—people who turned rotten long ago. As for the Zinovievist leadership, it constituted a Fronde of dignitaries who under the pressure of the Petrograd workers and a squeeze from our side went much further than they ever intended. Now they have returned to the nursery rooms they left behind them. However, hundreds of Petrograd workers did not follow their former leaders but remained with us. This fully justifies the bloc—both in its making and in its breaking.

I shall not dwell on the essence of the issue of the "left course" because I have already written concerning this in great detail in several letters to a number of comrades. Here I want only to add that in these letters I touched all too inadequately on the question of the methods of leadership—in the party, the state, the trade unions. This is quite correctly pointed out by Comrade Rakovsky in a letter which I received yesterday. Comrade Rakovsky advances to the forefront the idea that a correct political line is inconceivable without the correct methods for elaborating and realizing it. Even if on this or that question, under the influence of this or that pressure, the apparatus leadership should stumble onto the tracks of a correct line, there still are no guarantees that this line will be actually carried out.

"Under the conditions of the dictatorship of the party," writes Comrade Rakovsky, "gigantic power is concentrated in the hands of the leadership, such power as was never known to any political organization in history, and therefore the observance of Communist and proletarian methods of leadership becomes all the more indispensable inasmuch as every deviation from them, every falseness, is immediately reflected in the entire working class and the entire revolution. The leadership has become accustomed gradually to extend the negative attitude of the proletarian dictatorship toward bourgeois pseudodemocracy to those elementary guarantees of conscious democracy on which the party subsists and by means of which it is alone possible to lead the working class and the state."

On the other hand, under the proletarian dictatorship in which, as has been said, unprecedentedly vast power is concentrated in the hands of the leadership, the top brass, the violation of this spirit of democracy becomes the greatest and gravest evil. Lenin had already warned that our workers' state had become infected with "bureaucratic deformations." The danger of the party's being infected by them disturbed his thoughts up to the last moments of his life. He used to speak often of the kind of relationship the party leadership should maintain with the trade unions and the workers in general ("gear wheels," "transmission belts"). Let us recall his indignant protests against certain manifestations of rudeness ("fist-play," etc.), and against the individual failings of leaders, which to a superficial view are insignificant. Lenin's indignation is best understood if one takes into consideration that what he had in mind was to preserve within the party just the opposite methods of leadership. In the same connection should be understood his warm advocacy of culture—the struggle against Asiatic morals—and finally his intentions in creating the Central Control Commission.

"When Lenin was alive," continues Comrade Rakovsky, "the party apparatus did not wield one-tenth of the power it now possesses, and therefore everything that Lenin feared has now become tens of times more dangerous. The party apparatus has become infected with the bureaucratic deformations of the state apparatus, and there have been added to all this the deformations elaborated by the false bourgeois parliamentarian democracy. As a result, a leadership has arisen which instead of a conscious party democracy fosters: (1) garbled versions of the theories of Leninism adapted for the purpose of entrenching the party bureaucracy; (2) abuse of power, which with respect to Communists and workers under the conditions of dictatorship cannot fail to assume monstrous proportions; (3) fraudulent tampering with the entire party electoral machinery; (4) utilization of methods during discussion periods of which bourgeois-fascist authorities could be proud but never a proletarian party (strong-arm squads, hecklers who disrupt meetings, speakers torn from the platform, etc.); (5) the absence of comradely bonds and conscientiousness in personal relations, etc., etc."

It is from this that Rakovsky deduces all those monstrous processes which have in recent months finally come out into the open (the Shakhty case, the Artemovsk case, the Smolensk case, and so on). People who approach isolated economic measures separate and apart from the political process and political activity as a whole will invariably and always make mistakes. Comrade Rakovsky very appropriately reminds us that politics is concentrated economics.

You have of course noticed that our press refrains almost

entirely from printing the reactions of the European and American press to the events inside our party. This alone should lead one to gather that these reactions are not suited to the style of the new course. On this score I now possess not only conjectures but printed evidence, graphic in the extreme. A comrade has sent me a page clipped from the February 1 issue of *The Nation,* an American periodical. After briefly summarizing the latest events in our country, this most prominent left democratic journal says:

"This action brings to the front the question: Who represents the continuation of the Bolshevik program in Russia and who the *inevitable* reaction from it? To the American readers it has seemed as if Lenin and Trotsky represented the same thing and the conservative press and statesmen have arrived at the same conclusion. Thus, the *New York Times* found a chief cause for rejoicing on New Year's Day in the successful elimination of Trotsky from the Communist Party, declaring flatly that 'the ousted Opposition stood for the perpetuation of the ideas and conditions that have cut off Russia from Western civilization.' Most of the great European newspapers wrote similarly. Sir Austen Chamberlain during the Geneva Conference was quoted as saying that England could not enter into negotiations with Russia for the simple reason that 'Trotsky has not yet been shot against a wall.' He must be pleased by Trotsky's banishment . . . At any rate, the mouthpieces of reaction in Europe are one in their conclusion that Trotsky and not Stalin is their chief Communist enemy" [*The Nation,* February 1, 1928].

*The Nation,* we see, considers Thermidor, or the reaction against Bolshevism, inevitable (the article is entitled "Russia's Thermidor?"). In conclusion, it states flatly: "No doubt Stalin's tendency to depart from the rigorous Bolshevik program must be defended as a concession to the will of a majority of the people."

*Pravda* sometimes tries (it has tried this before) to quote isolated voices in the Social Democratic press who pick up our criticism just as they are now picking up the official "self-criticism," as *Pravda* itself admits. As if genuine class lines were determined by the petty intrigues of the Social Democratic press, which tries to warm its hands on our disagreements by picking now from this end, now from the other. The basic line of the Social Democracy is determined by the fundamental interests of bourgeois society. But the Social Democracy is able to play the role of the last prop of the bourgeois regime precisely because it is not at all identical with fascism, as is sweepingly asserted in the Soviet press, but on the contrary is able on all *nonfundamental* questions to play with all the colors of the rainbow. Social Democracy can utilize an opportunity to roar against reaction and slap genuine revolutionists approvingly on the back (so long as they remain in the minority), and swallow swords and fire—in a word, fulfill its function as the extreme left wing of bourgeois society. That is why it is necessary to *know how to read* the Social Democratic press. It is necessary to distinguish the basic line (basic for the bourgeoisie) from all the verbal political charlatanism which is basic for the Social Democracy itself, for it thrives on that.

As regards the solid capitalist press, it has no reasons for playing hide-and-seek on questions concerning the Communists and the proletariat. That is why the article from *The Nation* is of interest to us not only in and of itself but also for the reactions it quotes from the world of imperialist politics. There we have a serious and not an accidental or episodic verification of the class line. It is all the less accidental because more than a year ago the publication of the Council of French Heavy Industry evaluated in absolutely the same way the internal tendencies in our party and our country. Moreover, this was done not in a newspaper but in a bulletin intended for a comparatively narrow circle of the initiated.

That is all for the time being on questions of politics. Our personal situation is on the whole satisfactory despite the persistent malaria which beseiges Natalya Ivanovna much more cruelly than it does me. We hope to get rid of it by moving up higher, into the mountains. The preparations for moving were begun in May, but no apartments were available at the time, and the month of May itself brought only cold and rain. But now we have already moved to the mountains; the place is eight versts [five and one-half miles] from the center of the city. There are many gardens and it is cooler here than below in the valley. Our younger son has been living with us for more than a month. Our daughter-in-law (the wife of our older son) arrived from Moscow more than a week ago, so that our family has greatly grown.

Unfortunately things are not favorable in the rest of our family. One of my two daughters, Nina, is gravely ill with galloping consumption. I telegraphed Professor Gautier and a few days ago received his reply: "Galloping type. Incurable." My daughter is twenty-six years old, she has two babies, her husband Nevelson is in exile. From the hospital my daughter wrote me on March 20 that she wished to "liquidate" her illness in order to return to her job, but her temperature was high: $38^0$ C. [$101^0$ F.]

Had I received this letter in time I could have telegraphed her and our friends to have her stay in the hospital. But the letter she mailed on March 20 was delivered to me only on June 1—it was in transit for seventy-three days, i.e., it remained for more than two months in the pocket of a Deribas or an Agranov [GPU agents] or some other scoundrel corrupted by impunity. My oldest daughter, Zina—she is twenty-seven—has also been "running a temperature" for the last two-three years. I should like very much to have her here, but she is now taking care of her sister. Both of my daughters have of course been expelled from the party and removed from their jobs, although my older daughter, who used to be in charge of a party school in Crimea, was transferred a year ago to a purely technical post. In a word, these gentlemen are diligently occupying themselves with my family after smashing my secretariat.

You doubtless recall that my best collaborator, Glazman, a splendid party member, was driven to commit suicide by vile persecutions as far back as 1924. The crime remained of course unpunished. Now my three remaining collaborators are being cruelly persecuted. They all went with me—as did Glazman—through the entire civil war. Sermuks and Poznansky decided on their own responsibility to go to Central Asia in order to be with me. Sermuks was arrested here on the second day after his arrival. They kept him in a cellar for about a week, allowing him twenty-five kopeks a day from his own funds, and then shipped him to Moscow whence he was exiled to the autonomous region Komi [in the near-Arctic north of Soviet Russia]. Poznansky was arrested in Tashkent and exiled to Kotlas. Butov remains in jail to this day . . .

I warmly shake your hand,

Leon Trotsky

P.S.—Have gone through the draft program of the Comintern. What a wretched document! There is no unity of thought, no firmness in structure, all the walls have yawning revisionist cracks, the roof is full of holes . . . what a sorry edifice! At the same time it is all plastered and painted up with "cheerful" revolutionary colors—all our remarks have been taken into consideration, not in essence but merely for purposes of camouflage.

Bukharin's first draft [1922] was rejected precisely on account of its narrow national construction (see our "documents" in

*Pravda,* January 15, 1928 [last paragraph]). Now *Pravda* is boasting that the new construction is strictly internationalist, "not like the Social Democrats," and that "we" take our point of departure from the world economy and not the national economy. (Here too is an attempt to imitate what we said.) But the essence is not there—only one patch upon another. I am writing a detailed criticism for the Sixth Congress and making an attempt to keep them from adopting this fatal document.

# RUMORS FROM MOSCOW

## June 1928

*NOTE: A circular letter to leading Oppositionists, reporting symptoms of the impending split between the Stalinist center and the Bukharinist right as well as evidence of how sympathetically the Opposition was regarded among the workers. Wages and working conditions were set by annual "collective agreements" between workers represented by the official trade unions and the managers of the various industries or industrial units. An official campaign for the successful conclusion of negotiations leading to these agreements was apparently being conducted, because such negotiations often led to labor disputes and even strikes.*

*By permission of the Harvard College Library. Translated from the Russian for this volume by George Saunders.*

Dear Friend:

I have received three letters with "news," partly "rumors" circulating around Moscow. Two of the three correspondents assert that these are "the absolute truth." I am passing along excerpts from the three letters without any changes. I take no responsibility upon myself [for the accuracy of the contents]. But a great deal is highly plausible.

### First Letter

It was reported as a fact more than a month ago that Kaganovich had sent a letter to Moscow (to whom is not known) in which he cursed Stalin and showed himself an ardent Rykovist. They say that after that, Stalin wanted to remove him but did not succeed in doing so.

I have heard from a great many people that the first underground Rykovist document has come out. Nobody knows really what its content is, but the fact of its existence is considered *indisputable*.

They say that when several delegates from the Red International of Labor Unions (RILU) were visiting Stalin, they asked him: "What will happen now with the Opposition?" Stalin at first pretended that he didn't understand what they were talking about and then asserted that there was no Opposition, that Zinoviev, Kamenev, Pyatakov, etc., had defected and that there in his desk he [Stalin] had statements from Preobrazhensky, Radek, I. N. Smirnov, Beloborodov, and yet another person.

The overall decline in wages for Moscow province is somewhere around 25 percent; in some economic sectors, 50 percent. This information comes from a report of the Moscow Province Council of Trade Unions.

They say that Stalin offered a "bloc" to Kamenev and Zinoviev, but they declared that there could be no talk of any bloc as long as all the exiles had not been returned, in particular Trotsky. (Hm . . . hm . . .) To this Stalin replied that he could demonstrate with documents that he had voted in the Politburo against the deportation of Trotsky and that when the deportation occurred, he, Stalin, had not even been in Moscow. (He was in Siberia.)

At the CC plenum Stalin made a motion that the Higher Technical Educational Establishments be transferred to the jurisdiction of the Supreme Council of the National Economy (Vesenkha). (He made the motion in connection with the Shakhty affair.) Rykov was opposed to this motion. The votes divided roughly as follows—two-thirds were for Rykov, some abstained, and one-fourth or one-fifth were for Stalin. There is an assumption that some Stalinists didn't understand that the vote was so to speak a test case, and they voted according to conscience, not just out of fear.

When Stalin first proposed to the Politburo that Syrtsov be removed, no vote was held, because Bukharin had come down with an intestinal ailment. The second time, that is, when the vote was held, Stalin found himself alone with Molotov [in favor of Syrtsov's removal].

While Stalin was on his trip to Siberia, he brought Syrtsov back with him from Siberia and in Moscow, forced him to request his own dismissal. The question was raised in the Politburo once again, but Stalin lost again. Meanwhile, of course, he replaced Syrtsov's whole apparatus.

Before the [April] plenum a so-called party activists' meeting was held, consisting of full and candidate members of the Politburo and some members of the CC. Long debates took place there and resolutions were worked out, which were later adopted "unanimously" at the plenum. At this same meeting of the "activists" Stalin proposed that the question of restoring Zinoviev and Kamenev to party membership be brought before the plenum. This question was removed from the agenda by an overwhelming majority vote. In this connection it was reported to me as a fact that Rykov declared that if this question was to be raised, then it should be about the real Opposition, and not these scoundrels.

It was also passed on to me that the Stalinists and Rykovists speak of each other in unbelievable tones.

As a way of checking on Bukharin and M. I. [Maria Ilyichna Ulyanova, Lenin's sister], Yaroslavsky sits on *Pravda* [i.e., on its editorial staff].

In the Politburo now, according to the rumors, there are three groups. The third is embodied by Bukharin himself.

The Rykovists spread the rumor that Rykov wept when Trotsky was expelled from the party.

## Second Letter

. . . On June 10, a special CC plenum will be convened, at which the Comintern program will be discussed. At this plenum a speech by Bukharin about a new "Trotskyist" danger, in the person of Stalin, is possible.

The timing of the Sixth Comintern Congress has not yet been set because, first, they want to have the actual results of the elections in Germany and France, and second, the roles of Stalin and Rykov as reporters at the congress have not yet been divided.

Rykov is demanding for himself a report on "Ten Years of Soviet Power." Stalin will not agree to that because he is afraid that through this report he'd be letting Rykov take the congress into his hands. In spite of that, Rykov is preparing the report and his secretariat talks about it openly.

People assume that the congress will have the character of an enlarged plenum, i.e., will consider only current issues that have accumulated. (Not likely. The question of the program will be on the congress agenda.—L.T.)

In Leningrad, about three weeks ago, a narrow factional meeting of activists was convened, at which Slepkov spoke, having been sent there by Bukharin. Slepkov declared on Bukharin's behalf that with the left course Stalin was leading the party and country to disaster, that Stalin's new policy was nothing but "Trotskyism," and that it was necessary to take up arms and wage the fiercest possible ideological battle against Stalin. Slepkov's speech was supported by a member of the CC, Stetsky. Among those present there proved to be an "informant," who let Kirov know immediately, and Kirov denounced the whole affair to the "higher-ups." After a few days "organizational measures" ensued in relation to Slepkov. He was removed from *Bolshevik* and *Pravda* and exiled to the post of head of Agitprop in some remote part of Yakutia.

Stetsky's fate as a CC member will depend on the relationship of forces at the plenum that has been called for June 10.

Such quick reprisals against Slepkov are explained by the fact that Stalin, owing to Rykov's illness and the fact that Bukharin was temporarily relieved of his duties in order to work on the Comintern program, turned out to be in the "majority."

The Rykov faction is obviously taking shape not only in Moscow but also in the outlying regions. In the recent period Stalin has tried to "clean out" the Moscow party organization, which has turned out to be entirely for Rykov, with Uglanov in the lead, Ryutin being the only exception. Thus, Bauman has already been removed from the Moscow Committee. After Kaganovich's letter to friends, in which he wrote that the CC under Stalin's leadership had brought about sorry results as far as grain deliveries go, and that in the future the party should orient toward Rykov as the only talented leader, Stalin wanted to remove Kaganovich and wanted to earmark Uglanov for assignment to the Ukraine in order to purge Moscow more easily. But he was told that that wouldn't do, and Stalin evidently gave in.

The relationship of forces, in the event of a discussion, would not—in the general opinion—favor Stalin. That was confirmed by the vote at the April CC plenum on the Higher Technical Educational Establishments.

*The differences in the Politburo are no longer a secret to anyone, and neither side tries very hard to conceal them.* Thus at the April CC plenum a statement was submitted on the spot to the presiding committee over the signatures of eight CC members inquiring about the dissension in the Politburo. They asked that both Stalin and Rykov speak on this question so that—we are told—the "dispute" would not, after the fashion of previous years, come crashing down "like an avalanche on the head" of the party. This statement was passed over in total silence, and people heard about the submission of the statement only from the remarks of those who had submitted it.

When Stalin reported on the plenum at the Moscow activists'

meeting, a note was submitted to Stalin, among other notes, with the question, "Is it true that in the recent period you have found yourself in the minority on the Politburo?" To this Stalin replied, literally, "to be in the minority is no disgrace. Even Vladimir Ilyich was often in the minority." Nevertheless, he thanked the authors of the note for their sympathy.

### Third Letter

. . . The mood among the masses, in connection with the collective agreements is obviously one of opposition. But they have a fear of being identified with the openly organized Opposition, because they are afraid their demands would be rejected under the pretext of the struggle against the Opposition. The attitude of the workers toward the official trade union organizations is scornfully hostile. On all questions, even the pettiest, the workers go directly to the secretary of the party cell, saying they want to deal directly "with the boss and not with the frontman." The workers are very interested in the Opposition . . . Defections [from the Opposition] among workers are almost nonexistent; in the entire Moscow party organization barely three dozen or so have submitted statements [of capitulation].

There was an interesting incident at the Bogorodskaya textile mill during the meeting to celebrate the tenth anniversary of the Red Army. The person who gave the report, who had come from Moscow, proposed, after his dry report, that a bureaucratic resolution of approval be passed, sending greetings to the CC and to the "leader" Voroshilov, and so on. The secretary of the cell was foolish enough to ask the meeting whether anyone wanted to state an opinion. At that point a worker-Oppositionist stood up, an old partisan fighter in the civil war, who has great authority among the workers although he has been expelled from the party. He asked for the floor. First he proposed that everyone rise to honor the memory of those who had fallen, including Sklyansky and Frunze; and then he proposed that the meeting include in its resolution the sending of a telegram of greetings to the leader of the Red Army, Trotsky, and to include in the telegram of greetings to the CC the demand that Trotsky be restored to leadership work in the Red Army. The person who had given the report jumped up on a table and began to shout hysterically that this was obvious "counterrevolution" and demanded that this not even be put to a vote. The members of the presiding committee of the meeting, along with the secretary of the cell, were thrown into confusion, and the worker appealed directly to the meeting. He requested that workers who had fought in the civil war raise their hands, then asked them the question: "Who was the leader of the Red Army and whose orders did you recognize and carry out at the front?" Everyone answered: "Trotsky." In reply to which the official speaker tried to "argue" that the leader of the Red Army had been the CC and—Voroshilov. He was met with laughter and the vote was two thousand plus for the addition to the resolution, with two hundred opposed or abstaining. The next day the cell secretary was removed and new elections were scheduled for the bureau of the cell . . .

They say that after the announcement of the "left course" Kamenev and Zinoviev, when they were in Moscow, went to see Bukharin with offers to support the new course in every way. To which Bukharin replied that they should stay put and not be so hasty. "We've gotten along fine without you this far."

Zinoviev gave an "interesting" characterization of the "Trotskyist" Opposition, in a conversation with ——. The Trotskyist Opposition, he said, consists of three component parts: (1) the Old Bolsheviks from way back, like Pyatakov, Preobrazhensky, I.N. Smirnov, and Serebryakov; (2) some very talented individuals educated in the spirit of Western Social Democracy, who in the past were good revolutionaries but who did not have anything in common with *our* party—Trotsky, Radek, Rakovsky; and (3) the bulk of the Opposition, university students for the most part, a petty-bourgeois element. Now, he said, *we* will bring the third group back to the party. On the whole, the first group has already defected and only "isolated individuals" remain.

—— is with the Safarov tendency, and Zinoviev tried to persuade him to hand in a statement saying that "to orient toward Safarov is simply laughable," to which the Safarov supporter pointedly replied: "Laughable maybe, but not shameful." (By now it's shameful as well, in view of Safarov's conduct.—L.T.)

At the recent congress of the RILU, before the resolution for the congress was passed, there was the following discussion in the Russian delegation. After Lozovsky read the resolution aloud, Tomsky took the floor, criticized the resolution quite sharply (although the resolution had been drafted by the Politburo), and began to introduce additions and "corrections" in an obviously right-wing spirit, which would have negated the resolution completely. The delegation was inclined toward adopting these amendments. Then Lozovsky took the floor and announced that if even one of Tomsky's amendments was passed, he would immediately withdraw from the RILU and from all official work in general. The matter was referred to the Politburo for reconsideration. Every member of the Russian delegation was called in to the Politburo separately and told not to "make a fuss"; thus Lozovsky's resolution passed . . .

During a visit to Moscow, the Padishah of Afghanistan, Amanulla Khan, among other places, visited the new Red Army and Navy building. There he was met, they say, by Postnikov, who explained to the shah that the portraits hanging in the halls were of various leaders of the Red Army. This one, he said, was our "savior" in the civil war; that one was "the most important leader of the civil war," and so on. Having heard these explanations and looking over the portraits, the Padishah asked the invidious question: "Why no portrait of Trotsky? Wasn't he a participant in the civil war?" Postnikov was somewhat embarrassed and mumbled that "that" would be found in "hallways further along." He dispatched the commandant of the building to contact Voroshilov for instructions by phone. The latter ordered a portrait to be hung and the Padishah was satisfied. Eyewitnesses say that the portrait stayed up for an "entire" half hour . . .

At the opening of the Communist League of Youth (Komsomol) Congress in the Bolshoi Theater, Oppositionist Komsomol members on the fourth balcony sent sailing down about two thousand copies of an open letter to the congress from Opposition Komsomol members. The congress was stunned. Some handed in their copies of the leaflets to the presiding committee; some did not. The mood of the congress was not "of the calmest." Especially since another incident occurred: The Social Democratic youth league sent an invitation asking the Komsomol to attend its forthcoming congress, and the CC of the Komsomol accepted it. They say that Chaplin and Shatskin submitted a protest on this point to the presiding committee, which was not made public.

In the recent period the GPU has made many arrests among Opposition Komsomol members.

In Moscow now there is one more "person who has been struck"—Agranov. The Oppositionist comrade Zage hit him in public at a movie theater—and was arrested there and then.

*          *          *

That's all. I pass it on for what it's worth. It sounds very much like the truth—if not all of it, then almost all.

I firmly shake your hand,

Yours,
L. T.

# A CRUDELY EMPIRICAL TURN

## June 24, 1928

*NOTE: A circular letter. Preobrazhensky's first, conciliatory, proposal was that the Opposition should ask official permission to call a conference of all its members to discuss the new situation created by the "left turn" and to decide upon the Opposition's policy. For this proposal he came under heavy attack, and he evidently abandoned it. In this letter, Trotsky compares that proposal to "calling for a new Zemsky Sobor," a sixteenth- and seventeenth-century "consultative body" that met only at the tsar's pleasure, had no authority, could discuss only what the tsar wanted it to discuss, and could offer advice only when it was requested.*

*Preobrazhensky replaced his first proposal with an appeal to the Sixth Comintern Congress that contended that many of the differences between the Opposition and the party majority had become outlived as a result of the left course in the International. Trotsky, in this letter and in others, answers these arguments.*

*In the meantime, in early June, Safarov and Vardin, having appealed for reinstatment in the party, were informed by the Central Control Commission under Yaroslavsky that their declarations were inadequate; the next day, Yaroslavsky published an article in* Pravda *reminding Oppositionists that the six-month grace period set by the Fifteenth Congress in December was drawing to a close, and that applications for reinstatemnt in the party, accompanied by unequivocal recantations, would be considered only during the remaining days.*

*In the meantime, the Stalin-Bukharin draft program for the Comintern was published and Trotsky gives his initial assessment of it. In this letter, he also outlines his plans for the declaration to the Sixth Congress, which he will now begin to draft.*

*Finally, Trotsky learned that his younger daughter, Nina, had died of tuberculosis in Moscow on June 9.*

*By permission of the Harvard College Library. Translated from the Russian for this volume by Tom Twiss.*

Dear Friend:

Some comrades to this very day are toying with the idea of a conference, which was put into circulation by Preobrazhensky. Vardin (whom Sosnovsky calls deceased, though to be honest I don't know if he was ever alive) wrote to the CCC about our forthcoming application for a conference. With such an application one could apply only to make people laugh. However, I think that now argument is no longer necessary. Not only because the author himself has given up the idea, but also because certain events have occurred which define clearly enough both the limits and the mechanics of the "left course."

Completely correctly, Sosnovsky approaches all these questions from the point of view of the party regime. Rakovsky insists on this most tirelessly. And right now this is the only correct and reliable criterion. Not because the party regime is the independent source of all other phenomena and processes. No, to a large degree the party regime is a derivative factor. But at the same time it has a huge—and at certain moments, decisive—*independent* significance. Here, as everywhere, are dialectics. But since the party is the *sole instrument* by which we can consciously affect social processes, for us the criterion of the seriousness and depth of the turn is first of all the refraction of this turn within the party.

One noteworthy symptom was the case of the Kharkov machinist Bleskov, about which Sosnovsky has written a great deal. No need for me to repeat it. Even more significant is the decision in the case of Safarov and others of the "deceased." The CCC clearly and precisely established the limits of self-criticism: only the young can make mistakes. The elders not only are right today, but they always were right. Moreover, the Communist who recognizes the *current correctness* of the CC but does not recognize that it was correct yesterday not only does not have the right to give lectures about yesterday in a party school, he does not have the right to be a member of the party. You know, this decision alone shows how crudely empirical the turn is in relation to the kulak—crudely empirical and at the same time panic-stricken. Not the slightest connections are made between one thing and another. Moreover, they no longer even feel any need to make connections.

For if this need were even slightly felt, Yaroslavsky's decision in the affair of Safarov and the other deceased would be completely impermissible. Whoever does not learn this will make the most ridiculous mistakes.

One can say that there is an "objective logic of the situation" which will have to force its way, etc. But in the first place the objective logic also existed two years and three years and one year ago. While "objective logic" is cutting its teeth, it often happens that a lot of time goes by, during which the historical baby becomes quite feverish. It is possible to help the objective logic along, but not by changing our own subjective logic. That is, we must say what is and not discover that teeth are being cut when the gums are only starting to itch. Even if it be granted that objective logic will surely lead *certain* people in a *certain* period to understand what must be understood—even in that case the obligation of the revolutionary wing is not to praise people for what they have understood (that is, empirically conceded in panic), but to say loudly and clearly what they have not understood. And what they have not understood is nine-tenths, ninety-nine hundredths. And that endangers the little that has been understood. This is why Preobrazhensky's new proposal concerning the appeal to the congress seems to me to be a step backward even in comparison with his first proposal, although he has renounced the daydreamer Slavophile tradition of calling for a new *Zemsky Sobor*.

Another thing has happened which I consider decisive. That is the appearance of the *draft program*. We must understand that this is a bigger question than the question of the grain collections, an area where they can go back and forth ten more times—so long as the party remains silent—before the objective logic finally cuts its political teeth. The draft is a catastrophe. I am making the most conscientious effort to warn the congress of the consequences of this draft by analyzing all its component elements. Basically, this analysis sums up our collective work of the past few years. But I am compelled to take the responsibility for this analysis, precisely in view of the "unsuitable timing" of a Slavophile-type "assembly," which always proved to be ill-timed because it was "the overstimulated product of captive thought."

I consider the draft program a catastrophe in spite of the fact that there are no terrible remarks about our heresy in it. But there are none because, after all the zigzags that have been performed, it is difficult to say in precise programmatic form exactly what that heresy consists of. I tried to do this for the authors of the draft and had to put my pen down helplessly. It is all the more difficult to do this because three-quarters of the draft is spent on trying to imitate this heresy, but the contraband quality of the attempt is still there. The program studiously pretends to be a program of international revolution. In reality it is a program for the construction of socialism in one country, i.e., a program of social patriotism, not of Marxism. The disguise of left phrases changes nothing. The chapter on strategy draws none of the lessons flowing from the experience of the last decade. This signifies the sanctioning of the disastrous policies of the past five years. The section on the East sketches out the perspective for China of a worker-peasant democratic dictatorship which will grow over into a proletarian dictatorship at a later stage. This is preparation for a new Kuomintangism. We must carry out an open ideological struggle against those who did not understand this last fall. In such questions delays and deals are criminal.

I am making my critique of the draft program in the form of an extensive document which I will send to the congress and to the discussion bulletin of *Pravda*. It comes out to be of pamphlet length, the equivalent of several printer's sheets. While writing it, I was struck very vividly by how well timed Zinoviev's departure was. He came to us at a good time to help us inflict a mortal blow on the legend of "Trotskyism"; and he left us over half a year before the Sixth Congress, which freed our hands to criticize the mistakes of 1923, the mistakes of the Fifth Congress, etc. You know, up till now this was our weakest spot: because of our "allies" we ourselves were guilty for a while of national narrow-mindedness. Now we can fully correct this.

But how absurdly this ill-fated strategist acted in relation to his own capitulatory "line." If he had waited a few months he would have been able to seize onto the left turn and at the same time break with us on the question of our attitude toward the Sixth Congress. He would have left the bloc with some semblance of dignity and might have sown some confusion in the party ranks. But in his present woeful aspect he had done nothing but good for the party [ranks] and consequently for us, both in the way he came to us and in the way he left us. It is time to confer on him the rank of "socially necessary turncoat."

Now on the letter to the Sixth Congress. Since it is impossible to realize the idea of an "assembly," it will be necessary at the beginning of the letter to the Sixth Congress to say approximately the following:

Because of the conditions in which we find ourselves we are denied the opportunity to exchange views and formulate a collective declaration to the Sixth Congress. The present declaration was written by me personally, and I bear personal responsibility for it. However, on the basis of extremely incomplete correspondence with a significant number of cothinkers, I consider it unquestionable that *basically* the present letter expresses our collective view.

I see no other way. Regarding the *content* of the letter, I already outlined this in the proposal that I sent. Regarding the *tone,* we must not change our tone in relation to the party and the Comintern: this is the tone of our inseparable bond and of our genuine party spirit. Regarding the *leadership,* its activities, and its mistakes, after the latest events (the Safarov affair, the draft program) a shift is necessary—not to the right, toward Slavophile daydreams, but strongly to the left, toward Westernizing realism. Now this will no longer be distrust "in advance," but distrust based on undeniable facts and rigorously argued proofs within a strictly party framework.

I firmly shake your hand.


P.S.—Word of my daughter's death took me by surprise during my work on the draft program, and the memory of her was joined forever for me with the problems of the international revolution. I have dedicated this work, devoted to the basis of the program of the Communist Party, to the memory of my daughter, who was a young but very staunch and loyal party member, our steadfast cothinker. By telegraph we received and are receiving expressions of sympathy from many friends.

Many thanks.

# DECLARATION TO THE SIXTH COMINTERN CONGRESS

## July 12, 1928

*NOTE: The Sixth Congress of the Comintern was held in Moscow July 17–September 1, 1928. Although Trotsky sent this declaration in his own name, it reflects the views of the Opposition as a whole. It was widely circulated among Oppositionists and was endorsed by hundreds of them in telegrams to the Sixth Congress.*

*This was one of five documents Trotsky sent to the Sixth Congress. The other four were: (1) "Criticism of the Draft Program; (2) "What Now?" (both of these are in* The Third International After Lenin*); (3) "The July Plenum and the Right Danger" (printed elsewhere in this volume), which hadn't been written yet, and was sent to the congress after the other four; and (4) "Some Documents Relating to the Origin of the Legend of 'Trotskyism,'" a November 1927 letter Trotsky had circulated when Zinoviev and Kamenev had issued a statement of their disagreements with "Trotskyism" preliminary to leaving the Opposition. This last document included replies from Preobrazhensky, Pyatakov, Radek, Rakovsky, and Eltsin, establishing the history of Zinoviev's and Kamenev's roles in creating the legend of "Trotskyism," and Trotsky's January 3, 1928, postscript (all in* The Stalin School of Falsification*).*

*On June 3, the front page of* Pravda *carried an appeal from the Central Committee to all party members, calling for greater inner-party democracy and for more self-criticism, and decrying insufficiencies of the Soviet apparatus. Trotsky cited this as "an open (though forced) admission of the unhealthy and insupportable character of the regime that has been created in our party" but pointed out that the self-criticism campaign had been "nothing but a way of venting rank-and-file discontent by denouncing errors of secondary importance and by sacrificing one or two hundred bureaucrats as scapegoats."*

*From* Contre le courant, *October 25, 1928. Translated from the French for this volume by David Keil and Robert Dees. Revised against the Russian original by permission of the Harvard College Library.*

The congress now convening is taking place after an interval of more than four years marked by international events of the greatest importance and by cruel errors of leadership. The Bolshevik-Leninist Opposition, to which the undersigned belongs, has expressed its opinion on these events and errors many times in a number of documents, articles, and speeches. The course of events has already confirmed or increasingly tends to confirm the outlook of the Opposition in all its fundamental and essential aspects (its assessment of the 1923 defeat in Germany and the prospect of a stabilization of capitalism; its views concerning an "era of democracy and pacifism," the evolution of fascism and Social Democracy, and the relations between America and Europe; the slogan of a Soviet United States of Europe; the strategic problems of the Chinese revolution and the Anglo-Russian Committee; questions relating to the economic development of the USSR; the question of building socialism in one country; etc.).

It is neither possible nor necessary, within the limits of this declaration, to go back over these questions, which we have already clarified sufficiently elsewhere. It is enough to repeat that all the errors of principle committed by the leadership are the result of their backsliding from a Marxist and Bolshevik line to a centrist line, which, until very recently, has been veering more and more to the right.

The incorrect orientation followed so stubbornly for several years has since 1923 been inextricably bound up with the degeneration of the internal regime in the Comintern and in a number of its sections, especially the AUCP. During this period, bureaucratization has acquired absolutely unheard-of dimensions and forms, which menace the very foundations of the party of the international proletariat. The bureaucratic spirit and arbitrariness of the party apparatus may be seen most obviously and incontestably in the fact that for more than four years the leadership dealt with world events of the greatest importance without convening a Comintern congress. During this time, the Executive Committee elected at the Fifth Congress underwent total internal reorganization, without authorization by any congress and with the total removal of the leadership group elected at the Fifth Congress.

The consequences of this mistaken course, as well as the painful defeats it has occasioned, are: delay in the growth of the Comintern and in the spread of its influence; weakening of the USSR's position internationally; and a slowing of the pace of economic development and socialist construction in the first workers' state.

The leftward movement of the masses which is now beginning in Europe, and which is still going through its first stages, poses problems of the greatest importance for the Comintern, requiring a radical change in its course and a regroupment of forces internally. Equally pressing demands are being placed upon the AUCP by the political and economic situation in the Soviet Republic.

The Sixth Congress is meeting at a time when the total collapse of the line followed by the leadership for the last few years is already becoming evident under the pressure of events; a shift to the left has been projected, both in a series of resolutions and in practical measures adopted by the Central Committee of the AUCP, and in certain decisions of the February plenum of the ECCI.

Some elements of this contradictory shift to the left are reflected in the draft program presented to the Sixth Congress. For that very reason the document has an extremely eclectic character and cannot in any way or to any degree serve as a guide for the international proletarian vanguard.

In two long documents written for the Sixth Congress, the undersigned attempted to present an assessment of the draft program, examined in the light of changes that have occurred in the international political situation (particularly in the last five years), as well as an assessment of the recent shift by the Central Committee of the AUCP, and by the February plenum of the ECCI, in connection with the situation in the USSR and in the Comintern. One of these documents has already been sent; the second will be sent to the Sixth Congress at the same time as the present declaration.

The aim of this declaration is to pose before the highest body of the Communist International the question of the readmission of the Bolshevik-Leninists (Opposition) to the party, on the basis of a clear and precise exposition of our views on the present situation and the tasks facing the Comintern.

The isolation forcibly imposed on the supporters of the "Plat-

form of the Bolshevik-Leninists (Opposition)," removed from the
capital and separated from each other by hundreds or thousands
of kilometers (deported to Siberia, Central Asia, etc.), totally
prevents them from drawing up a *collective* declaration. Letters
addressed to the exiled Oppositionists (even by registered mail)
arrive only in exceptional cases: one letter in three or four arrives,
and that after intervals of one, two, or three months. Under these
conditions I am obliged to sign only my name to the present
declaration. It is quite likely, even certain, that if there had been
a collective discussion, essential modifications would have been
made in this text. However, my correspondence with cothinkers—
even in its present truncated, strangulated form—permits me to
state with full certainty that, in all essentials, this letter expresses the views of at least the overwhelming majority, if not all,
of the supporters of the Platform of the Opposition, especially the
many hundreds of deportees.

A correct domestic policy in the USSR is inconceivable without
a correct policy for the Comintern. Therefore, for us, the question
of the Comintern's line, that is, the strategic line of the international revolution, stands above all other questions. However, a
situation has developed historically in which the key to the
Comintern's policy is the policy of the AUCP.

There is no point here in speaking of the conditions and causes
that justifiably gave the AUCP the role of the leading party in
the Comintern. It was entirely due to the leadership exercised by
the AUCP that the Comintern made truly colossal gains in the
first few years of its existence. But subsequently, the mistaken
policies pursued by the leaders of the AUCP and the bureaucratization of its internal regime, have meant that the fertile influence
of Bolshevism on the Comintern in the areas of doctrine and
politics has more and more been replaced and eliminated by
"combinations" concocted by the functionaries and administrators.

This explains both the lack of any congress for four years and
the vote at the February plenum of the ECCI in favor of a
resolution stating that "the Opposition in the AUCP is banking
on the downfall of Soviet power"; this allegation discredits only
those who inspired it in the Executive Committee and those who
voted for it; in no way does it tarnish the revolutionary honor of
the Bolshevik-Leninists (Opposition).

The present task is to preserve—or more precisely to bring
about the rebirth of—the decisive influence of Bolshevik ideas
and politics on the young parties of the Communist Interna-

tional, at the same time freeing them from the system of bureaucratic command. This task is inseparably connected with the task of changing the orientation and internal regime of the AUCP itself.

Basing ourselves in this way on an international perspective and on the fundamental interests of the Communist International, we shall focus our attention in the present declaration on the crisis of the AUCP, the groupings inside it, and the consequent duties of the Opposition, as we see them.

*         *         *

Only a superficial mind would fail to see the immense objective difficulties that exist, and that would confront *any* leadership of the AUCP, in the present situation. These difficulties are above all the result of fundamental causes such as the country's petty-bourgeois character and its capitalist encirclement. In addition to that, the errors committed by the leadership for the past five years have meant a persistent slowing of the pace, which in turn has meant a cumulative piling up of ever new difficulties. Placing the blame for errors does not eliminate their results, which in turn become an objective condition. Any leadership would have to take as its point of departure the present difficult objective situation, which is complicated to the extreme by the continued, stubborn piling up of error upon error.

This means that there is no simple and quick solution. We can even grant, up to a certain point, that a resolute rightward solution, widening the boundaries of the NEP and narrowing those of the monopoly of foreign trade, would bring quicker and more immediate results than a leftward course. But these results would lead in a quite different direction. Heavy imports of foreign goods and capital—following the abolition or limitation of the monopoly of foreign trade—lower prices for the products of [state] industry, the expansion of exports, etc., would all lead *in the period immediately following* to an attenuation of the disproportion, a narrowing of the "scissors," a certain regularization of the market, "enrichment" of the village (that is, of its upper layers), and even a temporary reduction of unemployment. But those would be successes along the road of capitalist restoration, which would integrate the USSR into the imperialist chain after several short stages. "Russia no. 2" would once again become imperialism's weakest link; the result would be a semicolonial existence. But before it became evident that the course to the right was a course toward a backward and dependent capitalist society—a society of horrible exploitation of the workers and new wars in the service of world imperialist masters—the immediate results of the right-wing policy might be accepted by a considerable part of the population of the countryside and even the cities, as a way out of the dead end that the economy now finds itself in, with constant shortages, waiting lines for bread, and mounting unemployment. It is just here that we find the political danger of the rightist orientation: after the painful experience of the centrist policies, a rightward course could produce deceptively "alluring" results during the first stage of the path leading directly into the abyss of capitalism.

There is not and there cannot be a *simple* left recipe making it possible *simultaneously* to emerge from these difficulties and to progress toward socialism. In general, within the boundaries of a single nation, it is impossible to completely overcome the difficulties resulting from the delay in the world revolution. This should be said clearly, firmly, and honestly, in a Marxist and Leninist way.

It is poor logic, however, to draw pessimistic conclusions for the USSR just because socialist construction is inseparably dependent on the international revolution. It is just as poor logic as to draw pessimistic conclusions about the German revolution from the fact that it depends directly on the successes of the dictatorship in the USSR. The very idea that pessimism flows logically from the fact that our socialist construction is dependent on international relations—that is shameful for a Marxist.

But although the fate of the revolution is a function of its international character, it does not at all follow that the party in each country is relieved of the duty to *do the maximum* in all areas. On the contrary, this obligation only increases, because the economic errors made in the USSR not only retard the building of socialism in our country, but strike in the most direct way at the world revolution.

If at the right time, that is, at the Twelfth Congress, a firm economic course had been taken, aimed at overcoming the disproportion through a correct policy of distributing the national income and stepped-up industrialization, our situation now would be immeasurably more favorable. Even in that case, of course, fundamental difficulties would still face us. But in the worldwide struggle that we are waging, timing is decisive. If economic development had been more rapid, and if as a result the relationship of forces between classes inside the country were more favorable to us, we would be moving much more certainly toward victories by the proletariat in the more advanced countries.

A [genuine] left course could not promise to build "full socialism" by our efforts alone. It could not even promise a complete triumph over the contradictions within the country, as long as world contradictions exist. But it could gradually establish more correct control over the domestic class contradictions—more correct from the standpoint of socialism under construction. It could quicken the rate of growth, through a more correct policy of distributing the national income. It could consolidate in a more systematic and serious way the proletariat's hold on the commanding heights of the economy. It could establish a clearer and firmer class line in all policies, it could develop closer ties with the work of the Comintern, and finally it could ensure the application of Marxist foresight and leadership to the fundamental problems of the world proletarian revolution. Taken all together, this is precisely what is needed for victory on a world scale.

A true left course would require an economic plan extending over a period of years, a plan that was well thought out, audacious, and far-reaching, which would not lurch from one extreme to the other, driven by maneuverist policies geared to conjunctural changes. Such maneuvering is absolutely necessary, but it can never be decisive. A left course would also require tremendous tenacity on the part of the leadership, the ability to swim against the stream, to maintain an overall strategic line through all the twists and turns imposed by tactics. But this requires genuine optimism on questions of the international proletarian revolution and—based on that unshakable foundation—a profound faith in the possibility of successful socialist construction in our country.

All that can be accomplished by the issuing of circulars from on high is a zigzag to the left. But it is impossible to carry out a true left course by issuing circulars. *To carry out a left, proletarian course, a Leninist course, our party must have a new orientation, from top to bottom, and a realignment of forces.* Those are processes that would have to develop in a serious way over a long period. The party must be allowed once again to have its own free, collective thinking, its own powerful and resilient will. The party must stop being afraid of the apparatus. We must achieve conditions such that the apparatus could not and would not dare try to intimidate the party. The party must once again become—the party.

A right-wing policy is possible, leading to obvious and relatively quick "gains"—for capitalism. A left policy is equally possible, a systematic policy of proletarian dictatorship, socialist construction, and international revolution. What is not possible as a durable and successful policy (*much less* as a Bolshevik policy) is a so-called "left course" employing the methods of centrist "combinationism," while keeping the party suppressed and continuing to smash away at its left wing. This kind of left-centrist zigzag, unless the party forces it to "grow over" into a genuine left course, will inevitably collapse; that will occur, moreover, long before practical results of any importance become evident. At that moment, all the cards may prove to be in the hands of the right wing, which would immediately win reinforcements at the expense of the present center, perhaps even finding its leaders among those who are now with the center.

Whoever thinks that the present left shift by the party apparatus has canceled out the right danger is radically wrong. On the contrary, *never has this danger been so great, so threatening, and so imminent as it is now.* The most dangerous moment for a wagon near the peak of a steep mountain road is when the front wheels have already gone over the top but most of the wagon, with the heavy load and the passengers, has not yet gone over. That is precisely when maximum efforts by the horses and the driver are required; but, most importantly, the "passengers" themselves must get out, grab the spokes of the wheels, and push with all their might. Trouble comes if the passengers are drowsing or hesitate uncertainly, or if the driver turns around and, using the whip of Article 58, drives away those who with their bare hands are moving the wheels forward or who have placed their backs against the rear of the wagon to act as brakes. It is at a moment like this that the wagon, with all its weight, can slip back and go crashing down the mountain. Never has the danger from the right been so great, so threatening, and so imminent as it is now.

What does the right danger signify in the present period? It is less the danger of an open, full-fledged bourgeois counterrevolution than that of a *Thermidor,* that is, a partial counterrevolutionary shift or upheaval which, precisely because it was partial, could for a fairly long time continue to disguise itself in revolutionary forms, but which in essence would already have a decisively bourgeois character, so that a return from Thermidor to the dictatorship of the proletariat could only be effected through a new revolution.

We have argued repeatedly, in particular at the plenum of the Central Committee in February 1927, that the centrist leadership, in striking at the left, would inevitably draw along behind it a longer and longer right-wing tail, both inside the party and far beyond its boundaries, ending with conscious and militant Thermidorians. We predicted that this weighty tail would inevitably strike at the head and that such a blow could become the starting point for a profound regroupment within the party, that is, more and more insolent self-assertion by the right wing, a sharper and more audacious shift to the left by the proletarian core of the party, and a more feverish lurching back and forth by the centrist apparatus faction, which would lose its forces little by little. The bloodless kulak revolt of 1927-28, which occurred with the assistance of members of the party who desired to "live in peace with all classes," is precisely a blow struck by the tail at the head.

*Pravda* itself has now officially admitted (in an editorial of February 15, 1928) that an influential Thermidorian or semi-Thermidorian wing exists in our party. And no subsequent qualifications can plaster over that admission. For, in a proletarian party, what else can people be but Thermidorians if they are ready at any moment to smash away at the Left Opposition but then want to live in peace with the kulak, who is drawing the middle peasant behind him in opposition to Soviet power? We do not mean by this that everyone who promotes this policy wants consciously to go all the way to Thermidor. No, the Thermidorians, and even more the semi-Thermidorians, have never been distinguished by a broad historical awareness; only that fact permits a great number of them to fulfill their role in the service of another class.

So then, a blow has been dealt by the tail to the head, a serious one but one that up to the present has had only the significance of a signal and a warning. Regroupments have begun in the party, though as yet they are very unclear and very insufficient. One of the expressions of this process is the tendency for the "left" maneuver executed from on high to become a serious zigzag to the left. Thus the two front wheels of the party—or perhaps only one of them—already seem to be over the top, but the wagon as a whole, with its heavy load, is still on an incline, which could become for it a terrible downward plunge.

*          *          *

What is the duty of the Opposition toward the party in this exceptionally critical situation? (Obviously, here we are talking about the true Leninist Opposition, and not those occasional fellow-travelers who are always ready to abandon their opinions if that is firmly demanded of them, preferring other ideas that are easier to defend.)

To respond more clearly to the question of the duty of the Opposition, one must begin with the worst variant: that is, the hypothesis that, by taking advantage of the errors committed year after year by the leadership, the chronic disorganization of the market, the high cost of living, unemployment, the way everything is yanked back and forth by fiat from above, and so on, the Thermidorian, kulak, bourgeois, bureaucratic tail may try, at the peak of some future hill, at a time of even greater difficulties, to strike a really serious blow at the head; that is, try to move from the present semilegal forms of capitalist sabotage to direct civil war.

Is this possibility excluded a priori? No. Unfortunately not. Especially if international complications arise. Anyone who would say that it is excluded would be treacherously lulling the party to sleep.

Might we have reason to fear that at the hour of danger a fairly large percentage of the stalwarts of false party monolithism in such places as Smolensk, Artemovsk, Shakhty, and even in Leningrad, even in Moscow, would waver, step aside, or commit outright treason? Not only *might* we have reason; we *must* fear it. The recent revelations barely lift the edge of the bureaucratic curtain. In this domain, the party must expect great dangers.

On the other hand, can anyone imagine an Oppositionist who would say: "They have created this situation with their policies; let them disentangle themselves!"? No, it's impossible to imagine such an Oppositionist, unless it were a White Guard agent, a provocateur who had penetrated the Opposition for destructive purposes. Oppositionists will fight for the party, for the dictatorship, for the October Revolution, as would be expected of the selflessly devoted revolutionaries they have shown themselves to be in defending the banner of Bolshevism under the most difficult historical circumstances, while persecutions and repressions fall on them thick as hail. The cadres of the Opposition have stood the test. If the bureaucratic stupidity of the party apparatus should prevent the Oppositionists from occupying their places in the ranks of the regular army at the moment of extreme peril, they would fight the class enemy as guerrillas, because a revolutionary defends the revolution when it is in need without waiting for an order. There would be no need to speak of this, if not for the vicious and hysterical shouting about the alleged defeatism of the Opposition, which "is banking on the downfall of Soviet power."

The claim that the conduct of the Oppositionists has no importance for the defense of the dictatorship because of their "weakness," is an especially bankrupt one now. If the Opposition is so weak, why have the apparatus, the press, the official orators, the professors of the party schools for five years, and the GPU in the last period taken up the fight against the Opposition as their principal task? Why do all the speeches, articles, circulars, instructions, and books take this fight as their starting point and return to it again and again? Whatever the strength of the Opposition's influence, actual and potential, present and future, one thing is incontestable: the party of the dictatorship of the proletariat can count on this detachment, which belongs to it, under all circumstances, completely and entirely.

However, another question of more burning immediacy remains: What can and should the Opposition do in the present crisis? Here too we want to pose all the questions squarely, to leave no room for any confusion or misunderstanding.

Can the Opposition support the right against the centrists, who formally hold power—in order to help overthrow them, to "avenge ourselves" on them for the odious persecution, the rudeness and disloyalty, the "Wrangel officer," Article 58, and other deliberately vicious deeds? There have been such combinations between the right and the left in [past] revolutions. Such combinations have also ruined revolutions. In our party the right represents the link which the bourgeois classes secretly hold onto, to drag the revolution onto the path of Thermidor. *At the present moment,* the center is trying to resist, or half-resist. It is clear: the Opposition cannot have anything in common with such combinationist adventurism, counting on the aid of the right to overthrow the center.

The Opposition supports every step, even a hesitant one, toward the proletarian line, every attempt, even an indecisive one, to resist the Thermidorian elements. The Opposition does so and will do so completely independently of whether the center, which continues to look to the right, wants it or not. The Opposition of course does not set any prior conditions for this, demands no agreements, concessions, etc. It simply takes account of the fact that the center's current zigzag runs parallel, though at a certain distance, to the strategic line of Bolshevik policy.

We have already said (most recently in our declaration, read by

Comrade Smilga at the Fifteenth Congress) that the Opposition, even if expelled from the party, does not consider itself released from its party duties, nor from responsibility to the country for the party as a whole. We can only repeat here entirely what we said before. This means in particular that, despite the persecutions, expulsions, Article 58, etc., each Oppositionist is ready as before to carry out the missions that the party entrusts to him, independently of his attitude toward its leadership and of the regime that this leadership maintains.

However, from the political point of view, can the Opposition be responsible to the party for the sudden turns currently carried out in the name of a correct Leninist course? No, it cannot. The Opposition's support for every correct move, even a half-hearted one, toward a proletarian line, will never be the mere yea-saying of the party philistine to the centrism of the apparatus (even if it is left centrism); the Opposition will never pass over in silence the centrists' inclination to do things only halfway, their incoherence, the errors they continue to commit, and will never hypocritically ignore their revisionist theories, which pave the way for new, even greater mistakes. While supporting against the right every step of the center toward the left, the Opposition should (and will) criticize the complete insufficiency of such steps and the lack of guarantees in the entire present turn, since it continues to be carried out on the basis of orders from on high and does not really emanate from the party. The Opposition will uncompromisingly continue to reveal to the party the immense dangers resulting from the inconsistency, the lack of theoretical reflection, and the political contradictoriness of the present course, which is still based on the bloc of the center with the right against the left wing.

Under these conditions, can the Opposition renounce its Platform? Now less than ever. To do that would be equivalent to renouncing the thoroughly thought-out, generalized, and systematic basis for a true left course; it would render the best service to the right, whose hopes and plans can only be based on the zigzags and incoherence of the centrist course. *A continued fight for the ideas and proposals expressed in the Platform is the only correct, serious, and honest way to support every step by the center that is at all progressive.* It is only on this condition that one can have any serious hope of seeing the party succeed, through internal reform, in transforming the left-centrist zigzag of the leadership into a true Leninist course.

Is this fight for the Opposition Platform compatible with party unity? Under a bureaucratic—that is, an unjust and unhealthy—regime, such a fight may prove temporarily to be incompatible with unity, as the expulsion of the Opposition from the party showed. But the circular issued by the Central Committee on June 3 is above all an open (though forced) admission of the unhealthy and insupportable character of the regime that has been created in our party over the last five years and which still must be radically changed. Under a healthy regime the most rigorous criticism of errors of principle committed by the Central Committee is perfectly compatible with party unity and iron discipline in action. The actual differences of opinion (now that they have undergone a gigantic testing by events) could be fairly easily overcome by the party, if it reconquered its elementary rights. All questions come together around this question [of party democracy].

Is fighting for the convictions laid out in the Platform of the Bolshevik-Leninists (Opposition) compatible with renouncing the factional methods used to defend these opinions? Under a regime which, according to the expression used by this same circular of June 3, is infected with "the most vicious bureaucratism," all criticism of the opinions of the Central Committee or of a provincial committee, a district committee, or a cell secretary, is branded as "factionalism," and often the critics were forcibly driven down the road to factionalism. Under a regime that was truly based on "self-criticism"—or, stated more correctly, on *party democracy*—the fight for the views expressed in the Platform would be entirely possible. The Opposition is totally willing to defend its views using only the strictly regulated norms of party procedure, as long as these are firmly based on the two closely interrelated resolutions of the Tenth Congress, the one banning factions and the one on party democracy.

Even now, after the recent manifestos and circulars, the Opposition has no illusions about the party regime. A simple-minded credulity, mistaking words for actions and contradictory manifestos for a consistent and firmly guaranteed left course, is a quality that never was and never will be found in a proletarian revolutionary, especially one who has gone through the experience, and seriously reflected on the history, of the last five years.

Never has factionalism eaten away at the party so much as now, after the attempt to mechanically amputate the Opposition. The right, the buffer group, the center, the two "repentant" halves of the leadership of the Leningrad Opposition, the Bolshevik-Leninists (Opposition)—these are the principal groups now existing in the party, without counting the subfactions. The centrism of the leading faction, because of its formlessness and the contradictory character of its ideas and policy, is a real breeding ground for all kinds of factionalism, both left and right. Superficial measures—manifestos, plus arrests—will not deliver us from this situation. Only a correct course, elaborated and carried out by the party as a whole, can triumph over the factionalism devouring the party.

A correct course can be achieved only by the methods of party criticism, focusing on the basic shifts in line and defects in the party regime that have appeared in the last five years. We must condemn a false policy in order to pave the way for a correct one. As for the "self-criticism" announced in manifestos and articles, up to now this is nothing but a way of venting rank-and-file discontent by denouncing errors of secondary importance and sacrificing one or two hundred bureaucrats as scapegoats. Criticism of the way policy is carried out is presented as good, healthy, and "businesslike." Criticism of the leadership is said to be destructive, pernicious, oppositional. If the "self-criticism" does not surpass these limits, the entire left-centrist zigzag will be nothing but a harmful fiasco.

To bring bureaucratically legalized "self-criticism" out of this dead end and onto the road of party democracy is the task of the party itself. On the success of this task depends the success of the deep reform without which the party will not lead the revolution out of the crisis it is in. To resolve this double problem—to restore the health of its own ranks and of the Soviet state—the party first of all and most of all needs clarity in its ideas.

Thus the duty of the Opposition is to raise its voice as part of the "self-criticism" which certain very influential centrist bureaucrats regard as only a safety valve for the accumulated dissatisfaction, but which in reality should become an integral part of the system of party democracy. Above all, the Opposition must help the party ranks (not only in the AUCP, but in the entire Comintern) to resist the bureaucratic desire to keep "self-criticism" from touching the fundamental problems of political line and of party leadership.

The experience with the quality of economic policy in the USSR, the experience of the German revolutionary movement in 1923-28, the experiences of the Chinese revolution and the Anglo-Russian Committee, must be illuminated, examined, and studied in every aspect. Without this there is no way forward.

At the same time, the Opposition has the duty to watch vigilantly, so that "self-criticism" (which, if it continues to develop, will inevitably run into more and more bureaucratic obstacles) does not turn in an antiparty direction and bring grist to the anarchists' and Mensheviks' mill. The opportunist policies and the bureaucratic regime unavoidably produce malignant reactions of this kind among the working masses. Only the Opposition can protect the party against this evil, or at least reduce this reaction to a minimum, by recreating, reinforcing the confidence of the workers in the party, by pitilessly rejecting all equivocation or apparatus-style adaptationism, by fighting openly for its full program—in a word, by steadfastly following the Leninist line.

So stated, our principled orientation saves us the trouble of refuting the idea attributed to us that the party has become Thermidorian, or that Thermidor, i.e., a counterrevolutionary coup d'état, is already an accomplished fact. The hysterical persistence with which this "idea" is propagated, although it has nothing in common with our position and benefits only our class enemies, merely testifies to the impotence of our adversaries in the struggle of ideas, born of the general inability of centrists to seize and to understand the living dialectic of the historical process.

On the same level are the attempts to attribute to us the view that the Comintern has ceased to be the vanguard of the world proletariat and needs to be replaced by some new international association.

We have stated all along, and we repeat, that we cannot take even a shadow of responsibility for those who think that the process of backsliding from the class line by the leadership of the AUCP and the Comintern (a process which unquestionably has taken place in the last few years) is an irreparable and irreversible process; or for those who do not see or who deny any revolutionary tendencies or forces in the AUCP or the Comintern and who, therefore, directly or indirectly turn their backs on those organizations.

In the same manner we decline all responsibility for the policy of running Opposition candidates parallel to those of the Communist Party, a policy which we condemned in advance and against which we warned in a letter sent abroad. Since this letter was published in *Pravda* (on January 15, 1928), the continuing allegations that we are in solidarity with the policy of parallel candidates merely represent one more of the many attempts [by the leadership] to rudely deceive its own party in order to justify, somehow or other, the use of repression.

We base all of our calculations on the fact that there exist within the AUCP, the Comintern, and the USSR enormous internal revolutionary forces, which now are suppressed by the false leadership and the onerous regime, but which, with experience, criticism, and the advance of the class struggle throughout the world, are perfectly capable of correcting the line of the leadership and assuring a correct proletarian course.

The current attempts by the leadership to escape the consequences of its own policies by taking a road to the left instead of to the right, repeating and in part using the ideas and the slogans of the Opposition, are carried out under pressure, as yet vague and unformed, from the proletarian core of the party; they constitute one of the proofs of the correctness of our general analysis and our calculations.

With all our strength we will help see to it that the internal forces of the party and the class bring about a rectification of policy with the fewest possible convulsions within the AUCP, the workers' state, and the International.

We totally reject the accusation that our previous declarations on stopping factional work were not sincere. Those declarations always assumed a minimum of good will on the part of the official majority, so that a party regime would be ensured under which it would be possible to defend one's point of view by the normal methods worked out during the entire past history of the party. It is always possible for the all-powerful bureaucratic apparatus, fighting for its inviolability and its permanence, to mechanically close to party members all paths except those of factional work. In formulating our declarations announcing our intention of renouncing factional methods, we always referred to the teaching of Lenin on the proletarian party, and on the fundamental conditions of its healthy existence. We referred in particular to the resolution of December 5, 1923, which said that bureaucratism pushes the best members of the party onto the path of isolation and factionalism [see "The New Course Resolution," in *Challenge 1923-25*]. For us this declaration was not, and is not, a mere formality. It expresses the essence of the question.

Even more inappropriate and vile are the accusations that the Opposition, even after the Fifteenth Congress, despite its declaration that it would submit to the resolutions of the party and stop factional work, in reality continued. The promise we made at the congress presupposed our continued membership in the party;

and consequently the possibility of fighting for our views within its ranks. Otherwise this commitment would only mean a renunciation of all political activity in general, a commitment to stop serving the party and the international revolution. Only completely corrupted bureaucrats could demand such a renunciation from revolutionaries. Only contemptible renegades could give such a promise.

Basing ourselves on these principled positions, we can have nothing to do with so-called Leninists who deceive the party, try to use diplomacy on the class struggle, play hide-and-seek with history, pretend to admit their errors while secretly claiming to have been right, create the myth of "Trotskyism," demolish it, then try to reconstitute it—in a word, apply to the party the policy of a "Brest-Litovsk," that is, of a temporary, insincere capitulation made in the hope of revenge. Such a policy is admissible toward a class enemy; but it is totally adventurist in relation to one's own party.

We feel repugnance toward the Byzantine philosophy of recantation, according to which concern for party unity would mean that, in our day and age, in the epoch of the proletarian dictatorship, one must renounce one's opinions or abandon the defense of those opinions if today's leaders consider them inadmissible, for reasons of prestige, or decide to use the resources of the state to victimize those who hold such opinions. We would consider ourselves criminal if we had carried out a bitter fight within the party for five years in the name of principles so elastic that we could renounce them on command or under threat of expulsion from the party. Serving the party is inseparable from fighting for a correct political line. Only a contemptible pseudo-member of the party would allow the fear of temporarily losing his party card, however painful that may be, to outweigh the duty to fight for the fundamental traditions of the party and for its future.

There are speeches to the effect that the current attitude of the Opposition (faithful to its convictions, fighting for them) is incompatible with its declarations on party unity. These speeches reek of duplicity. If we thought that the development of the party was completed at the Fifteenth Congress, there would then be no historical alternative to the creation of a second party. But we have already said that we have nothing in common with this evaluation. If in connection with the grain hoarding crisis, in passing and as if by chance, it became evident that within the party there exists a strong and influential faction that wants "to live in peace" with all classes; if, within a short time, the affairs of Shakhty, Artemovsk, Smolensk, and many others, came to light—this shows that the inevitable process of differentiation in the party, of self-clarification and self-purification, is yet to be accomplished; the genuine proletarian core of the party will still have sufficient opportunities to realize that our evaluation of party policy, of its composition, of the general tendencies of its development are confirmed by facts of decisive importance. Temporarily placed outside the party by a lying and unhealthy regime, we continue to live with the party, to work for its future. Because our line of conduct and our perspectives are correct, because our methods of fighting for the Leninist convictions have a true party character, no force in the world can tear us away from this party or oppose us to the international proletarian vanguard and the Communist revolution. Least of all can this be achieved by using Article 58, which dishonors only those who stoop to employing it against us.

The contradiction that obliges us to remain formally outside the party, while fighting on its behalf against those who disorganize and undermine it from within, is a contradiction formed by life itself in the course of history. It cannot be escaped by a juridical sophism leading only to the despicable repudiation of ideas. The contradiction that is imposed upon us is only a particular manifestation of deeper, more general contradictions; it cannot really be resolved except by applying Leninist methods to the fundamental problems facing the Comintern and the AUCP. Until then, the question of the Opposition will remain the touchstone by which to judge the party's political line and its regime.

The reprisals against the Opposition for its criticism of the Central Committee, a criticism completely confirmed by the facts and now unintentionally corroborated by the recent partial measures and decisions of the Central Committee itself, are the most flagrant examples of the worst methods of the apparatus regime and the worst aspects of the leadership of the party. New expulsions and deportations of Oppositionists still continue to terrorize the party, despite the reassuring circulars. The question of readmitting the Oppositionists to the party, returning the deportees, freeing the prisoners, becomes the essential proof, the infallible means of verification, and the first indicator of the seriousness and depth of all the recent moves toward the left. The party and the working class will judge not at all by words, but by deeds. This was the lesson of Marx, it was that of Lenin, it is that of the Opposition.

The Sixth Congress of the Comintern can, in large measure, facilitate the reestablishment of party unity by firmly advising the central institutions of the AUCP to immediately abrogate the application of Article 58 to the Opposition, an application based on rude political disloyalty and on a perfidious abuse of power. The reinstatement of the Bolshevik-Leninists (Opposition) in the party is an indispensable and inevitable condition for a genuine turn toward the Leninist road. This of course applies not only to the AUCP but also to all other sections of the Comintern.

Every Oppositionist, in retaking the place that is rightfully his in the party—from which, we repeat, no force nor any resolution can separate him—will do everything he can to help the party get out of the current crisis, and to overcome factionalism. There can be no doubt that such a commitment will have the unanimous support of all the Bolshevik-Leninists (Opposition).

# WHAT TO EXPECT
# FROM THE SIXTH CONGRESS

## July 17, 1928

*NOTE: A circular letter, written the day the Sixth Comintern Congress began. Perhaps the most important part of this letter deals with the Opposition's approach to the left turn. Trotsky's argument was that the Stalin leadership had been forced to adopt some of the Opposition's platform; that was certain to stimulate an atmosphere in the party that would be more receptive to the Opposition's ideas and criticisms. If the Opposition took a formalistic approach to the left turn, insisting that it was a maneuver that meant nothing, it would be unable to get the attention of the widening circles in the party membership that were beginning to question the right-center policies and seek an alternative. This would cut the Oppositionists off from the very people they were trying to reach and they would consequently miss the opportunity to build a core of Communists educated in Bolshevik theory and prepared for the future. This is a theme Trotsky would strike again and again in replying to the accusations of sectarians and ultralefts in the Opposition that Trotsky was giving too much credence to Stalin's left turn.*

*The Septemvirate Trotsky refers to in paragraph 4 was a secret faction consisting of the six members of the Politburo after Lenin's final withdrawal from work (excluding Trotsky), plus Kuibyshev, who was chairman of the Central Control Commission. The six others were Zinoviev, Kamenev, Stalin, Bukharin, Rykov, and Tomsky. This secret faction met and made all the major decisions for the party without its knowledge or consent; it functioned from early 1923 until Zinoviev and Kamenev broke with the others in late 1925.*

*The Sixteenth Congress, which Trotsky demanded be democratically prepared and honestly convened during 1928, was not actually held until June-July 1930, after the destruction of the Right Opposition (Bukharinists). Trotsky seems to be saying that his two demands for party democracy were included in "What Now?" Actually, they appear in his reply to Radek's theses.*

*The rumor that Trotsky refers to here that Ruth Fischer had been readmitted to the German CP was erroneous. The congress would approve a resolution expelling dissidents from the French and German parties.*

*By permission of the Harvard College Library. Translated from the Russian for this volume by Tom Twiss.*

Dear Comrades:

This letter represents an answer to a number of letters received from various places over the past few weeks. Its lateness is due to the fact that I was occupied during these weeks with work in connection with the Comintern congress. I managed to finish the work in time.

I sent the congress four documents in all: first, a critique of the draft program of the Comintern—about eleven printer's sheets; second, the letter "What Now?" which constitutes an evaluation of the present left shift in the light of the policies of the last few years; third, a supplement to the letter, documentary information on the origin of the legend—or rather, the fabrication of the legend—of Trotskyism; fourth, a "declaration" in the true sense of the word. The last document, which is comparatively short (less than a printer's sheet), is a formal document demanding the Opposition's reinstatement in the party. I distributed the text of the declaration fairly extensively to comrades so that they could, if they found it necessary, associate themselves with this declaration by sending telegrams to the presidium of the congress. Earlier still, I distributed a rough copy of the future declaration. The final text is clearer, more precise, and sharper, but in essence does not differ from the rough copy.

I am enclosing the table of contents of the two long documents sent to the congress [the "critique" and "What Now?"]. The work had, by necessity, an ordinarily hasty character. There are probably omissions. But as I had to write on questions which we have often discussed and thought out, jointly and alone, I have a notion that on the whole the works sent to the congress represent a sufficiently complete statement of all the views of the Opposition on the basic questions of an international and domestic character.

I have already written to some comrades to the effect that the departure of Zinoviev could not have happened at a better time.

Had he had the tenacity to wait a few more months, he could have capitulated while maintaining some semblance of "propriety," by seizing onto the "left course," on the one hand, and breaking with us over our evaluation of the Fifth Congress and the Comintern regime, on the other. In coming to us he dealt an irreparable blow to the legend of Trotskyism, revealing one or two of the "secrets of the Madrid palace" (the Septemvirate). But by his extremely timely departure from us he untied our hands for the necessary criticism of the Fifth Congress and the politics of the years 1924-25, which combined right premises with ultraleft adventurism.

I will try to send comrades, even one part at a time, the most essential sections of the critique of the draft program and the letter "What Now?" Included in that letter was a detailed characterization of the party regime and its methods of leadership—something that Kh. G. Rakovsky and I. N. Smirnov correctly insisted upon. As practical but essential proposals along the lines of self-criticism and party democracy I introduced two demands, in addition to the demand for the release and reinstatement of the Opposition: first, the convening of the Sixteenth Party Congress in the course of 1928 with firm advance guarantees of full discussion and proper elections; second, the immediate publication of all of Lenin's articles, speeches, and letters which have been hidden from the party (I have counted seven groups of documents of that kind). Unfortunately, I forgot to add yet another demand which will inevitably play a great role in the life of the party in the future: namely, the cutting of the party budget to one-twentieth of its present size, i.e., to five or six million rubles. The party budget is the main instrument of the terrible corruption of the apparatus and the basis of its omnipotence. We need an open budget, fully under party control. Conspiratorial expenditures can be specially set aside and presented for examination by a special commission of the party congress every year.

Of course, these three demands do not replace our Platform on questions of the party regime. But they provide a serious test of the sincerity and honesty of the leadership's steps toward party democracy.

On the question of the draft program I received very valuable comments from Comrades Rakovsky and Rosengauz. Unfortunately, both letters arrived too late, so I was not able to use a number of their observations. But in general the critiques made by these comrades completely coincide with my formulation of the problems relating to the program. There is nothing surprising in this as, for the most part, I only had to sum up our collective work.

The question of the Chinese revolution was not raised in the declaration, or in the letter "What Now?" but in the critique of the draft program, where one chapter out of three is devoted to China. This chapter is directed primarily against the radically wrong, even reactionary, resolution of the February plenum on the China question.

What can we expect from the congress? Comrade Rozanov (Kustanai) quite correctly writes that the congress will undoubtedly attempt to cover us with the heaviest and most authoritative of tombstones ("That he may not arise from the grave . . ."). Of course, the documents I have sent can only aggravate that sort of pious wish. Fortunately, that is hardly feasible: Marxism will rise from the paper grave "at twelve o'clock midnight" as well as at various other hours, and, like an irrepressible drummer, will sound the alarm. On international questions the congress will, in all probability, attempt to extend the left zigzag to other problems and countries. However, the point is that in the present "left course," just as at the Fifth Congress, right premises are combined with elements of ultraleft scholasticism and adventure. Then they did not want to understand the defeat of 1923 and the inevitability of an ebb. Now, they do not want to recognize the full depth of the defeat in China and the inevitability of an extended period of gathering of forces and preparation. Then, there was the Estonian putsch: now, the one in Canton. Then, there was the love affair with Radić and La Follette: now, there is the continuation of the line of "two-class parties."

Of course the February plenum has great symptomatic significance. It is an admission that the right-centrist course has ended in a blind alley. But from this to a Marxist line is still very far. In any case, a left course adorned by Article 58 looks very much like a completely healthy man whose nose has fallen off "for some reason."

They report that Ruth Fischer has been readmitted to the party, and the question of Maslow set aside until his conduct is reviewed by a party court. From this, one of the comrades concludes that a new course is beginning in relation to the left. No, it is not so. The readmission of German and even French Oppositionists to the party in the present situation would only be a military move on the path of further encirclement and further "isolation" of our group, which represents the basic kernel of international Marxism and Bolshevism at the present time. The Master and the apprentice [Stalin and Molotov], in their deep lack of principle, will sacrifice Thälmann for Maslow tomorrow if at that price they can inflict a new organizational blow on us.

We must always keep in mind that the European Opposition, as well as official communism, still does not have the necessary theoretically and politically tempered cadres. Here there can still be peregrinations and desertions and generally all sorts of "surprises." It would be simply ridiculous and unworthy to be frightened of them. Five years of official leadership, armed with the colossal authority of tradition and with inexhaustible resources, has mutilated Marxism and dislocated brains. A whole revisionist generation has been created, in whose consciousness a mass of reactionary theoretical trash is combined with bureaucratic adventurism. Many European Oppositionists also passed through this school, and they are far from being free of it. The whole field must be replowed deeply with the plow of Marxism. This is why the slightest theoretical conciliation from our side would signify political suicide.

A shift in the policy of the AUCP and the Comintern would have the deepest significance and could even become a historic landmark. But why? Because the right-centrist policies have reached an impasse; an openly right-wing policy has been made difficult (not impossible, but difficult) by the entire preceding work of the Opposition; an exit to the left is conceivable only by obvious, even if partial, borrowings from our Platform. The party cannot help seeing this. It is impossible for the process of criticism and reflection not to begin, or more correctly, not to deepen, within the party. In other words, the soil will become more and more receptive to our seed. That is why it is impermissible to have a formally negative approach to the left shift, to say: nothing has happened, only machinations; everything remains as before. No. The greatest events have happened and are happening; the shifts in the party reflect deep shifts in the classes; there is a great deal to indicate that the accumulating quantity is preparing to turn into some new quality.

Of course, this process will still have its ups and downs. But one thing is clear: even a few cadres—if they are armed with a clear understanding of the situation in its entirety, if they are imbued with an understanding of their historical mission, and if, at the same time, they know how or are able to learn how to march in step with the progressive movements in the party masses and the working class—given the inevitable future crises of the situation, such cadres can play a decisive role. In any case, you won't hold them down with a tombstone, so don't kid yourself . . .

In conclusion, some personal things about myself and others. Comrade Drozdov (city of Osh, Kirgizia) writes about rumors that I head a communal farm in Alma-Alta and even traveled to Zelensk "to some sort of conference." Rumors of so rapid a turn in my career are clearly exaggerated. But just as exaggerated are the concerns of a number of comrades about my health. Since our move to the "orchards," the malaria has gone away almost completely. There has been only one bout of fever. The summer conditions here are pleasant enough climatically. It is true we lived through a disturbing epidemic of dog rabies here. Fifty or sixty people bitten by dogs showed up at the clinic each day. But now that too is behind us. I can't complain at all about my ability to work. I have received a sufficiently serious supply of books, especially about India, from Moscow. I receive Russian papers and journals regularly, including the provincial ones. I receive quite a few foreign papers. Books arrive directly from foreign friends. In a word, I can work.

Communications have come from various places about extraordinary excesses by local administrations against many exiles. All comrades undoubtedly know about the Kudymkor events (Comrade Vyaznikovtsev and others), the Kustanai events (Ter-Oganessov and others), etc., etc., without end. Not infrequently, the insults and physical violence have an unusually shameless character. It seems to me we should communicate all such cases to the Sixth Congress, demanding that it set up a special commission to investigate these matters. In general, judging by the correspondence, the mood of the overwhelming majority of comrades is quite cheerful and strong. And this is the most important thing.

Warm greetings and best wishes to all.

Yours,<br>
L. Trotsky

# RADEK'S THESES

## July 17, 1928

*NOTE: While Trotsky was working on his criticism of the Comintern's draft program, Radek was also preparing theses for the congress, which he sent to Trotsky and seven other Opposition leaders at the same time that he sent them to the congress. This conciliatory document, analyzed here in some detail, asserted that the left turn carried out by Stalin was the same as the program of the Opposition. Trotsky at once circulated his criticism of Radek's theses; Radek withdrew the offending theses and he and Smilga, who had signed them, joined other Oppositionists in putting their names to Trotsky's declaration. Almost exactly one year later, on July 10, 1929, Radek, Smilga, and Preobrazhensky signed a document of capitulation.*

*The Shvarts mentioned in point 6 was the chairman of the All-Russia Miners' Union and a member of the Central Committee of the AUCP. By "Pyatakovism" and "Safarovism" (point 10) Trotsky meant capitulatory currents that disarm the masses by telling them that Stalin has realized a genuine left-wing program.*

*Radek's retreat on the question of Thermidor (point 18) is especially striking in that Radek, with Smilga, had been on the extreme "left" within the Opposition: when Trotsky was expelled from the Central Committee (in October 1927), Radek wanted to proclaim the beginning of Thermidor, and had to be restrained with the explanation that this was just a rehearsal and not a conterrevolutionary overturn accomplished by the bourgeoisie. Because he had anticipated a steady degeneration of the centrist leadership, he was not prepared for a left zigzag and was disarmed by it. The peace of Tilsit, which Lenin used by way of analogy with the Brest-Litovsk treaty, was concluded between France and Prussia in 1807. By its terms, Prussia lost territory to France and Poland, and was forced into virtual vassalage to France. In July 1927, Maretsky, a "Red Professor" and a disciple of Bukharin, had published a series of articles in* Pravda de-

*nouncing Trotsky's use of the Thermidor analogy, and arguing that the Soviet Union had a different correlation of classes than eighteenth-century France.*

*Kamenev's mistake of 1917 (point 21) refers to his public opposition, with Zinoviev, to the Bolshevik decision to launch the October insurrection. Like many other Old Bolsheviks, Kamenev disagreed when Lenin dropped his own formula of 1905 (the democratic dictatorship of the proletariat and peasantry) in favor of the struggle to establish a dictatorship of the proletariat in 1917.*

*From the* Militant, *August 1, 1929. Revised against the Russian original in the* Biulleten Oppozitsii, *July 1929.*

Three days ago I received the draft of Comrade Radek's theses, sent to the eight comrades. These theses have probably already been sent to the [Sixth Comintern] Congress so that the immediate practical purpose of my remarks is lost. But since we need clarity for the future as well, I consider it necessary to express an opinion on these theses.

1. First of all, the theses say: "Several months of antikulak agitation—that is a fact of the greatest political significance, which it would be complete political blindness not to recognize." In these words the polemical spear is pointed in the wrong direction. In my opinion, the following should have been said: "Several months of antikulak agitation, if they are not followed by a radical change in the line, will inevitably throw the party back considerably and will undermine the last vestiges of confidence of the ranks in all slogans and in all campaigns."

2. With regard to our capital outlay, Radek says: "Instead of investing basic capital in a series of undertakings in the same branch of production which would only show results several years later, concentration of funds is necessary in order to obtain goods with the least possible delay." This obscure proposition is apparently intended to convey the idea that funds should be transferred from heavy industry to light. This is part of the right wing's program. I see no reason why we should enter on that road. If it is a purely practical proposal, then it should be supported by figures: that is, it should be proven that in allocating funds, the necessary proportion between heavy and light industry is not being preserved. If a reallocation of funds were to be made only on considerations of the moment, it would mean to prepare a still greater crisis in two or three years. Improvisation in such a question cannot be allowed at all and, as has been said,

is only grist to the mill of the right. It is sufficient for us to demand the allocation of funds for both heavy and light industry.

3. With regard to the Stalinist argument that it is impossible to combat the kulak as long as the middle peasant has not been won over, Radek's theses say: "We still haven't won over the middle peasant sufficiently." This is to embellish the reality. With our policies we have lost the middle peasant, who is now being led by the kulak, something that is acknowledged by the February article in *Pravda*.

4. Coming out against the view that the left move is a mere maneuver, the theses say: "Whether or not this struggle will be carried to the end depends on the strength and the determination with which the working masses insist on the extension of this struggle." This, of course, is true, but it is too general. It comes out sounding like this: "The Central Committee did what it could, but now it is the turn of the masses." In reality what should be said is: "The measures undertaken from on high will result in an inevitable fiasco if the Opposition—in spite of the obstacles placed in our way by bureaucratic centrism—does not educate the masses and help them carry this struggle to the end."

5. "The center in the party," say Radek's theses, "by concealing the existence of this group—the right—only weakens the chances of the struggle for a correction of the party line." This is to put it very tenderly. The struggle against the kulak requires a struggle in the party against the right. While carrying on a "campaign" against the kulak, the center in the party covers up for the right wing and stays in a bloc with it. The theses remark reproachfully that this "only weakens the chances of the struggle." No, it dooms the struggle to inevitable defeat, unless the Opposition opens the party's eyes to this whole process.

6. The characterization of Shvarts as a "comrade keenly attuned to the proletarian masses" sounds strange. Did he protest anywhere against the infamous banishments under Article 58? It seemed to me that he "keenly" voted for these banishments.

7. With regard to self-criticism, the theses vow: "It is not a fraud and not a maneuver, because the speeches of a number of party leaders cry out with the greatest concern for the fate of the party and the revolution." Isn't this a reference to the recent speeches by the Master, containing showers of abuse addressed to the Opposition and the explanation that criticism of the administrative agencies is useful, while criticism of the leadership is harmful? I would say this: "If on the kulak question the purely combinatory maneuver represents 10-20 percent and the positive

measures forced by the bread shortage amount to 80-90 percent of the present zigzag, then on the self-criticism question the apparatus-maneuvered tricks amount even at the present moment to not less than 51 percent, and the remaining 49 percent represents the overhead expenses for the maneuver: sacrificial victims, scapegoats, etc., etc." There is hardly any reason for vowing with such assurance that there is neither maneuver nor fraud here.

8. Radek's theses refer to Stalin's speech to the students [May 28, 1928, in Stalin's *Works,* vol. 11, pp. 85-101], without mentioning that with regard to the kulak question the speech is also a complete renunciation of the February article in *Pravda,* and may mean the obliteration of the left zigzag also in this important, though particular, question. Incidentally, this speech is astounding for its illiteracy on economic questions.

9. Further on comes the explanation of why the center, as distinct from the right, was against inner-party democracy. Because, you see, our party is not 100 percent proletarian—(Stalin). Radek's theses accept this explanation at its face value, repeat it, and develop it. It comes out sounding as though the centrists were afraid that the insufficiently proletarian party would not comprehend their truly proletarian policies. This is inadmissible apologetics. The centrists felt that their Chiang Kaishek, Purcell, and kulak policy would not be accepted by the proletarian core of the party. That is why they have been and are strangling democracy.

10. "The only way to ensure inner-party democracy is to awaken the party ranks. If they do not take into their hands the matter of self-criticism" . . . etc. Again too general. In order that the ranks may actually participate in this matter, they must not allow the centrists to lull them to sleep. The centrists have considerable means for that even now. The one thing they don't have is "blissful trust" on our part. Pyatakovism and Safarovism are at present the most effective "opium" for the people. All the more frequent antidotes should be given by us.

11. Radek's theses draw the following conclusions with regard to self-criticism: (a) further extension of self-criticism; (b) curtailment of the party apparatus; (c) proletarianization of the apparatus; (d) prosecution of those who strangle democracy in the factory; (e) ridding the party of bourgeois and bureaucratic elements. All this is too general; every newspaper editorial repeats such things, but without furnishing any guarantees. As an afterthought, it is´ said: "Finally, the readmission of the

Opposition into the party is necessary." That is correct. But instead of these other points, which are too general, something far more concrete should be said: "(a) announce the date of the Sixteenth Party Congress, to be held during 1928, and provide firm guarantees for genuine self-criticism in the preparations for the congress; (b) immediately publish all the articles, speeches, and letters of Lenin that have been hidden from the party—I have named seven groups of such documents in my letter to the congress; (c) immediately reduce the party budget to one-twentieth of its present size, that is, to five or six million rubles, because the present budget is the financial basis for bureaucratic corruption and the autocratic ways of the apparatus. These demands do not, of course, exhaust the question of the regime, but they are perfectly concrete and would mark a step forward.

12. Matters are even worse when we come to the question of the Comintern. Radek's assessment of the February plenum as a great, in a way decisive, turn onto the road of Marxist policy, is fundamentally incorrect. The symptomatic significance of the February plenum is very great: it shows that the right-centrist policy has landed completely in a blind alley, and that the leadership is trying to find a way out not to the right, but to the left. But that is all. There is no unifying idea in the leftism of the February plenum. This leftism reminds one a great deal of the leftism of the Fifth Congress. No real conclusions have been drawn from the mammoth defeat of the Chinese revolution; instead there is the fanfare of boasting about the approach of the so-called new wave, with regard to the peasant movement—and this after the proletariat has been decimated. This whole perspective is false and the whole manner of approaching the question endorses adventurism. The little reservations warning against putsches are for self-justification in the future, nothing more. If there is a new wave, then the revolts in the provinces are not putsches. But what is really going on is the destruction of the remnants of the proletarian vanguard. Theoretically the Menshevik resolution on the Chinese question, though it was written in pseudo-Bolshevik terminology, will certainly, from the strategic point of view, complete the destruction of the Chinese Communist Party. The English and French resolutions cover up the traces of yesterday, combining elements of ultraleftism with right-wing premises. Here, too, there is much resemblance to the Fifth Congress, which tried to remove the question of the German defeat of 1923 from consideration by engaging in an arbitrary burst of ultraleftism.

13. Finally, Radek's theses say that those "who sincerely and honestly want to struggle for goals set by the Comintern and with the methods proclaimed by the last plenum of the ECCI should be readmitted to the Comintern." You can hardly believe your eyes when you read it.

The "methods" of the February plenum of the ECCI consist first of all of the approval of Article 58 and of the assertion that the Bolshevik-Leninists "are banking on the fall of Soviet power." Can it be that the resolution on the Opposition is of less historical significance than the resolution on the second ballot in France, or the dubious hodgepodge on whether or not the British Communist Party should enter the Labour Party? How could anyone forget about *that*? Can I be admitted to the Comintern if I am deeply convinced that in voting for the Chinese resolution the February plenum dealt another mortal blow to the Chinese proletariat, and that in voting for the resolution on the Opposition it gave expression, in the worst, most reactionary, and self-debasing way, to the tendency to employ treacherous, bureaucratic methods for "running" the party.

14. The theses put the question of "temporary agreements with liberals in colonial countries" word for word just as the draft program puts it; but the draft program, under a radical form, endorses Kuomintangism.

15. On the theory of stages, on the theory of two-class parties, on the theory of socialism in a single country, Radek's theses say that these are "tails" that should be removed. It is as if the Marxist man has already emerged full-grown out of the centrist monkey, but with one superfluous organ: "the tail." The good teacher and preceptor hints: Please hide your tail and all will be well. But that is to embellish reality in a flagrant manner.

16. The general appraisal of the draft program in Radek's theses is incorrect, that is, it is excessively good-natured. Contradictory, eclectic, scholastic, full of patches, the draft program is no good at all.

17. The general points of principle made in Radek's theses on the question of partial or transitional demands are quite correct. It is high time, however, that these general considerations were translated into more concrete language, that is, for us to attempt to outline a series of transitional demands which would apply to countries of different types.

18. On the question of Thermidor, Radek's theses quite unexpectedly say: "I shall not discuss here the question of the applicability of analogies between the French and Russian

revolutions." What does that mean? The question of Thermidor we formulated together with the author of the theses and with his participation. Analogies should be made within the strict limits of the purposes for which they are utilized. Lenin compared the Brest-Litovsk peace with the peace of Tilsit. Maretsky could have explained to Lenin that the class conditions of the Tilsit peace were entirely different, as he explained to us the difference between the class nature of the French and our own revolutions. We would then have called Maretsky by the name he deserved.

We took Thermidor as a classic example of a partial counterrevolutionary coup d'état carried out entirely under the revolutionary banner, but actually having a decisively antirevolutionary character. No one has mentioned or suggested a clearer, more striking, and more richly instructive historical analogy for explaining the dangers of backsliding. A tremendous international polemic has developed and continues around the question of Thermidor. What political meaning, then, does the above-mentioned sudden doubt about analogies between the French and Russian revolutions have? Are we sitting in a society of Marxist historians and discussing historical analogies in general? No, we are carrying on a political fight in which we have made use of the analogy with Thermidor hundreds of times, but always within the specific limits which we have clearly defined.

19. "If history proves," Radek's theses say, "that a number of party leaders with whom we crossed swords yesterday are better than the theories which they defended, then no one will be more pleased than we." That sounds awfully chivalrous: Noble leaders first cross swords and then weep tears of reconciliation on each others' bosoms. But here is the rub: How can leaders of the proletariat be better than their theories? We Marxists have been accustomed to appraise leaders by their theory, through their theory, by the ability of leaders to understand and apply theory. Now it would seem that there may be excellent leaders who are accidentally armed with reactionary theories on almost all the basic questions.

20. "The support we give to the shift that has begun," Radek's theses declare, "should consist of fighting ruthlessly . . . against all the evils against which the party is now mobilized." But it should not consist only of that. The pitiless unmasking of the half-measures and confusion of centrism in each practical matter or theoretical question constitutes the most important part of our support for any progressive steps of centrism.

21. I will not dwell on a whole number of less weighty

observations of a particular character. I will confine myself to just one more point—the supplement to the theses, which is devoted to the Chinese revolution. This supplement is written as if we were approaching the question for the first time and as if, in particular, we had not carried on a correspondence with Preobra-zhensky [see "Three Letters to Preobrazhensky," March-April 1928, in *Leon Trotsky on China,* pp. 276-90]. The theses have not a word to say in reply to any of my arguments. But that is only half the problem. Much worse is the fact that Radek's theses are written as if there had never been a Chinese revolution in 1925-27. All of Comrade Radek's arguments might have been success-fully formulated at the beginning of 1924; the bourgeois-democratic revolution is not completed; there are still several democratic stages to come; and only after that will it "grow over" [into a socialist revolution]. But the right and left Kuomintang, the Canton period, the Northern Expedition, the Shanghai coup, the Wuhan period—what are all those if not democratic stages? Or is it that since Martynov made a mess of these matters, we can simply leave them out of consideration? The theses see in the future what has in reality already been left behind. Or perhaps the theses hope to find "real" democracy? May we be told where?

The essence of the matter is that all those conditions which in our country united the agrarian revolution with the proletarian revolution are expressed still more clearly and imperiously in China. The theses demand that we "wait" for the democratic revolution to grow over into a socialist revolution. Two questions are combined here. In a certain sense our democratic revolution grew over into a socialist revolution only toward the middle of 1918. Yet power had been in the hands of the proletariat since November 1917. The argument sounds particularly bizarre com-ing from Comrade Radek, who argued so emphatically [last year] that there is no feudalism in China, no class of landowners, and that therefore the agrarian revolution would not be directed against the landlords but against the bourgeoisie. Survivals of feudalism are very strong in China, but they are indissolubly bound up with bourgeois property. How then can Comrade Radek now pass over this difficulty by saying that the bourgeois-democratic revolution "is not completed," repeating here the mistake of Bukharin, who in turn repeats Kamenev's mistake of 1917? I cannot help quoting once again Lenin's words against Kamenev, to which Beloborodov recently called my attention: "To be guided in one's activities merely by the simple formula, 'the bourgeois-democratic revolution is not completed,' is like taking it upon oneself to guarantee that the petty bourgeoisie is definitely capable of being independent of the bourgeoisie. To do so is to throw oneself at the given moment on the mercy of the petty bourgeoisie" [*Collected Works,* vol. 24, p. 51].

That is all I can say on Comrade Radek's theses. I think it is necessary to say it for the sake of clarity, without fearing the attempts of our "monolithic" opponents to exploit our differences of opinion.

# THE JULY PLENUM
# AND THE RIGHT DANGER

## July 22, 1928

*NOTE: Trotsky described this as a postscript to his letter "What Now?" addressed to the Sixth Comintern Congress, and sent it to the congress by express mail at the last moment.*

*The July plenum of the AUCP (July 4-12) gave the Bukharinists an apparent victory over the Stalin faction. The extraordinary measures against the kulaks were canceled: requisitioning of grain was halted and searches and raids forbidden. Perhaps most important, the price of bread was allowed to increase by 20 percent, directly benefiting the wealthy peasants at the expense of the city workers. Bukharin was chosen to be the only member of the Politburo who would speak at the forthcoming Sixth Congress. The left course was widely perceived to be in disarray.*

*Trotsky's information about the July plenum evidently was based on a report about the plenum made by Rykov to a July 13 meeting of Moscow party workers and printed in* Pravda *on July 15. Stalin's speech the same day to the Leningrad party organization was printed in the same issue, but presented a sharply different impression. Although Stalin emphasized that the origin of the difficulties lay in the predominance of small-scale agriculture, he reassured his listeners that the individual peasant holding still had a future: this may have been to alleviate fears, stimulated by the extraordinary measures, that NEP was drawing to an end and a new "war communism" was on the agenda.*

*However, Bukharin interpreted the outcome of the July plenum in a light less favorable to the right than Trotsky did. Behind the scenes, Stalin had been moving to gain control over the editorial boards of* Pravda *and* Bolshevik *from the Bukharinists; he had achieved a firm majority of the Politburo by adding Kalinin to his supporters (Kuibyshev, Molotov, Rudzutak, and Voroshilov) against Rykov, Bukharin, and Tomsky; and had made veiled criticisms of Bukharin in a speech before the former Bukharinist stronghold, the Institute of Red Professors. On July 11, while the plenum was still in session, Bukharin held a secret meeting with Kamenev to solicit his support and Zinoviev's in an alliance against Stalin (see Appendix to this volume). Trotsky would learn of this meeting only months later.*

*Among other things, Trotsky uses this article to refute Rykov's charges that the administrative excesses that marked the extraordinary measures were in line with the Opposition's "anti-peasant" program. The Opposition had called for a forced loan from the kulaks (in the Platform of the Opposition and again in its "Countertheses" for the Fifteenth Congress, both in* Challenge 1926-27*). Trotsky distinguishes between this demand and the Stalinists' administrative excesses. And he likens Rykov's program of diverting resources away from industry toward individual peasant agriculture to the program of the "Friends of the People" (Narodolyuby), a narrow provincial bourgeois element in late nineteenth-century Russia who played a role in the* zemstvos *(institutions of limited rural self-government established under the peasant reforms of Tsar Alexander II in the 1860s). The Narodolyuby also opposed big industrial-commercial development projects, such as the building of the Trans-Siberian Railroad in the late 1890s (a point made by Trotsky is his polemic against a Rykov supporter, "A Heart-to-Heart Talk with a Well-meaning Party Member," later in this volume).*

*Trotsky reminds the reader that Rykov was one of the "Old Bolsheviks" (i.e., veteran party member) who opposed the Bolshevik plan for the October insurrection, favoring instead a coalition government of Bolsheviks, Mensheviks, and others. When he calls the rights "Yudushka Golovlyovs," he is alluding to a character in Saltykov-Shchedrin's satirical novel* The Golovlyov Family *who typified the sanctimonious hypocrisy of a serf-owning landlord.*

*From the* Militant, *December 15, 1928. Revised against the Russian original by permission of the Harvard College Library.*

The report read by Rykov on July 13 at the meeting of Moscow party workers on the outcome of the July plenum of the Central Committee was an event of capital political importance. Here was expounded the program of the most authoritative representative of the right wing, carrying his banner to the tribune if not entirely unfurled, at least halfway.

In his report Rykov did not pause an instant upon the program of the Communist International; he did not even mention it. He devoted his speech exclusively to the question of the grain collections. Moreover it is not without good reason that his report was delivered in the tone of a victor. The right has issued entirely victorious from its first skirmish with the center, after four or five months of "left" politics.

The July plenum of the Central Committee marks Rykov's first victory over Stalin, gained to be sure with the assistance of Stalin himself. The essential idea of Rykov's report is that the shift to the left that occurred in February was only an episode due to extraordinary circumstances, that this episode ought to be buried and forgotten; that we must also lay on the shelf not only Article 107, but also what appeared in *Pravda* in February; that we must abandon the former course and turn not to the left but to the right—and that the more sharply this is done the better. To clear the road Rykov acknowledged (he could not do otherwise before the accusing facts) three of his small errors: "First, at the moment when the crisis arose I judged it to be less profound than it really was; but second, I thought that through the extraordinary measures we would succeed in completely overcoming this crisis of grain supply. We did not. Third, I hoped that the whole campaign of grain collection would be carried out by relying on the poor peasant and maintaining completely firm ties with the masses of middle peasants. Upon this point I was also mistaken."

And yet the entire grain collections crisis, with all the political phenomena that accompanied it, was foreseen by the Opposition in its countertheses, which accurately pointed out for Rykov all that he did not comprehend and did not foresee. It was just in order to avoid belated, hasty, uncoordinated, and exaggerated administrative measures that the Opposition proposed in good time a forced loan of grain from the rich elements of the villages. To be sure, that measure too would have been an exceptional one. But the entire preceding policy had made exceptional measures inevitable. If the loan had been made methodically and soon enough, that would have reduced to a minimum these administrative excesses which are too high a payment for very slight material results.

Measures of administrative violence have nothing in common with a correct course. They are the price paid for the incorrect one. Rykov's attempt to attribute to the Opposition a desire to eternalize these measures of *his,* derived from the period of war communism, is a malicious absurdity. From the very first the Opposition considered the encirclement of villages [to confiscate stocks of grain], the revival of [civil-war era] roadblock units [to intercept individuals carrying surplus grain to market], etc., not as the beginning of a new course but as the failure of the old. Article 107 on hoarding is not the instrument of a Leninist policy, it is one of the crutches of the Rykov policy. In trying to present as the Opposition's program administrative measures of economic disorganization for which he himself is entirely responsible, Rykov is behaving as all petty-bourgeois politicians do, for they always in such a situation stir up the peasant against the Communist by depicting the latter as a bandit and an expropriator.

What was the significance of the shift in February? It was an acknowledgment of the lagging of industry, of the threatening class differentiation in the country, and of the extreme kulak danger. What should logically have ensued in the way of a new line? A change in the distribution of the national income, diverting to industry part of what had gone to the kulak, thereby diverting it from capitalism toward socialism and accelerating the development of both light and heavy industry.

Contrary to the article which appeared in February in *Pravda* (which merely repeated the arguments of the Opposition on this question), Rykov discovers the cause of the grain collections crisis to be lagging development not of industry but of agriculture. To offer such an explanation is to mock the party and the working class. It is to deceive the party and working class in order to justify a turn to the right. It is the old orientation of the Ustryalovist professors.

It is perfectly obvious that our agriculture is incoherent, scattered, backward; that it has a barbarous character; and that this backwardness is the fundamental cause of all the difficulties. But to demand on this basis, as Rykov does, a diversion of financial resources from industry to individual peasant agriculture is to choose not only the bourgeois road but the road of the agrarian bourgeoisie, of the reactionary bourgeoisie. It is to become a Soviet caricature of the "anticapitalist" "Friends of the People" (Narodolyuby) in the *zemstvos* of the 1880s.

Agriculture cannot be advanced except with the aid of industry. There exist no other levers. Nevertheless our industry is frightfully backward in relation to the *existing* peasant agriculture, incoherent, scattered, and barbarous as it is. The lagging of industry is observable not only in relation to the general historic needs of the peasant economy but also in relation to the peasants' purchasing power. To confound these two questions, one having to do with the general historical backwardness of countryside as against town, the other having to do with the backwardness of the cities in face of the present need for commodities in the villages, is to capitulate and abandon the hegemony of the cities over the countryside.

Our agriculture in its present form is infinitely backward even in comparison to industry, which is backward enough. But to conclude from that, that this centuries-old consequence of the operation of the uneven development of the different parts of an economy can be overcome or even attenuated by reducing the already insufficient funds allocated for industrialization, would be like combatting illiteracy by shutting down the institutions of higher learning. That would be to tear out the very roots of historical progress. Although our industry has a type of production and technology infinitely superior to that of agriculture, not only is it not big enough to play a directive and transforming role—a truly socialist role toward the countryside—but it is not even capable of satisfying the current demand in the villages for manufactured goods, and it thereby retards the development of the villages. This was exactly the source of the grain collections crisis. It was in no way caused by the general historical backwardness of the country, or by an alleged too rapid advance of industry.

On February 15, *Pravda* informed us that three years of harvests "had not passed without leaving their mark," that the village had enriched itself—that is to say, especially the kulaks; that in light of the delay in the development of industry this inevitably resulted in the hoarding crisis. Directly contradicting this explanation, Rykov holds that the mistake committed during the last year by the party leadership was, on the contrary, to have excessively speeded up industrialization; that it is necessary to slacken the pace, diminish industry's share of the national budget, and utilize the funds thus made available as subsidies for the rural economy, especially in its predominant private property form. Through such measures Rykov hopes "in a very short time to double the yield per acre." But he says nothing about how this doubled yield would be sold on the market, that is to say, how it would be exchanged for the products of an industry whose rate of development will have grown still slower.

It is impossible that Rykov does not consider this question in his own mind. A doubled harvest would mean five or ten times more marketable produce from agriculture, and that in turn would mean a much greater disparity, relatively speaking, in the supply of manufactured goods. It is inconceivable that Rykov does not understand this very simple correlation. Why then does he not divulge the secret which is to enable him to triumph in the future over this disproportion, which is destined to grow monstrously? Because the time has not yet come. For politicians of the right, words are silver but silence is golden. Rykov moreover had already spent too much silver in his report. But it is not difficult to estimate the value of his gold. An increase in marketable agricultural products, faced with a backward movement in industry, would mean quite simply an increase in the import of manufactured goods from abroad, destined both for the towns and for the countryside. There is not and cannot be any other alternative. On the other hand, the necessity of entering upon this course will be so imperious, the pressure of the growing disproportion will be so menacing, that Rykov will decide to coin his gold reserve and will demand out loud the abolition—or a reduction that is equivalent to abolition—of the monopoly of foreign trade. This is exactly the plan of the right, which our Platform predicted and which now has been publicly stated, if not as a whole, at least in one of its very considerable parts.

As it appears from Rykov's whole speech, raising the price of grain is the first payment on that plan. This is above all a bonus to the kulaks. It permits them to draw the middle peasants behind them, with still more assurance, explaining: You see, we have made them pay us well for the damage caused by Article 107; it is in struggle that we will win our rights, as our teachers, the Social Revolutionaries, say. One cannot doubt that the functionaries who really know their business are consoling the politicians by assuring them that it will be possible to recoup the excess paid for grain upon other raw materials produced by the peasants, so that the balance of payments between town and country will not shift to the town's disadvantage. But such talk is pure charlatanry. In the first place, the worker consumes bread and not the raw materials utilized by the machine; raising the price of grain will thus strike directly at the budget of the worker. In the second place, we will not succeed in recouping our losses by purchasing other peasant products more cheaply, if the principle has been established of making up for the left zigzag by paying good rubles. In general, maneuvers of retreat are carried out with more loss than gain. This is still more true of a retreat as disorderly as that marked by the decisions of July as against the resolutions adopted in February.

Raising the price of grain, even conceived as an exceptional and extraordinary measure, as a kind of Article 107 in reverse, conceals in itself an enormous danger: it only accentuates the contradictions that gave birth to the hoarding crisis. This rise in prices strikes not only the consumers, that is, the workers and the poor peasants whose harvest is not sufficient for their personal consumption. It is not only a bonus for the kulak and the well-off middle peasant, but a still further increase in the disproportion. If industrial products were already in short supply under the old price of grain, the lack will be still greater after the rise in prices and the increase in the quantity of grain harvested. This will mean a new intensification of the goods famine and the continued growth of social differentiation in the countryside. To combat the hoarding crisis by increasing the price of grain is to enter decisively upon the road of depreciation of the *chervonets*—in other words, it is to quench your thirst with salt water. This would be so even if it were an isolated and exceptional measure. But in Rykov's mind this rise in prices is in no way an extraordinary proceeding. It is one of the essential parts of the Rykov policy of sliding back toward capitalism. Along this road currency inflation is only a technical detail.

On the subject of the danger of inflation, Rykov says with a meaningful air: "*For the time being* the purchasing power of the ruble continues firm." What does "for the time being" mean? It means: Until the sale of the new harvest at higher prices in the face of a shortage of industrial products. But when inflation ensues, Rykov will say to the workers, whose wages will inevitably fall in such a situation: "You remember I said to you 'for the time being.'" And then he will begin to develop the part of his program on which he now remains silent. It is impossible to solve the crisis by taking the road of a neo-NEP without striking at the monopoly of foreign trade.

At the same time that Rykov was celebrating this triumph, Stalin, the vanquished, made a speech in Leningrad. In his really impotent speech (it is really embarrassing to read it), Stalin portrays the inflationary bonus now accorded to the upper elements in the villages, out of the hides of the workers and poor peasants, as a new consolidation of the *smychka* uniting town and countryside. (How many of these consolidations have we had already!) Stalin doesn't even attempt to show how he intends to escape from the contradictions which are closing in on him. He has just got out of the difficulties produced by Article 107, and proceeds to tangle himself up in those of the rise in prices. Stalin simply repeats the same general phrases about the *smychka* which have already been repeated ad nauseam. As if the problem of the *smychka* could be solved by a phrase, a formula, a promise, as if one could believe (anyone, that is, except Stalin's docile functionaries) that if the next harvest is good, it will be able by a miracle to overcome the disproportion which has only been aggravated by the three previous harvests. Stalin is afraid of the Rykovist solution from the right, but he is still more afraid of the Leninist solution. He is waiting. He is turning his back and occupying himself with manipulating the apparatus. Stalin is losing time under the impression that he is gaining it. After the feverish shake-up of February we are now again in the presence of tail-endism in all its pitiable impotence.

Rykov's speech has a totally different tone. Whereas Stalin dodges the issue because he has nothing to say, Rykov leaves certain things unmentioned because he doesn't want to say too much. The policy of raising the price of grain (especially accompanied as it was by Rykov's explanation for the abandonment of the left zigzag in the spring) constitutes, and can only constitute, the beginning of a deep and perhaps decisive turn to the right. Legal barriers along the road to the right, such as the restrictions on renting out land and hiring farm labor, will be abolished with a stroke of the bureaucratic pen, along with the monopoly of foreign trade—unless the rights run up against the iron wall of resistance by the proletarian vanguard. The logic of a rightward course can very quickly become overpowering. Any illusions or false hopes whatsoever as to the "party loyalty" of the rights, any trusting to luck in general, any loss of time, minimizing of contradictions, failure to state things fully, or playing at diplomacy, would only be to lull the workers to sleep, to directly aid the enemy, to promote, whether consciously or unconsciously, Thermidor. With Rykov's speech commenting on the resolutions of the July plenum, the right wing has thrown down the gauntlet to the October Revolution. We must understand that. We must take up the gauntlet. We must immediately and with all our might strike the first blow against the right.

The right, in issuing its defiance, has indicated its strategy in advance. For this it did not need any great ingenuity. Rykov asserts that at the root of Stalin's left-centrist efforts lies "a Trotskyist lack of faith in the possibility of building socialism on the basis of the NEP, and a desperate panic before the peasant." The struggle against "Trotskyism" is the last, unspent ruble of all backsliders. But if these sorts of arguments were fairly stupid on Stalin's lips, they become a pitiful caricature on Rykov's. It is just here that he ought to have remembered that silence is golden.

It is those who distrust the conquest of power by the proletariat in peasant Russia who are really panic-stricken before the peasant. These heroes of panic were seen on the other side of the barricades in October. Rykov was one of them. As for us, we were with Lenin and the proletariat, for we never doubted for one instant that the proletariat was capable of leading the peasantry.

The Rykov policy of 1917 was only a concentrated anticipation of his present economic tactic. At present he proposes to surrender one after another the commanding heights of the dictatorship, which the proletariat already controls, to the elements of primitive capitalist accumulation. It is only because of the falsification of history, which has become such a standard practice in the past few years, that Rykov dares to describe as panic the uncompromising struggle carried out by the Opposition in defense of the socialist dictatorship. He attempts at the same time to pass off as political courage his disposition to capitulate to capitalism with his eyes wide open.

At present Rykov is directing his reactionary demagogy— perfectly adapted to the psychology of the small property-owner on the way to wealth—less against the Opposition than against Stalin and the centrists, who are bending toward the left. Just as in his time Stalin directed against Zinoviev all the attacks which Zinoviev had directed against "Trotskyism," so Rykov is now learning to repeat the same operation against Stalin. Whoever sows the wind reaps the whirlwind. You can't play with political ideas. They are more dangerous than fire. The myths, legends, slogans of an imaginary "Trotskyism" have not become attributes of the Opposition, but certain classes have seized upon them, and thus these conceptions have taken on a life of their own. In order to usurp power more broadly and deeply, Stalin had to agitate a hundred times more brutally than Zinoviev had done. Now it is Rykov's turn. One can imagine what persecutions the right is going to turn loose when relying openly upon the property instinct of the kulak. We must not forget that if the Rykovists formed the tail of the centrists, they have in their turn another, still heavier, tail.

Immediately behind Rykov come those who, as *Pravda* has already recognized, want to live in peace with all classes—that is to say, want once more to force the worker, the hired laborer, and the poor peasant to submit peacefully to the master. Behind them already looms the small employer, greedy, impatient, vindictive, his sleeves rolled up and his knife in his boot top. And behind the small employer, just over the border, waits the real boss, with dreadnoughts, airplanes, and poison gases. "We must not let ourselves become panic-striken. Let us go on building as we have in the past." That is what the Yudushka Golovlyovs of the right are preaching, lulling the workers to sleep, mobilizing the property-owners, preparing for Thermidor. That is the present position of the pieces on the chess board. Those are the real class mechanics of the present situation.

Rykov, as we have already said, deceives the party in stating that the Opposition would like to perpetuate the extraordinary measures to which we are reduced, to our shame, in the eleventh year of the proletarian dictatorship by the policy pursued since the death of Lenin. The Opposition has said clearly what its aims are in its documents sent to the Sixth Congress. But Rykov was perfectly right when he said "The main task of the Trotskyists is to prevent the triumph of the right wing." Precisely correct. The victory of the right wing would be the last step leading to Thermidor. After a victory of the right wing it would no longer be possible to rise again to the dictatorship by the sole method of inner-party reform. The right wing is the handle on which the enemy classes are pulling. The success of this wing will be but a temporarily disguised victory of the bourgeoisie over the proletariat. Rykov is right. Our main task now is to prevent the triumph of the right wing. In order to achieve this, it is necessary not to lull the party to sleep as the Zinovievs, Pyatakovs, and others are doing, but to sound the alarm ten times louder all along the line.

We say to our party and to the Communist International: Rykov is openly beginning to surrender the October Revolution to the enemy classes. Stalin is standing now on one foot, now on the other. He is beating a retreat before Rykov and firing at the left. Bukharin is clouding the mind of the party with the cobwebs of reactionary scholasticism. The party must lift up its voice. The proletarian vanguard must take its destiny in its own hands. The party must discuss broadly the three main lines: right, centrist, and Leninist. The party needs the reinstatement of the Opposition in its ranks. The party needs a congress honestly prepared for and honestly chosen.

# THE CONFLICTS ARE STILL AHEAD

## August 30, 1928

*NOTE: A letter to V.D. Kasparova in Kurgan. This letter casts some light on the evolution of Preobrazhensky and Radek and Trotsky's relations with them. It also provides a balanced assessment of the July plenum, pointing out that the plenum did not liquidate the centrists as it appeared to do but rather set the stage for new conflicts between them and the rights. Many of the leading capitulators, including Zinoviev and Kamenev, were given technical assignments in such agencies as the Centrosoyuz, or Central Union of Consumer Cooperative Societies.*

*By permission of the Harvard College Library. Translated from the Russian for this volume by George Saunders.*

Dear V.D.:

Your letter with excerpts from the letters of Karl [Radek], Ivan Nikitich [Smirnov], and others came yesterday. Many thanks— both for your letter and for the excerpts from the letters of others. Apparently a number of my letters didn't reach you—in particular the letter in which I roundly reviled our friend Teplov for sentimentality, Manilovism, and other obscene qualities. Now, however, I feel relieved, since we've straightened out our front very well, even beyond expectations. Well, what can one say? The centrists helped, as always. Needless to say, I totally agree with you about the necessity for a serious internal discussion on the basic questions. Nothing but good could come of it. And the "young ones" are already making rather wide use of the right of discussion. I received a number of angry letters from them for being excessively compliant toward Preobrazhensky. And in the main they are right. I was overly diplomatic, trying to avoid an internal discussion at a sharp moment on a sharp question— "under the fishbowl" [i.e., with the GPU reading the Opposition-ists' mail]. But I fully agree with you that in relation to Karl, the "young ones" have gone much too far. I must say, however, that

Karl did everything he could to "arouse the public." While pouring out letters with a number of very important formulations, he didn't write a word to Rakovsky or me or a number of other comrades. I began to receive protests from all quarters against Karl's letters and was obliged to answer that I didn't know anything about these letters. That put the young ones on their guard even more. The letter to Vardin, the agent of Yaroslavsky, could not help adding fuel to the fire. Moreover, many of the young ones, even in their exaggerations, learned a lot from Karl, who took the most extreme position on all these questions at the end of last year and commented in a more than disapproving way about some of his present allies. Needless to say, I am doing and have done what I can to pour oil on troubled waters, because the importance of Karl to us needs no explanation. The youth also understand that.

In addition to the critique of the program, the letter "What Now?" the declaration, and the documentary record on "Trotskyism," I have managed to send the congress a "postscript" in which I summarize some of the results of the July plenum. I hope that this addition reaches you also.

From this whole serious and significant episode in the development of the party and the revolution—I am referring to the latest left zigzag—the most compromised element to emerge has been vulgar and unprincipled conciliationism. It is clear to every thinking person that it is not Zinoviev, Kamenev, Pyatakov, and Company who are inside the party now, but you and I. We are participating actively in the party's life. Our documents are read by the delegations to the Comintern congress. The hundreds of signatures endorsing our declaration are a major political fact. But the former chairman of the Comintern and all his miserable group do not exist politically. Zinoviev himself is forced to declare that there is nothing left to do now but keep quiet and wait. These people reentered not the party, but Centrosoyuz. It has never occurred to you and me, however, despite all the dreadful separations, that we were moving away from the party. We are seated in it more solidly than last year and I think that over the next several months this will become clear to everyone.

Another element that has emerged totally compromised out of all this is centrism. Some of the young ones exaggerate in seeing the increase in grain prices as the last word of centrism. No, the conflicts are still ahead. The centrists still have the apparatus. Our statement that we support every step to the left, even a half-hearted one, remains in force. But this has nothing in common with any illusions concerning the centrists, any vulgar conciliationism, or any desire to gloss over the differences. Along this line no quarter!

My general conclusion: we have passed a serious test with top grades and have entered the senior class. After this a summer vacation would normally be expected. But I do not know if we will have one.

As for our health, things are not entirely satisfactory. Natalya and I both have completely succumbed to malaria again, and the intensified use of quinine has undermined the stability of my intestines, so that everything is in commotion.

Endorsements of our declaration continue to come from "back there" in [European] Russia as well. I have received telegrams to that effect from Moscow, Voronezh, Odessa, Kherson, and elsewhere. In drawing up all the documents I was greatly helped by the numerous letters, theses, etc., that I have received. I hope to continue to receive letters—from you too of course, V. D. What news from your son? How is his health? You don't say anything personal about yourself either in your letter.

I am following the congress with great interest. The main report on the international situation, etc., made a devastating impression on me. There was not one complete thought in it. Fragments, scraps, cigarette butts—and nothing more. In bad years [years of famine] they feed cattle with dried up, decomposing chaff. It only tickles the throat but gives no nourishment. That is the impression the report makes . . .

I firmly shake your hand and wish you all the best.

# THE LAW OF ZIGZAGS
# REMAINS IN FORCE

## August 30, 1928

*NOTE: A letter to S. A. Ashkinazi in Samarkand. Like many other rank-and-file members of the Democratic Centralist group, Ashkinazi signed Trotsky's declaration to the Sixth Congress. At the same time, the DC leaders, above all Vladimir M. Smirnov, were mounting fierce polemics against Trotsky for his policy of critical support to Stalin's "left turn."*

*After his capitulation, Pyatakov had been given a post in the State Bank. Zinoviev was assigned to the Central Union of Consumer Credit Societies.*

*Ashkinazi's sister and brother-in-law, Rebecca and Karl Griunshtein, were exiled in Cherdyn.*

*By permission of the Harvard College Library. Translated from the Russian for this volume by George Saunders.*

Dear S. A.:

Apparently only one letter of mine reached you. Needless to say, I was very pleased by your endorsement of our declaration. I hope that the final text of it reached you and also copies of the other documents sent to the congress, in particular a "postscript" dealing with the July plenum. Of course the declaration was the only collective document. The others were sent on my own personal responsibility.

It seems it was a month ago that I received from Moscow a collective telegram from a Democratic Centralist group there, unknown to me, to the effect that my attitude toward the left course removes the differences between us. On the other hand, I hear from various quarters that Vladimir Mikhailovich Smirnov and others are fiercely criticizing our "capitulationism." As long as discussion only was involved, such bad language was no great sin. But the documents are now available; a clear and definite attitude toward them must be taken.

Since the July plenum some comrades have declared: "So you see, nothing has come of it all." These comrades are right insofar as they criticize the vulgar conciliationist tendencies in our midst and the illusions about the centrists' ability to come out onto the Marxist road. Both conciliationism and gullibility have been cruelly punished. But these comrades are wrong to the extent that they think (if they do) that the July plenum has put the finishing touches on the relationship between the center and the right. No, the important disputes are still ahead, and they are bound to come to the surface. The law of zigzags to the right and to the left remains in force, but the pace of these zigzags is more likely to speed up than slow down. We must take a stand without any blinders on and keep a sharp watch for all the twists and turns in the situation. The party should know that, as before, we are ready to support every step, even an irresolute, half-hearted one, in the direction of the proletarian line, while of course maintaining our full ideological independence and critical ruthlessness in relation to all half-heartedness and flabbiness, not to mention bureau-cratic-apparatus-type trickery.

At the congress our documents were read by the delegations, and with great attention, according to the reports. They are being read around the country as well. I have already received, from such cities as Moscow, Voronezh, Odessa, and Kherson, tele-grams informing me of the endorsement of our documents by cothinkers. In the work of drafting these [documents], our active correspondence was of great importance. It allowed me to keep abreast of the moods and views of many dozens of comrades, not to mention that this correspondence placed a number of questions before me which I might otherwise have overlooked.

The question of our reinstatement in the party has today become inseparable from the question of the restoration of the correct line to the party itself. To think that one can make one's way back into the party and then, at a later time, wage a political struggle to restore it to health is—to put it mildly—naive. The experience with Zinoviev, Pyatakov, et al., speaks too eloquently on this point. These people are much less a presence *in* the party now than they were a week before their expulsion. At that time they expressed their views and a section of the party listened to what they had to say. Now they are forced to keep quiet. Not only are they unable to make criticisms; they aren't even allowed to voice praise. Zinoviev's articles are denied publication. The centrists are applying especially crude pressure on the Zinoviev group, demanding that they hold their tongues and not compromise the centrists. How is the presence of these repentant gentle-men in the party expressed? Isn't it this—that the doors of the State Bank and Centrosoyuz are opened to them? But in order to get a job in Centrosoyuz, it really wasn't necessary to first sign the Platform of the Opposition and then repudiate it. The fact of the matter is that our group is in the party now, and the Zinoviev group is outside it. The Safarovs and Vardins are allowed to be "in the party" only to the extent that they undertake to "work us over." And so these totally drained elements rush into the fray. And, it seems, the centrists haven't yet said to them: "Please don't compromise us with your excessive ardor."

I will write about the congress when it is over, or, more accurately, when the reports and necessary materials reach Alma-Ata. The general impression is dreary. Even Bukharin complained in his concluding speech that those who had spoken on the main report touched only, so to speak, on their own specific national concerns and needs, or as Gleb Uspensky once put it, "made a great fuss about their own personal problems," but the general problems of the proletarian revolution were left untouched. The impression given was that these were speeches not by the delegates of an international proletarian party but by national envoys and mediators. The systematic decapitation of all sections of the Comintern has not passed without leaving its mark. Even Bukharin's report was lacking in any unifying idea whatsoever. The whole report was made up of patches, like a beggar's pouch. A very dreary impression. But more about that later.

In the last few days I had a letter from Cherdyn. Summer there is deadly, and R. A. [Griunshtein]'s health is rather poor. She and Karl Ivanovich are strong in spirit, of course, as always. Natalya Ivanovna [Sedova] and I are also passing through a stage of malarial and all other kinds of ill-being. Apparently the approach of autumn is making itself felt. We really don't want to have to return to the totally contaminated city. Therefore we are trying to stay at our dacha as long as possible even though the malaria, it turns out, has access to these parts too.

I will end with that for now. I firmly shake your hand; and the same for your whole colony, to whom I hope you will show this letter.

# WHO IS LEADING
# THE COMINTERN TODAY?

## September 1928

*NOTE: An assessment of the Comintern leadership, written in the wake of the Sixth Congress. Trotsky's preface to the 1929 German edition of this pamphlet, entitled "The Faces Change, the System Remains," is in* Writings 1929, *pp. 379-82.*

*From the* Militant, *August 15-November 30, 1929, in a translation from the Russian that may have been by Max Eastman. This version is based on the* Militant *translation and on a translation made six or seven years later by John G. Wright.*

Nothing so clearly characterizes the transformation of the official party of the Soviet Union as its attitude toward the problems of the international revolution. For the majority of the apparatchiks the Communist International has become a government department that is exclusively the concern of those to whom it has been entrusted as an official duty. In the last few years, the leadership has systematically made the party unaccustomed to taking a real interest in the inner life of the international labor movement, particularly of the world Communist parties. It must be said frankly: The present treatment of the internal processes occurring in the world working class by the Soviet newspapers is distinctly inferior to the information that used to be supplied by the best publications of the Social Democracy *before the war.* It is not possible to put any faith in the present rigidly official information, which is always adapted to the momentary interests of the leading circles. There is not even a pretense of following the day-to-day development of the labor movement and its internal struggles. Certain processes are suppressed, while others, on the contrary, are deliberately exaggerated; but even this is done episodically.

After a long interval, during which one party or another seems to disappear almost entirely from the range of vision of our press, there suddenly appears a "new danger," a "new deviation"—a catastrophe! The reader, however, learns of this catastrophe only after the appropriate bodies concerned have "taken their measures." The reader (that is, the party) is simply informed that the catastrophe, whose approach he had been entirely unaware of, has been happily liquidated thanks to the decision adopted yesterday by the presidium of the International and that the conditions for the prosperous and "monolithic" development of the national section involved are again assured. The monotonous repetition of this procedure stupefies the reader and plunges him into indifference. The average party member begins to regard the successive catastrophes in the International, like those in his own party, as the peasant looks upon hailstorms or drought: nothing can be done about it, we must have patience.

It is obvious that this phenomenon is conceivable only because of the heavy defeats of the international revolution. Moreover, the import of these defeats is never explained to the masses of the party, so as not to disclose the bankruptcy of the leadership. The destructive power of such methods is colossal. Only the great ideological, moral, and political capital inherited from the past, and the fact of the existence of the workers' state created by the October Revolution, still makes it possible for the International to include in the ranks of its organization throughout the world (excluding the USSR) 400,000 to 500,000 members at the very most.

Theoretical dishonesty has become one of the most important weapons in the internal struggle. This fact alone is a sure indication of the deep-seated disease that is consuming the organism of the International. Ideological dishonesty in a revolutionary leadership is the same as sloppiness in a surgeon. Both inevitably lead to the infection of the organism. However, the theoretical dishonesty of a leadership is neither an accident nor a personal trait: it flows from the contradiction between the principles of Leninism and the actual policy of the Stalinist faction. The less its authority and cohesion, the greater its coercion. Discipline, as necessary as salt is to food, has in these last years been found to displace food itself. But no one has yet been able to live on salt. The selection of personnel takes place in conformity with the current line and the internal regime of the party. Communist fighters are more and more being replaced by bureaucratic department heads of communism. This is most clearly and crassly seen at the very focal point of Communist leadership: the central apparatus of the International.

Accordingly, it is of paramount importance to be aware of what kind of element, what political type, is represented by those who at the present moment hold the reins in the Communist International. I do not possess the general statistics and the political records of the bureaucracy of the International. But they are not essential. It is enough to indicate some of the most "conspicuous" figures that personify the present leading line and the present regime.

Since I do not propose to present a systematic study in these cursory notes, and since the gallery of the Stalinist International must begin somewhere, we will first of all name *Bela Kun,* without intending thereby to exaggerate his importance in either the good or the bad sense. In all justice, it must be recognized that Bela Kun, at any rate, is not the worst element in the leading circles of the International. He is flanked by two other Hungarian Communists: Varga and Pepper. All three play an international role, appearing almost continuously as teachers and guides of the national sections. Two of them, Kun and Pepper, are also highly qualified specialists in the struggle against "Trotskyism." The short-lived Hungarian Soviet republic still casts a certain luster of authority upon them. Still, it must not be forgotten that these politicians did not have to conquer power; it was simply thrown at their feet by a bourgeoisie that had landed in a blind alley. Having assumed power without struggle, the Hungarian leaders demonstrated that they were not big enough to keep it. Their policy was a chain of errors. Let us confine ourselves to mentioning two of the links: first of all, they forgot about the peasantry, failed to give it the land; second, to celebrate the happy occasion, they merged the young Communist Party with the Left Social Democracy as soon as the latter began fawning on the [new] state power. Thus they showed—and particularly Bela Kun—that the experience of the Russian revolution had taught them to understand neither the peasant question nor the question of the role of the party in the revolution. Of course, these mistakes, which cost the Hungarian revolution its head, can be explained by the youth of the Hungarian party and by its leaders' extreme lack of political preparation. But is it not astonishing that both Bela Kun and his Social Democratic shadow Pepper consider themselves justified in denouncing us, the Oppositionists, for underestimating the peasantry and failing to understand the role of the party? Where is it written that someone who, out of carelessness, has broken his neighbor's arms and legs, is therefore qualified for the position of Professor of Surgery?

At the Third Comintern Congress, Bela Kun, flanked by his indispensable adjutant, Pepper, took an ultraleft position. They defended the strategy employed in Germany in March 1921, of which Bela Kun was one of the principal inspirers. Their position was essentially this: unless the revolution is immediately summoned forth in the West, the Soviet republic is doomed. Bela Kun endeavored many a time to convince me to "take a chance" along this path. I flatly rejected his adventurism and, together with Lenin, explained to him at the Third Congress that the task of the European Communists was not to "save" the USSR by engaging in revolutionary street theater but to seriously train the European parties for the task of winning power. Today Bela Kun, with all the Peppers, feels called upon to accuse me of "lack of faith" in the vital forces of the Soviet republic and of "speculating" solely upon the world revolution. What is called the irony of history here assumes the aspect of pure burlesque. Really, it is no accident that the Third Congress proceeded to the accompaniment of Lenin's reiterated formula: "All this is nothing but the stupidities of Bela Kun." And when I sought, in private conversations with Lenin, to defend Bela Kun against excessively harsh attacks, Lenin answered: "I do not dispute that he is a fighter, but as a politician he is worthless; the comrades must be taught not to trust him."

In *Pepper,* we have the consummate type of the man who knows how to adapt himself, a political parasite. Such individuals have attached themselves and will always attach themselves to every victorious revolution as unfailingly as flies stick to sugar. No sooner had the Hungarian Soviet republic collapsed than Pepper endeavored to enter into relations with Count Karolyi. At the Third Congress he was with the ultraleft. In America he became chief promoter of the La Follette party and dragged the young Communist Party into the swamp up to its waist. It is hardly necessary to say that he became a prophet of socialism in one country and one of the most implacable anti-Trotskyists. Now he has made this his profession, as others run a matrimonial agency or sell lottery tickets.

On *Varga* I must repeat what I have said once before, that he is the consummate Polonius type of theoretician at the beck and call of any leadership of the Communist International. There is no question that his knowledge and analytical abilities make him a very useful and qualified worker. But there is not the slightest trace of revolutionary will or physical strength in his thinking. In this regard Varga is a miniature edition of a Kautsky. He was a

Brandlerist under Brandler, Maslowist under Maslow, Thäl-mannist under the void that is called Thälmann. Conscientiously and scrupulously, he always serves up the economic arguments for the political line of others. The objective value of his works is entirely limited by the political quality of the instructions upon which he himself has not the slightest influence. He defends the theory of socialism in one country, as I have said elsewhere, by invoking the lack of political culture of the Russian worker, who needs "consoling" perspectives.

*Manuilsky,* like Pepper, has a rather distinct notoriety even within the faction to which he now belongs. The last six years have thoroughly debauched this man, whose principal quality is his moral inconstancy. There was a time when he showed a certain promise, not theoretical or political, but literary. A certain flame, always feeble, burned in him. However, some kind of internal worm gnawed at him incessantly. Fleeing from himself, Manuilsky constantly sought someone to lean upon. He always had something of the "errand-boy" in him. Suffice it to say that for a long time he strove to remain attached to . . . Alexinsky. During the war, Manuilsky did not conduct himself badly. Nevertheless, his internationalism was always superficial. The October days were a period of vacillation for Manuilsky. In 1918, he proclaimed unexpectedly (for me, above all) that Trotsky had liberated Bolshevism from its national narrowness. But no one attached any great importance to his writings. Manuilsky lived quietly in the Ukraine as an administrator of little ability—distinguishing himself, however, as a fine narrator of anecdotes. Like all the present leaders, he came forward and began his rise only after the death of Lenin. His intrigues against Rakovsky served him as a springboard. The general esteem enjoyed by Rakovsky in the Ukraine was such that in 1923 no one dared to begin a campaign against him, despite all the urgings from Moscow. Manuilsky did dare. In private conversations, between two anecdotes, he would openly admit whose commission he was discharging and proclaim his contempt for his employer, and even more for himself. His acquaintance with foreign countries predetermined the arena that would be chosen for his future exploits: the Communist International. A compilation of what Zinoviev and Stalin have said about him wouldn't be a bad digest of political cynicism. On the other hand, matters would not be changed very much if one compiled what Manuilsky has said about Zinoviev and Stalin. At the Sixth Congress, Manuilsky appeared as the principal accuser of the Opposition. For anyone who knows the leading personnel and the past of the party, this fact by itself settles the question!

In the apparatus of the International and in the press, *Walecki* plays a very conspicuous role. In *Communist International* and in *Pravda* he frequently denounces Trotskyism from the "theoretical" and "philosophical" viewpoint. He was created by nature itself for this sort of task. In the eyes of the younger generation Walecki is simply a venerable unknown. The older generation has known him for a long time. At the opening of the century, Walecki made his appearance in Siberian exile as a fanatical supporter of the Polish Socialist Party (PPS). At that time Pilsudski was his idol. In politics, Walecki was a nationalist; in theory, he was an idealist and a mystic. He preached the theories of decadence, of faith in God and in Pilsudski. In our colony of exiles, he was isolated. When the PPS split as a consequence of the 1905 revolution, Walecki turned up as a member of the more "socialist" wing (the Lewico [Left]), only to begin defending, there and then, an extremely Menshevik position.

Even at that time he fought against the theory of "permanent revolution": He regarded as fantastic, and even insane, the idea that the proletariat could come to power sooner in backward Russia than in Western Europe. During the war he was at the very best to the right of Martov. One can be sure that five minutes before the October Revolution, Walecki was an irreconcilable enemy of Bolshevism. I have no information about when he became a "Bolshevik." But in any case it was not until after the Russian proletariat had taken power firmly in its hands. At the Third Congress, Walecki tacked about between the line of Lenin and the ultraleftists. Under Zinoviev he was a Zinovievist, only to change opportunely into a Stalinist. His mobility and elasticity are not yet exhausted. It is easy for him, with his light baggage, to change from one train to another. Today, this former nationalist, idealist, mystic, Menshevik teaches the working class how to fight to win power, despite the fact that he himself first heard about this only after power had been won. People of Walecki's caliber will never conquer anything. But they are perfectly capable of losing what has been conquered.

*Warski*'s past is infinitely more serious. For many years he marched behind Rosa Luxemburg, while Walecki always looked upon her with the blind hatred of a Polish chauvinist. But Warski assimilated the weak sides of Rosa Luxemburg much more fully than her strong sides, the best of which was her revolutionary inflexibility. In the end, Warski has remained to this day a "revolutionary" Social Democrat of the old type. This brought him close to Klara Zetkin, as could be seen clearly in the attitude they both took to the German events of 1923. Warski never felt himself quite at ease with Bolshevism. That explains his momentary "conciliationism," based on a misunderstanding, toward the Opposition of 1923. But as soon as the lines became clearly drawn, Warski found his natural place in the official ranks. The struggle of the epigones against "permanent revolution" and the "underestimation" of the peasantry induced the timorous Warski to interpret Pilsudski's victorious uprising as a sort of "democratic dictatorship of the proletariat and peasantry" and therefore to lead the Polish Communists into supporting this fascist coup d'état. This solitary example gives the measure of Warski's Marxist perspicacity and revolutionary firmness. Needless to say, having "confessed his error," he is today one of the pillars of Stalinism. How this old companion of Rosa Luxemburg—who was an internationalist to the marrow of her bones—teaches the Polish workers the construction of socialism in one country, I do not know. But it is highly doubtful that people of this type can teach the Polish workers how to wrest power from the bourgeoisie.

Let us, however, return to the central apparatus of the International, which Warski has left since he became a deputy in the Sejm [parliament].

For a long time *Klara Zetkin* has been a purely decorative figure on the presidium of the Executive Committee of the Communist International. This cruel characterization might not have been necessary if Zetkin did not serve as a pathetic cloak for the methods that not only compromise her but also bring the greatest injury to the cause of the international proletariat. Zetkin's strength was always her temperament. She never had any independence of thought. For a long time Rosa Luxemburg was her political pivot. Afterwards she looked for a new pivot in Paul Levi, and to a certain extent in Brandler.

After the days of March 1921, Zetkin did not simply revolt against the "stupidities of Bela Kun," but she defended essentially the "old, tested policy" of the continuous accumulation of forces. In a conversation that Lenin and I had with her, Lenin kept repeating to her, mildly but insistently: "The youth will commit many stupidities, but they will nevertheless make a good revolution." Zetkin exclaimed excitedly: "They will not even make a bad one." Lenin and I looked at each other and were unable to restrain our laughter.

Zetkin's brief and vague half-sympathies for the Opposition of 1923 were aroused only because I was against making the Brandler group the Comintern's scapegoat for the German catastrophe of 1923. During 1923, Zetkin showed all the traits of a good old Social Democrat: she understood neither the sharp change in the situation nor the necessity for a bold change in policy. In the main, Zetkin takes no part in deciding questions. But her traditional authority is necessary as a veil for the Manuilskys, the Peppers, and the Heinz Neumanns.

Among the men who in this last period have led the work of the International from the inner offices of the presidium of the Executive Committee, not the lowest rank is occupied by the representative of the Czechoslovak Communist Party, *Smeral,* who has today also become one of the inflexible knights of neo-Bolshevism. Smeral and inflexibility—that is like Tartuffe and sincerity, or Shylock and generosity. Smeral has passed through the solid Austrian school, and if he is to be distinguished from the Austro-Marxist type it is only by the fact that he has never risen even to that level. In the old Czech Social Democracy Smeral was in a semi-opposition, the nature of which was so much the more difficult to grasp since the "ideas" of Smeral always gave the impression of a spreading grease spot. One might say that Smeral countered the Czech social nationalism of Nemec and company with the idea of an Austro-Hungarian imperialist state, along the lines proposed by Renner, but without Renner's knowledge and talent. The Czech republic was realized in the meantime—not as the result of the policy of Benes, Kramar, and Nemec, but as a by-product of the operations of Anglo-French imperialism. However that may be, an independent Czechoslovakia made its appearance and the Austro-Hungarian Smeral landed in a political blind alley. Which way to turn? There were not a few workers who, in the beginning, were intoxicated with the Czechoslovak state. There were still more workers whose hearts beat faster at the thought of the Russia of October. But there were none at all who grieved after the Austro-Hungarian Empire. That was when Smeral made his pilgrimage to Moscow. I remember outlining to Lenin my analysis of the psychological mechanism behind Smeral's Bolshevism. Ilyich repeated with a thoughtful smile: "That's likely . . . you know, that's very likely . . . Types like that will come thronging to us now. We must keep our eyes open. We must test them at every step."

Smeral was profoundly convinced that renaming the Czech Socialist Party as the Communist Party exhausted the question.

At any rate, he did everything in his power to justify further the saying of Otto Bauer on the good Social Democratic parties in Europe: the Austrian Social Democracy and the Czech Communist Party. This year's "Red Day" has shown tragically that five years of Zinovievist, Bukharinist, Stalinist, and Smeralist "Bolshevization" have given the [Czech] party, especially in the way of leadership, nothing—absolutely nothing. On the other hand, Smeral has taken root. The deeper the leadership of the International sank ideologically and politically, the higher Smeral rose. Such people constitute an excellent political barometer. Needless to say, for this patented "Bolshevik" we Oppositionists are inveterate opportunists. But the Czech workers should be told clearly that Smeral will never lead them to the conquest of power.

Another variety of the same species that has been developed in the Hotel Luxe during the last five years is *Kolarov*. His past is more serious because for a long time he belonged to the Tesnyaki ("Narrow") Bulgarian Party, which endeavored to remain on Marxist ground. But in spite of its apparent intransigence, this was a Marxism of wait-and-see propaganda, a passive and rather inert Marxism. In international questions the Tesnyaki inclined much more toward Plekhanov than toward Lenin. The ruin of Bulgaria in the imperialist war, then the October Revolution, pushed them toward Bolshevism. Kolarov settled in Moscow. In the first years that followed the revolution, we avidly grabbed every foreign Marxist, or rather everyone we supposed to be a revolutionary Marxist. Bearing this title, Kolarov was drawn into the apparatus of the International as a possible general secretary. But within a few months we unanimously abandoned these hopes. Lenin summed up his impression of Kolarov in terms that I do not want to write down here. In 1923, Kolarov further revealed his limitations in the Bulgarian events. The same result. While Lenin was still in the leadership it was decided to remove Kolarov from any leading role in the International. But after Lenin's illness and death came the "revitalizing" struggle against Trotskyism. Kolarov immediately dipped himself in this baptismal font and came out reborn. He marched first with Zinoviev against Trotsky, then with Bukharin against Zinoviev; today he marches with Stalin against Bukharin. In a word, he is a watertight, fireproof, unsinkable Bolshevik of the Luxe.

*Kuusinen* is one of those who brought to ruin the Finnish revolution of 1918. Under the pressure of events and the masses, Kuusinen, in spite of his better judgment, found himself constrained to take a position for the revolution, but like the good philistine he was, he wanted to make the revolution according to the best vegetarian recipes. During the insurrection, with an eloquence all his own, he called upon the decent people to remain at home so that there would be no casualties. If, as in Hungary, events had thrown power at his feet, he would not have been quick to bend down and pick it up. But no one threw power to him. It had to be conquered. The situation was exceptionally favorable. All that was needed was revolutionary audacity and willingness to seize the initiative. In other words, those qualities were needed of which Kuusinen is the living negation. He showed himself literally incapable of taking the offensive against the Finnish bourgeoisie, who were then able to drown the heroic insurrection in blood. But to make up for it, Kuusinen developed considerable aggressiveness in relation to the left wing of the International, after he examined himself and discovered that, in the words of Shakespeare, he was no worse than those who were no better than he. Here, he risked nothing. He swam with the stream like those who commanded him. The petty logician became a great intriguer. Of the lies used by the epigones to poison the mind of the international working class in these last years, it can be said that the lion's share belongs to Kuusinen. That may seem paradoxical. But it sometimes happens that the lion's share falls to the hare. As was shown by his report on the colonial question at the Sixth Congress, Kuusinen has remained exactly what he was when he helped the Finnish bourgeoisie to slaughter the Finnish proletariat and later helped the Chinese bourgeoisie to smash the Chinese proletariat.

A very active role is now played in the International by such a person as *Petrovsky-Bennet*. It is individuals of this kind who make decisions today, since the official "leaders," regardless of how competent they are, do not bother themselves, so to speak, with the problems of the International. In practice, it is the Petrovskys who direct, taking good care to cover themselves, that is, by getting an authorized endorsement for themselves whenever needed. But we will see that further on.

Petrovsky is a Bundist-Menshevik of the special American type, i.e., the worst kind. For a long time he was one of the pillars of the miserable and pitiful Jewish yellow Socialist journal in New York, which became enraptured with the German victories before it licked Wilson's boots. Back in Russia in 1917, Petrovsky moved in the same Bundist-Menshevik circles. Like Guralsky, like Rafes, he rallied to Bolshevism only after the Bolsheviks had conquered power. He showed himself to be a diligent and adroit official in military work, but nothing more than an official. The late Frunze, an excellent soldier, but one who was not distinguished by any keen political judgment, told me more than once: "Petrovsky reeks of Bundism." Not only in questions of military administration but also in political questions Petrovsky invariably aligned himself with his superiors. More than once I said in jest to my deceased friend Sklyansky that Petrovsky is trying too hard to support me. Sklyansky, who valued Petrovsky's practical qualities and therefore defended him, replied to this complaint jokingly: "Nothing can be done about it; it's his nature." And, as a matter of fact, it is not a question of careerism in the narrow sense of the word, but of a self-sustaining instinct for adaptation, an urge for protective coloration, in short, organic opportunism.

*Rafes,* another variety of the same type, proved himself just as capable of being a minister of Petlyura as of being an adviser to the Chinese revolution. To what extent he contributed to the destruction of Petlyuraism by his support I will not try to judge. But that he did everything he could to bring the Chinese revolution to ruin is proved by every line of his reports and articles.

The native element of the Petrovskys, the Rafeses, and the Guralskys is behind-the-scenes bustle, matchmaking, and combinationism, diplomatic tricks around the Anglo-Russian Committee or the Kuomintang: in brief, floundering around the edges of the revolution. The flexibility, the adaptability of these people goes only so far; there is a fatal, built-in limit: they are organically incapable either of taking revolutionary initiative in action or of defending their views as a minority. And yet it is just those two qualities, which complement each other, that make a real revolutionary. Without the ability to stand obstinately in the minority, it is impossible to assemble a confident, firm, and courageous revolutionary majority. On the other hand, a revolutionary majority, even when once conquered, by no means becomes a permanent and irrevocable patrimony. The proletarian revolution marches over great heights and depths. There are dips in the road, tunnels, and steep declivities. And there will be an ample supply of these heights and depths for decades to come. That is why the continual selection of revolutionaries, tempering them not only in the struggle of the masses against the enemy but also in the ideological struggle within the party, testing them in the great events and at abrupt turning points, is of decisive importance for the party. Goethe has said that once you acquire a thing, you must win it again and again in order to possess it in reality.

During the first party purge, Lenin recommended that 99 percent of the former Mensheviks be thrown out. He had in mind Menshevism not so much as a conciliatory political line but rather as a psychological type—the adaptationism that constantly seeks protective coloration and is therefore ready to change its colors to Bolshevik red—so as not to have to swim against the stream. Lenin recommended that the party be pitilessly purged of those who adapt themselves. But after his death these elements began to play a great role in the party and a decisive role in the International. Guralsky crowned and uncrowned the leaders of the French, the German, and other parties; Petrovsky and Pepper directed the Anglo-Saxon world; Rafes taught the Chinese people revolutionary strategy; Borodin became state councilor to the national revolution. All are variations of one and the same basic type: parasites of the revolution.

Needless to say, Stalin's present "left course" has in no sense disquieted this public. On the contrary, all the Petrovskys joyously enter into this left course today, and the Rafeses fight against the right danger. In this left-centrist campaign, which is three-fourths inflated and purely formal, the adapters feel themselves like fish in the sea, demonstrating cheaply—to themselves and to others—what remarkable revolutionaries they are. At the same time, they remain, more than ever before, true to themselves. If anything can kill the International, it is this course, this regime, this spirit, incarnate in the Petrovskys.

One of the chief inspirers and educators of the International after Lenin has undoubtedly been *Martynov*—a wholly symbolic figure in the history of the revolutionary movement. The most consistent, and consequently the most dull-witted, theoretician of Menshevism, Martynov remained patiently sheltered from the revolution and the civil war in a comfortable refuge, as a traveler shelters himself from bad weather. He ventured forth into the light of day only in the sixth year after October. In 1923, Martynov suddenly surfaced by publishing an article in the Moscow review *Krasnaya Nov.* At a session of the Political Bureau, in the spring of 1923, I said in passing, half in jest, half in earnest, but at any rate as a bearer of ill tidings: "Watch out that Martynov doesn't worm his way into the party." Lenin, his two hands around his mouth like a trumpet, "whispered" to me so that he was heard throughout the room: "Everyone knows very well that he is a blockhead." I had no reason to contest this brief characterization, made in a tone of absolute conviction. I merely observed that it is obviously impossible to build a large party out of intelligent people only and that Martynov might get in accidentally under some other category. But the joke took a serious turn. Martynov not only wormed his way into the party, but he became one of the chief sources of "inspiration" in the Comintern. He has been brought closer and has been elevated—or rather, they have come closer to him and they have stooped to him—solely because of his struggle against "Trotskyism." For this he did not need reeducation. He simply continued to fight "permanent revolution" just as he had done for the previous twenty years. Formerly, he spoke of my underestimation of bourgeois liberalism and bourgeois democracy. He has not changed the cliché: he has only inserted the peasantry.

In the Menshevik journals of the period of the reaction, there were plenty of articles by Martynov designed to prove that "Trotskyism triumphed for the moment in October, November, and December 1905" (literally) when the uncontrolled elements ran riot and extinguished all the torches of Menshevik reason. The highest upsurge of the revolution—October, November, and December 1905—was designated by Martynov as its "Trotskyist" decline. For him the true upturn began only with the Imperial Duma, with the bloc with the Cadets, and so forth, that is, with the beginning of the counterrevolution.

Having weathered in his refuge an infinitely more terrible replay of the "elements running riot"—that is, the October Revolution, the civil war, revolution in Germany and Austro-Hungary, the Soviet upheaval in Hungary, the events in Italy, and so forth, and so on—Martynov came to the conclusion in 1923 that the time had come to relight the torch of reason in the Russian Communist Party. He began where he had left off in the period of Stolypinist reaction. In *Krasnaya Nov,* he wrote:

"In 1905 L. Trotsky reasoned much more logically and consistently than either the Bolsheviks or the Mensheviks. But the flaw in his argument was that Trotsky was 'too consistent.' The picture he painted was a *very precise anticipation of the Bolshevik dictatorship of the first three years of the October Revolution, which, as is well known, ended by landing in a blind alley,* after having detached the proletariat from the peasantry, with the result that the Bolshevik Party was obliged to beat a great retreat" (*Krasnaya Nov,* no. 2, 1923, p. 262; my emphasis).

Here Martynov tells, with total frankness, what it was that reconciled him to October: the great retreat of the NEP, which was, incidentally, rendered necessary by the retardation of the world revolution. Profoundly convinced that the first three years of the October Revolution were nothing but the expression of the "historic error of Trotskyism," Martynov entered the party and, without waiting for a moment, assumed the role of the heavy artillery in the struggle against the Opposition. This fact alone illustrates more eloquently than many theoretical arguments the profound evolution that has taken place in the upper circles of the party leadership in these last years.

Comrade B. Livshits, in his unpublished work "Lenin on the Dictatorship of the Proletariat and the Peasantry" (at the present moment, serious and conscientious works generally remain in the form of manuscripts; on ticklish questions only the shabby products of the apparatus are printed), gives an instructive political characterization of Martynov in a short note: "It seems to me," he says, "that the political biography of this man invites special attention. Very much so. He came to the Narodniks after their degeneration had begun, when epigones set the tone (toward the middle of the '80s). He came to Marxism and the Social Democracy only to preside over the backsliding of a section of the Social Democrats, from the platform of the Emancipation of Labor group and Lenin's Petersburg Union of Struggle to the platform of opportunist Economism. Then this old opponent of *Iskra* came over to *Iskra* (when it was actually becoming the pro-Menshevik "new" *Iskra*), at the moment when the remaining editors were backsliding from their old political positions. While seeming to play only secondary roles in this group (outside the editorial board of *Iskra*), he actually provided in his 'Two Dictatorships,' the platform for the opportunist-conciliatory tactics of the Mensheviks in the 1905 revolution. Subsequently this Menshevik of yesterday, this most venomous anti-Bolshevik, came over to the Bolsheviks, but here again it was just at the moment (1923) when their leaders were turning into epigones and were already backsliding from Bolshevik positions. Remaining here also in secondary roles (outside of the Political Bureau and the presidium of the International), he actually provided 'theoretical' inspiration for the struggle against the Bolshevik faction of the party; his articles and speeches constituted a platform for the opportunist and conciliationist tactics of the Stalinists in the Chinese revolution. . . . Truly, a kind of fatality seems to accompany this individual."

The "fatality" of this figure coexists excellently with its

involuntarily comic side. Slow and heavy of wit, created by nature for the baggage train of the revolution, Martynov is aglow with a noble passion: to make theoretical connections [to put two and two together theoretically]. Since he enters only into declining ideological currents or into declining branches of healthy currents, he manages, in his efforts to combine extremes, to bring every error to the height of absurdity. Having authored "Two Dictatorships" for 1905, he produced, in 1926-27, the formula "a bloc of four classes," thereby giving theoretical expression to the fact that the Chinese bourgeoisie, with the help of the International, had seated itself firmly astride three other classes: the workers, the peasants, and the urban petty bourgeoisie. In March 1927, Martynov raised the slogan of a "transfusion of workers' blood into the Kuomintang"—just at the moment when Chiang Kai-shek got down to the business of shedding the workers' blood. When the "Anglo-Russian" and "Chinese" discussions opened up in the party, Martynov relived his youth by serving up the old Menshevism, without modifications or additions, in its most intact and most stupid form. While others made haste to hunt up and invent a theory to justify the political backsliding, Martynov brought one out of his pocket, thought out long ago, all finished, only slightly forgotten. That gave him a manifest advantage.

Now this "fatal" figure is one of the chief inspirers of the Communist International. Supposedly he is teaching revolutionaries how to orient themselves in various situations, to foresee the further course of revolutionary developments, to select cadres in advance, to recognize a revolutionary situation at the proper time, and to mobilize the masses for the overthrow of the bourgeoisie. A more malicious caricature cannot be imagined.

There is a man who now works in the propaganda department of the International—and functions virtually as its director—a certain *Lentsner*. However insignificant a figure he may be, it is well to say a few words about him, as a by no means accidental part of the whole. For a certain time, Lentsner worked as an editor of my *Works*. I first became acquainted with him in this connection. He was a product of the Institute of "Red Professors." He had no revolutionary past. This by itself could not be held against him: he was young. He entered politics after the revolution was made. The worst of it was that the chaotic havoc wrought in every field made it possible for him to make his way as a "Red Professor" with a minimum of theoretical resources. In other words, the revolution for him signified above all a career. His ignorance particularly astonished me. In the annotations that he wrote, not only the thought but also the etymology and the syntax of the honorable "Professor" had to be revised. Above all, attention had to be paid to his excessive zeal: Lentsner resembled less a cothinker than a sycophant. In this period (1923) many impatient careerists and aspirants who had not yet found a place for themselves in the apparatus were still trying their luck here and there. Indulgence had to be shown for Lentsner's superficial knowledge, however, because the more capable workers were overwhelmed with work: at that time the Oppositionists had not yet been removed from their posts.

Lentsner prepared the material for *The Lessons of October* for me, verified texts, collected quotations under my direction, etc. When the anti-Trotskyist campaign, a long time in preparation, was launched and was formally connected with *The Lessons of October,* Lentsner began darting his eyes in every direction and within twenty-four hours he switched his position. To secure himself more safely, he used the material he had prepared in a diametrically contrary sense, that is to say, against "Trotskyism." He wrote a pamphlet, it goes without saying, on permanent revolution; this pamphlet was already on the press but at the very last moment the type was destroyed by the order of the Political Bureau: it was decided that it would really be too embarrassing to make arrangements with this personage. Nevertheless Zinoviev took him under his wing and wheedled him into the International. By the side of the Kuusinens and the Martynovs, Lentsner became one of the leaders of the daily work of the International. This Red Professor writes leading articles in the official review of the International. The few lines that I have read sufficed to convince me that Lentsner does not know to this day how to write two consecutive words correctly. But apparently there is no one among the editors of *The Communist International* to look after not only the Marxism, but even the grammar of the writers. These Lentsners are characteristic of the apparatus of the International.

*Lozovsky* occupies a leading place in the Red International of Labor Unions and an influential one in the Communist International. If, in the beginning, under the old leadership of the party, his role was purely technical—and even in this capacity was held in serious doubt and regarded as temporary—it is no less true that in this last period Lozovsky has reached the very front ranks.

Lozovsky cannot be denied certain aptitudes, a quickness of wit and a certain flair. But all these faculties have an extremely fleeting and superficial character in his case. He began, I believe, as a Bolshevik but withdrew from the Bolsheviks for many years and became a conciliator. An internationalist during the war, he worked with me in Paris on *Nashe Slovo*[Our Word], where he always represented the extreme right-wing tendency. In the internal questions of the French labor movement, as in the questions of the International and of the Russian revolution, he inclined invariably to the right—toward pacifist centrism. In 1917, he was the only one of the *Nashe Slovo* group that did not join the Bolsheviks. He was a fierce enemy of the October Revolution. He remained an enemy until 1920, I believe, mobilizing a part of the railway workers and trade unionists in general against the party. He did rally to the October Revolution earlier than Martynov; but at any rate, it was not only after the revolution had been made but also after it had been defended against the most menacing dangers. His knowledge of languages and of life in the Western countries carried him, in those years when the assignment of personnel was still very chaotic, to the Red International of Labor Unions. In the Political Bureau, when we found ourselves faced with this fact, we all—Lenin first of all—shook our heads; we consoled ourselves by saying that he would have to be replaced at the first opportunity. But the situation changed. Lenin fell ill and died. The changing of landmarks began, carefully prepared behind the scenes by the apparatus. Lozovsky floated to the surface. He found himself right in his element. Had he not polemicized against me during the war in defense of Longuetism and petty-bourgeois democracy in Russia? Had he not polemicized against the October Revolution, the Red terror, the civil war? After a brief pause, he resumed the struggle against "Trotskyism." That assured his position in the Red International of Labor Unions and immediately created one for him in the Communist International. At the height of the Martynovist course, Lozovsky even stood on the left wing to a certain extent. But that is dangerous neither for Lozovsky nor for the International; for, despite all his apparent rashness, Lozovsky is perfectly aware of the limits beyond which leftism ceases to be encouraged. As frequently happens, an impulsive spirit mingles in Lozovsky with a conservatism in ideas. In a stirring article he can call upon the workers of South Africa or the natives of the Philippine Islands to overthrow their bourgeoisie, and forget his own counsel an hour later. But in every serious instance where he is responsible for decisions that must be made, Lozovsky invariably makes for the right. He is not a man of revolutionary action; he is an organic pacifist. The future will demonstrate this more than once.

The question of the leadership of the young parties of the East, which have colossal tasks before them, forms the darkest page of the International after the death of Lenin.

It is enough to say that there a leading role is given to *Raskolnikov*. Contrary to those whom I have named before, he is incontestably a fighting revolutionary, a Bolshevik with something of a revolutionary past. But only the frightful devastation of the leading ranks could bring things to the point where Raskolnikov turns up as a leader of—Russian literature and the Asiatic revolutions. He is just as ill-suited for the one as for the other. His deeds were always better than his speeches and articles. He expresses himself before thinking. It is certainly not bad to have him on your side in a civil war. But it is bad to have him on your side in an ideological conflict. When he returned from Afghanistan in 1923, Raskolnikov was bursting with eagerness for battle on the side of the Opposition. I had to hold him back very insistently, for fear that he would do more harm than good. For this reason or for another, he became an active fighter a few days later—in the other camp. I do not know if he studied the East very much during his sojourn in Afghanistan. But he did write lengthy memoirs of the first years of the revolution, in which he thought it necessary to devote not a little space to the author of these lines. In 1924, he revised his memoirs—which had already been published—and where he had put a plus sign before he now put a minus sign, and vice versa. This revision has such a primitive and puerile character that it cannot be taken seriously even as a falsification. At bottom, his is an essentially primitive manner of thought. Raskolnikov's activity in the domain of proletarian literature will constitute one of the most amusing anecdotes in the history of the revolution. But that subject does not interest us here. Raskolnikov's work as the director of the Eastern department of the International has a much more tragic character. It is enough to read Raskolnikov's foreword to the report of T'an P'ing-shan to be convinced once more of the facility with which certain persons relapse into political ignorance when conditions are favorable. To T'an P'ing-shan's Menshevik report Raskolnikov wrote a eulogistic Menshevik foreword. It must of course be added that the report of T'an P'ing-shan was approved by the seventh plenum of the Executive Committee of the International [November 1926]. Just think of what pains and resources are wasted to lead people off the right road. Raskolnikov is not so much the responsible inspirer as he is the victim of this whole mechanism. But his unfortunate role as leader becomes, in turn, a source of the greatest mishaps and victims.

The Indian movement is represented in the International by *Roy*. It is doubtful if greater harm could be done to the Indian proletariat than was done by Zinoviev, Stalin, and Bukharin through the medium of Roy. In India, as in China, the work has been and is oriented almost totally toward bourgeois nationalism. In the whole period since Lenin, Roy has conducted propaganda in favor of a "people's party" which, as he himself has said, should be "neither in name nor in essence" the party of the proletarian vanguard. This is an adaptation of Kuomintangism, of Stalinism, and of La Folletteism to the conditions of the national movement in India. Politically this means: through the medium of Roy, the leadership of the International is holding the stirrup for the future Indian Chiang Kai-sheks. As for Roy's conceptions, they are a hodgepodge of Social Revolutionary ideas and liberalism flavored with the sauce of the struggle against imperialism. While the "Communists" organize "workers' and peasants' parties," the Indian nationalists are seizing hold of the trade unions. In India the catastrophe is being prepared just as methodically as it was in China. Roy has taken the Chinese example as a model, and he appears at the Chinese congresses as a teacher. It is not necessary to say that this national democrat, poisoned by an adulterated "Marxism," is an implacable foe of "Trotskyism," just like his spiritual brother T'an P'ing-shan.

Things are no better in Japan. The Japanese Communist Party is invariably represented in the International by *Katayama*. As fast as the leadership of the International was drained, Katayama became one of its Bolshevik pillars. To tell the truth, Katayama is by nature a complete mistake. Unlike Klara Zetkin, he cannot even be called a decorative figure, for he is totally devoid of any adornment. His conceptions form a progressivism very lightly colored by Marxism. By his whole make-up, Katayama is incomparably closer to the ideological world of Sun Yat-sen than to that of Lenin. This does not prevent Katayama from expelling the Bolshevik-Leninists from the International, and in general from deciding the destinies of the proletarian revolution by his vote. In return for his services in the struggle against the Opposition, the International supports Katayama's fictitious authority in Japan. The young Japanese Communists look upon him with deference and follow his teachings. Why? It is not for nothing that there is a Japanese proverb: "Even the head of a sardine can be worshipped; the main thing is to have faith."

In the meantime, endless attempts are being made in Japan to unite the various "workers' and peasants' parties" of the right, center, and left, which constitute, all of them to the same degree, an organized assault upon the political independence of the proletarian vanguard. The diplomatic notes and counter-notes, the unity conferences and counter-conferences, increase and multiply, absorbing and corrupting the very few Communists, diverting them from the real work of rallying and educating the worker-revolutionaries. The press of the International gives hardly any news of the real revolutionary work of the Japanese Communists, of the illegal work, the building of the organization, the party's proclamations, etc. On the other hand, we learn almost every week of new steps by a new committee for the reorganization of the left workers' and peasants' party in the direction of a union with the left wing of the centrist workers' and peasants' party, which, in turn, approaches the left wing of the right party, and so on without end. What has Bolshevism to do with this? What can Marx and Lenin have in common with this obscene trafficking?

But we will have to return more basically to the burning questions of the East from another point of view.

\*     \*     \*

As can be seen, the general spirit of the changes that have taken place in the leadership of the International appears in full light in the procession of its responsible figures. The International is led by the Martynovs, by the conformers of every description. The French have the political expression *rallié,* which means "one who has become reconciled." The need for such a term was born of the frequency of political revolution. If the republicans had to become reconciled to the empire, the royalists and the Bonapartists, in their turn, had to get used to the republic. They did not do this right away, but only after convincing themselves of the stability of the republican regime. They are not the republicans who fought for the republic, but those who graciously accepted positions and stipends from it. They are the ones who are called *ralliés.* But one must not think that this type is peculiar only to the bourgeois revolution. The basis of *ralliément* is not the revolution but its victory, and the state created by this victory.

It goes without saying that true fighters, especially in other countries, not only among the younger generation but in a certain measure also among the older generation, have rallied and are rallying to the October Revolution. But the present regime in the International does not permit them to rise to the level of independent leaders, not to speak of revolutionary chiefs. It removes, sweeps away, deforms, and tramples under foot all that is independent, ideologically firm, and inflexible. It needs conformists. And it finds them without much difficulty, groups them together, and arms them.

The *ralliés* include people of many shadings, from politically dull but honest elements, devoid of perspicacity and initiative, to out-and-out careerists. But even the best of these *ralliés* (as psychology suggests and experience proves) demonstrate toward new revolutions the same qualities that they showed before and even on the eve of October: lack of foresight, of creative initiative, and of real revolutionary courage. The Kolarovs, the Peppers, the Kuusinens, the Waleckis, the Martynovs, the Petrovskys, the Lozovskys, and the other heroes who overslept, missed, or destroyed one, two, three, and even more revolutions, are undoubtedly saying to themselves: "Let a new revolution come our way and this time we will prove ourselves." It is like the unlucky hunter who swears after every miss that he will take better aim at the next bird. Remembering their faults and uneasy at the idea that they have not been forgotten, these postrevolutionary revolutionists are always ready, on a sign from above, to prove their fearlessness to the four corners of the earth. That is why missed revolutionary situations alternate with no less tragic revolutionary adventures.

The best that can be done with all the varieties of Martynovs, Kuusinens, and Peppers is to keep them a good long distance away from the institutions where the destinies of the revolution are decided.

*         *         *

One can object that all the figures I have enumerated above are only of the second order and that the "real" leadership is concentrated in the Political Bureau of the Russian Communist Party. But that is an illusion. Under Lenin, the *immediate* leadership of the affairs of the International was entrusted to Zinoviev, Radek, and Bukharin. In the solution of all questions of any great substance Lenin and the author of these lines took part. Needless to say, in all the fundamental questions of the International, the key was in the hands of Lenin. *Not one of the present members of the Political Bureau,* with the exception of Bukharin, *took the slightest part in the leadership of the International,* and naturally that was not by mere chance. The nature of this work presupposes not only a certain theoretical and political level, but also the direct knowledge of the internal life of the Western countries and the knowledge of languages, permitting one to follow the foreign press continually. In the present Political Bureau, no one possesses even these formal qualifications, with the exception of Bukharin, who, while Lenin lived, was only a candidate member of the Political Bureau.

Lenin's Testament, at first glance, gives *Bukharin* a somewhat contradictory characterization. On the one hand, he is spoken of as "a most valuable and major theorist of the party"; on the other hand it is pointed out that "his theoretical views can be classified as fully Marxist only with great reserve, for there is something scholastic about him (he has never fully understood dialectics)" [*Collected Works,* vol. 36, p. 595]. How can a nondialectician and a scholastic be a theoretician of a Marxist party? I will not dwell upon the fact that the Testament, written for the party with a definite aim, is permeated with the desire to "balance off"—to a certain extent—the comments on the leading figures of the party: Lenin carefully withholds any too marked praise just as he softens too harsh a judgment. Still, this has reference only to the form of the Testament and not to its essence, and it does not explain how the Marxist works of a writer who has not mastered dialectics can be "valuable." Nevertheless, the characterization given by Lenin, despite its seeming contradiction meant to sweeten the pill a little, is not contradictory in essence and is entirely correct.

Dialectics does not do away with formal logic, just as synthesis does not do away with analysis, but is, on the contrary, supported by it. Bukharin's mode of thought is formally logical and abstractly analytical through and through. His best pages are in the domain of formally logical analysis. Wherever Bukharin's thought moves along the furrows already dug by the dialectical blade of Marx and Lenin, it can give valuable *partial* results, even if they are almost always accompanied by an aftertaste of scholasticism. But where Bukharin penetrates independently into a new sphere, where he is obliged to combine elements borrowed from different fields—economics and politics, sociology and ideology, or in general, the base and the superstructure—he manifests a completely irresponsible and untenable arbitrariness, pulling generalizations out of the clouds and juggling the ideas as if they were balls. If you took the pains to assemble and classify chronologically all the "theories" that Bukharin has served up to the International since 1919, and especially since 1923, you would end up with a scene from some Walpurgis Night, with the wan shades of Marxism being whipped about wildly by the icy winds of scholasticism.

The Sixth Congress of the International brought the contradictions of the apparatus regime to its ultimate expression, and therefore to the point of absurdity. Outwardly, the leadership seemed to belong to Bukharin: he made the report; indicated the strategical line; presented the program and saw it adopted—no trifle, that—and, lastly, opened and closed the congress with general summaries. His domination seemed complete. And in the meantime everyone knows that the real influence of Bukharin upon the congress was next to nothing. The interminable babblings of Bukharin were like bubbles thrown up by a drowning man. In the meantime, without regard to the spirit of the reports—nay, even counter to this spirit—a regrouping went on among the delegates and their factional organization was consolidated. This monstrous duplicity disclosed what a secondary, subordinate, and even decorative role is played after all by "ideology" under the bureaucratic regime of the apparatus.

But now that there is no longer any reason to speak of the leadership of Bukharin, inasmuch as the main point of the Sixth Congress was to liquidate him, there remains *Stalin*. But here we fall from one paradox into another: for the man who is called today, with some justice, the leader of the International, did not even show up at the congress, and in his most recent speeches disposed of the questions of the program and the strategy of the International with a few meaningless phrases. And that again is no accident.

There is no need at all to dwell upon the grossly empirical character of Stalin's policy. With more or less belatedness, it is only the passive reflection of subterranean class impulses. The strength of apparatus centrism for a certain period and under certain conditions lies in an empirical adaptation. But that is precisely its Achilles' heel.

Those who do not know him find it difficult to imagine the primitive level of Stalin's scientific knowledge and theoretical resources. When Lenin was alive, it never occurred to any of us to draw Stalin into discussions of theoretical problems or strategic questions of the International. The most he ever had to do was to vote sometimes on this or that question whenever the differences of opinion among the Russian leaders of the International necessitated a formal vote in the Political Bureau. In any case, up to 1924 it is impossible to find a single article, a single speech of Stalin dedicated to international problems. But this "special feature"—the fact that he was not bound personally by any ideological obligation or tradition to the fundamental theoretical and international questions—rendered him only all the more fit to lead the policy of retreat when the classes crushed by the October Revolution began to rise again in our country and to exert pressure upon the party. Stalin became necessary when the October film began to run backwards. "Every social epoch," said Marx, invoking the words of Helvetius, "demands its great men; when they do not exist, it invents them" (*Class Struggles in France*). Well, Stalin is the great man "invented" by the period of the reaction against October.

It is known that Marxism does not at all "deny" the personal factor in history; on the contrary, better than any other doctrine, it is capable of elucidating the historical function of an outstanding personality. But the fetishism of the personal factor is entirely alien to Marxism. The role of a personality is always explained by the objective conditions contained in class relationships. There have been historical periods in which, according to the expression of an intelligent enemy, Ustryalov, "to save the country," an outstanding mediocrity and nothing more proved necessary. In his *Eighteenth Brumaire,* Marx showed, according to his own words, "how the class struggle created the circumstances and the conditions that permitted a mediocre and vulgar personage to play the role of a hero." Marx had in mind Napoleon III. The social subsoil of this Bonaparte's power was the dispersed mass of small peasant proprietors, in a situation where the bourgeoisie and the proletariat neutralized one another's influence. Essential elements of such a situation exist among us also. It is entirely a question of the mutual relationship of forces and the trends of development. We are still fighting to influence those trends. But in the meanwhile it is incontestable that the further the Stalinist regime goes, the more it appears as a dress rehearsal for Bonapartism.

Small-mindedness and contempt for questions of principle have always accompanied Stalin. In 1925, the Tiflis party paper, *Zarya Vostoka* [Dawn of the East], did him a bad turn by publishing his letter of January 24, 1911. In this letter Stalin calls Lenin's bloc with Plekhanov for the struggle against the liquidators and the conciliators a "foreign tempest in a teapot"—neither more nor less—and then continues:

"In general, the workers are beginning to look upon the groups in emigration with disdain; let them get into a rage to their hearts' content; we, however, think that whoever really has the interests of the movement at heart, works—the rest will take care of itself. My opinion is that the result will be best." [This letter is not in Stalin's *Works*. It was intercepted by the tsarist police and published along with other police files on Stalin in *Zarya Vostoka* on December 23, 1925. Stalin had first used the term "tempest in a teapot" to describe Lenin's philosophical polemics with Bogdanov in a June 1908 letter.]

Thus, in 1911, Stalin disdainfully left it to Lenin to "get into a rage" in his struggle against liquidationism. As for the group that Lenin formed ideologically, Stalin called it contemptuously "a foreign tempest in a teapot." What disgusting hypocrisy is Stalin's retrospective intransigence today concerning the old ideological disputes.

But it is not only a matter of 1911. In the spring of 1917, the semidefender of the Fatherland, Stalin, was in agreement in principle that the party should unite with the defender of the Fatherland, Tseretelli. In the minutes, concealed up to now, of the party conference in April 1917, we read:

"Order of Business: Tseretelli's proposal for unification.

"Stalin: We ought to go. It is necessary to define our proposals as to the terms of unification. Unification is possible along the lines of Zimmerwald-Kienthal."

To the fears expressed by certain delegates to the conference, Stalin replied:

"There is no use running ahead and anticipating disagreements. There is no party life without disagreements. We will live down trivial disagreements within the party."

The differences with Tseretelli appeared to Stalin as "trivial disagreements," just as six years earlier Lenin's theoretical struggle against liquidationism seemed to him "a tempest in a teapot." In this cynical contempt for political principles and in this conciliatory empiricism lies the whole basis of the future alliances with Chiang Kai-shek, of the collaboration with Purcell, of the theory of socialism in one country, of the two-class workers' and peasants' parties, of the unity with the Martynovs, the Peppers, and the Petrovskys for the struggle against the Bolshevik-Leninists.

Let us quote another letter of Stalin, written on August 7, 1923, on the situation in Germany: "Should the Communists at the present stage try to seize power without the Social Democrats? Are they sufficiently ripe for that? That, in my opinion, is the question. When we seized power, we had in Russia such resources in reserve as (a) the promise of peace; (b) the slogan: land to the peasants; (c) the support of the great majority of the working class; and (d) the sympathy of the peasantry. At the moment the German Communists have nothing of the kind. They have of course a Soviet country as a neighbor, which we did not have; but what can we offer them? . . . If the government in Germany were to topple over now, in a manner of speaking, and the Communists were to seize hold of it, they would end up in a crash. That, in the 'best' case. While at worst, they would be smashed to smithereens and thrown way back. The whole point is not that Brandler wants to 'educate the masses' but that the bourgeoisie plus the right-wing Social Democrats [are] bound to turn such lessons— the demonstration—into a general battle (at present all the odds are on their side) and exterminate them [the German Communists]. Of course, the Fascists are not asleep; but it is to our advantage to let them attack first: that will rally the entire working class around the Communists (Germany is not Bulgaria). Besides, all our information indicates that in Germany fascism is weak. In my opinion the Germans should be restrained and not spurred on." [This letter is not in Stalin's *Works*; the translation is from Trotsky's *Stalin*, vol. 2, p. 182.]

To this amazing document, which we must refrain from analyzing here, it must simply be added that in the spring of 1917, before the arrival of Lenin in Russia, Stalin did not pose the question of the conquest of power in any more revolutionary a manner than he did in 1923 with regard to Germany. Is it not evident that Stalin is therefore the most qualified person to brandish the thunderbolts over Brandler and the right wing in general?

As to Stalin's theoretical level, finally, it is enough to recall that, in seeking to explain why Marx and Engels rejected the reactionary idea of socialism in one country, he declared that in the epoch of Marx and Engels "*there could be no question of the law of uneven development in the capitalist countries.*" There could be no question of it! That is what was written on September 15, 1925!

What would be said of a mathematician who came to maintain that Lagrange, Hauss, or Lobachevsky could not yet know of logarithms? With Stalin this is no isolated case. If the chopped-up eclecticism of his speeches and his articles is examined, one will perceive that they consist almost entirely of such pearls and diamonds of almost virginal ignorance.

In his attacks, first against "Trotskyism," then against Zinoviev and Kamenev, Stalin always struck at the same target: the old revolutionary emigrés. The emigrés are people without roots who think only of the world revolution. . . . But today new leaders are necessary, who are capable of realizing socialism in one country. The struggle against the emigrés, which is in a sense the continuation of Stalin's 1911 letter against Lenin, is an integral part of the Stalinist ideology of national socialism. Only a complete ignorance of history allows Stalin to have open recourse to this manifestly reactionary argument. After every revolution, the reaction began with the struggle against the emigrés and foreigners. Were the October Revolution to recede to another stage on the Ustryalovist road, the next, the third set of leaders would certainly set themselves to hunting down the professional revolutionaries in general: for while these cut themselves off from life, going underground, those others, the new "leaders," were always rooted in the soil!

In truth, never did the provincial-national narrow-mindedness of Stalin appear so brutally as in this scheme to make the old revolutionary emigrés into bogeymen. For Stalin, emigration signifies the abandonment of the struggle and of political life. It is organically inconceivable to him that a Russian Marxist, having lived in France or the United States, should have engaged in the struggle of the French or the American working class, not to speak of the fact that most of the time, the Russian emigrés performed important functions in the service of the Russian revolution.

It is curious that Stalin does not observe that his "well-rooted" blows against the old "uprooted" emigrés strike first of all at the Executive Committee of the International, which is composed of foreign emigrés in the Soviet Union where they are invested with the leadership of the international labor movement. But it is upon himself, as "leader" of the International, that Stalin is striking the most painful blows: for it is impossible to imagine a more consummate "emigré"—that is to say, a more isolated one—than he is toward all the foreign countries. Without any knowledge of the history and the internal life of the foreign countries, without personal knowledge of their labor movements, without even the possibility of following the foreign press, Stalin is today called upon to hammer out and to settle the questions of the world revolution. In other words, Stalin is the most perfect incarnation of the caricatured type of emigré pictured in his imagination. That also explains why the incursions of Stalin into the field of international questions, beginning with the autumn of 1924 (the day and the date can be established without difficulty), have always this episodic, broken, accidental character, without being any the less injurious for that.

It is not by chance that Stalin's thoroughly cynical empiricism and Bukharin's passion for playing with generalizations have marched side by side for a relatively long period. Stalin acted under the influence of direct social impulses; Bukharin, with his little finger, set heaven and hell into motion in order to justify the new zigzag. Stalin regarded Bukharin's generalizations as an unavoidable evil. In his heart, he believed as before that there was no reason to get excited over theoretical "tempests in a teapot." But ideas in a certain sense live their own life. Interests become fastened to ideas. Basing themselves upon interests, ideas weld people together. Thus, while serving Stalin, Bukharin nourished the right group theoretically, while Stalin remained the practical organizer of the centrist zigzags. Therein lies the reason for their parting of the ways. At the Sixth Congress, this split became all the more scandalously obvious, the more they tried to disguise it.

Stalin's real, but not purely formal, interest in the International is determined by the anxiety to get the necessary support from the leading cadres for the next zigzag in domestic policy. In other words, what is demanded from the International is apparatus obedience.

At the Sixth Congress, Bukharin read from a letter of Lenin to Zinoviev and himself in which he warns them that if the sensible but not necessarily obedient people in the International are driven out and replaced by obedient idiots, they will certainly destroy it. Bukharin risked bringing forward these lines only because they were necessary to defend himself against Stalin. In actuality, Lenin's warning, which rings so tragically today, embraces the regimes of Zinoviev and of Bukharin, as well as of Stalin. This part of Lenin's legacy has also been trampled under foot. *At the present moment, not only in the Russian Communist Party but in all the foreign Communist parties without exception, all the elements that built up the International and led it in the period of the first four congresses have been removed from leadership and cut off from the party.* This general change of the leading cadres is of course not accidental. The line of Stalin requires Stalinists and not Leninists.

That is why the Peppers, the Kuusinens, the Martynovs, the Petrovskys, the Rafeses, the Manuilskys, and their sort are so useful and irreplaceable. Adaptation is their native element. In seeking to obtain the obedience of the International, they realize their highest destiny. For many of these parasites, the maximum of bureaucracy has become the preliminary condition for their maximum personal "freedom." They are ready to make any kind of right-about-face, on the condition that they have the apparatus behind them. At the same time they feel themselves to be the direct heirs of the October Revolution and its harbingers throughout the world. What more do they need? Verily, they are building an International in their own image.

This "work," however, contains a fatal deficiency: it does not take into account the resistance of the material, that is to say, the living masses of the workers. In the capitalist countries, the resistance appears much sooner, for there the Communists have no apparatus of coercion. Despite all their sympathy for the October Revolution, the working masses are by no means disposed to put confidence in every cudgel appointed as a leader or to worship the "head of a sardine." The masses cannot and do not want to understand such apparatus machinations. They learn from great events. But now they see nothing but mistakes, confusion, and defeats. The worker-Communists feel the atmosphere growing cold around them. Their uneasiness is transformed into ideological ferment, which becomes the basis for factional groupings.

It is clear: the International has entered a period in which it must pay heavily for the sins of the last six years, in the course of which ideas were treated like worthless bank notes, revolutionaries like functionaries, and the masses like an obedient chorus. The gravest crises are still to come. The ideological needs of the proletarian vanguard are breaking through, bursting the barrel-hoops of the apparatus. The false monolithism is crumbling to dust in the International more rapidly than in the Russian Communist Party, where the holding devices of the party apparatus have already been entirely replaced by economic and governmental repression.

It is not necessary to point out the danger represented by factional splitting. But up to now no one has succeeded in overcoming factionalism by lamentations. The conciliationism about which they complain so much in all the resolutions is still less capable of weakening factionalism. It is itself a product of the factional struggle and, at the same time, the partly processed material for new struggles. Conciliationism is unavoidably called upon to differentiate itself and to be reabsorbed. Every palliation or concealment of differences of opinion would only increase the chaos and give the factional formations a more durable and painful character. The growing turmoil of factionalism can be overcome only by means of a clear line of principle. From this standpoint, the present period of avowed ideological struggle is a profoundly progressive reality. One should remember, however, to compare it not with the abstract ideal of "unity" but with the bitter reality of these last years.

Three basic lines have come to light on an international scale. The line of the right, which is a hopeless attempt to resuscitate, under new conditions, the prewar Social Democracy, in the best case of the type of Bebel (Brandler and others). The line of the left, which is the continuation and the further development of Bolshevism and the October Revolution. That is our line. Finally, the line of the center (Stalin and his partisans), which wavers between the two principal lines, shrinking back from one at one moment and from the other at the next, devoid of any principled content of its own and always, in the last analysis, serving as a screen for the right wing.

Personal regroupings will take place, even in the higher circles. As for the bulk of the Communist masses, inside and outside of the party, the process in which they will define their position still lies entirely ahead. The problem is, therefore, to win the masses. This struggle must be endowed with the greatest intransigence. The masses will never be won by hints or by half-words. The dialectic of development is such that the International can be saved from the peril of factional collapse only by a bold, firm, and intransigent grouping together of the international faction of the Bolshevik-Leninists.

# REMARKS AFTER
# THE SIXTH CONGRESS

## September 9, 1928

*NOTE: Apparently a circular letter, Trotsky's initial assessment of the Sixth Congress on the basis of incomplete information. The Comintern luminaries mentioned in this letter are described fully in "Who Is Leading the Comintern Today?" in this volume.*

*The Anti-Imperialist League (point 12) functioned under Comintern auspices from 1927 to 1929. Albert Purcell was a leader of the General Council of the British Trades Union Congress during the General Strike of 1926. James Maxton was a left-wing Labourite and chairman of the Independent Labour Party, 1926-31 and again 1934-39.*

*The Malakhov faction (point 20) is described in "A Heart-to-Heart Talk with a Well-meaning Party Member," September 12, 1928 (pp. 244-45).*

*From the* Militant, *March 15, 1929. Revised against the Russian original by permission of the Harvard College Library. The addendum, which was omitted from the* Militant, *was translated from the Russian for this volume by Marilyn Vogt. The "three additional remarks" are based on Osip Pyatnitsky's organizational report to the Sixth Comintern Congress.*

Dear Comrade:

You ask me my opinion of the congress. Up to now I have at hand neither the final text of the program nor the resolutions of the congress, with the exception of the one on tactics adopted after the reading of the report by Bukharin. This I received yesterday. As is known, the drafts of the resolutions were not published—this in order to prevent "outsiders" from comparing them with the final text. Thus many of the speeches appear to allude to something "unknown to anybody." A final judgment can be formed only after receiving all the resolutions. For the moment I will confine myself to some provisional remarks.

1. The congress has attempted to inaugurate a new line of conduct without abandoning the old. Automatically, the two clash. In many questions, starting from revisionist opportunist premises, we arrive at conclusions that are sometimes opportunist, sometimes ultraleftist. The congress changed its color during the very month while its sessions lasted, or rather it has increased its "leftward" coloring. The most opportunist interpretation of the capitalist stabilization was contained in Bukharin's first report, but at the end of the theses concluding this same report some phrases are added "on the possibility of abrupt historical changes," which were taken word for word from our documents but without any exposition of the tendencies characterizing the imperialist epoch.

In spite of the influx of new colonial elements, especially from across the Atlantic, and the lively impulses breaking through in the speeches and proposals of numerous delegates, the general spirit of the leadership of the congress, and of its resolutions, was that of eclecticism and epigonism.

2. Although, I repeat, I do not yet possess the final text of the program, it is already clear that things have not gone beyond attempts to disguise the worst parts. The program is a deadly dangerous consecration of eclecticism. It therefore will become the source of all sorts of festering sores—not only revisionist and opportunist but also ultraleftist. Like the resolutions of the congress in general, it inaugurates a period of profound differentiation within the Comintern.

3. The congress conducted its work while looking over its shoulder at the Opposition. It was held under the banner of defense—of defense against us. Hence its peculiar tone of insecurity. On every question it made prudent reservations. Those who want to, will act on the theses; those who do not, will avail themselves of the reservations. The Opposition constituted one of the most important "sectors" in the hall, although it seems we had no representative there. Only on the question of the program did one of the delegates, Comrade Alfonso from Indonesia, speak clearly from our standpoint (*Pravda,* no. 191).

4. The question of the stabilization was decided differently at different moments of the congress, this again being due to the influence of our attitude on that point. For Europe and America stabilization is presented as "organic" and not "accidental" (Bukharin). This absurd position easily allows inferences breaking with every principle of the Leninist analysis of the imperialist epoch (see the second chapter of my criticism of the program). At

the same time it is announced that "in China the revolution is continuing." Anyone who thinks that after the defeats already suffered, China is going through a fairly extended period between two revolutions is denounced as a liquidator.

5. No program of transitional, fighting demands was offered for this period of "organic" stabilization, except for the slogan of struggle against war.

6. The slogan of struggle against war was issued in a mechanical, isolated fashion—a real Bukharinist fashion. The parties are urged to "concentrate all their forces" on this struggle. As if there were a special secret way of fighting against war other than correct revolutionary policies in the struggle against the bourgeoisie and its state.

Bukharin poses the question of the struggle against Social Democracy in exactly the same way. It's as if he were saying, "We have already learned many things, but we have not yet learned how to fight Social Democracy." As if this were a special "art," independent of a correct revolutionary line in general.

7. While no program of transitional demands is offered, the struggle for the seizure of power is, on the other hand, indefinitely postponed. They present, as one of the most important tasks incumbent on the European Communist sections, the struggle for the Chinese revolution. But there is no revolution at present in China; there is a counterrevolution. We cannot know when the revolution will have a rebirth there. In Europe even the perspective of a revolution has been totally dropped in practice.

8. Kuusinen's report on the colonial and semicolonial countries is absolutely shameful. The poor devil has merely regurgitated the entire undigested program of Menshevism. Martynov had the pleasure of hearing himself talk exactly as he used to twenty years ago. The mere fact that the congress did not drive Kuusinen from the podium with an old broom itself is a dire warning.

9. The question of "peasant" parties and "worker and peasant" parties was left pending. They didn't dare touch the Peasants International. Some voices, to be sure, were raised in favor of creating parties of this kind, which the Communist parties would enter. The objections, timid and limited, were not objections in principle. I do not yet know whether this question was broached in any way in the resolutions. And yet this is a question of life and death for the colonial Communist parties, and for the whole Comintern.

10. The slogan of the "democratic dictatorship of the workers and peasants" is definitively transformed into a suprahistorical

abstraction for four-fifths of humanity (Asia, Africa, Latin America). The debates of the congress, even according to the expurgated, polished, and whitewashed reports appearing in *Pravda,* make it evident that the democratic dictatorship of the proletariat and peasantry signifies the path of the Kuomintang in all its possible historical variations.

11. I must quote here on this subject the truly refreshing words of Martynov: "According to the opinion of Comrade Bennet [D. Petrovsky], in India we are on the eve of a transformation of the bourgeois and democratic revolution into a socialist revolution. But this is just what Radek said about China. What becomes then of the struggle against imperialism, the struggle for national liberation, the stage of the anti-imperialist dictatorship of workers and peasants? They disappear."

The struggle against imperialism "disappears" because it is conducted under the dictatorship of the proletariat. In the same way with us the agrarian revolution ought to have "disappeared" because it was not made till after the October insurrection.

12. The "Anti-Imperialist League" remains a sort of super-Kuomintang, an arena in which adventurers and careerists from the colonial and imperialist countries may refresh their reputations at the expense of the oppressed nations, especially the proletariat of those nations. It suffices to point out that one of the representatives of this charlatans' masquerade is the English semi-Purcell, Maxton, whom our Tass publicizes as it recently did Purcell.

13. By simply declaring the Chinese revolution "in process of continuation," the leaders have relieved themselves of the necessity of furnishing the Communist Party of China a program of action for the Stolypin period of Chiang Kai-shek, through which China is now passing. The absolutely necessary transitional demands have not been raised: a Constituent Assembly, expropriation of land belonging to the "landed gentry," eight-hour day, abrogation of unequal treaties. The struggle for these slogans, also conducted in the parliament (if a parliament is established), should lead, the moment the revolution begins anew, to the creation of soviets and the battle for the dictatorship of the proletariat supported by the urban and rural poor. Our sorry strategists, however, "leap over" the reactionary stage that has now set in in China's historical evolution. They attempt to stuff all holes with the panacea of the democratic dictatorship, which in that country can only have a reactionary significance favoring the Kuomintang.

14. The report of Manuilsky is remarkable only for the personality of the reporter. Things must have gone pretty far when they put on this harlequin, whom no one takes seriously (his masters less than others), introducing him as the attorney general and guardian of Marxist doctrine and Bolshevik tradition. Here the struggle against the Opposition has descended to the level of collecting anecdotes. This is an imprudent step. A group which designates Manuilsky to defend its ideas is reaching the end of its rope.

15. Varga's report, with cautious deviousness, presents material from the point of view of "socialism in one country," but in such a way that he will not be rendered entirely responsible for this theory. Varga is theoretically much too educated not to know that this whole conception cannot stand up.

In the spring of 1926, when I was in Berlin, Varga said to me literally, in the presence of Lapinsky and Krestinsky, the following words: "Obviously, this theory is false, but it gives the Russian worker a view of the future and sustains his morale. If the Russian worker were sufficiently mature to be inspired by international perspectives, we would not have needed the theory of socialism in one country." In a word, this is a pious lie of the priest, but it offers salvation.

In the Communist International Varga is a theoretician like Polonius in *Hamlet*. He is ready to demonstrate theoretically that the clouds on the horizon resemble a camel, or a whale, or, if it pleases the prince of the moment, even "socialism in one country," or in general whomever and whatever you wish. The Communist International already possesses a whole army of Poloniuses of this kidney.

16. The theses announce "the full Bolshevization and internal consolidation" of the parties of the Comintern, and "the overcoming of the internal struggle." The congress, however (even as seen through the bars set up by the editorial censors) presents a picture of an entirely different character. A violent and muffled struggle is developing all along the line. Factional groupings, more or less clearly formed, revealed themselves at the congress in the delegations from Germany, England, Poland, the United States, Rumania, Yugoslavia, etc. The delegation of the USSR naturally was no exception. On the contrary, it is the one which transplants splits into the other parties. In a multitude of speeches complaints were heard about sharp factional battles "which are not justified by any major political differences."

17. No one took the trouble to ask, however, why these factional struggles are eating away at the "internally consolidated" Communist International. The answer is nevertheless clear. At present, the Communist International is based on a bloc composed of the right and the center, or, to speak more precisely, on a bloc between an opportunist faction, a left-centrist one, and an as-yet-unformed proletarian one. The situation in the USSR and the regime in the Communist International have retarded the development of the differences between these groups, but the class struggle makes a bloc between forces straining in different directions insupportable. That is where the bitter factional struggles come from in the apparent absence of "major political differences."

18. Much was said at the congress about the integration of the Social Democracy with the capitalist state. Incontestably, the Social Democratic and trade union bureaucracy is forced, because of the situation of the petty-bourgeois layers caught between the imperialist bourgeoisie and the proletariat, to assume at all critical moments, in all important questions, direct responsibility for the bourgeois state. But, at the same time, the Social Democratic bureaucracy leaves room for new petty-bourgeois layers to occupy the intermediate positions.

These are taken in part by the left Social Democracy, but to an even greater extent by the right wing of the Comintern. In China and in England we have seen this phenomenon in its most complete and classic form. But the same tendencies exist also in other countries. It is the Communist Party of the Soviet Union which forms the basis of this situation.

In the left-centrist groupings of the Comintern we frequently see a distorted refraction of proletarian tendencies that cannot attain legal expression under the present regime, in view of the mechanical destruction of the Opposition.

A differentiation between the proletarian and petty-bourgeois tendencies in the Comintern is absolutely inevitable, and the entire process still lies ahead.

19. The theses concerning the "victory over the Trotskyist Opposition" hinge upon that. It has already been said above that the whole congress took place under the banner of defense against us. We have already resumed the attack in the ideological domain on the whole international front. Only hopeless imbeciles can imagine (and hypocritical bureaucrats can confirm) that the resolutions of the Sixth Congress, which approve those of the

Fifteenth Congress of the Communist Party of the Soviet Union, signify "the end of the Opposition." The end is still far off. The Opposition has only begun.

20. The resolution makes a pitiful attempt to foist upon us the group of adventurers of Suhl, who, with the workers duped by them, have passed from the Opposition to the Social Democracy. I will not explain here why good revolutionary workers are sometimes dragged along into all sorts of blind alleys which they cannot get out of by themselves. The blame lies upon the leadership of the Comintern. Obviously, it also touches us indirectly: we have not been able up to the present to state our views clearly, resolutely, and concretely enough in regard to the situation in each country. But one thing is clear: a certain group, which, for a brief lapse of time, had come to us by way of our former allies in the bloc (Zinoviev and Company), went over to the Social Democrats. We are neither more nor less responsible for it than are the leaders of the present regime for the events of Smolensk, Artemovsk, Shakhty, etc., which took place under their "monolithic" leadership. If we bear the responsibility for the defection of the Suhl group, our accusers must answer for the Malakhov faction.

21. The congress has again shown the illusory nature of vulgar adaptationism. By minimizing differences of opinion, by adopting a hypocritical tone, one can slip into the Centrosoyuz but not into the Comintern. *The reestablishment of the unity of the Comintern must be preceded by a profound internal differentiation.* The present leaders cannot carry this out; they will be its first victims. They know it well. The naive peacemakers also will receive only blows and bruises. No concessions to cheap peacemaking! On the contrary, relentless struggle for the reestablishment of the revolutionary unity of the Comintern through a clear demarcation of lines on a principled basis!

The profound differences of opinion which rend the Comintern, and which even appear throughout the censored report of the Sixth Congress, prove that it is impossible to speak of our isolation. The muffled factional struggle in all the parties will be transformed, under the pressure of events and of our criticism, into a battle between well-defined political lines. The proletarian line will adopt *our* principles as the only possible ones.

These are my provisional impressions after reading the reports in *Pravda*. With sincere greetings,

Yours,

L. D. Trotsky

### Three additional remarks

1. It is best of all to gear our theoretical research work to the text of the program of the Comintern with the aim of producing by the time of the Seventh Congress a genuinely Marxist draft program. I am writing about this in more detail in a letter to several comrades.

2. The number of members in the whole Comintern, excluding the All-Union Communist Party, was given in Pyatnitsky's report as 583,000. This number is strikingly small. But even this turns out to be a gross exaggeration. It comes out that this number includes the 100,000 members of the Chinese Communist Party. Meanwhile, from the discussions at the congress, it is apparent that the Chinese Communist Party has lost its workers and that the "100,000" are peasants who joined the party during the agrarian movement. If the Chinese Communist Party has retained to the present day one-quarter of its official membership, this is very good. There are obvious exaggerations in the listings for other parties as well. One may suppose that the total membership of the Communist parties in the entire world (other than the AUCP) barely exceeds 400,000.

3. The call to reestablish the unity of the Comintern and the AUCP after a general demarcation of lines demands a brief clarification. I received a very timely reminder of this old slogan in a letter of Comrade Palatnikov's. In essence all the documents of the Opposition were imbued with the idea of this slogan. But now it is necessary to refresh this old formulation. The stage when, sitting in the Central Committee, we still tried to persuade the centrists and rightists to "change their ways" has receded irretrievably into the past. Our task for a long time now has been not to convince the leadership, but to explain to the party that this is not a leadership but bankruptcy. We are not forgetting that there are many valuable elements in the party apparatus which the party will need. But it is possible to fight for influence over them only through the merciless and irreconcilable opposition of the Leninist proletarian core of the party to the opportunist-centrist leadership. Attention to the struggle of the rightists against the center must not obscure for us the fact that the rightists live and get stronger only by the grace of the centrists. The idea, half-admitted by *Pravda* in a moment of enlightened consciousness (February 15), that the All-Union Communist Party

contains two potential parties—one bourgeois conciliationist, which is raising its head ever higher, and the other proletarian—this idea must become the foundation of the policy of a general demarcation of lines. An alliance of two classes, according to Leninist conceptions, not only does not demand but does not allow the transformation of the All-Union Communist Party into a "two-class" party developing in a Kuomintang direction. We need a one-class party. And this can be achieved now only by means of a general internal differentiation—not according to the line drawn by the apparatus under pressure from the bureaucrats and the new bourgeoisie, but along class lines, which the Opposition has theoretically projected and must politically realize, leaning on the proletarian core of the party and the working class as a whole. This concerns not only the All-Union Communist Party but the Comintern.

# MAX EASTMAN: A FRIEND OF THE OCTOBER REVOLUTION

## September 11, 1928

*NOTE: A letter to N. I. Muralov in Tara. Max Eastman (1883-1969) was a writer and editor and an early sympathizer of the Left Opposition. He translated several of Trotsky's books and was the first to acquaint the American public with the issues of the Trotsky-Stalin struggle. Trotsky compares him to John Reed, another American journalist who supported the Russian revolution and wrote the account* Ten Days That Shook the World. *In 1925, Eastman's book* Since Lenin Died *was published, containing the first true account of the inner-party struggle. It also had the first public report of Lenin's Testament, letters dictated in December 1922 and January 1923 giving Lenin's final evaluation of the other Soviet leaders and calling for Stalin's removal from the post of general secretary. The Testament was suppressed in the Soviet Union until "de-Stalinization" in 1956. When Eastman's book arrived in the Soviet Union it created a scandal. To avoid a confrontation with the Politburo majority over this issue, Trotsky disclaimed responsibility for the book and denied the authenticity of Lenin's Testament (see "Letter on Eastman's Book," in* Challenge 1923-25, *p. 310). In October 1926, possibly at the indirect urging of some Russian Oppositionists, Eastman published the text of the Testament in the* New York Times. *Trotsky used this letter to Muralov to set the record straight about Eastman.*

*In the late 1920s Eastman developed differences with the Marxist movement; in the following decade he rejected socialism altogether and moved to the right, eventually becoming an anticommunist and an editor of* Reader's Digest.

*From* New International, *October 1934, in a translation by John G. Wright.*

Dear Nikolai Ivanovich:

I received your inquiry about Comrade Max Eastman, who is played up from time to time as a bogey by our press, being almost depicted as a hireling of the bourgeoisie, selling it the state secrets of the USSR. This is a shameless lie. Comrade Max Eastman is an American revolutionist of the John Reed type, a devoted friend of the October Revolution. He is a poet, writer, and journalist; he came to the Soviet republic during the initial difficult years of its existence, learned the Russian language here, and came into intimate contact with our internal life in order to defend the Soviet republic better and with greater assurance before the masses in America.

In 1923 Max Eastman sided with the Opposition and openly defended it against political accusations and especially against insinuations and slanders. I will not here touch upon those theoretical differences that separate Comrade Eastman from the Marxists. But Eastman is an absolutely irreproachable revolutionist, whose entire conduct is proof of his ideals and political honesty. In this respect he is several heads higher than many of the functionaries who are hounding him. Eastman held to the opinion that the struggle waged by the Opposition was not energetic enough, and he inaugurated a campaign abroad on his own accord and risk.

Having no access to the official Communist press and desiring at any cost to give the widest possible publicity to Lenin's Testament, Eastman handed it over to an American bourgeois newspaper. Every one of us, both before and during the Soviet period has had more than one occasion to resort to foreign bourgeois newspapers in order to give one bit of news or another the wide circulation which we could otherwise not obtain. Lenin on more than one occasion utilized such publicity in the form of interviews given to foreign journalists. It must also be added that except for an absolutely insignificant minority, American workers read only the bourgeois press. Lenin's Testament is not a state or party secret. It is no crime to publish it. On the contrary, it is a crime to keep it hidden from the party and from the working class. Today, the minor and casual remarks that Lenin wrote for his own personal use (for example, notations on book margins) are being printed by the hundreds, provided these notations can be used even indirectly against the Opposition. But kept hidden are many hundreds of articles, speeches, letters, telegrams, and notations made by Lenin if they tend directly or indirectly to discredit the present leadership or favor the present

Opposition. It is difficult to conceive of a ruder and more disloyal handling of Lenin's ideological heritage. Had the Testament been given timely publication in our party press, it could have been freely reprinted by any bourgeois newspaper. But inasmuch as the Stalinist censorship had placed a ban on Lenin's Testament, as well as on hundreds of his other works, Eastman turned to the bourgeois press. There was nothing at all underhanded in such a utilization by Eastman of a newspaper for the sake of publicity. Even on the pages of a bourgeois newspaper Lenin's Testament remains Lenin's Testament.

But, the slanderers say Eastman "sold" this Testament. Yes, the bourgeois paper paid for the material it got. But did Eastman appropriate this payment and use it for his own personal purposes? No. He donated it all to the cause of the French Opposition so that this same Testament of Lenin and other documents shamefully kept hidden from the party and the proletariat may be published. Does this act place the least splotch on Eastman's reputation? Not the slightest. On the contrary, Eastman's entire behavior shows that he was motivated exclusively by ideological considerations.

During the time when the Opposition still figured on correcting the party line by strictly internal means without bringing the controversy out in the open, all of us, including myself, were opposed to the steps Max Eastman had taken for the defense of the Opposition. In the autumn of 1925 the majority in the Political Bureau foisted upon me a statement concocted by themselves containing a sharp condemnation of Max Eastman. Insofar as the entire leading group of the Opposition considered it inadvisable at that time to initiate an *open* political struggle, and steered toward making a number of concessions, it naturally could not initiate and develop the struggle over the private question of Eastman, who had acted, as I said, on his own accord and at his own risk. That is why, *upon the decision of the leading group of the Opposition,* I signed the statement on Max Eastman, *which was foisted upon me by the majority in the Political Bureau* with the ultimatum: either sign the statement as written, or enter into an open struggle on this account.

There is no cause to enter here into a discussion of whether the general policy of the Opposition in 1925 was correct or not. It is my opinion even now that there was no other way during this period. In any case, my statement on Eastman at that time can be understood only as an integral part of what was then our line toward concilation and peacemaking. That is how it was interpreted by all those members of the party who were in the least informed or who did some thinking. This statement casts no shadow, either personal or political, upon Comrade Eastman.

As far as I know from news that has reached me about Eastman in the past year, he remains right now what he has been: a friend of the October Revolution and a supporter of the views of the Opposition.

With Bolshevik greetings,
L. Trotsky

# A HEART-TO-HEART TALK WITH
# A WELL-MEANING PARTY MEMBER

## September 12, 1928

*NOTE: In his May 1, 1929, preface to* La Révolution défigurée, *Trotsky described this as "a little pamphlet that I wrote in exile . . . in reply to a letter remonstrating with me from a well-meaning opponent. I think that this document, which circulated widely in manuscript, gives the book exactly the proper conclusion, by revealing to the reader the final stage in the struggle preceding my exile [abroad]" (see* Writings 1929, p. 127). *The well-meaning opponent was one Shatunovsky, a member of the Bukharin-Rykov faction.*

*"Depersonalized dispatch," also called the "Rudzutak reform," refers to the organization of transportation to avoid shipment of similar products in two opposite directions (for example, the dispatch of wheat to Moscow from Leningrad at the same time as wheat was sent from Leningrad to Moscow). The application of this formula to Rudzutak, who was commissar of railways from 1924 to 1930, is an allusion to his frequent and unnecessary trips, which were the object of public ridicule.*

*For Order No. 1042, see* Challenge 1923-25, pp. 109-23. *The concessions policy discussed in this pamphlet was the policy, elaborated under Lenin, of giving foreign investors concessions in Soviet industry, with part of the proceeds going to the Soviet government. In the case cited here, Chubar, who held important party and government posts in the Ukraine and was also chairman of the metallurgy committee of the Supreme Council of the National Economy, was promoting manganese from the Ukranian deposits at Nikopol although that meant increasing the financial losses of the industry as a whole.*

*The Wrangel officer was a GPU agent introduced into the Left Opposition at the end of 1927 in an attempt to discredit the Opposition through its alleged association with White forces (Wrangel had been a White Guard general who was the last commander in chief of the counterrevolutionary forces in the civil war).*

*Kardo-lenta was a Soviet textile trust.*

*Moshe Frumkin, a deputy commissar of finances and an outspoken rightist, was the focus of Stalin's campaign against the rights until Bukharin, Rykov, and Tomsky were publicly identified with the right wing in 1929.*

*"Peasant philosophers" was a term used by Stalin in the spring of 1928 to designate unnamed right-wing Communists.*

*In the last paragraph, Trotsky explained the elementary idea that he would be willing to make an agreement with the right wing against the Stalin faction to restore inner-party democracy, because that would establish the preconditions for the workers to regain their control over the party. Trotsky was criticized for this idea, and in December he defended his formulation in the article "On the Topics of the Day."*

*From* La Révolution défigurée, *in the compendium* De la Révolution *(Minuit, 1963). In French this pamphlet was entitled "Reponse à un contradicteur bienveillant" (Reply to a friendly critic). Translated from the French for this volume by David Keil, and revised against the Russian text in the Library of Social History.*

Dear Comrade:

I have received your August 6 letter from Zaporozhye, where you are staying temporarily. I have no reason to doubt that you wrote with the best of intentions. I have even less reason to doubt that the road straight to Thermidor is paved with just such intentions. A good deal more energetic work is being done today on fixing up the roads to Thermidor than on our "good old Russian" country roads.

You would like to convince me of the harmfulness of the Opposition in general and of "superindustrialism" in particular. As a graphic example you cite the Dneprostroi project [at Zaporozhye], where you now happen to be. You write: "Striking proof of this (that is, the harmfulness of excessive industrialization), may be found in your decision (?) to force the pace of the Dneprostroi project, which will not really be needed for a long time to come and which, besides, is being built according to a plan that is absolutely illiterate."

You then bring in a large number of other considerations, piling them on top of one another and making your whole letter (if I may speak frankly) a rather chaotic mess. But in every case you come back to this same Dneprostroi, which has proven to be, as you put it, a "litmus paper, an infallible means of determining exactly what it is that you"—that is, I—"propose to do."

I am answering your letter because it seems to me typical in the highest degree of the present party philistine's way of thinking, which has two characteristic traits: an inability to put two and two together in theoretical matters; and as a result, a careless attitude toward the facts.

The Marxist method of thinking is very rigorous and demanding: it does not tolerate gaps, omissions, or the crude fitting together of parts. That is why it pays such strict attention to facts, does not take things on say-so or rely on memory, but checks the primary sources. The philistine way of thinking, on the other hand, is trivial and approximative; it wanders and gropes around without looking ahead and naturally has no need of great factual accuracy. Especially not in politics; least of all in factional politics. And if you're caught red-handed, you can always say you heard it from the grapevine, from one of your cronies, and heard it with your very own ears. Unfortunately, your letter falls into this category.

It is obvious that everything you say about Dneprostroi you have heard from a gossipy friend, who is obviously anything but reliable. You write that my "decision to force the pace of the Dneprostroi project is being carried out." What decision is that? In what capacity and by what authority could I put through such a decision? Especially in 1925, when all decisions were made behind my back by the factional Septemvirate and then went through the Politburo purely for the sake of form.

Listen to what actually happened. In the summer of 1925, the Council of Labor and Defense passed a decree—which I had nothing to do with—naming a Dneprostroi commission under my chairmanship. In principle, the question of building a hydroelectric station had been decided *two or three years earlier*. The appropriate agency had done a great deal of work in drawing up estimates and making other preparations and had submitted a finished plan. I had absolutely no connection with all that. My commission, according to the decree of the Council of Labor and Defense, had the task of checking the agency's plan and its estimates over a period of two or three months, so that the budget for 1925-26 could include the first expenditures required for this project. In this case, as in many others, I defended the viewpoint that, given our poverty, it was better to spend two extra years estimating and double-checking than to spend two extra months on construction. Precisely for that reason I sought and managed to obtain a one-year *extension* on the deadline fixed for my commission's work. As you can see, this hardly resembles "forcing the pace." The best personnel, nationally and internationally, were brought in to check the estimates for the project. A wide exchange of views took place in the press among technicians and economists. For my part, I put no pressure on the commission, in which all Soviet economic institutions were represented, still less on the press; nor could I have exerted such pressure, in view of the overall situation in the top circles of the party and the soviets. After all, this was in 1925-26, when the history of the party and the October Revolution had already been rewritten, when Molotov had become a theoretician, and Kaganovich was running the Ukraine.

It is true that both in the press and at Central Committee meetings I opposed the banal arguments, based on purely philistine reasoning, that in general Dnesprostroi was more than we could handle. This is the same kind of argument the moss-backed "Friends of the People" used in their day against building the Trans-Siberian Railway, which it may be said in passing was an infinitely more difficult enterprise for Russia at that time than Dneprostroi is for us. Nevertheless, the solution to the general problem of the pace of industrialization cannot by itself resolve the particular question of when and in what proportions Dneprostroi ought to be built and, in general, whether it should be attempted. The commission I led was assigned only to prepare the information required to resolve this question. But it did not even get that far. One of the sidelines in the struggle against "Trotskyism" was the struggle against Dneprostroi. The directors of various institutions, especially the railways, of which you speak so unfavorably, considered it their duty to use every means to sabotage the commission's work. The only rule guiding certain sages of the state, as you undoubtedly know, is to say "shaven" when I say "shorn." Because of the early stage the work was in I had not stated a definite opinion on the project or on the period of time in which Dneprostroi should be finished. So the agencies simply dragged things out, created disruptions, engaged in sabotage, and spread "rumors." In the end I asked to be relieved of the functions of chairman of the commission. The request was granted. After that, within an extraordinarily short time, in a few weeks, the commission carried out all its work, formulated its conclusions, and had them adopted by the Council of Labor and Defense.

It is quite possible that the commission allowed itself to be guided by the noble desire to show that it did know what it was doing. Probably it also received an encouraging word from on high. At that point things actually did move at a "forced pace." But I had nothing to do with the final checking of the plans and figures, still less with the schedule that was set.

While I was chairman of the commission, Stalin, and consequently Molotov, intervened as resolute opponents of Dneprostroi. Speaking in the tone of the "peasant philosophers," Stalin uttered axioms of this type: for us, building Dneprostroi would be like a poor peasant buying a gramophone. When after my resignation, a 180-degree turn occurred, and I expressed my surprise at this in the Central Committee, Stalin explained that earlier a half-billion rubles were involved, whereas now it was a question of no more than 140 million. All this is recorded in the transcript of one of the plenums of the Central Committee. Stalin showed quite simply in this way that he understood nothing about the actual fundamentals of the problem and that the interest he showed in Dneprostroi was limited to considerations of personal combinations. Comrades had talked of the half-billion rubles in regard to new factories which were to consume the energy from Dneprostroi. In round numbers, their cost was fixed at that time at 200-300 million. Adding on Dneprostroi, the total was about a half-billion. But these factories were themselves part of the construction plans of the respective branches of industry. It was not Dneprostroi that needed them, but they that needed Dneprostroi.

The last word on the subject of these new factories ought to have been left to the chemical industry, the metallurgical industry, etc. In my time, the commission had only begun to examine this problem. As soon as I had left, it was resolved instantly; obviously someone sprinkled magical waters on the commissioners' heads.

From this short sketch, which is easy to check against documents, it becomes evident how lightmindedly you have taken the road of mythmaking.

There is no reason for you to be especially embarrassed, however. You are not the first, and you will not be the last. There are dozens and hundreds of other . . . mythmakers. The most striking example—the classical example, it might be said—is the myth about the Putilov works. Almost every educated person in the world now knows that in 1923 I wanted to "close" this establishment. It would appear that this crime is the opposite of the one you accuse me of: on the Dnepr River I am supposed to have decided to "build" what we didn't need, and on the Neva River I am supposed to have decided to close something that was indispensable to us. I think you know that the Putilov question played an enormous role throughout what was called the struggle against "Trotskyism," especially in its first phase. Many reports and resolutions, not only of our congresses and conferences, but also of the Communist International, contain allusions to this. At the Fifth Congress, the French delegation, during a private meeting with me, questioned me closely about why I wanted to close a factory that constituted one of the iron ramparts of the dictatorship of the proletariat. Even a resolution of the Fifteenth Congress once again mentions the Putilov works.

The following is what actually happened. Rykov, the newly appointed chairman of the Supreme Council of the National Economy—Rykov, and not I—came to the Politburo with the proposal that this establishment be closed down; according to the figures of the Supreme Council of the National Economy, he said, this factory would not be needed during the decade to come and consequently would be an intolerable burden upon our metallurgical industry. The Politburo voted *in favor* of closing it down, I along with the others. I had no connection with the Supreme Council of the National Economy, or the State Planning Commission, or Leningrad industry. I made no proposal of my own on this point. As a member of the Politburo, I was obliged to make a decision on the basis of Rykov's report. The general problem of industrialization cannot by itself resolve the particular question of Putilov any more than it can the question of Dneprostroi. Stalin too voted for closing the Putilov works on the basis of Rykov's report. Later  however, because of a protest by Zinoviev, the question was reconsidered and a new decision reached, outside the Politburo, by use of factional methods. In any case, at a subsequent Politburo meeting Rykov accused Stalin of making a deal with Zinoviev on the basis of considerations having nothing to do with economic efficiency.

That is the real story of my "attack on the Putilov works." What is remarkable is that the resolution of the Fifteenth Congress, repeating the Putilov legend, was adopted on a report by Rykov. And yet my whole "crime" had been to vote for a proposal made by him, Rykov! Incredible, you say? But really, it's nothing compared to everything else that has gone on.

While writing this letter, I happened to look at a pamphlet published by the State Publishing House, written by a certain

Shestakov and entitled, *To the Peasants: On the Resolutions of the Fifteenth Congress*. There on page 49 I learn that Trotsky "submitted a statement to the Central Committee of the party, when he was on it, demanding the closing down of the huge Putilov and Bryansk factories." It does not state why he demanded this. The fact is merely asserted to unmask the Opposition's pretended "love for the workers." As if to say: this is what they're really like, these superindustrializers; they want to hurt the workers, and so they demand the closing of the "huge Putilov and Bryansk factories." In regard to Putilov, I have told you what I know. As for the Bryansk matter, never having heard of it, I can enlighten you no further. Perhaps it was simply added to round out the collection. In general, it would be difficult to imagine any more insolent and wanton libel than is found in this semi-official pamphlet on the resolutions of the Fifteenth Congress. A great many literary scoundrels, capable of anything, have sprung up in our times. In 1882, Engels wrote to Bernstein, "That is what our literary gentlemen are like. Exactly imitating the bourgeois men of letters, they believe that they have the privilege to study nothing and give their opinions on everything. They have created for us a literature that, in its ignorance of economics, its pure greenhorn utopianism, and its brazen arrogance, has no equal." This has a horribly up-to-date sound. But the Shestakovs have left even the literary men of that epoch far behind both in their ignorance and in their official utopianism, and above all in their arrogance. At the moment of danger, these gentlemen without honor or conscience will be the first to betray; and in the event of the defeat of the proletariat, in the same style with which they prettify the official line, they will sing the praises of the conquerors.

\*         \*         \*

You are opposed to taking any measures on a large scale. "Ours are not the times for great tasks," you say. And with a certain irony you write: "The only major reforms now under way are in transport, where our reforms have destroyed the tracks, are destroying the locomotives, and have put the railroad cars on the list to be destroyed next." Further you write: "All of this is called 'depersonalized dispatch,' centralization of repair shops, etc."

One could conclude from the text of your letter that here too the guilty party is . . . the Opposition. It's like the refrain in that old song, remember? "Who's always to blame? It's always Paulina."

OK. We are responsible for the closing or near closing of Putilov and even of the Bryansk factory. And we are also to blame for inaugurating or nearly inaugurating the Dneprostroi project. But how in the world can we be responsible for Rudzutak's "depersonalized dispatch"? Isn't it possible that there's a direct line of descent here from order No. 1042, which according to Lenin and Dzerzhinsky, saved the locomotives and the cars, but which, in 1924, that is, four years later, was denounced as having caused, or almost caused, the destruction of the railways? Don't you think you could demonstrate that it was I who "lured" Rudzutak onto the path of constant "depersonalized dispatch" to and fro? If your own resources aren't sufficient to carry out this historico-philosophical task, you can turn to Yaroslavsky, Gusev, and the other "keepers of the heritage"; they will furnish you immediately with everything you need—and more!

Since you are trying to approach general economic questions by taking up particular cases (and I have no objection to this method in principle), I propose that you focus your attention on one other example. Industrialization is intimately linked with the policy of concessions. Lenin attributed enormous importance to concessions policy. But in fact the results obtained have been modest to say the least. There are obviously objective reasons for that. But in this area as well, methods of leadership play a not insignificant role, a role that is undoubtedly not of the last rank in importance. Here is an example that I advise you to research well (better than you did the Dneprostroi question). Moreover, you could make use of the era of self-criticism to place this case before the court of party opinion. But you will have to hurry: self-criticism is already on the way out.

My example has to do with our extraction of manganese. Our largest deposits of this metal, those at Chiatura, are, as you know, leased to the American Harriman, as a concession. The ones at Nikopol we exploit ourselves. As a person familiar with metallurgical questions, you probably know that manganese has a very particular application, and as a result its market is strictly limited. Manganese from Nikopol is of a completely inferior quality, is much more difficult to extract, and costs a great deal to transport. According to the rough calculations that I made at one time in collaboration with the most qualified experts in the matter, the profit differential per ton of manganese compared to Chiatura is about eight to ten rubles. That means that when a ton from Chiatura yields a profit of four to five rubles, a ton from Nikopol incurs a loss of about four to five rubles. In accordance with the concession contract, we receive a certain amount of money for each ton sold by the concession-holder. With each ton from Nikopol that we sell ourselves we lose money. If the state considers it necessary to keep the entire manganese industry in its own hands without leasing out concessions (the late Krasin defended this thesis, and he may have been correct), it is necessary to reduce the work at Nikopol to the minimum and develop Chiatura to the maximum. Then we would be assured of large profits. But we have acted in exactly the opposite way: after leasing out Chiatura, we have begun to develop Nikopol, investing some of the millions that, as everyone knows, are burning holes in our pockets. In this way we achieve a dual purpose: we sell the Nikopol manganese at a loss and, by exporting this unprofitable product, we shrink the overall manganese market and thus reduce our profit on each ton of Chiatura manganese sold by the concession-holder. In a word, through our loss at Nikopol we cause ourselves a further loss at Chiatura.

How did this complex system of self-sabotage arise? In such cases, there is much talk among us about miscalculations or oversights, and it always turns out that some distant relative is to blame, and wherever possible, someone from the poor side of the family. However, there was no error in this case. All the calculations had been done in advance. All the institutions had been informed. The documents related to this question, with the exact mathematical computations, are there in the appropriate archives. It was our Soviet "feudalism" that played a fatal role here; just as we have been taught concerning China, feudalism inevitably intermingles with bureaucratism and mandarinism and sometimes even originates out of them. Chubar and other mandarins of the Ukraine persisted in developing the Nikopol manganese because they viewed it from their own local standpoint. The Kharkov point of view came into conflict with that of the state as a whole. In a regime of centralized proletarian dictatorship, the question could have been resolved easily enough for the good of the entire Soviet Union, and consequently for the good of the Ukraine. But when methods of bureaucratic feudalism are applied, everything is turned upside down. Due to considerations that had nothing to do with manganese, it proved to be quite impossible to do anything that might upset Chubar; that might have changed the "relationship of forces." What was involved here was not an economic miscalculation, but a political calculation that had only one fault: it was rotten to the core.

At the moment I have no information on the work at Nikopol or its relationship to the work at Chiatura. But the general situation on the world market, as I understand it, can hardly have produced the miracles for Nikopol that the Kharkov leadership counted on, in defiance of all good sense. This can only mean losses in the millions. That is only a supposition on my part. Perhaps you will check into it and publish your results? If it turns out that I am mistaken, I will be the first to be pleased.

But let us return to Dneprostroi. In view of your slovenly approach to the facts, I have no reason to believe you when you say that Dneprostroi was begun prematurely. Your second assertion, that it is being constructed badly, is much more plausible. But what do I have to do with that? You shouldn't go anticipating the Gusevs, Kuusinens, Manuilskys, Peppers, Lyadovs, and other political leeches, who will demonstrate that I am responsible, not only for the errors at Dneprostroi, but also for those on the Turkestan-Siberia railway, which is being built in the vicinity of where I live now.

You keep saying, "Think about it, reflect on Dneprostroi, and revise your industrialization program, into which you have unfortunately lured the party."

"Lured"? How? Superindustrialism has been condemned by every august assemblage. The party has rejected it with all the required monolithism. The literary leeches have written hundreds of pamphlets about this. Mountains of "study outlines" have been distributed throughout the country and, it might be said, throughout the world. They are always on the same theme: "Trotskyism" equals robbing the peasant for the sake of superindustrialization. Now, all of a sudden, it seems that Trotsky has "unfortunately" lured the party into supporting this criminal program. Allow me to ask you: in that case, what are you, an opponent of the Opposition, implying about the party, especially its leadership? How could you give a vote of confidence to such a leadership?

Further on you write: "Attempts have been made to speak your language to the peasants. What is the result? The *smychka* between the peasants and workers has been disrupted for years to come. But the army is peasant, and the country is peasant; collectivization is a screen for getting loans from the peasants; industrialization will require a century."

These few candid lines contain a whole program—more than that: a whole conception of the world. Only . . . what stray breeze could have blown you into the party of Marx and Lenin, with this world outlook? But don't worry; you are virtually the hero of our times. You put down in writing exactly what is in the hearts of tens of thousands in the upper circles. A profound alteration has taken place in the party of Marx and Lenin, and your reactionary, philistine letter is just one of the innumerable manifestations of this.

"Attempts have been made to speak your language to the peasants." Who attempted? The Central Committee. Then permit me to ask you: Why did it "attempt" this? It started out by condemning, rejecting, expelling, and deporting. Then it changed its mind: "What the hell, let's give it a try." Again I ask you, what are you implying about the Central Committee? How do you view its policy? Its political morality? Your position is not so good. Or is it that the position of the Central Committee is not so good? But that is precisely what we have been saying.

You say: "Attempts have been made to speak your language to the peasants. What is the result? The *smychka* between the peasants and workers has been disrupted for years to come." Permit me: it is precisely on the question of the *smychka* that our whole discussion has revolved. It is the Opposition "that does not want a *smychka* with the peasantry." The first Manuilsky to come along could prove that to you. And all of a sudden, we find that the leadership has supposedly disrupted this *smychka* for years to come, simply because it wanted to indulge itself in a little "Trotskyism." What a confused mess.

Your misfortune is that the continual, dreary, endlessly repeated, and fundamentally unprincipled sessions where people are "worked over" have made you unaccustomed to thinking things through, being accurate, and reasoning in an honest way. Just as the Ford assembly line wears on the nervous system, the mass-produced "study outlines" wear down one's ability to think. You round out the confusion of your politics with a jumble of high-sounding commentaries. Yet you can't get around the fact that the Opposition published its Platform and its countertheses for the Fifteenth Congress. All these questions were analyzed quite clearly and in as concrete a way as was possible in such documents. Instead, you attribute to us, as though it were our program, those panicky "measures," accompanied by fits of administrative ecstasy, which were the product of the entire preceding wrong course. Is that not so? If not, then what did bring them about? If it were admitted that as a result of a correct socialist policy it was really necessary, ten years after October, to resort to such destructive and arbitrary measures (which are said to be the same as "war communism," for what reason I do not know), that would mean there is no way out of the situation. That would be a condemnation of the dictatorship of the proletariat as a whole and of socialist methods for running an economy. That would mean handing all the cards over to the Mensheviks and the retainers of the bourgeoisie in general. That is exactly what our entire crowd of ideological leeches tend to do, despite their intentions. As they would have it, everything is fine, everything is excellent, right up to the moment when suddenly everything goes badly. Why does the trouble arise so suddenly in the middle of smooth sailing; why, when the *smychka* between the peasants and the workers is being systematically consolidated, do these "measures" appear out of nowhere and disrupt the *smychka* "for years to come"? Our leeches don't worry about that question. It is nevertheless the question that decides the fate of socialism.

You are talking nonsense, sir, when you say that attempts have been made to speak *our* language to the peasants. These measures of desperation did not come from our Platform but from that fact that you did not listen to our Platform when you should have. And there are still blowhards and underhanded types who tell the workers that "the Opposition obstructed" the grain collections, that it "distracted people's attention." What did it distract people's attention from? From the grain collections? But it was precisely the Opposition that talked about them; it was you who distracted the party's attention from the grain problem to the Wrangel officer! Watch out that tomorrow you won't be forced to repeat this "maneuver" on a much broader scale.

"The army is peasant and the country is peasant; collectivization is a screen for getting loans from the peasantry; industrialization will require a century." In these few words your whole foundation is exposed to the world. Why don't you finish what you are saying? The logical conclusion of your argument goes like this: "We were a little early, a wee bit premature, in undertaking the October Revolution. We should have waited roughly another century. To establish Soviet power only to end up with a peasant army in a peasant country and a collectivization that is only a screen for getting loans from the peasants? No. For results like that, the costs were far too great. We were too hasty, much too hasty, alas, with the October Revolution."

That's the point of view that comes out ever so clearly, once you throw off the tangled mass of "study outline" verbiage and start speaking from the heart.

In conformity with your whole manner of thinking, you immediately add: "I think that now you yourself doubt that the necessary conditions exist for the establishment of Soviet power in China."

On that I can give you one reply: the philistine has grown bold and scratches his belly in public. Of course, philistinism remained unextinguished within many revolutionaries not only after October but even before as well. Until now it merely stayed hidden; now it comes back to the surface, not only among the intellectuals, but also among many former workers who have raised themselves above the masses, received titles, made names for themselves, and can look down on the masses, whether Russian or Chinese.

"But with *our* population," they say, "is anything else possible? What kind of industrialization can you have with a bunch of peasants? As for the Chinese, isn't Soviet power more than those ugly mugs can handle?" The reactionary philistine has devoured the revolutionary; all that's left of some are the horns and hooves; of others, not even that.

Honorable comrade, you are repeating the wise maxims that the philistines of every stripe threw at us thousands and thousands of times; not only before the October Revolution, not only ten or twelve years before, when we said that in tsarist, slave, peasant, backward Russia, the revolution could lead to proletarian power earlier than in the most advanced capitalist countries; not only then, but even in 1917, after February, on the eve of October, during October, and during the first hard years that followed. Just count on your fingers: nine-tenths of the current "optimistic" leaders, builders of "full socialism," did not even believe in the possibility of the dictatorship of the proletariat in Russia; and to support their lack of faith, they cited the ignorance of the Russian peasants, exactly as you do for industrialization and for soviets in China.

Do you know what that is called? How it could be characterized in one word? *Degeneration.* For others, however, for many others, it is *rebirth*, a return to their original petty-bourgeois nature, which was temporarily driven down by the hammer of the October Revolution.

The petty bourgeois cannot engage in politics without myths, legends, and even gossip. Invariably, facts turn on him in their most unexpected and disagreeable form; he is organically incapable of embracing great ideas; he has no staying power; therefore he sets to plugging the holes with conjecture, fabrication, and myth. With the backsliding from the proletarian line to that of the petty bourgeois, mythmaking becomes even more indispensable, for in this process one must work without letup to camouflage oneself, to make some slapdash connection between yesterday and today, to trample on traditions while pretending to preserve them. In such periods theories are created to compromise ideological adversaries on the personal level; at the same time masters of this art emerge. Faith in the political omnipotence of slander flowers in full glory. Gossip multiplies, develops more and more details and categories, and is canonized. A body of authors of study outlines is created, strong in the knowledge of their own irresponsibility. From the external point of view, this all gives truly miraculous results. In reality, these results are due to the pressure of other classes, transmitted by the intermediary of the "masters" of the apparatus, intriguers, and authors of scholastic documents that lull the consciousness of their own class and thus diminish its force of resistance.

By chance I have come across some lines that I wrote almost twenty years ago (in 1909):

"When the curve of historical development rises, public thinking becomes more penetrating, braver, and more ingenious. It learns to distinguish immediately the essential from the insignificant and to evaluate the proportions of reality at a glance. It grasps facts on the wing and links them with the thread of generalization. . . . But when the political curve indicates a drop, public thinking succumbs to stupidity. It is true that daily life contains persisting debris of general phrases that are reflections of past events. . . . But the internal content of these phrases flies to the winds. The priceless gift of political generalization vanishes somewhere without leaving a trace. Stupidity grows in insolence and, baring its decayed teeth, heaps insulting mockery on every attempt at a serious generalization. Feeling that it is in command of the battlefield, it begins to resort to its own methods."

There is no need to hold it against me if your letter has produced this association of ideas. But since the shoe fits, you should wear it.

To explain his confusion, his blunders and errors, the petty bourgeois needs not only myths in general, but also a constant source of evil. You probably know that the Evil One is the mythological incarnation of human weakness. In the present world situation, who is weaker ideologically than the petty bourgeois? He sees demonic forces in various things, depending on his national conditions, his historical past, and the place destiny has accorded him. When he is, if we may express ourselves in this way, an unadulterated bourgeois, the source of all the trouble in his view is the Communist who wants to rob the peasants and all the honest toilers in general. If he is a democratic philistine, the universal evil seems to him to be fascism. In a third case, it is the Krauts, the foreigners, the *métèques,* as they say in France. In a fourth case, it is the Jews, etc., and so on ad infinitum. In our country, for the *average* apparatchik, the petty bourgeois armed with a briefcase, this universal source of evil is "Trotskyism." Personally, you represent simply a "well-meaning" variety of this type. If Dneprostroi is being built badly; if Rudzutak is carried away with "depersonalized dispatch"; if quite a few dangerous complications have been created in the process of using Article 107 to hurriedly correct the errors made year after year—"Trotskyism" is guilty. What else? Engels once wrote that anti-Semitism is the socialism of fools. Applying this term to our conditions, "anti-Trotskyism" is the communism of . . . people who are not terribly bright. In other words, the authors of the anti-"Trotskyist" mythology know perfectly well what's really going on, but their hope is that the simple people's attention can be distracted from the errors of the leadership and turned toward the universal source of evil in the world, that is, toward "Trotskyism." What place do you personally occupy in this machinery of deceivers and deceived? You are somewhere in the middle, functioning as a transmission belt.

*        *        *

You write: "As a friend I fervently urge you to stop. Don't be wiser than the party. Make mistakes along with the majority, this same majority of functionaries, apparatchiks, and philistines, corrupt and degenerate; even if this majority really was degenerate and corrupt, you would not, in any case, be able to transform it, or to replace it with anything else."

What amazing lines! It would be impossible to make up better ones. And you didn't even have to make them up. You simply let your inner self, the party philistine, speak up. So allow me to remind you that the spirit of revolutionary collective work is one thing, and the philistine herd mentality is another. The spirit of revolutionary collective work must be conquered ever anew; the herd mentality is there to be taken, ready made, from the past. You have certainly heard the talk about [Trotsky's] "individualism," "aristocratic behavior," etc.? This is the vicious, gossipy expression of the philistine herd mentality, on the one hand, and of bureaucratic cronyism, on the other.

Above all, the party needs a correct line. It is necessary to know how and to *dare* to defend this line against the majority of the party if necessary—even against a *real* majority—and thus to help this majority correct its errors. If worse comes to worst, it is not even so shameful to be wrong with the majority if the majority makes its mistakes on its own, if it checks itself in the light of experience and learns. But there isn't the slightest hint of that. For a long time now the apparatus has made the mistakes *for* the majority and has not allowed the majority to correct itself. Here lies the quintessence of the present "leadership"; that is the heart and soul of Stalinism.

You think that the existing majority must simply be taken as it is. If the party had been infused with this spirit, would it have been able to make the October Revolution? Could it have even dreamed of that? No. This spirit is the product of the last five years. Before the October Revolution the collaborationist elements, conciliators, and opportunists, with their limp and worthless petty-bourgeois spirit, attached themselves to other forces: the liberal cultural movement, legal educationism, the patriotism of the war period, and "revolutionary defensism" after February. At present all those elements protrude from beneath the banner of apparatus "Bolshevism"; they have been welded together and trained in the work of baiting the Opposition, that is, proletarian Bolshevism.

How many of the present venerable defenders of October, who are "protecting" the revolution against the "anti-Soviet" [Left] Opposition, were on the other side of the barricades during the October Revolution? And after it, during the civil war, how many of them disappeared to parts unknown? Count them. Opportunism invariably tries to base itself on an already constituted force. Soviet power is such a force. Every opportunist, petty bourgeois, or philistine is drawn toward it, not so much because it is Soviet as because it is power. Pseudorevolutionaries of every stripe, former revolutionaries who have been devoured by the philistine dormant within them, former workers who have become swaggering dignitaries, the Martynovs and Kuusinens past and present, by holding fast to the status quo, can present themselves, and even think of themselves as the direct heirs of October.

Among all these former revolutionaries an especially significant place is now held by certain onetime Bolsheviks. It would be good to take a census of them some day. These are people who adhered to Bolshevism around 1905 as revolutionary democrats; who left the party when the counterrevolution came along; who tried, with some success, to become part of the June 3 regime; who rose to prominence as engineers, physicians, and businessmen; who became cronies and relatives of the bourgeoisie; who went into the imperialist war as patriots, together with the bourgeoisie; who were carried by the wave of military defeats into the February revolution; who tried to make the largest possible place for themselves in the "democratic" regime; who showed their teeth to the Bolshevik disrupters of "law and order"; who were furious enemies of October; who put their hopes in the Constituent Assembly; but who—when the Bolshevik regime began to consolidate itself in spite of everything—suddenly remembered 1905, reestablished their "party record," took up the defense of the new order and the old traditions; and who now are abusing the Opposition with the same expressions they employed against the Bolsheviks in 1917. There are many people like that. Just take a look at the Society of Old Bolsheviks; a good half of it, to say the least, is made up of such intransigent "militants," who have behind them a brief interim of some eight, ten, or twelve years spent among the bourgeoisie.

What is most unbearable to all these bureaucrats, who have found a stable situation for themselves, gained weight, and become somewhat dull, is the idea of "permanent revolution." They are not thinking of 1905, of course, or artificially resurrecting old faction fights long relegated to the archives. What is Hecuba to them? The problem is definitely of our era, of the here and now; for them it is a question of breaking free from the chain of events shaking the world. They want to secure their positions through a "prudent" foreign policy, to build what can be built, and to call it socialism in one country. The philistine wants order, tranquillity, and a more moderate pace, both in economics and in politics. The quieter you go, the easier things are. So don't get all excited; we'll get there on time. Don't go leaping over stages. The country is peasant. And in China there are four hundred million "ignorant" peasants. It will take a century to industrialize. Is it worth knocking our heads against the wall over platforms? Live and let live. That is what underlies the hatred of "permanent revolution." When Stalin said that nine-tenths of socialism had already been built here, he gave supreme satisfaction to the narrow-minded and self-satisfied bureaucracy: we've built nine-tenths; and the one-tenth that's left—we'll certainly finish building that. During the last years of his life, Lenin feared above all this mutul reassurance of the apparatchiks and bureaucrats armed with all the resources of the leading party and the state apparatus.

And you urge us to capitulate to these philistine elements, to this enormous historical regurgitation produced by the as-yet-poorly digested October Revolution? Well, you are addressing the wrong people. You say, "Rethink your position." Well, we have thought it over again. Your letter only reveals once again the immense historical superiority of the several thousand persecuted Bolshevik-Leninists over the flabby, formless, mindless mass of functionaries, bureaucrats, and, to put it simply, leeches. If we had reached your conclusion that "it is impossible to transform" the existing structure, we would not have resigned ourselves; we would have started building anew, that is, taken the good bricks out of the old walls, hardened new ones in the kiln; and used both to erect a new edifice in a new location. But, luckily for the revolution, your successes have not proceeded that far. We will find the means to make an alliance with the proletarian core of the party, with the working class, no matter how much you persecute us and no matter how much you try to fence us off. We abandon to you neither the Bolshevik tradition nor the proletarian cadres of Bolshevism.

*        *        *

By the way: a day or two before my departure from Moscow, I received a visit from one of the philistines of exalted rank, who wanted to express his sympathy and condolences in some way, or rather sought to compensate for his sad-sack, philistine impotence and discomfort in face of the ominous processes under way in the party and in the country. This exalted party man stated during this farewell visit that he considered all the policies of the Central Committee correct; as for the view that the party regime has its faults, "that," he said, "is true. And deportation is completely scandalous." That is pretty much how the brave official expressed himself. Of course, it must be admitted, there were no witnesses. When I asked him, "How has a bad regime carried out a good policy?" my guest replied: "You see, there have been isolated errors, but 'we' will rectify these things. Everyone, really everyone, that I have talked with," the dignitary confided, "of course condemns the Opposition, but is outraged by the deportations. We will get them reversed." I laughed at my visitor and spoke a few harsh words to him, as I recall, the same kind you have obliged me to use with you. "You won't get them reversed; in fact, tomorrow you will endorse the deportations, because you don't have any fight left in you." Naturally, that is what happened.

I recently received a letter from another, slightly less important "official"; this one, you see, complained that I wasn't keeping up an amiable correspondence with him. To be sure, he doesn't "agree" with me, he says, but that's not a good reason. Then he immediately changed the subject and began telling about the changes at the office and about how Ivan Kirylych had gained weight and was playing the violin.

One other "favorably disposed" official communicated her advice to me: "You only live once," she said, "so you shouldn't put up all kinds of opposition and get yourself sent into exile." The wives of the ex-Jacobins of the Directory period reasoned exactly the same way—though more with their hips than with their heads, it's true. If you tell this official, who is only going to "live once," that she stinks of Thermidor, she will recite such a lovely quotation from the collected works of Vretsky or Brekhetsky that Yaroslavsky himself would be moved.

And now you come along, you who in your way speak more "ideologically" and even with a certain élan, and at once you want to correct my ways by citing Dneprostroi. All of you—I say "all," because your names are legion—seem to forget completely that it is you, precisely you, who have sent hundreds of my comrades and myself to prison and exile. If you were told that to your face, you would look surprised. "Yes, certainly we voted for something. True, we didn't protest. But to say that we sent you— really, that's exaggerating." The party philistine prefers in such cases to play the role of Pontius Pilate, benevolently picking his nose. If hundreds of excellent revolutionists, sturdy, tenacious, committed to their principles, most of them heroes of the civil war, have recently been sitting in the same jail cells as embezzlers, speculators, and in general, sinister scum of every kind; if they are now warming up the old tsarist exile colonies with their bodies—then according to you it is simply a sad circumstance, an imperfection of the mechanism, a misunderstanding, an excess of zeal by the lower echelons. No, dear friends, you will not escape! *You* are responsible for that and you will have *to answer for it yet.*

We, the Opposition, are now in the process of training a new historic levy of true Bolsheviks. And you, through dishonest slander and repression, are putting them to the test, helping us make the selection. There are those who are afraid to be in the same cell with embezzlers and speculators. These are the ones who "repent," who confess their errors. For them the guards open the prison doors. Are these the best elements? Are these revolutionists? Are these Bolsheviks? Yet these are the ones who will occupy the posts from which authentic revolutionists have been pulled.

More and more a selection of conformists is taking place in the party. The Opposition is abandoned by skeptics, tired people, people of little faith, bargain-rate diplomats, or simply people overwhelmed by family problems. They swell the number of hypocrites and cynics who think one thing and say something else out loud. Some justify this with the argument of "state necessity." Others simply toil away in harness, poisoned forever because it is impossible to express their opinions in their own party. In the meantime, Yaroslavsky and the other gravediggers draw up the statistics on "Bolshevization." The real mass of workers, in the party and outside it, inwardly take their distance from the apparatus, keeping to themselves, growing bitter. That is the most threatening process, the main process, the decisive one. More than anything else the Stalinist faction is now working to the advantage of the Mensheviks and anarcho-syndicalists, preparing the ground for them in the working class. Trying to keep the workers tied to the apparatus by allowing them a teaspoonful of self-criticism once a year is a hopeless business. Only the Opposition, which fights to the death not only against Menshevism and anarcho-syndicalism—that goes without saying—but also against Stalinist centrism and the officious spirit of the apparatus, is able to express the needs and aspirations of the best part of the working class, keeping it under the banner of Lenin.

\*    \*    \*

You are certainly aware of the Malakhov affair: for several years, this member of the Central Control Commission carried out thefts and took bribes in grand style. There are black sheep in the best of families, you will say. Undoubtedly, a philistine inclined to philosophize will always try to get out of a difficult spot with some familiar saying. I venture to think, however, that the Central Control Commission, *as it was conceived,* is too distinguished a family and the "black sheep's" presence in it was of too long duration for that explanation to work. Another thing. The entire trust of the Kardo-Lenta, at least the top officials, must have known about Malakhov's escapades. Surely those who were linked with him in daily life also knew about them. Or can it be that Malakhov had neither friends, nor relations, nor intimates in the Central Control Commission? In that case, how could he have gotten to such an elevated institution? He didn't fall from the sky, did he? There were those, then, who knew and who kept quiet, and they were pretty numerous. Colleagues and subordinates kept quiet: the first profited, the others were afraid. They were doubly afraid, because Malakhov was a member of the Central Control Commission. He could affect people's fates. That is why Malakhov was able to steal for so long and with so much ingenuity and success: precisely because he was a member of the supreme tribunal judging the morals of the party. That is the dialectic of bureaucratism!

And yet, you know, this very same Malakhov judged and expelled us, the Oppositionists? In between a bribe of several thousand rubles and an orgy in the company of speculators, he took part in the judgment against Rakovsky, I. N. Smirnov, Preobrazhensky, Mrachkovsky, Serebryakov, Muralov, Sosnovsky, Beloborodov, Radek, Griunshtein, and many others, and found them to be "traitors to the cause of the proletariat." Malakhov also expelled Zinoviev and Kamenev and, after their "repentance," pardoned them, and sent them to work at Centrosoyuz. What a turn the dialectic takes!

I hardly doubt that when Rakovsky or Mrachkovsky was being judged a traitor to the proletariat, it was Malakhov who made the most sanguinary comments. As early as the Fourteenth Congress, when I was seated at the presidium, I first noticed Moiseyenko. He had been placed in the first row with several other Ukrainian ventriloquists to sabotage the Leningrad Oppositionists' speeches with their shouts. I expressed the following hypothesis to my neighbor Kalinin: "I do not know why he (Moiseyenko) is so zealous; I wonder if he has something to be ashamed of!" At that time this was only a very uncertain intuition, a "working hypothesis," so to speak, but later came verification; it turned out that in fact, Moiseyenko, who enriched the transcripts of conferences and plenums with phrases from the garbage pail hurled against the Opposition, indeed belongs to the same Malakhovist religion. More than once, in the last few years, in letting myself be guided by the same psychological intuition, I have succeeded in touching the essence of things. If an apparatchik brays too arrogantly, lies, slanders, and raises his fist against the Opposition, in nine cases out of ten it is a Malakhovist bluffing to distract attention from his own guilt. That's the kind of dialectic we have here.

You have the audacity to argue that that's the way things are and that's the way they always will be. "It didn't start with us; it won't end with us either." Not so, good sir! *We* are the ones who started it. Or more exactly *you,* that is, the party regime that you support. It is the self-sufficient regime of bureaucratism, *rude* and *disloyal.* Do you remember who gave this definition? It was not some impotent moralist, but the greatest revolutionist of our century. A *disloyal* regime—that is the greatest of all dangers. Of course, we do not recognize immutable norms of morality nor those imposed from outside. The end justifies the means. But the end must be a class end, a revolutionary, historic one; for that the means cannot be either disloyal, dishonest, or repugnant. This is because disloyalty, bad faith, and dishonesty can temporarily bring very "useful" results, but they undermine the very basis of the revolutionary power of the class and the internal confidence of its vanguard if they are applied over a long period of time. Thus we pass from trick quotations, and the suppression of authentic documents, to the Wrangel officer and Article 58. Once again, what is involved here is politics, above all preserving the political "prestige" that has been shaken by a whole series of opportunist fiascos. Of course, in the Kardo-Lenta case, the stakes are lower and the means in relation to the end are different. But the Malakhovs from the Kardo-Lentas protect themselves by staring deeply into official eyes and saying: "Look, I'd give my life to help you, but you've got to look out for me too." The seeds of rudeness and disloyalty, if they are sown so methodically, will sprout. Whoever sows the Wrangel officer will reap Malakhov. If only the number were limited to one! But this harvest yields a hundredfold, even a thousandfold.

When you have thought about all this, and understood it all, we will be able to chat in a different manner.

*       *       *

Since you have shown so much interest in my situation in relation to the party, allow me to become a little bit interested in yours. You speak continually about the party and its majority. But the ideas that you yourself express are those of a clandestine faction. You accuse the Central Committee of taking the "Trotskyist" road in industrialization. This is the voice of the "Rykovist" faction, the right-wing faction. You assert that in agrarian policy, the Central Committee spoke the language of the Opposition at the beginning of this year. Those are the very words of Rykov. You think that such ventures as Dneprostroi constitute "criminal destruction of our resources." But it is the Central Committee, that is, its majority, that is responsible for these ventures. The extraordinary measures applied in the countryside have disrupted the *smychka* between the peasants and workers for years to come, according to you. Therefore the policy of the present majority of the Central Committee is worth absolutely nothing. In other words, you are openly undermining the party leadership. Only your undermining leads *toward the right,* in the spirit of the political people whom Stalin has begun to designate vaguely by the term "peasant philosophers." I do not know if you officially belong to this faction. But no adult will doubt that your letter is entirely imbued with the opinions and state of mind of this grouping and that it is completely *oppositional,* that is, *right oppositional.* You are a Rykovist. As a Rykovist, you attack the Opposition, but you are aiming at Stalin. As the proverb says: "Strike one to hurt the other."

How then do you picture future relations between the Rykovist faction of "peasant philosophers," deeply rooted in the country, and the Stalinist faction of the golden mean, which holds the reins of the apparatus in its hands? Stalin's secret polemic with Frumkin calls to mind the first steps in the struggle between the lefts and the right-center bloc. Officially, of course, total unanimity reigns. It is said that, as proof of this unanimity, the authorities even distributed a notice to the [Comintern] congress delegations explaining that the rumors concerning "so-called" differences within the Politburo were invented by the "Trotskyists." But that is only a schoolboy imitation of more illustrious models. In April 1925, the Central Committee sent all the party organizations a circular stating that the rumors of differences on the peasant question within the "Leninist nucleus" were put into circulation by the same "Trotskyists." Only by this circular, however, did the majority of Oppositionists learn that the differences were rather serious if they required disavowal by this means. The author of this circular, as I recall, was Zinoviev, who several months later was to sign documents of quite a different nature. Don't you think that here too history might repeat itself a little? A certain wise person once said that when history goes to the trouble of repeating itself, it usually replaces drama with farce, or at least introduces farcical elements.

It must be said that however dramatic the general situation may be, the rehashed statements about monolithism sound like a rather pitiful comedy, in which no one believes, neither actors nor spectators. This is all the more true inasmuch as the dénouement is bound to take place not so many months from now. The faction of "peasant philosophers" is strong in the country, but it is afraid of the party and its proletarian core. It does not talk out loud; not publicly, at least. Up to now, the Thermidorians take this liberty only in private conversation or in letters; yours, for example.

I do not know if the fight will break into the open in the near future or if for the time being it will develop quietly within the monolithic bureaucratic regime. That is also the reason why I do not presume to guess what the "majority" will be at the next stage. Do you, on the other hand, promise to line up with whatever "majority" exists, even if this majority has disrupted the *smychka* between the peasants and the workers for years to come? Or do you intend to seriously struggle against superindustrializing, even at the risk of an abrupt change in your place of residence? Because the Yaroslavskys are vigilant. They have great resources in their hands, not in the domain of ideas, of course, but resources that in their own way are also effective, at least for now. They will try to strangle you, while in essence carrying out your policies, although only by installments. And on this path, against you or even with you, they could perhaps expect complete success if the Opposition did not exist. But it does exist. And you will have more than one occasion to see this.

*    *    *

You will ask: "But what are your conclusions, then?" We have explained the essential conclusions elsewhere; I will not repeat them here. But I will draw some partial conclusions here.

The regime existing in the party in the last several years has brought the whole party into a state of illegality, so to speak. The Stalinist faction clandestinely decides all the most important party matters. Your faction, Rykov's, also operates by these underground methods. As for the Opposition, it is not necessary to say anything. This whole situation is the reason why the Opposition exists. The only righteous souls who still adhere to legality, presumably, are Zinoviev and Safarov. But if these are the saints, then who are the sinners? So then, shouldn't we restore the ruling party to a condition of legality in a common effort? How? you will ask. Very simply: by giving the party back its rights.

It is necessary to begin by sharply reducing to about one-twentieth the party budget, which has grown monstrously, and which has become the financial basis for the bureaucratic arbitrariness that is dominant in the party. The party must have a budget that is strictly controlled and accounted for. Secret revolutionary expenditures should be checked each year by a special commission of the congress.

Preparations for the Sixteenth Congress should be organized in such a way that, unlike the Fifteenth, Fourteenth, and Thirteenth, it would be a congress of the party and not of the factional apparatus. Before the congress, the party should hear all the factions into which it has been splintered by the regime of the last few years. The whistle-blowers, disrupters, and fascists should by common agreement be sent to work on the new state farms, but without Article 58 being applied to them. Since there is still a good way to go before achieving a true liberation of the party, it is necessary to introduce the secret ballot into all elections leading up to the Sixteenth Congress.

These are strictly practical proposals. On the basis of these proposals we would even be willing to negotiate with the rights, because the implementation of these elementary preconditions of party principle would give the proletarian core the opportunity to really call to account not only the rights but also the centrists, i.e., the main support and protection for opportunism in the party.

Those are some of the conclusions that unexpectedly come from . . . Dneprostroi.

# THE SIXTH CONGRESS
# AND THE OPPOSITION'S TASKS

## September 18, 1928

*NOTE: Trotsky continued to assess the Sixth Congress as new information about it reached him. On August 22 the congress had heard reports from Varga and Manuilsky on the state of the USSR, endorsing the policies of the AUCP leadership and condemning the expelled Opposition. Earlier, Kuusinen had presented long theses on the colonial and semicolonial countries.*

*The citation from Lenin about "obedient idiots" that Bukharin read at the Sixth Congress was intended to minimize the concession that Bukharin had made in agreeing that the right deviation was the main danger. Bukharin hoped an impersonal "right deviation" would be opposed by ideological means, rather than organizational ones directed against individuals.*

*In this letter, Trotsky explains the dynamic of the "left turn" in terms of the pressure brought on the Stalinists by the leftward movement of the workers in Europe, as well as by the effect of the Opposition's work. He also broaches the subject of the evolution of the leadership of the Democratic Centralist group, discussing the arguments of V. M. Smirnov, the group's most outspoken leader, and takes up the relation between international politics and the fate of the Soviet republic. He returns to Smirnov's letter in the next selection.*

*The letter from Rakovsky to Valentinov, dated August 2, 1928, is in English in* New International, *November 1934.*

*By permission of the Harvard College Library. Translated from the Russian for this volume by Ron Allen.*

Dear Friend:

Almost all of the newspaper accounts of the congress have been received. Still lacking are the theses of rotten Kuusinen's rotten report. Evidently, they are still mulling over these theses in order to give them a more "uplifting" appearance. The general picture of the congress is becoming clearer and clearer, but that does not make it more comforting. The cutting edge of the congress was, of course, not the eclectic, hastily worked-out program, which will need to be radically revised, but the resolution regarding the Opposition. We didn't expect anything else. It was clear to us that the leadership would attempt to seal its handiwork beneath the heaviest of "tombstones." Now this attempt has been made. The prediction has become a fact. Conclusions must be drawn.

I made some general remarks regarding the congress in the previous letter. Now I want to fill them out. Of course we're not speaking here of a thorough balance sheet. That task will demand substantial time from all of us, for it will be necessary to say everything that the interests of the Communist movement require but the congress did not say. Here I want to confine myself to what seem to me to be some indisputable considerations flowing from the central resolution of the congress on the Opposition.

What was the leadership's scheme in relation to the Opposition on the eve of the "era" of repression? To eliminate the Opposition with one swift blow. "We'll expel the leaders, a hundred people, then exile twenty, and that will be the end of it." A typical mistake for bureaucrats: overestimating the power of the apparatus to influence events.

There was an additional part of the scheme, one that was deliberately provocative in nature: to use repression and slander to bring the leaders of the Opposition to the point where they would make statements or take actions that, if only after the fact, would "justify" reprisals against them in the eyes of the masses of workers and would establish an impassable barrier between the Opposition and the working class core of the party.

Neither part of the scheme was realized. There have been thousands of expulsions, hundreds of arrests and deportations. But the end is not in sight, for the Opposition continues to come forward in speech and in print. The capitulations have had a purely individual character. From below there is an influx of fresh elements. On the other hand, even the provocation failed to work. The Opposition did not take the road of "ultimatism" toward the party, did not turn its back on it, and when the "left" shift was projected said: We are honestly ready to help the party, i.e., the proletarian core, turn this left shift into a correct Bolshevik course.

Then there followed the right turn of July, which revealed how totally unsound conciliationism was and which rendered completely hopeless the perspective of smashing the ranks of the Opposition and isolating its leadership.

These were the conditions under which the congress convened. In the debit column of the ECCI there were: the most brutal defeats worldwide, gross miscalculations flowing from the false line, the necessity on the eve of the congress to convulsively change policies in France and Britain in the direction of the Opposition, the two-way zigzag in domestic policy—as if on orders—exactly on the eve of the congress. (This February-July zigzag looks terribly like a diagram to illustrate the Platform of the Opposition.) An extremely unfavorable situation had developed for the Central Committee of the AUCP. Only a *strong* and *authoritative* leadership, capable of thinking about the future, could have reversed itself, i.e., reopened the door for the Opposition and thus corrected the mistake of the Fifteenth Party Congress, which had by no means produced the results expected. But the weak Central Committee, politically compromised, devoid of moral authority, had need of "strong" measures. What was extorted from the congress through the strong-arm methods of Bukharin, Kuusinen, and Manuilsky, a threesome personifying every kind of weakness, was in its own way quite symbolic. The reckless resolution regarding the Opposition—they were going for broke—is the very clearest expression of the weakness and ideological bankruptcy of the leadership.

There was one other circumstance calling for an "irreversible" decision. In the party and the working class a strong protest has been growing against the deportations, which turn the notorious "self-criticism" into half-comedy and half-provocation. The leadership, devoid of authority, wants something to hide behind in advance of this growing wave of protest. "Until the next congress," they want to say, "nothing can be done." Yet everyone knows from the experience of the past four years that when necessary a decision of a Comintern congress is more easily annulled than a decision of a provincial Soviet Executive Committee.

One question remains: How is it that the congress agreed to such a decision? And this question has two sides: (1) the composition and level of the congress, and (2) the situation in which it was held.

This is what they told the congress: The fate of the Comintern depends on the fate of the USSR, and the fate of the USSR is connected with the leadership of the ruling party; support this leadership to the end, close your eyes, and vote.

If the Sixth Congress had risen to its tasks and had taken into account the lessons of the Fifth Congress, when the Zinoviev group had already performed this sort of experiment on the Comintern, the congress would have understood that its task is not to save the "prestige" of any given leadership, but to help the ruling party reestablish a leadership capable of coping with the historical tasks. But this is where the question of the Comintern itself comes in, and of the level of the Sixth Congress. In what condition has it emerged from the right-centrist laboratory of the last five years?

From Pyatnitsky's report we finally learn that in the Comintern there are four million members. Of them, there are 1.75 million in the parties and 2.25 million in the Communist Youth. At first glance the figures don't seem too discouraging. But it soon becomes clear that of the total number of party members the USSR accounts for 1.2 million, so that in all the remaining parties in the world there are fewer than 600,000. In the Communist Youth in the USSR, membership has surpassed two million, so that in the remaining countries in the world the Communist Youth has fewer than 200,000. Thus all the parties of the capitalist world account for about one-third of the Comintern, while the AUCP accounts for two-thirds. The Communist Youth outside the USSR makes up about one-twelfth of the Communist Youth International. The last figure is absolutely devastating; the progress of the movement, the progress of revolutionary ideas, is always measured by the influx of youth. For youth is— no offense to the bureaucrats and philistines—the barometer of its class. If one keeps in mind the above figures on the Comintern and the Youth International, which have finally been stated for all to hear, and the degree of their thorough dependence on the AUCP, then it is not hard to understand how much the Comintern, with its present composition, is prevented from taking an independent position with respect to each succeeding leadership of the AUCP.

The fact is that the first congresses were immeasurably more independent with respect to the Leninist leadership than the Fifth Congress was with respect to the Zinovievist leadership, or the Sixth Congress with respect to Bukharin and Manuilsky. It is enough to recall that during the Third Congress Lenin, greatly alarmed, discussed with me (in a "factional" manner) the question of what tactics we would hold to in case we were to find ourselves in the minority at the congress on the basic strategic question of the moment. And this danger did threaten us. Now, Manuilsky runs no risk at all of being left in the minority. In order to achieve such a happy result, it was necessary over the course of five years to systematically disorganize and remove from power the leadership of the Communist parties.

In Germany the Brandler Central Committee was removed. Later, the Maslow-Fischer Central Committee was expelled. Both of these Central Committees were far from irreproachable. A leadership could have been fashioned out of them only by a process of long experience. Still, both of them were far superior to the Central Committee of Thälmann.

In France the central groups of several Central Committees were expelled—Loriot, Souvarine, Rosmer, Monatte, Treint, Suzanne Girault, and others. Again in France, a Central Committee could be formed only as the result of a serious party selection on the basis of the party's own experience and with the careful and thoughtful assistance of the Comintern. The present Central Committee headed by Sémard is incomparably inferior to the ones which came before it.

In Belgium on the eve of the Sixth Congress an outright party coup was carried out, banishing from the party the founding group of Overstraeten, around which the party was created. Vujović had told me that on the eve of the Fifth Congress everything possible was done to overturn the Overstraeten group: but it was so intimately linked with the party that even the Zinoviev leadership did not succeed with a coup. Now the Belgian party is shattered and Overstraeten has been replaced by Jacquemotte, who recently emerged from the Social Democracy.

In Italy the single serious leadership put forward was the group of Bordiga, the virtual founder of the party. How many times have I heard from so many of the current Poloniuses testimonials about Bordiga as a "true leader." Now "Bordigism" is said to have been "overcome," i.e., the party leadership has been shortened by a head, if not worse. In Italy, as everywhere, the bets are placed on the obedient and, consequently, mediocre bureaucrat. But the mediocre bureaucrat won't conquer the world. All too often what he worries about is not so much conquering the world as not losing his post.

And to think that Bukharin was incautious enough, for his own private reasons, to present to *this* very congress the quotation from an unpublished letter in which Lenin warned Zinoviev and Bukharin that if they were to expel intelligent, but not necessarily obedient people, replacing them with "obedient idiots," they would ruin the Comintern for sure. But the very plan that Lenin outlined in his letter, presented as a *reductio ad absurdum,* has now been carried out three-quarters of the way.    Right now Smeral is one of the leading figures of the Comintern. The devastating experience of "Red Day" has shown what the Smeral leadership of the Czechoslovakian Communist Party is like. "What brought this person to us?" Lenin once asked me about Smeral, having in mind my close acquaintance with the internal life of the old Austrian Social Democracy. (I lived in Austria from 1907 to 1914.) "Smeral turned out to be a Communist," I answered, "only because during the war he, together with Renner, had placed all their bets on the Habsburg monarchy, not on a Czech republic. When the republic was founded nevertheless, he found himself in a desperate position in the face of national 'public opinion,' and so he bought a train ticket to Moscow." "That is very, very likely," Lenin repeated, in reply to my explanation. Smeral was tolerated as a temporary foothold. Now, a chief leader of the Comintern, he is expelling Rakovsky, Radek, and others. But he remains the very same Smeral, and events will show this to be so.

The provincial Social Democrat Kuusinen, who knifed the Finnish revolution in 1918 and learned nothing from the experience; Rafes, a former minister under Petlyura, now a "director" of the Chinese revolution; Martynov, who needs no references—these are the permanent central officials and day-to-day inspirers of the Comintern. The politics of backsliding are inevitably linked with reliance on lesser figures.

Thälmann, Sémard, Jacquemotte, Smeral, Ercoli [Togliatti], and the rest, are aware of their own weakness, of course, and know that—as a result of the struggle for self-preservation in the AUCP leadership—the strong groups in all of the parties have been thrown out of leading positions and even out of the Comintern. The newly appointed leaders understand that they can hold on to their posts only by piling on the "extraordinary measures." That is why they themselves have a "material interest" in decisions which seem to be "irreversible." Here their inner weakness comes to the assistance of the present weak leadership of the AUCP. And the result is clear: weakness multiplied by weakness has given the Sixth Congress the false appearance of "iron strength."

Much was said at the congress about the disproportion between the political influence of the Communist parties and their numerical size. Insofar as such a disproportion exists (and it is grossly exaggerated, in order to disguise the terrible numerical weakness of the Communist parties) it does require explanation. The fact is that there is a fundamental disproportion between the tasks and opportunities of the Comintern, on the one hand, and the character of its leadership, on the other. The Comintern is living off the capital accumulated by the October Revolution. The pull of the masses toward communism is great (although it does not increase continuously, as the official optimists would portray it). Objective contradictions push the masses toward communism. But the false course, the worthless regime, the bureaucratic boasting, the unwillingness and inability of the bureaucrats to learn, the substitution of orders for ideological life—these are the reasons for the stagnation, even the outright decline in membership and, in many cases, in the political influence of the Communist parties.

The difficulty with which an authentic leadership cadre is formed is too well known. Bourgeois society rescued itself after the imperialist war, first of all, because the revolutionary movement had insufficient Communist parties and, secondly, because the Communist parties had insufficiently mature leaderships. Thoroughly false and simply stupid catch-phrases are now being circulated to the effect that the problem is not in the leaders but in the masses and that we are putting our hopes in "collective leaderships," etc. This way of counterposing leaders and masses has nothing in common with Marxism. The proletariat needed Marx and Engels and Lenin. No bureaucratic party collective of any sort could have replaced them. It took more than a week, even more than a year, for the Second International to produce such leaders as Bebel, Jaurès, Victor Adler, etc. It is not by chance that during the imperialist war, partly even before the war, people such as Loriot, Monatte, Rosmer, Souvarine, Brandler, Bordiga, Overstraeten, etc., came forward. It is possible to back them into a corner and cause them to make mistakes. But to replace them through Pyatnitsky's organizational department is an impossible task. After all, the overwhelming majority of the delegates to the Sixth Congress—i.e., the chosen of the chosen— came to communism (for the most part from the Social Democracy) *after* the October Revolution, and many of them in just the last few years. A majority of the delegates, 278 people, were present for the first time at a Communist congress. The policy of banking on the bureaucrat is supplemented by banking on inexperience, unpreparedness, immaturity, and blissful trust. All of this passes for "collective leadership." But over this atomized "collective" rises one-man rule, which bases itself not on representation of the correct line but on the apparatus.

By its policies and regime during the past years the Comintern has systematically cleared the way for the Social Democracy, helped it to consolidate, and rendered immeasurable services to the General Council of the Trades Union Congress [in Britain] and to Amsterdam. When we point this out, the perpetrators of this historic crime dare to speak of our "Social Democratic deviation." *The Social Democracy could not wish for any better helpers than those in the present leadership.* Following this course there is no way out. But the expulsion of the Opposition has only strengthened this course.

The "irreversible" decision of the Sixth Congress shows how far things have gone, how badly the wagon is stuck, and how deep the processes from below must be in order to drag the Comintern's wagon out of the swamp onto the road—through open, systematic, and uncompromising struggle against the official leadership.

Under difficult circumstances there is nothing more dangerous than illusions, than prettifying the situation, cheap conciliationism, or a lulling reliance on the "objective course of events." If the Opposition did not now render all necessary aid to this objective course of events, with all its energy, fully conscious of its responsibility, then it would itself become only a pitiful relief valve for the centrist bureaucrats, who are bringing the Comintern and the October Revolution to ruin.

\*     \*     \*

A process of leftward movement by the working masses in Europe could be of decisive significance for the tempo of our successes within the USSR and, considered more broadly, for the entire fate of the proletarian dictatorship. We expected a rightward domestic shift immediately after the Fifteenth Party Congress (see "At a New Stage" [in *Challenge 1926-27*]). That was a partial mistake of ours, one of a completely secondary character, within a correct overall prediction. After the party congress, on the contrary, a left zigzag ensued and lasted about half a year, although the zigzag in the international arena has not concluded, even now. The "leftism" very likely reached its highest point in February, as shown not only by the February editorial in *Pravda* but also by the decisions of the February plenum of the ECCI. There is a most immediate connection between the two. The first stage of the leftward movement of the workers in Europe has already made the Stalin-Martynov policy of "united front" impossible once and for all for the Communist Party. Regular praise on the part of the Social Democracy and bourgeoisie for Stalin's "realism" was embarrassing to the official Communist position. It became necessary to prove that the Opposition was not being exiled for being leftist. This sectarian and factional requirement coincided with the exacerbation of the grain collections crisis. A quick way out of this crisis could have been found toward the right, i.e., by beginning "July" in February. As we have said, that is what we expected, underestimating to a certain degree the difficulties we ourselves had created for any turn to the right. Moreover, we did not pay enough attention to the conjunctural "international" needs of the ruling centrist group, which were intensified greatly by the leftward movement of the European workers, especially on the very eve of the congress.

The leadership's domestic course and its international course in February were of the same kind, mainly *left-centrist*. In July came a divergence: the domestic course turned rightward while the course of the Comintern remained left-centrist, combining within it, as has been the custom, all of the gradations from open opportunism to ultraleftism. That is what the program is like also. The continuing link between the domestic and international courses is the deadly hostility toward the left, genuinely Bolshevik wing, which finds its expression in the crucially important resolution of the congress dealing with the Opposition.

The Sixth Congress, despite all the work of preparation, selection, and camouflage, despite the compulsory unanimity, revealed a deepgoing process of differentiation within its ruling stratum. In the period ahead this process will deepen further in connection with the general course of the class struggle and the leftward movement of the working masses. The "July" duality in relation to the domestic and international courses will loom larger and larger and become evident to all. The factional groupings in the Comintern will grow stronger, not weaker. All this will create a great receptivity within the proletarian vanguard to both our ideas and our slogans. The Sixth Congress has not concluded the history of the Opposition, but has instead begun a new and more significant chapter.

*        *        *

Our foremost responsibility is to *understand* that we represent an international current, and that only as such do we have the right to exist and to count firmly on victory. In connection with this it will be necessary, though annoying, to dwell on the latest discoveries of the ultraleft theoretician V. Smirnov. A letter of his, which is circulating hand to hand and which I received several days ago, has so much the flavor of unbridled Safarovism that one's natural desire is to dismiss it. But in the letter there are some points of principle which are deeply hostile to Marxism and require elucidation in the interest of those few, but nevertheless healthy, revolutionary workers who still follow Smirnov.

In his letter Smirnov attempts to scoff at my contention that the defeats of the German revolution, the General Strike in Britain, the Chinese revolution, etc., are "directly and immediately"—as he writes—reflected in our proletariat, intensifying the centrist tendencies in it. "How? In what way?" asks the bewildered ultraleft critic. It would seem to any conscious revolutionary, more so to a Marxist, that there just isn't any question here. For a long time our party trained the workers to consider the October Revolution a part of the world revolution, and to count upon imminent aid from the Germans and the British, who have a higher level of technology and culture. "Endure" and "hold out"—these were the kinds of slogans we had in the early years. In 1923, especially the second half, the expectation of a revolutionary outcome in Germany was at its highest intensity. Our newspapers, our orators, spoke of nothing else. To think that the expectation of a German revolution did not touch to the quick all that was most advanced and thoughtful in our working class is to look upon the masses with the arrogant eyes of the old radical student who in his soul thinks that only the collective-bargaining agreement interests the worker. In fact the very question of the improvement of the workers' collective-bargaining agreements in 1923 was connected with the victory of the German proletariat. The smashing of the German revolution was a most severe blow to our workers, weighed down upon them, put off their hopes for a change in their destinies until a more distant future. It intensified a narrow concern with local job issues, increased atomization and passivity, and allowed a regurgitation of chauvinism, Black Hundredism, etc., to occur. And in response to this (although not only to this, to be sure) there came down from on high the theory of socialism in one country.

The bloc with the General Council was long touted as a means of salvation. Purcell was elected an honorary machinist and many other things. The British General Strike again raised the hopes of our workers—and again disappointed them. All of this was a blow to the revolutionary consciousness of the masses in the most direct and immediate way. A deep psychological reaction affecting the masses becomes a political factor of great significance. Domestic failures—the living standard, the regime, the growing elements of dual power—are amplified by blows which are international in character and reduce the vigor of the proletariat as a class.

The Chinese revolution, as far as one can tell, because of its massive size, scope, and duration, once again seized our masses with the tensest expectations. Its horrendous defeat was a domestic catastrophe here. Though perhaps invisible to the superficial view, it was no less real a catastrophe for our proletariat. How can one fail to understand this? How can one fail to see it? How could one conceive of a revolutionary leadership that failed to take account of the deep molecular processes going on among the masses themselves?

Can it be, however, that the rotten leadership is a justifiable explanation for these processes? Only a fatalistic metaphysician who thinks that the leadership only "reflects" the processes at work in the masses could argue like that. The dialectician knows that the leadership, within very broad but still finite limits, affects these processes, can accelerate, decelerate, or divert them. This can be seen most clearly from the single fact that these same defeats in Britain, Germany, and China were the immediate results of opportunist leadership. The centrifugal processes within the working class, which have intensified because of these defeats, do not alleviate the responsibility of the leadership to the slightest degree; nor do they in the least release us, the Oppositionists, from the necessity of actively counteracting the hostile tendencies, i.e., from the obligation to swim against the stream. However, these processes also explain the temporary, but still rather prolonged, "successes" of the right-centrist, nationally limited leadership and the very possibility of the "triumphant" organizational defeats of the Opposition. On the other hand, only a clear understanding of the objective processes on an international scale (and the consequences of defeats become in the consciousness of the workers an "objective" factor themselves)— only that understanding can provide the necessary orientation for victory over centrism and the most rapid possible means of overcoming the present deepgoing centrifugal tendencies in the working class of the USSR.

To be sure, matters can in no way be reduced solely to the effects of the defeats of the foreign proletariat, which, as has been said, are causally connected to our domestic leadership. Our Platform and a series of other documents of the Opposition have pictured domestic social and political shifts in the USSR as being at one and the same time both the causes and the results of the ruling policy. Related to this is the problem which for the sake of brevity I tentatively designated the political mobilization by the right-centrist "head" of a "tail" consisting of petty-bourgeois, bureaucratic, and newly propertied elements (especially in the struggle against the Opposition), which would inevitably have as a consequence that the bourgeois "tail" would strike increasingly heavy blows at the centrist apparatus, the "head." Connected with this, in particular, is the problem of Soviet bureaucratism. Here too V. Smirnov, just like Safarov or Slepkov, tries to discover on our part a wish to hide behind the "imagery" of head and tail, that is, of this condensed representation, a kind of mnemonic device, symbolizing the class relations which we have already analyzed. In this he discovers an attempt by us to retreat from class analysis. Doesn't this border on buffoonery? After all, has V. Smirnov himself added anything, however small, to the analysis made by the Opposition—other than his own increasing "abstraction from the international factor"?

An exceptionally interesting and significant letter from Comrade Rakovsky to Comrade Valentinov dated August 2, 1928, is devoted to the question of the special mechanics of degeneration and the methods of leadership under the dictatorship, i.e., to internal, "superstructural," but *directly decisive* factors. In a word, this letter maps out for investigation some topics of exceptional importance.

The point is, however, that the domestic processes in our country since the end of the civil war have been evolutionary in character. The accumulating changes have taken place more or less unnoticed. The upheavals in the world were, on the one hand, shocks that revealed or disclosed "all at once" the changes that had taken place, including ideological changes; on the other hand, those shocks greatly accelerated or decelerated the pace of change. In order to understand the dialectical interaction between "internal" and "external" factors, it is enough to imagine what impact a war would have on our internal relations, what political shifts it would disclose, and what realignments of forces it would produce.

The history of the Democratic Centralism group, which in its majority consists of staunch revolutionaries, has its own "dialectic." Separated from the Opposition and compelled to turn in upon itself ideologically, because of the inadequacy of its leadership forces, it began to turn its back on international questions. Some of its representatives directly accused us of "distracting" people's attention from domestic problems to Chinese questions.

So the theoreticians of the group, having fallen into introversion and sectarianism, are, as the German expression goes, trying to make a virtue of their own misfortune. Now V. Smirnov has gone so far as to refuse to understand *how and in what way* the defeats of the international proletariat can have an effect on our proletariat, i.e., he refuses to understand why major revolutionary, as well as counterrevolutionary, successes always produce powerful international ripples, why victory for a revolution in one country encourages revolutions in other countries and conversely. You can go no farther down the line of ultraleft nationalist narrow-mindedness. To top it all off, after backing himself into a corner, Smirnov has completely lost his spiritual equilibrium and seeks to find in a Marxist explanation of the processes at work in the proletariat a "justification" for centrism or the makings of a path to capitulation. This is already the purest Safarovism, though turned inside out. But we have already seen the outside and the inside of Safarov and found nothing of worth.

*    *    *

But let us return to more important questions.

As a result of four years of struggle we compelled the ECCI at the very last moment, right before the raising of the curtain, to hastily alter the draft program from one of a national type to one of an international type. At the congress Bukharin explained that the reason for this catastrophic (even if purely superficial) capitulation to the Opposition was the circumstance that, after all, for the first time delegates from Africa and South America had come to a Comintern congress and that this was no joke, and that accordingly the program had to be given African-American scope. It seems that Bukharin first learned from these newly arriving delegates that in the age of imperialism it is less permissible than ever to "abstract from the international factor." The world hegemony of the United States was also "noted," after a delay of several years, and mechanically included in the program. As with the history of all the domestic questions, this shows that the initiative for research on worldwide economic and political processes and on the interaction of these processes with the social and political shifts in the USSR continues to be the responsibility of the Opposition.

This means that we must get down to serious work. A proper division of labor should be carried out—in the sense of a detailed, concrete, day-to-day study of all the basic aspects of our domestic life, of the life of various capitalist countries, the colonial countries, their economics, politics, trade union movements, national struggles, militarism, etc. We must make proper use of our time to train skilled cadres for the AUCP and the Comintern. Accurate, well-organized correspondence with all the local areas, accurate reading of the newspapers, including provincial newspapers, with the aim of selecting materials on particular questions and from a particular point of view—all this will bear invaluable fruit. It will be necessary for comrades who have a predisposition for this or who have relevant facts to get to work on foreign languages. To be sure, this division of labor must have an *international* character. All "sentinels" should attentively follow unfolding processes and alert one another in good time.

Of course, even in exile this work must not have an archival or academic character, but must be intimately joined with the activity of the Communist parties and the struggle of the working masses. *On every major question a firm Bolshevik notch must be made in the consciousness of the vanguard workers.* Something has already been done in this regard, of course, on the questions of industrialization, the kulak and the grain collections, the bureaucratic regime, the events in Germany, Britain, China, etc. But life doesn't stand still. It is impossible to continue to live on interest from capital, as does the current leadership of the Comintern, which squanders the fixed capital of the Bolshevik Party. Intense, systematic, collective work is needed. Revolutionary tenacity must now manifest itself in such work, regardless of the unfavorable conditions. Without a correct orientation there can be no correct political line. Moreover, only a correct line will allow the Bolshevik-Leninists, on every major question that affects the masses, to make ever deeper notches in the consciousness of ever broader circles of advanced workers.

On the one hand, this work thus assumes the character of theoretical research in the very broadest sense of the word, i.e., within the reach, however limited, of the very youngest and least trained Oppositionist, and on the other hand, this work will acquire a propagandistic character, again in the very broadest sense of the concept, including militant agitation. At a certain stage theoretical research and propagandistic work must completely cross over into *politically effective,* i.e., mass work, or to put it differently, merge with the party and the working class. When and at what stage? Of course, this can't be predicted. In different countries at different stages. Our epoch is one of sharp turns. This applies to the workers' movement as a whole, and, consequently, to the Opposition—and to it especially. In order that we do not miss the moment when our ideas can be linked with a mass shift in the Comintern and the working class, it will be necessary to observe the basic rule of all politics, all the more of revolutionary politics: *our voice must be heard on every immediate or general historical question which affects the interests of the working class.*

In his concluding speech at the congress, Bukharin declared that the resolution on the Opposition signifies our "political death." These brave words are the product of cowardice, weakness, and a need for self-consolation. In politics no one ever took Bukharin seriously; he never took and never will take himself seriously; these "intimidating" words of his can be taken seriously least of all. It was not without reason that Zinoviev himself with great accuracy—he should be awarded this justice—called Bukharin a hysteric and stated that anything could be expected from him, up to and including the taking of monastic vows.

When Tseretelli was thundering at the Kronstadters in the early summer of 1917, I warned him that when some White general started soaping the rope intended for Tseretelli's own neck, it would be the Kronstadt sailors that he would call upon for help. As is known, during Kornilov's uprising this prediction came true with far greater accuracy than we could have supposed at the time.

The policies of the current leadership are leading to greater complications. The bourgeois Ustryalovist noose is being braided tirelessly for the neck of the proletarian dictatorship. When the matter becomes serious—and I fear that this will happen sooner than it seems—the best elements of the current apparatus will have to summon us to help. We forewarn them of this. There is no need to say that we will find our way even without their summons. All that is necessary is that the proletarian vanguard hear our voice day after day and know that in spite of the hysterical howling we are more alive than ever. It is also necessary at the same time not to allow ourselves to become isolated for even an hour from the centers of the workers' movement and to join in the life and struggle of the revolutionary vanguard. And for this we need to do continuous systematic work on ourselves and for others, on the basis of a correct division of labor and firm ideological cohesion.

Best regards,
L. Trotsky

# NO POLITICAL CONCESSIONS
# TO CONCILIATIONIST MOODS

## October 2, 1928

*NOTE: A letter to Boris Eltsin, one of the "intransigent" Oppositionists. This letter is especially interesting because of its analysis of the conciliationist moods that gripped sections of the Opposition.*

*On September 11, Nikolai Uglanov, a supporter of Rykov and Bukharin and head of the Moscow party organization, made a report on the economic situation to a meeting of the Moscow party committee. The report was carried belatedly in* Pravda *on September 21. He avoided the subject of the grain collections and did not refer to the campaign against the kulaks, but he did include an aggressive attack against the Opposition and derided its analysis of right and centrist tendencies in the party leadership. The committee adopted a resolution along these lines. For downplaying the campaign against the kulak, the committee was reprimanded in a lead article in* Pravda, *September 15. On September 25, Uglanov spoke to the Moscow party committee again, this time explicitly insisting that the cause of the economic trouble was the lagging of agriculture behind industry. But Uglanov and other Bukharin supporters were outmaneuvered by the Stalinists. On the very day that Trotsky wrote this letter, the Moscow party committee sent an open letter to party members repudiating its September resolution. This was the beginning of the open campaign against the right wing and its supporters.*

*In the meantime, since the end of summer, Trotsky's health had worsened and rumors began to reach him that he was to be moved again. Oppositionists from all over the USSR began sending telegrams to Moscow protesting the unhealthy climate he was forced to live in and the lack of adequate medical care. Some exiles planned a collective hunger strike in his defense. Trotsky insisted that these plans be called off lest such actions jeopardize*

*the Oppositionists involved in them. He also rejected the notion
that the authorities would move him again.*

*In October the postal blockade became stricter and Trotsky
began to be cut off from cothinkers and friends.*

*By permission of the Harvard College Library. Translated from
the Russian for this volume by George Saunders.*

Dear Comrade Eltsin:

I have not written you for a long time, and am to blame for
that. To tell the truth I thought Lyova was keeping you more or
less abreast of things. And apparently that was the case.

In your last letter you wrote mainly about Oppositionist
conciliators. You call for us to come out more decisively against
them. With your basic idea, that there cannot be any concessions
in this area, I am of course in full agreement. To the extent that
conciliationism has tried to find political expression for itself, in
the form of definite proposals, theses, etc., it has met with our
fairly unanimous rejection. As a result we straightened out our
front not at all badly vis-à-vis the Sixth Congress. Not counting
Serebryakov, who is sinking more and more into philistinism, all
the comrades signed our declaration to the congress. By this I in
no way mean to say that all the comrades are of the same mind.
Undoubtedly there are small shadings of difference, as well as
fairly substantial ones. We have seen that comrades afflicted
with conciliationism have begun to seek not only points of
agreement with the centrists (dreaming up such points where
they don't exist) but also points of difference with us, centering
fatally around those same old fateful themes: two parties and—
permanent revolution. It is absolutely clear that what we are
dealing with here is a mood, that is, something very resistant to
arguments. To decide in advance that these moods are unaltera-
bly bound to take political shape, and to draw the logical
conclusions, would now be premature to say the least. It would be
totally impermissible to push comrades in this direction when
they have been seized by intangible conciliationist moods or
otherwise thrown off their footing. We are passing through a
fairly steep dip in the historical process, and a wavering in the
moods of some comrades, however unpleasant that may be, is
inevitable. In some equilibrium will be restored, and in others it
will be lost completely. One thing is clear: there can be no
*political* concessions in this area.

You of course have read Uglanov's speech. It is the "juiciest" of
all the official speeches of the recent period. Especially good is

the part dealing with the "new question" of the Opposition. Other reports supplement this part of Uglanov's speech and provide evidence that the mole of history is tunneling away, in spite of all and sundry thundering articles. Q.E.D.

The comrades now are very preoccupied with the question of my transfer from Alma-Ata. I do not expect this. Where would they send me? Rakovsky, who was sent to Astrakhan by order of the Central Committee, is denied the right to go to Kislovodsk for a cure, which is absolutely necessary for him. Now after a number of telegrams and protests, the leaders consider it less possible than ever to make concessions. After all, the question of "prestige"—that fetish of the weak—has been squarely posed. I am feeling considerably better now and am again carrying a normal workload. How stable this improvement is, only autumn will show. At any rate I maintain the perspective of continued residence here. Comrades who have sent telegrams and protests should limit themselves to that. Further steps would not be advisable from a practical point of view. They would not achieve their aim and might needlessly complicate the situation for many of our friends. I insist on this very firmly.

Are you working systematically on anything? The congress distracted me a little from the plans I had made for research work. I hope to return to those this winter, if the course of events allows. I firmly shake your hand and wish you all the best.

# ANALOGIES WITH THERMIDOR

## October 20, 1928

*NOTE: A letter to Karl Radek. By the late summer it had become apparent that the rightward course taken at the July plenum (canceling the extraordinary measures, allowing the price of bread to rise) was at an end, and the "left turn" was about to resume. This gave encouragement to the conciliators among the Oppositionists, and Radek in particular began circulating apologies for the capitulators. At the same time, Radek wrote a long attack on permanent revolution, which he circulated to Oppositionists but avoided sending to Trotsky. Trotsky received a copy second-hand and sent this ironic reply, which is of interest in part because of the light it throws on Radek's evolution throughout this period and in part because of the information about the relations with Zinoviev as far back as August 1927, when the Opposition leaders were preparing what became the "Statement of the Thirteen" (see* Challenge *1926-27, p. 291).*

*By permission of the Harvard College Library. Translated from the Russian for this volume by George Saunders.*

Dear K. B.:

I received your essay on the "democratic revolution" from Moscow, in the same way that in general, since the very beginning of this exile, I have been one of the last to learn of your views, and have learned of them almost exclusively second-hand. Please don't take this to imply that I have any claims against you. For my part I will continue as I have thus far to include you among the first to receive everything I write.

On the present occasion I am sending you a copy of some writings of your own, which I accidentally came across among my papers. Despite the fact that one of these works is fourteen months old and the other nearly two years old, their timeliness is beyond question. The first work is the counterdraft you wrote of theses on the August [1927] plenum, in opposition to Zinoviev, who was guilty [in his theses] of idealizing the party apparatus and attempting to drag "anti-Trotskyism" in as ideological preparation for his [later] renegacy. Our group [i.e., the 1923 Oppositionists] was in agreement with your theses, which I personally considered superb (for that particular moment). We agreed, however, to sign Zinoviev's theses (with amendments), in order to put Zinoviev in the position of having to break over programmatic and tactical questions, that is, in the writing of the Platform, and not over the two hobby horses he was raising artificially—"two parties" and "Trotskyism."

Besides that, I am sending you as an appendix an excerpt from another work of yours, "The Thermidorian Danger and the Opposition." In view of the fact that you recently dredged up the question of the admissibility of analogies with Thermidor [in theses to the Sixth Congress], it is not unbeneficial to remind you of how you yourself replied to such doubts a year and a half or two years ago.

# THE DANGER OF BONAPARTISM AND THE OPPOSITION'S ROLE

## October 21, 1928

*NOTE: A circular letter. The plenum Trotsky refers to was not held until November. This is Trotsky's first comment on and analysis of the July 11 meeting Bukharin had held with Kamenev to plead for a rapprochement with the Opposition, against Stalin (see Appendix to this volume). According to Isaac Deutscher (in* Prophet Unarmed, *p. 441n), Kamenev met with some Moscow Trotskyists on September 22. It was probably then that he showed the Trotskyists his record of the July 11 conversation with Bukharin and urged Trotsky to make a statement offering reconciliation with Stalin on the basis of a struggle against the right. The Moscow Trotskyists probably sent the record of the Bukharin-Kamenev meeting and an account of their meeting with Kamenev to Trotsky, who received it some weeks later. This October 21 letter is Trotsky's first reference to Kamenev's meeting with the Moscow Trotskyists.*

*Mikhail Kalinin and Kliment Voroshilov ("Klim") were full members of the Politburo. Kalinin was known to be a Bukharinist; Voroshilov, commissar of war, was a supporter of Stalin, but the Bukharinists considered him a potential supporter because of unrest in the peasant army. Both, however, lined up firmly with Stalin at the July plenum.*

*As Bukharin became more isolated within the leadership, Molotov emerged as Stalin's major spokesman and "theoretician." Lev Mekhlis was one of Stalin's personal secretaries.*

*"Kolya Balabolkin" was a mocking name for Bukharin. Kolya is short for Nikolai. Balabolkin is a last name made up from the Russian word* balabolka *(a chatterbox; blabbermouth; one who talks excessively and foolishly). Trotsky seems to have begun using this name for Bukharin after reading the account of his July 11 conversation with Kamenev.*

*On September 30, 1928,* Pravda *carried a major article by*

*Bukharin, "Notes of an Economist," which was an attack on industrialization and the five-year plan and an assault on the Stalin group under the guise of "Trotskyist superindustrializers." This bold attack leads Trotsky to analyze the antagonism between right and center and its importance to the Opposition, and to explain the pressures that could force the centrists to make a bloc with the Left Opposition, contrasting his perspective to that of the conciliators. He also speculates on the strength of the right-wing forces and on the forms of Thermidor and Bonapartism. Semyon Budenny, a Stalinist, was a leading military figure. Andrei Bubnov, an Old Bolshevik and Central Committee member, had been head of the Political Directorate of the Red Army since 1924, when he had replaced the then-Oppositionist Antonov-Ovseenko.*

*Here Trotsky raises the demand for the secret ballot as something that the workers, intimidated by the arbitrary practices of the apparatus, would see as a means for fighting back.*

*From the* Militant, *February 1, 1929. Revised against the Russian original in the Library of Social History.*

Dear Comrades:

I am writing to you in advance of the October plenary session [of the Central Committee], or at least before the news of the session has reached Alma-Ata. I have nothing new to tell you. I merely wish to summarize what I have already said, and to give you the criteria by which to judge the impending session.

It is reported that Zinoviev said that Stalin had triumphed in July. From the political point of view that is absurd. Centrism weakened itself politically by its compromise. The right and left wings were simply given renewed impetus. But the development of the apparatus has its own logic, which so far has not coincided with the general shifts of power in the party and the working class, and is even contrary to it.

By surrendering his political position Stalin split the right wing. He "broke loose" from it (temporarily) Kalinin and Voroshilov, who are wholeheartedly for the new proprietors and for "order," but who, so far, have been afraid of being left face to face with Rykov, Bukharin, and Tomsky as "leaders."

The situation from the point of view of the apparatus is bad enough for the right. Stalin, having *retreated politically* and assured himself of his majority, attacks organizationally. It suffices to note that Molotov's candidacy for the post of actual chairman of the Comintern (in place of Bukharin) is already regarded as a serious question. Yes, yes, we once jokingly suggested that Stalin would put Mekhlis in as chairman of the Comintern. The reality is not far from the jest. Kaganovich is supposed to be replacing Uglanov, against whom charges are pending in the Central Control Commission (incitement of Communist League of Youth comrades against Stalin). But the real situation of the right appears in the fact that—according to a Moscow story—Bukharin secretly runs to Kamenev and promises to "swap Stalin and Molotov for Kamenev and Zinoviev." Kamenev of course would declare himself ready for this operation, but he understands that Bukharin's political promises are worth no more than his economic prognoses. If things were going well for him, this leader of the Comintern, the almighty Balabolkin, would not go running to the men who were expelled from the party only yesterday, while glancing nervously over his shoulder at his own shadow.

What is Stalin thinking? It is not difficult to guess. If I get out of these difficulties by means of centrist measures, then I will denounce the panicky right-wingers as capitulators, and drop them a peg or two lower in the organization. If, on the other hand, the situation gets worse, then I will steer to the right myself, that is, I will weaken the right faction by robbing it politically. I will declare that it has invented the disagreements, that it is trying to split the party, and thus lower it a peg. If these right measures do not work, I will make my right allies responsible for the failure, give them the boot, and again steer a course to the left by giving Kamenev and Zinoviev a little longer leash— since they are waiting docilely like whipped dogs, who "know better" than to dare to go along with Balabolkin. And so, we shall see . . . That is Stalin's scheme. Its strength lies in the apparatus. Its mortal weakness is that it does not take into account what the bosses do, i.e., the classes. But as long as the classes are silent, Stalin's scheme will work.

If the main outlines of Stalin's plan are already evident to us from afar, they are certainly clear to the right. That is why the rights have become so upset. They do not want to let themselves be eliminated bit by bit. But they are very afraid that if they come out into the open, Stalin will wipe them out at one blow.

Stalin's method was made even clearer to them during the [Comintern] congress. The number of hours Bukharin spoke at the congress was in inverse ratio to his influence, which fell from day to day. In the first place, the right policy of the USSR is distasteful to the foreign party bureaucrats in view of the radicalization of the masses and the pressure of the Opposition. In the second place, the apparatus is in the hands of Stalin, and in the Comintern the religion of the apparatus is no weaker than in the AUCP. During the congress the absent Stalin took three-fourths if not nine-tenths of the assembled apparatchiks away from Bukharin. It was not necessary for Stalin to be present. He had nothing to say. The bargaining was done for him by the impersonal mechanism of power.

It is evident that the rights, whether they wish to or not, are forced to jump into the cold water—that is, they must try to carry their fight against Stalin outside of the apparatus. This explains the publication of Bukharin's article "Notes of an Economist." That was the courage of despair. It is possible that Rykov and Tomsky sent Bukharin out as a scouting party. (The article is a product not only of theoretical weakness, but also of complete political impotence.) This move has done the right nothing but harm. A "real" right wing, determined to carry the struggle outside the boundaries of the bureaucratic hencoop, would have barked out: "New proprietors, unite; or the socialists will rob you!" Such appeals were made in the struggle against the Opposition, but even then they had a rather colorless and ambivalent ring to them. Nevertheless, in order to seriously oppose itself to the center, the right would have to start thundering at the top of its voice, like the Black Hundreds, like Thermidorians. But Bukharin still doesn't have the stomach for that. He has put his toe into the cold water, but he is afraid to plunge in. He stands there and trembles at his own bravery. Meanwhile, Rykov and Tomsky watch from a safe distance, to see what will happen, in order at the proper moment to dive into the bushes. This is the positioning of the most important actors on the bureaucratic stage.

One may say that all this is not very important. But that would be false. Naturally, if the classes should speak out loud, if the proletariat should pass over to a political attack, the positioning of these apparatus actors would lose nine-tenths of its meaning; in fact, they would drastically change their positions, moving in one direction or another. But we are passing through an as yet unfinished era in which the apparatus remains all-powerful, while elements of dual power continue to build up within our country. Stalin and Rykov and Bukharin are the government. And the government plays a role of no little importance. It is necessary to study the positioning of the bureaucratic players closely, but from the standpoint of class rather than from that of the apparatus.

*    *    *

How can the right danger "really" materialize? That is a question of great importance. The main thing is that the right wing has its chief support outside of the party. The right wing is more weakly represented in the apparatus than the center is, but in contrast to the centrists it has a solid class support in the country. Still, how can the strength of the right wing actually be put into effect? In other words, how can the new proprietors come to power?

At first glance, it seems reassuring that the political parties of the possessing class are shattered, that the new proprietors are politically atomized, that the right wing inside the party, fearing the proletarian core and still restrained by the past, cannot decide to rely openly upon the new proprietors. Naturally, these are all advantages that we inherit from the past, but they are by no means absolute guarantees. The conditions necessary for Thermidor to materialize can develop in a comparatively short time.

We have already more than once called attention to the fact that the victorious bourgeois counterrevolution must take the form of fascism or Bonapartism, but absolutely cannot take the form of bourgeois democracy, of which the soft-headed Mensheviks dream. Kamenev has never understood that to this day. In his recent conversation with our comrades, Kamenev described the situation in the country as if before long "Kerensky would be at the gates." Decidedly not. If one must mention Kerensky, then it would be better to say that right now, under the right-centrist regime, the country is passing through a "Kerensky period in reverse." The function of the historic Kerensky period consisted in this: that on its back the power of the bourgeoisie passed over to the proletariat. The historic role of the Stalin period consists in this: that on its back the power is sliding over from the proletariat to the bourgeoisie. In general the post-Lenin leadership is unwinding the October film in reverse. And Stalinism is Kerenskyism moving from left to right. In a country which has been shaken by the greatest of all revolutions, a bourgeois order could not possibly assume a democratic form. For victory, and for the maintenance of this victory, the bourgeoisie would need a supreme and purely military concentration of power, rising "above all classes," but having as its immediate point of support the kulak. That is Bonapartism. Thermidor is only a stage on the road to Bonapartism. The stage does not have to be realized completely. The counterrevolution, like the revolution, can "leap over" one or another step.

In a Thermidorian overturn, and still more in a completely Bonapartist one, the *army* would play a major role—in the second case, the decisive role. For this reason, we must follow with the greatest attention the processes that are taking place in the army. We must not forget that in the June report to the Moscow conference of party workers, the right "leader," referring to his friend Klim, said: "If you again resort to extraordinary measures, the army will answer with an insurrection." That is a very significant formulation—half *prophecy* and half *threat*. Indeed, it may be three-quarters threat. But who is making the threat? The new property-holders, through the commanding apparatus of the army. The army apparatus, through Klim. Here you have the prime candidate for the role of Bonaparte, if one can speak of him that way—Klim. It would be extremely naive to object that he would make far too drab a Bonaparte. There have been different Bonapartes. There was not only Napoleon I, but also Napoleon III, who was a very pitiable specimen. When the possessing classes find it necessary, they will—to use one of Stalin's expressions—"make a prince out of any old filth." Yes, events can develop in such a way that Klim (one of these Klims) may spring forth as a "prince." He would certainly be a third-rate type of Bonaparte. But that would not prevent him from destroying the revolution. True, they say that Klim has gone over from a right position to the right center, and is supporting the "Master." But such combinations at the top are formed and can be torn apart in twenty-four hours by an impetus from without. Moreover, it does not have to be Klim. If he won't do it, then Budenny. There will be no shortage of Bonapartes.

The Master says: "These cadres can be removed only by civil war." Klim adds: "If you workers make too much fuss, remember that a great power stands behind me." Both these statements are elements of Bonapartism. In the first case speaks the party-state apparatus, which considers itself higher than everyone else, higher even than the army. In the second case speaks the military apparatus, which tomorrow will feel compelled to "put the civilians in their place."

A bloodless victory of the centrists' party apparatus over the right would not do away with the Thermidorian-Bonapartist perspective, but would only change and postpone it. An independent victory of the centrists without the Opposition, without the masses, can succeed only through increased repression, through a further narrowing of the mass base of centrism, through a further fusion of the centrist faction with the apparatus of governmental repression, including ultimately the commanding apparatus of the army, in which party life died out long ago, since no one is permitted to hold other opinions there than those which Bubnov is ordered to propagate. As a result of such "fusion," will the Master himself eventually mount the white horse, or will he be found lying under Klim's horse? From the class standpoint that is quite an unimportant question.

We thus come to the conclusion that a "victory" of the right would lead directly along the Thermidorian-Bonapartist road, while a "victory" of the centrists would zigzag along the same road. Is there any real difference? *As a final historical consequence,* there is no difference. Centrism represents only a variety of conciliationism (in the given case, toward the new proprietors, toward bourgeois society, which is attempting to form itself anew). But this is only as a final historical consequence. At the present stage, however, centrism reflects on a much larger scale the broad strata of those who have "risen" from the working class. The right has its roots in the new property-owners, chiefly the peasant proprietors. It would be a very crude mistake, a Democratic Centralist type of blurring of political distinctions, to ignore the struggle between these two elements.

The centrists do not want to break openly with the workers. They fear this break much more than the right, which above all does not want to offend the property-owners. Just this relation between the upper layers of the working class and the new proprietors is the basis of the groupings in the apparatus, no matter how confusing the cross-currents in the party, no matter how great may become the "difficulties" between personalities (Stalin, Bukharin, Rykov, Tomsky). We must distinguish between the two groupings in order to follow the separate stages of the struggle, in order to understand the meaning of the struggle and its limitations. This struggle has of itself no great significance, but it breaks the bureaucratic fetters, brings the hidden to light, impels the masses to think, and widens the arena for their active intervention.

The July plenum was an important moment in the retreat of the centrists. But it would be stupid to think that this was the *last* stage in the struggle, that the centrists have *finally* capitulated, and that henceforward the right enjoys a position of "monopoly." No, under the pressure of contradictions, the struggle will inevitably break out again and play no small role in the history of the party and of the revolution.

But from this one can by no means infer that the centrists in their struggle with the right wish to rely upon the Opposition. Upon neither the defectors from the Opposition nor the Opposition itself. Never. The centrists fear the Opposition more than they fear the right. The centrists struggle with the right, but steal from its program (as Balabolkin complains in all directions, both left and right). To say that a bloc with one or another part of the present center would never be possible under any circumstances would be ridiculous doctrinairism. Many of the present centrists will still veer to the left. If anyone had told us in 1924 that we would form a bloc with the Zinoviev people, few would have believed it. But it happened that the struggle of the Leningrad centrists against the attack of the kulaks brought them to a bloc with us, and to the adoption of our Platform. Similar zigzags are not impossible with the ruling centrists of today, if class pressure compels them to break openly and definitely with the right, and if circumstances properly trim off their tail. Such historical possibilities are not to be excluded. They can become steps on the way to a further development and strengthening of the Bolshevik line, just as the bloc with the Zinoviev people did. But it would be losing one's head entirely to steer a course at present toward a bloc with the centrists as they now are, instead of systematically, uncompromisingly, implacably opposing to the centrists the proletarian core of the party. In the long run these two tendencies will obliterate the difference between the overwhelming majority of the Opposition and its small minority, which is given to dreaming how beautiful it would be if a nice bloc could be formed with the centrists who have rethought their positions, and that such a bloc would save us from the expense of difficulties, upheavals, and dangers in the development of the party and the state. But alas, the too rich experience of the past testifies that such a supposedly more economical course would prove to be the costliest one of all and that those who summon us to this course are themselves slipping into centrism.

The bureaucratic apparatus struggle of the centrists with the right can be employed as a starting point for a thoroughgoing party reform only if there is a decisive intervention by the masses. Only the Opposition can organize this intervention by the masses in a truly Bolshevik way, because the Opposition is politically independent of both the right and the centrists and owing to this independence is able to make use of every stage of the struggle between them.

*       *       *

A few words in this connection about the advice and counsel of our new friend Kamenev (in the above-mentioned conversation). Kamenev, you know, finds that "L. D. [Trotsky] should hand in a document in which he would say: Call us, we will work together. But L. D. is a stubborn man," etc., etc. Kamenev is really not so naively good-natured and of course does not himself believe what he says. He knows perfectly well that such a declaration would not alter the legal position of the Opposition, it would merely deal it a political blow which would lower it to the level of the Zinoviev people. The latter have won themselves a disgraceful half-amnesty which denies them any political life whatever. And this only thanks to their break with us. Kamenev understands this very well. His conversations and his flirting have only one goal—to frighten Stalin, who is already mistreating his future "allies" a little too contemptuously. Kamenev wants to raise his own price so that at a new opportunity he can betray us again, but under conditions that are more favorable for himself. In the end, however, only complete fools could yield to his blandishment. Among us there will be no two opinions on this. Especially noticeable is Kamenev's sorrow over my "frequent" and "harsh" attacks upon his capitulation. "People must work together." "We should not revive old quarrels." "It is too bad that a split has arisen." "Life has confirmed all the positions of the Opposition." Kamenev sings well—with coloratura. That he sings without fear of Yaroslavsky testifies to the weakening hold of the apparatus and to the growing opportunities for the Opposition. We put this in our books on the credit side. But only one inference can be made from it: *we must strike twice as hard, three times, ten times as hard, against the capitulators.*

*       *       *

The question of the intervention of the masses in the [intra-bureaucratic] conflict is above all a question of the mobilization of the working class around all questions of domestic and international life, beginning with the simplest and most pressing problems.

In a number of letters we have run across arguments to the

effect that the Opposition lacks a platform on the "labor question." What does this mean exactly? Is our Platform obsolete? The "labor" section of our Platform was drawn up with particular precision and concreteness. I'm afraid that its application is simply being forgotten. It seems as if many comrades have forgotten the Platform. They do not apply it, they do not seek counsel in it, and for that reason they are always demanding new documents. Continuity must be restored. Every speech by a Bolshevik-Leninist should be based on the Platform, with specific quotations being given whenever possible, if there are quotations applying to the question under discussion. Theses over no matter what question of the day, little or big, should begin with a quotation from the Platform. This document was built out of a vast collective experience, and all the formulations were carefully thought out and discussed. The application of the Platform to all questions will have a great influence in the direction of discipline, especially among the youth.

It stands to reason that there may be deficiencies in the Platform, obsolete assertions or erroneous details which need to be changed, corrected, or supplemented. But we must formulate these additions and corrections clearly and accurately on the basis of the Platform itself.

The question of how to apply the Platform at any given stage or to any particular question—for instance, the next round of collective-bargaining agreements—will always involve specific difficulties, which can be solved only with the participation of the comrades on the spot, in the factories and the various trades. Our most important guiding idea, the decisive criterion in this field, is *the increase of real wages.* As to the extent of this increase, negotiations must be carried on with the managers, with the soviet, party, and trade union institutions. A strike is, as the resolution of the Eleventh Party Congress declared, an extreme measure but absolutely not an illegal, antiparty, or antisoviet measure [see "The Role and Functions of the Trade Unions Under the New Economic Policy" in Lenin's *Collected Works,* vol. 33, pp. 187-88]. The participation of the Bolshevik-Leninists in a strike, even in the leadership of a strike, may prove to be the party duty of those Bolshevik-Leninists, when all other means for obtaining the legal, that is, the actually realizable, demands of the masses have been exhausted. The extent to which these demands are actually realizable can be determined, as we have said, by negotiations in which the workers' representatives listen to all the various explanations and actually examine the books.

Who shall conduct these negotiations? That depends on how dissatisfied the masses are and how vigorously they are pressing forward. In appropriate cases, the Bolshevik-Leninists will demand the election of special commissions and delegations to conduct negotiations with the regional trade union administration or the party province committee, and to visit the editorial offices of the papers and ultimately all the highest institutions, with written records being kept of the proceedings during all these visits and a full report being given to a general assembly of all the workers represented.

The mood of the workers is such as to require of us the greatest determination and activity. Only *we* can lead the suppressed dissatisfaction into the correct soviet and party channels. The present passivity of the masses, due to many causes, testifies in part to a wavering and indecisiveness of the masses themselves, since many of the old ways have disappointed them and new ones have not yet been found. This standing at the crossroads can naturally not last long. A new crystallization process is bound to begin among the masses and it may under certain conditions go forward with dizzying speed. And around what pole will this process take place—the bureaucratic? No, that is impossible. If we are not the pole around which this process turns, then it will be the Mensheviks, the Social Revolutionaries, the anarchists. And that would mean that the October Revolution would be derailed completely. Only the Bolshevik-Leninists can protect the revolution against this, by going boldly to the masses, knocking over, when necessary, the roadblocks the bureaucrats set up.

Going to the masses does not mean yielding to spontaneism, as the Democratic Centralists are inclined to do. They would either break their necks with an adventurist policy, which would be only half bad, or they would unwittingly help the enemy to break the neck of the revolution, which would be much worse. The policy of the last five years has created anew in the working masses an antisoviet mood, partly not yet formulated, partly already formulated—that is, directed toward private property. The activity of the masses must be so mobilized that a differentiation along the class line goes continually forward among them. To the antisoviet voices, especially to those which are articulate, conscious, and malicious, we must react much more alertly and decisively than the apparatus does. At every new outbreak of dissatisfaction we must first of all unmask the Mensheviks, the Social Revolutionaries, the anarchists, to the extent that they try to put their oar in. We can and must react to such attempts of the agents of the bourgeoisie with a direct appeal to the workers.

We need not doubt that with the growth of our activity and our influence upon the left wing of the working class, the attempts of elements alien to us, and even our class enemies, to align themselves with us and even clothe themselves in our colors, will grow more frequent. We must be on our guard, and denounce these elements publicly whenever possible. It is necessary that our flanks and rear be marked off by an absolutely clear line, so that the masses can know when they are encountering us and when they are encountering someone else.

This is especially so with regard to the Democratic Centralists. You will remember that even in our ranks there were individual comrades who looked upon the question of Democratic Centralism from a sentimental standpoint ("They are pretty good fellows, just the same"). Some of them did not want to see the distinctions in our political lines. It is worth remarking that precisely those comrades who yesterday were still proposing a complete union with the Democratic Centralists today stand upon the conciliatory wing, and rave and shout against "Democratic Centralism" in our own ranks, often understanding by Democratic Centralism the development of our principled line.

Although it is annoying to waste time upon secondary questions, we must nevertheless occupy ourselves a little with these Democratic Centralists, in order to be clear about the sectarian character of their policy and the adventurism lodged within it. Since the "leaders" of Democratic Centralism, whom we have until now left to themselves (and in that we have been right), have talked themselves out to the end, they have given us good weapons against themselves. We will take away the best elements from them with the help of their own documents, especially with the letters of V. Smirnov. We must not neglect even the smallest wound; otherwise poison threatens the whole organism. We will win the workers away from them with a courageous and determined policy in the weightiest questions, on the one hand, and with a campaign of clarification, on the other.

\*       \*       \*

All the material I have received testifies that the slogan of the secret ballot in the party and the trade unions can and must be raised. Self-criticism has evolved to the point of half-comedy and half-provocation. That is clear to everyone. In our "partial" slogans—our transitional slogans, so to speak—we must express the mood of the workers and their not yet very boldly articulated wish to get rid of pressure from above. . . . "Why didn't you vote against it?" . . . "If there had been a secret ballot, it would have been different." That is to be heard everywhere.

Whether it will come to the secret ballot or whether the intolerable contradictions will be solved in some shorter way, "leaping over" certain stages, is a separate question. But for the moment, the slogan of the secret ballot is a vital question in the party and the trade unions, since it expresses the fact of bureaucratic pressure, that is, class pressures upon the workers through the apparatus. The slogan of the secret ballot is the best expression for the struggle now beginning against dual power at the present stage. The open ballot was introduced in its time so that the enemy could not vote against the proletarian dictatorship. The element of dual power in the country has created conditions in which the workers cannot vote for the dictatorship, through fear of pressure from the bourgeoisie reflected through the apparatus. That is the heart of the matter. The apparatchik stands at the rostrum and watches the hands of the voters, or the worker's wife pulls him by the sleeve: "Better not vote." In these circumstances, to say that the secret ballot supports passivity and indecisiveness is a surrender to idealistic doctrinairism. Whoever poses the question in that way puts the slogan of the secret ballot not in relation to the existing situation, from which we must still find a way out, but in relation to an idealized situation where all workers vote courageously and firmly according to their convictions.

If one develops this position to its logical conclusion, one must abolish the slogan of the secret ballot even in a capitalist society, in order better to develop "activity" and "courage." In China one could of course summon the brave-hearted workers to open voting, but the next morning they would lose their heads for it. Therefore in China the slogan of secret ballot (in all elections) can have an extraordinary significance, since this slogan is dictated by the relation of class forces. Although the social regime in our country has a different *foundation,* nevertheless this foundation is already in great part overgrown with weeds. It is not true that the character of our elections and voting is determined today *only* by the amount of courage and decisiveness of the workers. No, it is already to a great degree determined by the *changed relations of class forces.* This change finds its objective expression in the governmental apparatus, in its whole mechanism. Stalin has truly said: "These cadres can be removed only by civil war."

Naturally there is in these words also a certain bureaucratic boasting and intimidation. In the face of a real upsurge from below the apparatchik will duck; he will not let it come to a civil war. In any case this course—the course of a reform through powerful pressure of the masses—must be tried out to the end. At the present stage the slogan of the secret ballot drives the masses forward toward activity and away from passivity. At any and every meeting where there is talk of self-criticism, of party democracy, and so forth, the Bolshevik-Leninists must and can say: "In order to have self-criticism you must remove the pressure, make it possible for us to vote according to our convictions, without fear of loss of employment—that is, secretly. Then all the apparatchiks will be held in check."

We must begin with the party, then go on to the unions. As to the soviets, where different classes take part in the voting, the question must be left to wait until we have gathered the necessary experience.

\*       \*       \*

As regards the general perspectives of the struggle, both domestic and international, I must limit myself here to general remarks, reserving the right to come back to these questions in the near future, in order to treat them more concretely, and also with reference to the more important individual countries, as I have already done in part with reference to China ["The Chinese Question After the Sixth Congress," in *Leon Trotsky on China*, p. 345]. A considerable part of the documents we sent to the congress was devoted to an explanation of the relation of our domestic struggle to the international struggle. The theoreticians of Democratic Centralism do not understand this relation—they have in general no line on international questions. They make accidental, purely adventurist blocs with people who have broken altogether with Marxism, people like Korsch and Company. In his latest pronouncements, V. Smirnov is merely a left caricature of Stalin.

Europe is now passing through a phase of a rather lively strike movement. This wave is to a certain extent economically "belated," since it coincides with an obvious decline in economic prosperity. The belatedness of the strike wave was caused by the previous heavy defeats, the growing influence of the Social

Democracy, and the bureaucratic passivity in the policy of the Comintern. A further economic decline is sure to bring the economic struggle into the political field and thereby favor the leftward movement of the workers. It will have a different tempo in different countries. But an extraordinary sharpening of the political situation in certain European countries is not impossible even in the near future. This depends to a large degree upon the depth, the duration, and the extent of the coming crisis, not only in Europe but also in the United States. America will overcome its crisis at Europe's expense, and can, with its pressure on individual countries, Germany in the first place, bring them to immediately revolutionary situations. Here again is revealed the fundamental, long-term contradiction, that between the tasks of the epoch and the maturity of the Communist Party. The danger of missing new revolutionary situations has absolutely not been eliminated or even diminished. The adventure with Thälmann is of course no accident. The present regime is a hothouse for Smolensk cases on an international scale. And these gentry, the people of Smolensk and Hamburg, condemn us and expel us. Their work consists of befouling the banner of communism and destroying the Comintern. The more they do this, the more they demonstrate the gigantic mission of the Opposition on an international scale. We must bend all our energies to form genuine Bolshevik cadres through experience in the struggle with bureaucratism, to develop them and bring them to maturity. That will be the chief difference between the third five years of the Comintern and the second. Five years were necessary in order to bring the weightiest questions and differences out of the bureaucratic underworld onto the world arena. That point has now been reached. No power can cancel out the positions and counterpositions that have now been presented. The revolutionary cadres of the foreign parties can grow only through their own experience. We will not make any attempt to run the International Opposition by command in the manner of the Executive Committee of the Comintern. A broadly extended and systematic exchange of theoretical and political experiences, a collaboration in the sphere of Marxist analysis of ongoing processes, and a working out of slogans for action—that is the place to start. The first serious steps have already been taken, in connection with the Sixth Congress. We must develop these steps, broaden them, and deepen them.

The outcome of our domestic struggle is inseparably bound up with these worldwide processes. Only a fool could draw from that the conclusion that, this being the case, the existing domestic policy and in particular the domestic policy of the Opposition are a matter of indifference for the fate of the October Revolution. We do not promise the building of socialism in one country; that is known. We have never said and do not say that we possess a wonder-working formula which will remove the contradictions of socialist development under capitalist encirclement. What we have to offer is a correct orientation, a correct prognosis, and the correct class line deriving from it. The axis of our domestic policy is the maintenance of power in the hands of the proletariat—or more accurately, the return to the proletariat of this power, which has been usurped by the apparatus, and a further reinforcement of the dictatorship of the proletariat upon the basis of a systematic improvement of the daily material living conditions of the working class. There are no other formulas and none are needed.

The Opposition has a correct line. The task is to make this the line of the proletarian vanguard. To this end we must be wholly imbued with a consciousness of the great historic mission which is ours, and we must act with genuine Bolshevik courage.

# HOW TO CRITICIZE THE CENTRISTS

## October 22, 1928

*NOTE: A letter to Oppositionists exiled in Cheboksary, the capital of the Chuvash republic, on the Volga river eighty miles west of Kazan. This letter provides something of a refinement on Trotsky's description of the left turn and its implications for Opposition policy.*

*Trotsky was working on a polemic against Stalin, Bukharin, and Zinoviev on permanent revolution and other questions of Marxist theory, when he received, at about the time of this letter, Radek's lengthy memorandum ("on the democratic revolution") criticizing Trotsky's concept of permanent revolution and expressing apprehension that the Opposition would lose its influence if it remained isolated from the party.*

*Trotsky set aside his contemplated work "against the official ideology of the era of reaction" to answer Radek, according to the introductory section of Trotsky's* Permanent Revolution *(dated "October 1928"). Apparently he adapted substantial parts of his draft for use in* Permanent Revolution.

*By permission of the Harvard College Library. Translated from the Russian for this volume by George Saunders.*

Dear Cheboksary Comrades:

I am replying to your letter of September 22 with some delay because I have been very busy during the last few weeks. I will answer point by point.

1. My health in the recent period has become considerably better—after prolonged use of quinine. I am again working without interruptions. I am getting ready for a big hunting trip. Whether the malaria will return this fall, the future will tell.

2. I am very pleased by your comments on the "Criticism of the Draft Program." Unfortunately the work had to be written extremely rapidly. After it was sent off, I found quite a few deficiencies in it, and since then I have found here in my files

quite a few transcriptions, quotations, and documents, which could be used to good advantage to supplement and make more precise what was said in the critique. Well, but what can you do?—we'll say it another time.

3. I hope that "The Chinese Question After the Sixth Congress" reaches you [see *Leon Trotsky on China,* pp. 345-401]. This work is devoted to the immediate perspectives and tasks in China and, in particular, presents the arguments for the Constituent Assembly slogan.

4. You raise the question of "permanent revolution," so to speak from a retrospective standpoint, i.e., looking back on the past. Yes, the question has been posed and it must be answered. I have a rough draft on this question, aimed against Stalin and Bukharin, who have never understood Lenin's approach to the question, or mine, and who counterpose the two approaches precisely in the fundamental area that brings them closest together. When I free myself of the most urgent tasks, I will take up "permanent revolution," that is, finish that old draft. No less than two or three weeks will be needed for that, however, because it is a vast subject.

5. You give me a pretty good "working over" for the ways I have defined the "left course." You quite skillfully pick apart, I must confess, all the imperfections of my terminology in regard to the centrist zigzag. In one case I speak of a "turn," in another, a "shift"; in one place of a turn "being carried out," and in another, of one that "has been carried out"; and so on. All that is true, but here you tend, ever so slightly, to substitute grammar for politics. No science has yet worked out a precise terminology for such centrist zigzags. A turn (of course, a turn to a *certain* degree) was carried out in February; that is, a change of direction occurred in the line. But this left turn is still "being carried out," since it is being extended to other areas and to other parties (e.g., the Czechoslovak party). When you are dealing with an unfinished process, and an internally contradictory one at that, you may fall into schematism if you chase after precise and finished terminology and put periods where they should not be.

Thus, your letter could be understood to mean that the struggle of the rights against the centrists is over and that July drew the final balance sheet. Comrade Nevelson's letter grants the possibility that at a certain new stage the centrists could come close to us (of course, only under the influence of major objective causes: contradictions, mass pressure, etc.). I discuss this topic in more detail, however, in the letter to a number of comrades enclosed with this [see "The Danger of Bonapartism and the Opposition's Role"] and therefore I won't repeat.

6. Comrade Nevelson, in his letter about the direction of our fire, comes to the absolutely indisputable conclusion that the main fire must be directed against centrism as the camouflage and source of support for the rights within the party. Unfortunately, Comrade Nevelson did not notice that *that is what we have been doing all along.* Against whom did we aim our fire in all our articles and speeches, in the Platform, etc.? Against Stalin. And against Bukharin, to the extent that the latter identified himself with Stalin. In our Platform a few dozen lines were devoted to the rights. We simply indicated their presence. For the workers no more than that was needed. In their naked, openly revealed form, the rights do not draw the workers behind them. All the fire of our criticism, all along, has been concentrated almost exclusively on the centrists.

But there is another and no less important aspect of the matter that cannot be left out of sight. The centrists rest, through the party apparatus, upon the undifferentiated mass of party members, including the worker members. The rights rest, through the Soviet [i.e., government] apparatus, on the new property-owners. Thus far the center and the right have spoken and acted "monolithically." Stalin uses all the power of the propertied elements against us, and against Rykov he uses the support of the workers. A break between the center and the rights would mean a class fissure, with the propertied elements dragging Rykov much farther to the right, and the workers dragging Stalin much farther to the left. In the long term, there could be a civil war between us and the army of the rights, and a common front between us and the army of the centrists. I deliberately speak of armies, i.e., of classes, and not of the little groupings at the top. It would be sheer suicide to soften our criticism of centrism with the aim of drawing closer to the masses who today are following the centrists. However, it is entirely correct and politically expedient in appealing to these masses to say: "You fear a split? You fear upheavals? Then let us try to make the turn that is being or has been carried out by your leadership—which you have confidence in but we do not, not in the slightest—let us try to make this turn (whether completed or in process) into a starting point for a genuine left course. We are ready to assist you in every way along this path. To start with, let us present the leadership with such and such modest demands (return of the Oppositionists to the party, honest preparation for a new party congress, a reduction in the party budget, etc.) and in that way let us test the political line and the just plain honesty of the leadership." Such an approach to the audience is absolutely correct. All Oppositionists in a cell or at a workers' meeting would take exactly this approach if they are Bolshevik-Leninists and not frenzied Democratic Centralists who have turned their backs on the party, having decided that "the party is a corpse" (V. Smirnov). To the extent that such a tone in my approach to the audience troubles you, to that extent, it seems to me, you are not right. There are no concessions of principle in this approach. For it is not excluded that the left zigzag can be transformed into a left course (it was not excluded yesterday and it can prove not to be excluded tomorrow)—on one very small condition: the growing activity of the masses and the growing influence of the Opposition on those masses.

I will end with that. I am afraid that I have written too much and in some places have overstated the case in regard to both the past and the present. However, please don't take it to heart. I can only be gladdened by such attentive and meticulous reading by you of all our documents. Meticulousness is a good old Marxist tradition.

I firmly shake your hands and wish you all the best.

# AN ULTRALEFT CARICATURE
# OF STALIN

## October 22, 1928

*NOTE: A short letter on the relations between the Democratic
Centralists and the conciliationist current in the Opposition. The
"otzovists" (recallists) were a dissident group of Bolsheviks after
the 1905 revolution who advocated the recall, or withdrawal, of
the Social Democratic deputies elected to the Duma (parliament)
on the grounds of the Duma's extremely reactionary character;
they favored doing underground work only. Trotsky uses the term
broadly to refer to the sectarian abstentionists of 1928.*

*By permission of the Harvard College Library. Translated from
the Russian for this volume by George Saunders.*

Dear Comrade Teplov:

I was very glad to receive direct news of you at last. I confess
that in one of my letters I came down rather hard on you in
connection with your assessment of the left course. I had received
from V. D. [Kasparova] an extensive excerpt from your letter.
Now the question has been made superfluous, as I see from your
letter of September 28, and so there is no reason to return to it.
That the Stalin zigzag introduced more than a few fissures into
the unthinking mass of party members, which constitutes the
basis of the centrist line and the bureaucratic regime—of that
there can of course be no doubt. As for how long it will take for
the hidden processes to come to the surface, it is not easy to
guess.

You hope that the changes in the working class section of the
party will become evident in the next four or five months. That is
not excluded—on one condition: that the vacuum that will be left
behind in the mass consciousness by retreating centrism will be
filled up in time by the Leninist line. The activity and independence of the Opposition are the most important conditions for any
political progress. That is why I responded with such alarm to the

statements of some comrades, yours included, when elements of a new line within the Opposition began to be projected.

Your short, second letter of October 7 was devoted to the Democratic Centralists. They have come onto the agenda now in all the exile colonies. There is word to the same effect from Moscow, referring to Kharkov and other places. Even before receipt of your letter, with the copy of V. Smirnov's letter, I had commented in several letters on the latest discoveries of this man, who is a fine revolutionary but who has never, not on one single question, taken an independently correct position, who moreover, at the present time, seems to have set himself the conscious task of doing an ultraleft caricature of Stalin. If there are Democratic Centralist moods in our ranks, that should become evident now in an absolutely clear and distinct form. None of us will show any indulgence to such tendencies. In each individual case all we have to do is determine whether some temporary psychological excess is involved, especially as a result of the struggle against conciliationist tendencies, or whether we are dealing with true ultraleftism, with all its sins: ignoring the party and its internal processes; smug, self-satisfied sectarianism; "otzovism"; and adventurism. In the first case we have to explain in a comradely way; in the second, we have to draw a line of demarcation.

It would not be superfluous, however, to recall that precisely the most prominent representatives of conciliationist or semiconciliationist moods in relation to centrism, until the most recent period, as late as January of this year, were emphatic opponents of our making a clear demarcation between ourselves and the Democratic Centralists. They favored not only joint work with the Democratic Centralists but even total merger. And if we reflect on this well, it is not hard to understand that the 180-degree turn from fusion with Democratic Centralism to semi-conciliationism toward centrism is not at all accidental.

I'll stop with that for now. Enclosed is a letter of a general character, written in reply to several comrades on the "current" moment, so to speak [probably the letter of October 21].

I feel considerably better. The last three weeks I've been working without "interruptions." Getting ready for a big hunt. I would like to hope that autumn—my accursed enemy—would have mercy on me this time. Warm regards to all the comrades at Ishim.

# OUR DIFFERENCES WITH
# THE DEMOCRATIC CENTRALISTS

## November 11, 1928

*NOTE: A letter to Borodai in Tyumen. Borodai was a member of the Democratic Centralist group, also known as the Group of Fifteen. Timofei Sapronov was a Democratic Centralist leader. Aleksandr Shlyapnikov was a leader of the Workers' Opposition, a syndicalist tendency in the AUCP that had opposed the New Economic Policy.*

*From* New International, *April 1943, in a translation by Max Shachtman from the French Opposition journal* Contre le courant, *May 6, 1929. Revised against the Russian original in the Library of Social History.*

Dear Comrade Borodai:

I have just received, after almost a month's delay, your letter of October 12 from Tyumen. I am replying immediately by return mail, in view of the importance of the questions you raise. Taking your point of departure from the standpoint of the Democratic Centralist group to which you belong, you put seven questions and demand that the answers be "clear and concrete" and "not nebulous." An altogether legitimate wish. Only, our way of being concrete should be dialectical, that is, encompass the living dynamics of evolution, and not substitute ready-made labels which at first sight seem very "clear" but are in reality false and devoid of content. Your way of putting the questions is purely formal: "Yea is yea, and nay is nay, and all else is from the devil!" Your questions must first be put upon a Marxian basis so that correct replies may be made.

1. After setting forth the character of the social composition of the party and its apparatus, you ask: "Has the party degenerated? That is the first question." You demand a "clear" and "concrete" reply: Yes, it has degenerated. However, I cannot answer that way, for at present our party, both socially and

ideologically, is extremely heterogeneous. It includes elements that are entirely degenerated, others that are still healthy but amorphous, others that have hardly been affected by degeneration, etc. The regime of apparatus oppression, which reflects the pressure of other classes upon the proletariat, and the decline of the activism of the proletariat itself, renders very difficult a daily check upon the degree of degeneration of the various strata and nuclei of the party and of its apparatus. But this check can and will be achieved *in action,* especially by our active intervention in the internal life of the party, by tirelessly mobilizing its living and viable elements.

Naturally, such intervention is out of the question if the point of departure is that the party as a whole has degenerated, that the party is a corpse. With such an evaluation of the party, it is absurd to address oneself to it, and still more absurd to wait for it, or for this or that section of it, that is, primarily, for its proletarian core, to heed or to understand you. To conquer this core, however, is to conquer the party. This core does not consider itself—and quite rightly—either dead or degenerated. It is upon it, upon its tomorrow, that we base our political line. We will *patiently explain* our aims to it, basing ourselves upon experience and facts. In every cell and at every workers' meeting, we will denounce as a falsehood the slander of the apparatus which says that we engage in plots or are trying to create a second party; we will state that a second party is being built up by the Ustryalov people in the apparatus, hiding behind the centrists; as for us, we want to cleanse Lenin's party of the Ustryalovist and semi-Ustryalovist elements; we want to do this hand in hand with the proletarian core, which, aided by the active elements of the proletariat as a whole, can still become master of the party and save the revolution from death, by means of *a profound proletarian reform in every field.*

2. "Is the degeneration of the apparatus and of the Soviet state a fact? That is the second question," you write.

Everything that has been said above applies equally to this question. There is no doubt that the degeneration of the Soviet apparatus is considerably more advanced than the same process in the party apparatus. Nevertheless, it is the party that decides. At present, this means the party apparatus. The question thus comes down to the same thing: Is the proletarian core of the party, assisted by the working class, capable of triumphing over the autocracy of the party apparatus, which is fusing with the state apparatus? Whoever replies in advance that it is *incapable* thereby speaks not only of the necessity of a new party on a new foundation but also of the necessity of a second and new proletarian revolution. It goes without saying that it can in no way be stated that such a perspective is out of the question under all circumstances. However, it is not a question of historical divination but rather of not surrendering to the enemy and instead reviving and consolidating the October Revolution and the dictatorship of the proletariat. Has this road been tried to the very end? Not at all. At bottom, the methodical work of the Bolshevik-Leninists to mobilize the proletarian core of the party in the new historical stage has only begun.

The arid reply—"Yes, it has degenerated"—that you would like to get to your question about the degeneration of the Soviet state would contain no clarity in itself and would open up no perspective. What we have here is a developing, contradictory process, which has yet to be resolved in one direction or the other through the struggle of living forces. Our participation in this struggle will have no small importance in determining its outcome.

3. "Taking the present situation in the country and the party as a whole, do we still have a dictatorship of the working class? And who possesses the hegemony in the party and in the country? That is the third question," you ask further.

From the preceding replies it is clear that you put this question also inexactly, not dialectically but scholastically. It is precisely Bukharin who presented this question to us dozens of times in the form of a scholastic alternative: *Either* we have Thermidor and then you, the Opposition, should be defeatists and not partisans of defense, *or,* if you are really partisans of defense, then acknowledge that all the speeches about Thermidor are nothing but chatter. Here, comrade, you fall completely into the trap of Bukharinist scholastics. Along with him, you want to have "clear," that is, completely finished, social facts. The developing, contradictory process appears "nebulous" to you. What do we have in reality? We have a strongly advanced process of *dual power* in the country. Has power passed into the hands of the bourgeoisie? Obviously not. Has power slipped out of the hands of the proletariat? To a certain degree, to a considerable degree, but still far from decisively. This is what explains the monstrous predominance of the bureaucratic apparatus oscillating between the classes. But this state apparatus depends, through the medium of the party apparatus, upon the party, that is, upon its proletarian core, *on condition that the latter is active and has a correct orientation and leadership.* And that is where our task lies.

A condition of dual power is unstable, by its very essence. Sooner or later, it must go one way or the other. But as the situation is now, the bourgeoisie could seize power only by *the road of counterrevolutionary upheaval.* As for the proletariat, it can regain full power, overhaul the bureaucracy, and put it under its control by *the road of reform of the party and the soviets.* These are the fundamental characteristics of the situation.

Your Kharkov colleagues, from what I am informed, have addressed themselves to the workers with an appeal based upon the false idea that the October Revolution and the dictatorship of the proletariat are already liquidated. This manifesto, false in essence, has done the greatest harm to the Opposition. Such declarations must be resolutely and implacably condemned. That is the bravado of adventurers and not the revolutionary spirit of Marxists.

4. Quoting from my postscript on the July victory of the right wing over the center, you ask: "Are you thus putting entirely within quotation marks the 'left course' and the 'shift' that you once proposed to support with all forces and all means? That is the fourth question."

This is downright untruth on your part. Never and nowhere have I spoken of a *left course.* I spoke of a "shift" and a "left zigzag," contrasting this conception to a genuine left course, that is, a consistent proletarian line. Never and nowhere have I proposed to support the alleged left course of the centrists, nor did I promise to support it. But I did propose and promise to support by all means every step that centrism really took toward the left, no matter if it was a half-measure, without ceasing for a single instant to criticize and unmask centrism as the fundamental obstacle in the way of awakening the activism of the proletarian core of the party. My "postscript" was precisely a document exposing the political capitulation of the centrists to the right wing during the July plenum. But I did not and I do not hold that the history of the development of the party and particularly the history of the struggle of the center against the right wing came to an end at the July plenum. We are right now witnesses of a new centrist campaign against the right-wingers. We must become independent participants in this campaign. Naturally we see right through all the hypocrisy and duplicity, the perfidious halfwayness of the apparatus in the Stalinist struggle against the right-wingers. But behind this struggle we see profound class forces which seek to break a path for themselves through the party and its apparatus. The driving force of the right wing is the new evolving proprietor who seeks a link with world capitalism; our right-wingers are timid and mark time, for they do not yet dare to straddle this war-horse openly. The functionary of the party, the trade unions, and other institutions, is the rampart of the centrists: in spite of everything, he depends upon the working masses and seems to be obliged in recent times to take these masses into account more and more: hence the "self-criticism" and "the struggle against the right." It is thus that the class struggle is refracted and distorted, but nevertheless manifested in this struggle; by its pressure, it can transform the quarrel between the centrists and the right-wingers in the apparatus into a very important stage in the awakening and enlivening of the party and the working class.

We would be imbeciles if we took the present campaign against the right-wingers seriously. But we would, on the other hand, be pitiful scholastics and sectarian wiseacres if we failed to understand that hundreds of thousands of workers, party members, do believe in it, if not 100 percent then at least 50 or 25 percent. They are not yet with us, to be sure. Do not forget that; do not become ensnared in sectarian trivia. Centrism holds on not only because of oppression by the apparatus, but also because of the confidence or the half-confidence of a certain part of the worker–party members. These workers who support the centrists will enter the struggle against the right much more readily than they did the struggle against the Opposition, when they had to be dragged along with a rope around their neck. A serious and intelligent Oppositionist will say, in any workers' cell, in any workers' meeting: "We are summoned to fight against the right wing— that's a wonderful thing. We have called on you to do this for a long time. And if you're thinking of fighting seriously against the right wing, you can count on us to the limit. We will not be strikebreakers. On the contrary, we'll be in the front lines. Only, let us really fight. Down with the masks! The leaders of the right wing must be named out loud, their right-wing deeds must be enumerated," etc. In a word, the Oppositionist will push the proletarian core of the party forward like a Bolshevik, and he will not turn his back upon it on the pretext that the party has degenerated.

5. "Is it still possible to entertain illusions about the Stalinists'

ability to defend the interests of the revolution and of the working class? That is the fifth question."

You put the fifth question just as inexactly as the first four. To entertain illusions about the centrists means to sink into centrism yourself. But to shut your eyes to the mass processes that drive the centrists to the left means to enclose yourself within a sectarian shell. As if it was a matter of whether Stalin and Molotov are capable of returning to the road of proletarian policy! In any case, they are incapable of doing it by themselves. They have proved it completely. But it is not a question of divining the future fate of the various members of the Stalinist staff. In this field, all sorts of "surprises" are possible. Didn't the former leader of the Democratic Centralists, Osinsky, become an extreme right-winger, for example? That doesn't interest us at all. The correct question is this: Are the tens and hundreds of thousands of workers, party members, and members of the Communist League of Youth, who are at present actively, half-actively, or passively supporting the Stalinists, capable of correcting themselves, of reawakening, of welding their ranks together "to defend the interests of the revolution and of the working class"? To this, I answer: Yes, this they are capable of doing. And they will still be capable of doing this tomorrow or the day after if we know how to approach them correctly; if we show them that we do not look upon them as corpses; if, like Bolsheviks, we support every step, every half-step, they take toward us; if, in addition, we not only do not entertain "illusions" about the centrist leadership but expose them implacably, by dint of the daily experience of the struggle. At the moment, it must be done by the experience of the struggle against the right wing.

6. After characterizing the Sixth Congress and describing certain phenomena inside the party, you write: "Is not all this Thermidor with a dry guillotine? That is the sixth question."

This question has been answered concretely enough above. Once more, do not believe that Bukharinist scholasticism turned upside down is Marxism.

7. "Do you personally," you ask me, "intend to continue in the future to call the comrades belonging to the Group of Fifteen by the splendid epithet of 'honest revolutionists,' and at the same time to separate yourself from them? Is it not time to terminate the petty quarrel? Is it not time to think about consolidating the forces of the Bolshevik guard? That is the seventh and last question."

Unfortunately, this question is not put quite correctly either. It is not I who separated myself from the Democratic Centralists, but this grouping that separated itself from the Opposition as a whole, to which it belonged. It is on this ground that a subsequent split took place in the Democratic Centralist group itself. That is the past. Let us take the very latest phase, when the most serious exchange of opinions took place among the exiled Opposition, resulting in the elaboration of a whole series of responsible documents that received the support of 99 percent of the Opposition. Here, too, the representatives of the Democratic Centralists, without contributing anything essential to this work, once more separated themselves from us, by showing themselves to be more papist than the Pope, that is, than Safarov. After all this, you ask me if I intend to continue in the future to "separate" myself from the Democratic Centralists! No, you approach this question from the wrong end. You represent things as if, in the past, the Zinovievs, the Kamenevs, and the Pyatakovs prevented unification. You are mistaken on this score, too. One might conclude from your remarks that *we,* the 1923 Opposition, were for the unification with the Zinovievists, and the Democratic Centralist group was against. On the contrary. We were much more cautious on this question and we were much more insistent in the matter of guarantees. The initiative for the unification came from the Democratic Centralists.

The first conferences with the Zinovievists took place under the chairmanship of Comrade Sapronov. I do not say this as a reproach at all, for the bloc was necessary and a step forward. But "our yesterdays must not be distorted." After the Democratic Centralist group separated itself from the Opposition, Zinoviev was always for a new unification with it; he raised the question dozens of times. As for myself, I spoke against it. What were my reasons? I said: We need unification, but a lasting and serious unification. If, however, the Democratic Centralist group split away from us at the first dip in the road, we ought not rush into new corridor fusions, but leave it to experience to check the policies and either deepen the split or prepare the conditions for a genuine, serious, durable unification.

I contend that the experience of 1927-28 would certainly show how absurd were the suspicions and insinuations of the Democratic Centralist leaders toward the 1923 Opposition. I counted above all on the principled documents we addressed to the Sixth Congress to facilitate the unification of our ranks. That is what did happen in the case of a number of comrades of the Democratic Centralists. But the recognized leaders of your group did everything in their power not only to deepen and sharpen the differences of opinion but also to poison relations completely. For my own part, I take the writings of V. Smirnov calmly enough. But in recent times I have received dozens of letters from comrades who are indignant to the highest degree over the character of these writings, which sound as if they were specially calculated to prevent a rapprochement and to maintain at all costs a separate chapel and his own status as pastor.

But apart from the whole past history of who separated from whom, of how it was done, of who honestly wants unity in our ranks and who seeks to keep a parish of his own, there still remains the whole question of the *basis in ideas* of this unification.

On this score, Comrade Rafail wrote to me on September 28:

"Our friends of the Group of Fifteen have begun to conduct a furious campaign especially against you, and there is a touching harmony between the editorial in *Bolshevik,* no. 16, and Vladimir Mikhailovich Smirnov and other comrades of the Group of Fifteen. The fundamental error of these comrades is the fact that they attribute too great a value to purely formal decisions and combinations in the upper spheres, particularly to the decisions of the July plenum. They do not see the forest for the trees. Naturally, these decisions are, during a certain phase of development, the reflection of a certain relationship of forces. But in any case, they cannot be looked upon as determining the outcome of the struggle, which continues and will continue for a long time. Not a single one of the problems that provoked the crisis has been resolved; the contradictions have worsened. Even the official editorial in *Pravda,* on September 18, had to acknowledge this. In spite of the 'steel hammer' that drives an 'aspen-wedge' into the Opposition every day (how many times already), the Opposition *lives* and has the will to live; it has cadres tempered in battle, and what cadres! To draw, at such a moment, conclusions like those of the Group of Fifteen is false to the bottom and exceptionally harmful. These conclusions create a demoralizing state of mind instead of organizing the working class and the proletarian core of the party. The position of the Fifteen can only be passive, for if the working class and its vanguard have already surrendered all their positions and conquests without a struggle, then on whom and on what can these comrades count? You do not organize the masses to revive a 'corpse,' and as to a *new struggle,* given the situation of the working class as they picture it to themselves, the time it will take is much too long and this will lead inevitably to the position of Shlyapnikov." I think Comrade Rafail is perfectly right in characterizing the situation the way he does.

You write that the proletariat does not like nebulous half-measures and diplomatic evasions. That is right. And that's the reason why you must finally put two and two together. If the party is a corpse, a new party must be built on a new spot, and the working class must be told about it openly. If Thermidor is completed, and if the dictatorship of the proletariat is liquidated, the banner of the second proletarian revolution must be unfurled. That is how we would act if the road of reform, for which we stand, proved hopeless. Unfortunately, the leaders of the Democratic Centralists are up to their ears in nebulous half-measures and diplomatic evasions. They criticize in a very "left" manner our road of reform—a road which, I hope, we have shown by deeds is not at all the road of Stalinist legality—but they do not show the working masses any other road. They content themselves with sectarian mutterings against us, and count meanwhile on spontaneous movements. If this line were to take firm hold, it would not only destroy your whole group, which contains not a few good and devoted revolutionists, but, like all sectarianism and adventurism, it would render the best service to the right-centrist tendencies, that is, in the long run, to bourgeois restoration. That is why, dear comrade, before uniting—and I am for unification with all my heart—it is necessary to establish the ideological delimitations, based upon a clear and principled line. It is a good old Bolshevik rule.

With communist greetings,
L. Trotsky

# CRISIS IN THE RIGHT-CENTER BLOC

## November 1928

*NOTE: A large part of this article is in answer to Stalin's October 19 speech at the meeting of the Moscow Committee and the Moscow Control Commission, entitled "The Right Danger in the CPSU (B)," in English in Stalin's Works, vol. 11, pp. 231-48. At this meeting, the Stalinists continued the process of eroding the base of the rights in the key party organization in Moscow (see "No Political Concessions to Conciliationist Moods," October 2, 1928). Uglanov, a supporter of Bukharin, was not replaced as Moscow party secretary by Molotov until after the November plenum of the Central Committee, but his cothinkers were replaced with Stalin's supporters in October.*

*The "vital practical questions" that constitute the Stalinists' charges against the rights, which Trotsky summarizes and analyzes in point VI (D), were itemized by Stalin in his October 19 speech.*

*Trotsky's discussion in paragraph 3 of the two-front fight the Stalinists claimed to be waging—against right and left equally— is in reply to Stalin's November 19 speech at the plenum of the CC and the CCC (in his Works, vol. 11, pp. 255-302).*

*At the end of point IV Trotsky refers to an article in Pravda by Ya. Yakovlev, a member of the presidium of the CCC and deputy president of the Workers and Peasants Inspection. This agency, which Lenin set up to conduct systematic criticism of shortcomings in government agencies, was enlisted by Stalin as part of the campaign of "self-criticism."*

*From New International, December 1941 and February 1942, in a translation from the French journal Contre le courant (March 22, 1929). Revised against the Russian original by permission of the Harvard College Library.*

## I. A New Chapter

The campaign against the right constitutes in a certain sense the opening of a new chapter. This campaign is distinguished from others by an extraordinary amount of noise and tumult—with a total absence of concrete form politically. Above all, it is literary camouflage for the organizational operations of the Stalinists behind the scenes; it is an attempt to justify this work before the party. Moreover, the campaign cannot take concrete form politically, because that would require the enumeration of the sins committed in common by the center and the right. But at the same time the campaign indicates a crisis (a serious crisis, though not yet the collapse of the ruling bloc). The backsliding up to now has prepared the transition of quantity into a new quality. The open social degeneration of important groups and layers of the party is evident everywhere. Centrism is frightened (particularly under the blows of the Opposition) at the sight of the "ripest" fruit of its work. But centrism is bound hand and foot—by its acts of yesterday, by its "national socialist" approach to problems, by its piecemeal policy, by its theoretical poverty. In attacking the right it is particularly mindful not to wound itself. That accounts for the character of deep duplicity of the whole campaign: if from the practical point of view it may mean the elimination from the party of the most arrogant Ustryalovist elements and the retarding or abatement of the backsliding and degeneration, at the same time it also means a new disorganization of the mind of the party, by further weakening the Marxist method and by preparing even more confused and more dangerous new stages in the development of the party.

Stalin and Molotov attempt to present the matter as though their line is the same irreconcilable struggle against the liquidators of the right as against the "defeatists" of the left.

The central idea of the present campaign, that Marxist politics in general consists of a struggle against the right and against the left with the same irreconcilable spirit, is thoroughly absurd. To the right of Marxist politics stands the mighty world of imperialism with its still enormous agency of collaborationists. There is the enemy. To the left of the Marxist line there can be only wrong tendencies within the proletariat itself, infantile disorders in the party, and so forth. The most extreme expression of this false "leftism" is anarchism. But anarchism's strength and influence are all the smaller and less significant the more resolutely, the more determinedly, the more consistently the revolutionary party fights against opportunism. That is precisely the special historical merit of Bolshevism. In its annals, the struggle against the left always bore an episodic and subordinated character. The Stalinist formula of a struggle "with the same intransigence" against the right and the left is not a Bolshevik formula but the traditional formula of petty-bourgeois radicalism, whose entire history has been nothing but a struggle against "reaction" on one hand and against the proletarian revolution on the other.

The Social Democracy of today has taken over this tradition in all its nuances. *The formula of struggle against the right and left as a guiding formula characterizes, generally speaking, every party that maneuvers between the main classes of modern society.* Under our present conditions, this formula is the political passport of centrism. Otherwise it would be entirely impossible to solve the following question: How could the Stalin-Molotov faction constitute an indissoluble bloc with the right faction of bourgeois restoration? And furthermore: How can it continue, in practice, to maintain this bloc to the present day? The answer is very simple: The ruling bloc was not an unnatural alliance of Bolshevism with bourgeois restoration but an alliance of backsliding right-centrism with Ustryalovism. There is nothing unnatural in such a union. A bloc of centrists of various shades with open conciliators and even with real traitors for a sharp struggle against the left is to be found at every step in the history of the whole working class movement. When Stalin and Molotov today make a "furious" characterization of the right wing, partly by copying from the Platform of the Opposition, they best characterize themselves, their line, and their group. Without at all realizing it they are exercising a fatal "self-criticism."

But perhaps the situation has now radically changed after the declaration of the so-called implacable struggle against the right deviation? For the moment it would be thoughtless, at the very least, to draw such a conclusion. The Leninist wing has been sent beyond the Urals and the Caucasus; the right wing occupies leading positions. That is what is decisive. One thing is clear: the period of carefree existence for the bloc between the center and the right is finished. The February shift of centrism has its internal zigzags: from February to July, from July to November, and so forth. Those comrades judged very hastily who thought that the July plenum put an end to the fight of the centrists and the right and that the contradictions between them had lost all political significance. No, this is wrong. Nevertheless, it would be still more erroneous to consider the rupture irreversible. Finally, only an absolutely thoughtless person could regard a return of centrism to the road of the right as impossible.

From this general characterization of the campaign as one shot through with duplicity arise the tasks of the Bolshevik-Leninists. On one hand, they will support every real, even if timid and insufficient, step toward the left taken by party militants under centrist leadership; on the other hand, they will oppose these militants to the centrist leadership itself, so as to expose the lack of principle and incompetence of that leadership. But these tasks will be accomplished basically by the same method. Support for every move toward the left will be expressed precisely by the Bolshevik-Leninists formulating clearly and distinctly the real aim of the struggle in every concrete case, by propagating genuine Bolshevik methods, by exposing the mediocrity and fakery of the centrist leadership. There can be no other support. It is also the most effective.

The fact that our overall tasks are quite clear does not relieve us of the duty to examine the new stage more closely and more concretely in the light of the general development of the party and the revolution.

## II. Five Years of Social-Political Reaction on the Basis of the Proletarian Dictatorship

We must say clearly and distinctly: The five years after the death of Lenin were years of social and political reaction. The post-Lenin party leadership became an unwitting, but all the more effective, expression of this reaction, as well as its instrument.

Periods of reaction, as distinct from those of counterrevolution, arise without changing which class rules. Feudal absolutism knew periods of "liberal" reform and periods of counterreform strengthening serfdom. The rule of the bourgeoisie, beginning with the epoch of the great revolutions, knew alternating periods of stormy advance and periods of retrogression. This among other things determined the succession of different parties in power during various periods of the domination of one and the same capitalist class.

Not only theory but also the living experience of the last eleven years shows that the rule of the proletariat can go through a period of social and political reaction as well as through a period of stormy advance. Naturally, it is not a matter of reaction "in general" but of reaction on the basis of the victorious proletarian revolution, which stands opposed to the capitalist world. The alternation of these periods is determined by the course of the class struggle. The periods of reaction do not change the basis of class rule—that is, they do not signify the passage of power from one class to another (that would mean the counterrevolution)— but they signify that there is a change in the relation of class forces and a regrouping of elements within the class. In our country, the period of reaction that followed the period of powerful revolutionary advance was called forth chiefly by the fact that the former possessing classes, defeated, repulsed, or terrorized, were able, thanks to objective conditions and to the errors committed by the revolutionary leadership, to gather their forces and pass gradually to the offensive, using mainly the bureaucratic apparatus. On the other hand, the victorious class, the proletariat, not supported from without, encountered ever new obstacles and difficulties; it lost the strength and spirit of the first days; differentiation set in, with a bureaucracy emerging at the top and acting more and more in its own interests, and with tired or completely despairing elements breaking off down below. Correlative to the decreased activity of the proletariat came the growing activity of the bourgeois classes, above all, those strata of the petty bourgeoisie striving to advance by the old ways of exploitation.

It is unnecessary to demonstrate that all these processes of internal reaction could develop and gain in strength only under conditions of cruel defeats of the world proletariat and an ever stronger position of the imperialist bourgeoisie. In turn, the defeats of the world revolution in the last five or six years were decisively determined by the centrist line of the leadership of the Communist International, a line that is especially dangerous in the context of great revolutionary crises.

One might reply: How can you call this period of economic growth in the country, socialist construction, and so forth, a period of reaction? But this objection is not to the point. Economic construction is a contradictory process. The first stage of growth following the years of collapse and famine, the stage of reconstruction, was just the one that created the conditions for the existence of social and political reaction. The famished working class was inclined to believe that everything would continue to go forward without hindrance. They were even persuaded of this from above. But in the meantime contradictions developed within this process of growth, contradictions accentuated by the blind and false policy of the leadership and resulting in a decline in the relative social weight of the proletariat, weakening its feeling of self-confidence. Of course, as a result of the progress of industry, which reassembled the proletariat in the shops and factories and renewed and supplemented its cadres, the social premises for a new revolutionary proletarian advance were created. But this already belongs to the next stage. Certain symptoms are at hand which permit the belief that this political revival has already begun and is one of the factors that drove the centrists to introduce "self-criticism," to begin the struggle against the right, and so forth. It is not necessary to add that the sliver of steel which is the Opposition and which no surgeon in the world can remove from the body of the party, is also working in this direction. Both of these circumstances (the revival of the working masses and the vitality—so "unexpected" by those at the top—of the Opposition) open up, unless all signs fail us, a new period, and it is no accident that it coincides with the struggle of the center against the right. The preceding period, which developed on the ground of the reconstruction process and all its illusions, was characterized by a decline in the proletariat's activism, by the revival of the bourgeois strata, the strangulation of workers' democracy, and the systematic destruction of the left wing. In other words, it was a period of social and political reaction.

From the ideological point of view it was marked by the struggle against "Trotskyism." With this name the official press designates heterogeneous and often absolutely incompatible ideas, debris from the past, Bolshevik tasks of the present, counterfeit quotations, and so forth. But in general this name was given to everything which the backsliding official leadership felt obliged to dispense with at each stage in its degeneration. Social and political reaction, despite the complete empiricism of its leadership, is unthinkable without the revision and rejection of the clearest and most intransigent ideas and slogans of Marxism. *The international character of the socialist revolution and the class character of the party:* these are two ideas that are insupportable in their fully stated form to the politicians of the reactionary period, who swim with the stream. The struggle against these two fundamental ideas was conducted, at first apprehensively and in a roundabout manner and then more and more arrogantly, under the pretext of a struggle against "Trotskyism." The results of this struggle were two miserable and contemptible ideas of the leadership which will remain forever the disgrace of the reaction against the October Revolution: the idea of socialism in one country, or national socialism, and the idea of two-class workers' and peasants' parties, that is, Chernovism. The first of these ideas, which serves above all to conceal a policy of following at the tail of economic events, has brought great dangers to the October Revolution. The second of these ideas inspired the theory and practice of the Kuomintang and strangled the Chinese revolution. Stalin is the author of both these "ideas." They are his sole theoretical assets.

As already stated, the difference between a period of reaction and one of counterrevolution is that the first develops under the rule of the class in power while counterrevolution means a change of which class rules. But is is quite clear that while reaction is not the same thing as counterrevolution, it can prepare the necessary political conditions for it and can appear as an introduction to it. If we keep to the broad historical scale, that is, leave aside all secondary considerations, it can be said that the division of the ruling bloc into centrists and right-wingers became openly manifest just at the phase when the methods of social and political reaction began to turn into directly Thermidorian methods.

It is superfluous to explain that the present struggle of the centrists against the right not only does not contradict our prognosis of a Thermidorian danger but, on the contrary, confirms it completely, in the most official manner, so to speak. The Opposition never thought that the sliding toward Thermidor would be uninterrupted, uniform, and equal for the whole party. We predicted dozens and hundreds of times that this backsliding would mobilize the enemy class, that the heavy social tail would strike at the head, the apparatus; that this would provoke a division not only in the broad party ranks but also in the apparatus; and, finally, that this division would create new and more favorable conditions for the work of the Bolshevik-Leninists, an activity directed not only against the open conciliators but also against centrism.

Thus the present campaign is a confirmation of a *particular* prediction of the Opposition which is closely bound up with its *general* prognosis concerning the danger of Thermidor.

### III. The Bureaucratic Regime as an Instrument of Reactionary Tendencies and Forces

Like all other processes in the party, the struggle of the centrists and rights must be considered not only from the broad angle of class tendencies and ideas but also from the narrow angle of the bureaucratic regime. It is no secret that the noisy and hollow struggle of "ideas" against the right is only the accompaniment to the machinations being prepared by the apparatus against Bukharin, Rykov, and Tomsky. This question is not without importance if one considers the positions that this trio occupy in the present system of the party and the soviets. Rykov and Tomsky have always felt a "sympathy, an almost unwholesome attraction," for opportunism. In the October days this was shown openly and clearly. But when life in the party was healthy and its leadership was correct, their opportunist penchant was limited to themselves. The same must be said of Bukharin too, with his passing from ultraleft to ultraright capers. If we consider this question from the personal standpoint (as Lenin did, for example, in his Testament) it must be said that Stalin's falling out with this trio was predetermined even before the trio found themselves on a right platform. This rupture, resulting from the tendency of the bureaucratic regime toward personal power, was predicted with perfect precision by the Opposition more than two years ago, in September 1926, when there was no talk at all about any struggle against the right. The Opposition document "Party Unity and the Danger of Split" said: "The aim of all these discussions and organizational measures is the complete defeat of the nucleus which until recently was called the Leninist Old Guard, and its replacement by the one-man rule of Stalin, relying on a group of comrades who always agree with him.

"Only a dullard or a hopeless bureaucrat could think that the Stalinist struggle for 'party unity' is capable of really achieving unity, even at the price of smashing the old leadership group and the entire present-day Opposition as a whole. From everything that has been said it is clear that the closer Stalin seems to come to his goal, the farther he is from it in fact. One-man rule in the administration of the party, which Stalin and his most intimate circle call 'party unity,' requires not only the defeat, removal, and ouster of the present United Opposition but also the gradual removal of *all authoritative and influential figures in the present ruling faction.* It is quite obvious that neither Tomsky, nor Rykov, nor Bukharin—because of their past, their authority, etc.—is capable of playing the role under Stalin that Uglanov, Kaganovich, Petrovsky, et al. play under him. The ouster of the present Opposition would in fact mean the inevitable transformation of the old group in the Central Committee into an opposition. A new discussion would be placed on the agenda, in which Kaganovich would expose Rykov, Uglanov would expose Tomsky, and Slepkov, Sten, and Company would deglorify Bukharin. Only a hopeless dullard could fail to see the inevitability of this prospect. But at the same time the more openly opportunist elements in the party would open fire against Stalin as one too much infected with "leftist" prejudices, one who hindered a more rapid and unconcealed retrogression" [*Challenge 1926-27,* pp. 116-17].

In verifying this prediction after more than two years only the allusion to Uglanov and Slepkov has proved erroneous. But in the first place this is only a detail, and secondly, have patience: they will make good their "mistakes."

Let us hear now how our wise Tomsky is now obliged to confess that he understands nothing, that he foresaw nothing, that his good faith was abused. Here is what a well-informed comrade writes on the matter:

"In talking with his friends, Tomsky complained: 'We thought that after we were finished with Trotsky we would be able to work peacefully; but now it appears (!!) that the same methods of struggle are to be applied against us.'"

Bukharin expresses himself in the same way, only more pitifully. Here is one of his declarations, absolutely authentic, about the Master [Stalin]: "He is an unprincipled intriguer who subordinates everything to the preservation of his own power. He abruptly changes his theories depending on whom he wants to get rid of at the moment," and so on.

These unfortunate "leaders" who understand nothing and foresee nothing are naturally inclined to see the principal cause of their mishaps in the perfidy of their opponent. So they attribute to his personality gigantic proportions that it does not really possess. The fact is that the backsliding from a class line leads inevitably to the omnipotence of the bureaucratic machine, which in turn seeks a representative who is "adequate" for it. The regroupings within and between the classes created the conditions for the victory of centrism. What was demanded from the apparatchiks who came forward under the old banners was above all else that they not understand what was taking place and that they swim with the stream. For this, men of the empirical type were needed, who make their "rules" for each occasion. The Stalins, the Molotovs, and others, lacking entirely in theoretical horizon, appeared as those least immune from the influence of the invisible social processes. If we examine individually the political biographies of these elements who before, during, and after October occupied second- or third- or tenth-rate positions, and who have now come to the fore, it would not be difficult to demonstrate that in all important questions, when left to themselves, they leaned toward opportunism, Stalin included. The historical line of the party must not be confused with the political line followed by a part of its cadres that rose to the top with the wave of social and political reaction of the last five years. The former was realized in the course of a sharp struggle of tendencies within the party, by constantly overcoming internal contradictions. In this struggle the elements at present in the leadership played no determining role; for the most part they represented the yesterdays out of which the party was passing. That is just why they felt themselves lost in the decisive days of October and had no independent role. Still more: at least half of the present leaders who call themselves the "Old Guard" were on the other side of the barricades in October; the majority of them had a patriotic or pink pacifist position during the imperialist war. There is no reason to believe that these elements, as the history of recent times has shown, could constitute an independent force capable of resisting the reactionary tendencies on a world scale. It is not for nothing that they have so easily assimilated the Martynovs, the Larins, the Rafeses, the Lyadovs, the Petrovskys, the Kerzhentsevs, the Gusevs, the Krzhizhanovskys, and others. It is precisely this section which, in the opinion of Ustryalov, is most capable of gradually bringing the ruined country back to "order." Ustryalov takes the remote example of the "time of troubles" (end of the sixteenth and beginning of the seventeenth centuries) and refers to Klyuchevsky, who said that "the Muscovite state emerged out of its frightful troubles without resorting to heroes; it was saved from misfortune by excellent, but mediocre, people" (Klyuchevsky, 1923 ed., vol. 3, p. 72.) One can doubt the "excellence" of the present candidates for saviors from trouble ("permanent" revolution). But otherwise the quotation by Ustryalov is not without merit and hits the nail on the head. In the final analysis, the Master, with his qualifications for intrigue and downright treachery, is nothing but the incarnation in a single personality of the apparatus that has no personality. His triumphs are the victories of social and political reaction. He has helped it in two ways: by his blindness to the deepgoing historical processes and by his tireless combinations behind the scenes, in a direction suggested to him by the realignment of class forces against the proletariat.

The hopeless struggle of bureaucratic centrism for a "monolithic" apparatus, that is, a struggle for one-man rule in reality, leads under the pressure of class forces to ever new splits. All this does not take place in a vacuum: the classes fasten themselves on to the splits produced in the leadership, they widen them, they fill the bureaucratic groupings with a certain social content. The struggle of the Stalin group in the Political Bureau against the trio, the struggle of centrism against the right, has become the focal point of the pressure of the classes; if it grows, it can (and at a certain stage it must) be transformed into open class struggle. And such a development could bode no good—for centrism at any rate.

## IV. What Is Centrism?

The question of the social basis of the groupings in the Communist Party of the Soviet Union is quite naturally stirring the minds of the comrades who can reflect and learn; that is, above all, the Bolshevik-Leninists. This question must not, however, be considered mechanically and schematically, with the intention of allotting each faction a well-defined social basis. We must remember that we have before us transitional forms, incomplete processes.

The main social reservoir of international opportunism, that is, of class collaborationism, is the petty bourgeoisie, as a broad, amorphous class, or more correctly, a stratified accumulation of numerous subclasses left over from precapitalist production or newly created by capitalism, and forming a series of social rungs between the proletariat and the capitalist bourgeoisie. During the rise of bourgeois society this class was the protagonist of bourgeois democracy. Now this period is long passed, not only in the advanced capitalist countries of the West, but also in China, in India, and so forth. The complete decline of the petty bourgeoisie, its loss of independent economic importance, deprived it forever of the possibility of working out an *independent* political representation that could lead the revolutionary movement of the working masses. In our epoch the petty bourgeoisie oscillates between the extreme poles of contemporary ideology: fascism and communism. Precisely these oscillations give the politics of the imperialist epoch the character of a malarial curve.

Class collaborationism in the workers' movement has a more persistent quality precisely because its direct proponents are not the "independent" parties of the petty bourgeoisie but rather the labor bureaucracy, which sinks its roots into the working class by way of the labor aristocracy. The ideas of collaborationism, thanks to their origin and the sources from which they are fed, have experienced a historical change through the intermediary role of the labor bureaucracy; these ideas passed over from their old defenders to the new, assuming a socialist tinge; with the collapse and putrefaction of the old democratic parties they received a new vitality on a new class basis.

The labor bureaucracy, by its conditions of existence, stands closer to the petty bourgeoisie (officialdom, liberal professions, and so forth) than to the proletariat. Nevertheless it constitutes a specific product of the working class movement; it is recruited from its ranks. In their primitive aspect, collaborationist tendencies and moods are elaborated by the whole petty bourgeoisie; but their transformation, their adaptation to the peculiarities, to the needs, and above all to the weaknesses of the working class—that is the specific mission of the labor bureaucracy. Opportunism is its ideology, and it inculcates and imposes this ideology upon the proletariat by utilizing the powerful pressure of the ideas and institutions of the bourgeoisie, by exploiting the weakness and immaturity of the working masses. The forms of opportunism to which the labor bureaucracy resorts—open collaborationism, centrism, or a combination of both—depends upon the political traditions of a country, on the class relations of the given moment, on the offensive power of communism, and so forth and so on.

Just as under certain circumstances the struggle between bourgeois parties can assume a most violent and even sanguinary character, while remaining a struggle for the interests of property on both sides, so the struggle between open collaborationism and centrism can assume an extremely violent and even desperate character at certain times, remaining within the limits of petty-bourgeois tendencies adapted by the labor bureaucracy in *different ways* for the maintenance of their position of leadership in the working class.

Up to August 4, 1914, the German Social Democracy bore an essentially centrist character. The right stood in opposition to the leadership, as did the left radical wing, which was not clearly formed. The war showed that centrism was incapable of leading the party. The right seized the helm without encountering any resistance. Centrism revived only later, in the form of an opposition. The situation is the same at present in the Third [Communist] International and in the Amsterdam International. The main strength of the international labor bureaucracy is its durable collaborationist wing. Centrism is only an auxiliary spring in its mechanism. The exceptions existing in certain parties, as in Austria for example, are essentially only of a potential character and only prove the rule.

It must be added that since the war the right, together with the center, is much closer to the bourgeois state than was the right in the period before the war (particularly in Germany). Thereby room was made for a centrism that was more radical, less compromised, more "left" than the so-called left Social Democracy. The policy of postwar left-centrism appeared in large measure under the name of communism (in Germany, in Czechoslovakia, in England, and so forth). Great historical events will inevitably lay bare this situation, perhaps in a catastrophic manner.

Now, how do things stand under the workers' state, which is obviously inconceivable without a labor bureaucracy, and at that, one that is more numerous, more broadly ramified, and infinitely more powerful than those in the capitalist countries? What about the line of the leadership of the Communist Party of the Soviet Union, which, in recent years, has slid from the class to the apparatus, that is, to the bureaucracy?

The simplest and easiest way of testing the policy of the Central Committee of the Communist Party of the Soviet Union is on the international field, for there the peculiarities of the situation of the ruling party in the country of the dictatorship of the proletariat are suspended, the new character of the situation cannot mask the class tendencies, the political line can be judged on the basis of well-established Marxist criteria. The policy of the Central Committee in China was not centrist, but Menshevik, and rather right Menshevik; that is, it was closer to the Menshevism of 1917 than to that of 1905 (direct submission to the leadership of the bourgeoisie plus open restraining of the revolutionary offensive of the masses). The policy of the Central Committee in England was of a right-centrist character in the decisive period of the struggle (support to the opportunists and traitors plus a half-hearted criticism at home). In Germany, in Czechoslovakia, in France, and so forth, the policy bore a left-centrist character, repeating under new conditions the policy of the prewar Social Democracy. In Poland, during Pilsudski's coup d'état, the line of the leadership was somewhere between the English and the Chinese examples, that is, between right-centrism and out-and-out Menshevism. In general it can be said that the centrism of the leadership of the Communist Party of the Soviet Union sank more decisively into the Menshevik rut the more revolutionary was the situation, the more it required political perspicacity and audacity. It can adorn itself with "leftism" only in the noise and bustle of political trivia. In this way a supreme, unchallengeable test has been made, on the international level, of the entire line of the post-Lenin leadership.

However, enough experiences have been accumulated up to now in the country itself to be able to recognize and expose centrism even without the international criteria.

The labor bureaucracy, which has grown to such enormous proportions among us, has elaborated a quite new theory in recent years with which to approach all essential questions, above all, the question of its assessment of its very own self. The general thrust of this approach is as follows: Since we have the dictatorship of the proletariat, the proletarian character of all the social processes is guaranteed a priori and forever. Since we have a workers' state, the peerless Molotov has instructed us, how can it be brought closer to the workers? Since we have the dictatorship of the proletariat, then we also have a proletarian kulak, who by his inherent nature is growing into socialism. Since we have the socialist revolution, how can we be threatened by the danger of Thermidor, that is, of bourgeois restoration? Since we have Soviet power, the uninterrupted growth of socialism is assured, irrespective of whether the situation of the working class in this period is improved or worsened. And finally, since we have a Leninist party, how can the "Leninist" Central Committee make mistakes? Isn't all criticism directed against it condemned in advance to play the role of a right or left "deviation," according to which side the secretariat of the Central Commitee sees itself criticized from? *Materialist dialectics,* as a means of assessing the driving forces of the proletarian dictatorship, has been replaced at every point by *immanent idealism,* which has become the specific philosophy of the party and Soviet bureaucrats in their struggle for the stability and permanence of their own positions, for absolute power, and for independence from control by the working masses. The fetishism of the self-sufficient, autonomous apparatus and its functionaries—whose existence has become an aim in itself, who cannot be removed by a decision of the party but "only by civil war" (Stalin)—that is the axis of the immanentist philosophy which sanctifies the practical steps of usurpation and prepares the way for genuine Bonapartism.

The radical change in the fundamental ways of assessing social phenomena attests to the new social role of the labor bureaucracy, and the Soviet bureaucracy in general, in relation to the proletariat as well as to the other classes. Parallel with its independence from the proletariat, this bureaucracy becomes more and more dependent upon the bourgeoisie. The fetishization of the workers' state "as such" is a mask for this dependence. Everything proceeds here according to law. Hence follows with iron logic the organic predilection of our bureaucracy for the petty-bourgeois leaders, for the "solid" trade union bureaucrats of the whole world (China, England, Poland; the orientation of Tomsky, Kaganovich, and others toward Amsterdam, and so forth). This international affinity among all labor bureaucracies, which arises organically, is neither negated nor eliminated by even the most ultraleft zigzags of centrism.

Of course, the labor bureaucracy in the West develops its activity on the basis of capitalist property. In our country, the labor bureaucracy has grown up on the basis of the dictatorship of the proletariat. But from this deep contradiction one cannot conclude, as both theory and experience have shown, that there is an immanent, that is, inherently guaranteed, contradiction between our labor bureaucracy and that of the capitalist countries. The new social basis—which, considered by itself, is immature and does not have any *absolute* durability—does not guarantee the new character of the superstructure, whose degeneration can, on the contrary, become an important factor in the degeneration of the basis itself. In these fundamental questions the scholasticism of Bukharin ("Yea is yea, and nay is nay, and all else is from the devil!") only serves to cover up the processes of social degeneration. The Jacobins also considered themselves the natural antagonists of the monarchy and of monarchist Caesarism. Nevertheless, Napoleon later recruited his best ministers, prefects, and detectives among the old Jacobins, to whom he himself had, moreover, belonged in his youth.

The social and historical origin of our bureaucracy, without insuring it as we have said above against degeneration, nevertheless gives the ways and forms of this process an uncommon singularity; in the given situation it gives the centrist elements an obvious and undeniable predominance over the right, lending to centrism itself a special, extremely complicated character, which reflects the various stages of backsliding, the various states of mind, and the different methods of thought. That is why the speeches and articles of the leading centrists remind one most often of a manuscript written in Russian, Latin, and Arabic letters. This explains the frightful illiteracy, not only theoretical, but also literary, of most of the centrist writers. It is enough to read *Pravda* these days. After the apostles of centrism partake of the grace of the Secretariat they immediately begin to speak in tongues. This is surely a sign of the power of grace. But it is virtually impossible to understand them.

It may be objected: If the present leading tendency in the Communist Party of the Soviet Union is centrism, how can one explain the present sharp attitude against the left Social Democracy, which itself is nothing but centrism? This is not a serious argument. Our right also, which, according to the opinion of the centrists, is following the road to the restoration of capitalism, proclaims itself the irreconcilable enemy of the Social Democracy. Opportunism is always ready, when conditions demand it, to establish its reputation on a clamorous radicalism to be used in other countries. Naturally, this exportation of radicalism consists for the most part of words.

But the hostility of our centrists and rights against the European Social Democracy is not entirely composed of words. We must not lose sight of the whole international situation and above all of the huge objective contradictions between the capitalist countries and the workers' states. The international Social Democracy supports the existing capitalist regime. Our domestic opportunism, which arose on the basis of the proletarian dictatorship, is only *evolving* in the direction of capitalist relations. Despite the elements of dual power in the country and the Thermidorian tendencies in the Communist Party of the Soviet Union, the antagonism between Soviet power and the bourgeois world remains a fact of the greatest importance that can be denied or neglected only by "left" sectarians, anarchists, and those tending toward anarchism. The international Social Democracy, by its whole policy, is obliged to support the designs of its bourgeoisie against the Union of Soviet Socialist Republics. This alone creates the basis of a real, and not merely a verbal, hostility, despite the rapprochement of the political line.

Centrism is the official line of the apparatus. The vehicle of centrism is the party official. But the officialdom is not a class. It serves classes. Then what class line is represented by centrism?

The reviving property-owners find their expression, timid though it is for the present, in the right faction. The proletarian line is represented through the Opposition. By the method of elimination we get . . . the *seredniak*—middle peasant. And in reality centrism in our country has shed its skin of Bolshevism by clinging to the idea of winning the middle peasant. The Leninist slogan of the alliance of the ruling proletariat with the middle peasantry has been replaced by the fetish of the middle peasant as the highest criterion of proletarian policy. And to this day, the centrists will not leave I. N. Smirnov in peace, because he was the one who in the autumn of 1927 developed the correct thought that the alliance of the proletariat with the middle peasantry is predicated on the readiness of the party, in time of need, to have a temporary falling-out with the middle peasant in order to carry through a correct proletarian policy and thereby to create new conditions for a more durable and more lasting alliance with the middle peasants. For such an alliance is possible not on the basis of some sort of equable class line but only on the basis of the proletarian line. The partial concessions to the middle peasants can bear only an auxiliary character. The attempt to find a middle line [between the proletariat and middle peasantry] can result only in an increasing orientation toward the kulaks and the bourgeoisie in general. The middle peasantry cannot have an independent line or an independent party. An "independent" peasant party is always in reality a bourgeois-kulak party. Our centrism, theoretically poverty-stricken, with its short memory, has not understood this. For this reason it has generalized from its own ill-defined essence, being neither this nor that, to create the reactionary, caricatured idea of a "two-class workers' and peasants' party" (Stalin). In reality, the two-class party signifies the Kuomintang, that is, the political muzzling of the workers and peasants by the bourgeoisie.

The Stalinist idea of the workers' and peasants' party is the most important inspiring idea of the right wing. In broad bureaucratic circles, especially in the Ukraine, no little has been said recently of the party possessing a reserve: to go back from the proletarian dictatorship to the formula of 1905, that is, to the democratic dictatorship of the proletariat and the peasantry. The party, by including the right wing as part of itself, has really become a two-class party. And a retreat to the position of the dictatorship of the proletariat and peasantry could mean only the restoration of capitalism and nothing else.

Since the middle peasantry was made the highest criterion,

rather than the strategic proletarian line, the rights quite logically drew pro-kulak conclusions from the independent principle of middle peasant policy. To the extent that he stands opposed to the proletariat, there can be no other road for the middle peasant than the kulak road. In the course of the last few years the centrists have hidden their heads from these conclusions in the statistical rubbish especially prepared for them by Yakovlev and Company. This does not prevent the same Yakovlev today, in his veiled polemic against Bukharin, from zealously cribbing arguments from the old notebooks of the Opposition, pretending that these were notes from a desk pad at the Workers' and Peasants' Inspection (see *Pravda,* no. 253, Ya. Yakovlev, "On the Question of the Economic Tasks of the Next Year: From Notes on a Desk at the Workers and Peasants Inspection"). Even if Yakovlev occupies himself only with "splinters" and "fragments" of the Opposition's Platform, this alone proves sufficient to deal with the "Notes of an Economist." But the kulak crawled out of the statistical rubbish in the grain collections crisis. Today the centrists vacillate between Article 107 and the raising of the grain prices. Simultaneously they erect as before the naked idea of the middle peasantry as the main principle that separates them from the Opposition. They only show thereby that they have no point of social support and no independent class policy. The line of centrism is the zigzag line of the bureaucracy between the proletariat and the bourgeoisie while the dissatisfaction of both classes grows irresistibly. The hybrid policy of centrism slowly but surely prepares its liquidation, which is possible in two directions, that is, by issuing forth along the proletarian or the bourgeois road.

## V. What Is the Right Wing?

Matters stand more simply and clearly with regard to the right wing.

The Thermidorian tendency in the country, in the broadest sense of the term, is the private-property tendency, as opposed to proletarian socialism. That is the most general definition of the Thermidorian tendency, and at the same time the most fundamental. The petty bourgeoisie is its driving force, but which petty bourgeoisie? That which is most addicted to exploitation, that which strives for position, that which is being transformed, or tends to be transformed, into the middle bourgeoisie, that which seeks its ally in the big bourgeoisie, in world capitalism? The central figure in this Thermidorian army is the kulak, the "natural-born" conveyer of the moods and aspirations of Bonapartist counterrevolution.

Inside the ruling apparatus and party, as an ally or semially of the property-owners of Bonapartist inclinations, is the official who has become "totally ripe for the plucking," i.e., wants to "live in peace with all classes." There exist social causes for this: materially or intellectually he is related to the new proprietor; he himself has grown fat; he wants no commotion; he regards with raging hatred the perspective of "permanent" revolution; he has had more than enough of the revolution, which, God be praised, is happily in the past and now permits him to harvest its fruits. National socialism—that is his doctrine.

This firmly established official, as we said above, is the ally of the Bonapartist kulak. However, even between them there is a difference that is very important for the present stage. The kulak would like to discard the whole hated system by using the army or through an insurrection. The bureaucrat, however, whose continuing welfare is linked with the Soviet apparatus, is opposed to the open Bonapartist road; he is for the path of "evolution," of a camouflaged Thermidor. We know from history that Thermidor was only a step leading to the Bonapartist coup d'état. But that was not understood at that time. The active Thermidorians would have sincerely rejected as a base slander any suggestion that they were merely paving the way for military-bourgeois usurpation.

This shifting relationship between the two sections of Thermidorians is the cause of the weakness of the right wing. To take up the gauge of battle, it must openly mobilize all the propertied elements and instincts in the country. This was readily done during the struggle against the Opposition; but the bloc with the center and the banner of the party served to conceal it. The powerful tail constituted by the proprietors and encouraged by the leadership during these past years, exerted pressure from every direction upon the party, helping to terrorize the proletarian core and to demolish the left wing. But since the struggle began openly between the centrists and the right, even though conducted with half-measures, the political situation has changed abruptly. It is the centrist apparatus that now speaks in the name of the party. This mask can no longer be assumed by the rights in this struggle. They can no longer base themselves upon the proprietors anonymously. They must now publicly and openly straddle a new war-horse.

In the lower ranks of the right faction, the difference between the party bureaucrat and the kulak presents hardly any difficulties in the way of common action. But the higher one goes, and the nearer the industrial sections and the political centers, the more obstacles are encountered by the right—living ones, embodied in the dissatisfaction of the workers; and dying ones, the [revolutionary] traditions. The present leaders of the right are not yet "ripe enough" to publicly straddle the proprietors' war-horse against the official party. Driven into a blind alley by the pressure of the apparatus, the bureaucrats of the right either resign, or else, like Uglanov, they make moving pleas that they should not be "crippled."

The "unripeness" of the Thermidorian wing of the party, the absence of political connection between this wing and the reserve formed by the proprietors, explains the easiness of the present victory of the centrists over the right. Instead of military operations there is an apparatus parade and nothing more.

There is also another reason for this "easiness." But this reason has its roots in the relations between the centrist apparatus and the proletarian core of the party, whose head was stuffed for more than five years so as to incite it against the left wing; for this purpose it was terrorized by the pressure of the bourgeois classes. And yet the result of all this is that at the end of the sixth year of struggle, they are obliged anew to call for an *intensifed offensive* against the so-called "remnants" [of the left wing]. In contrast to that, the proletarian core is ready to struggle against the right, not out of fear but out of conviction. And even though the present campaign [against the rights] is entirely impregnated with bureacratism that completely suppresses the initiative of the masses; even though "sentinels" have been posted ahead to indicate with their red pennants the limits within which the centrist parade shall proceed; even though the masses are disoriented, perplexed, and unprepared, especially in the provinces—the proletarian core of the party nevertheless supports the centrist apparatus incontestably *in this struggle,* if not actively, at least passively; in no case does it aid the right.

These are the essential reasons why the centrists have vanquished the right so easily—inside the party. But these same reasons explain the whole meagerness and superficiality of this triumph. To understand this better, let us examine more closely what they are disputing about.

## VI. Differences Between Center and Right

A proletarian revolutionist cannot be an empiricist, that is, he cannot let himself be guided only by what happens under his nose at the moment. That is why the struggle against the right is of importance to us not only from the point of view of the immediate budget questions, credits to be allocated for collective farming in 1929, and so forth, around which the struggle seems to hinge (although even on these points they keep within the bounds of allusion and commonplaces), but above all from the point of view of the general ideas that it introduces into the mind of the party.

What then is the ideological baggage of the centrist struggle against the right?

### A. The Danger of Thermidor

Above all, let us examine what the right danger essentially consists of. As our guide on this point, as well as on the others, let us take the fundamental (and alas! the most insipid) document of the whole campaign: the speech of Stalin at the plenum of the Moscow Committee and the Moscow Control Commission on October 19, 1928. After recounting the differences with the right—of which more later—Stalin concludes by saying: "A victory of the right deviation in our party would mean an enormous strengthening of the capitalist elements in our country. And what does the strengthening of the capitalist elements in our country mean? It means weakening the proletarian dictatorship and increasing the chances of the restoration of capitalism" [from Stalin's *Works,* vol. 11, p. 235].

In this case, as in all others where Stalin turns upon the right, he does not devise his own gunpowder but uses the weapons forged in the arsenals of the Opposition, dulling their sharp Marxist edge as much as he can in the process. And really, if one takes Stalin's characterization of the right seriously, it appears as the nub of Thermidorian reaction inside the party. The danger of counterrevolution is nothing other than the danger of "the restoration of capitalism" in our country. The Thermidorian danger is a masked form of counterrevolution, accomplished in its first stage through the right wing of the governing party: in the eighteenth century through the Jacobins; today through the

Bolsheviks. Insofar as Stalin, by repeating what was said by the Opposition, declares that "a victory of the right deviation would . . . [increase] the chances of the restoration of capitalism," he is only saying that the right wing is the expression of the Thermidorian danger in our party.

But let us hear what he says a few lines further on about the left wing, about the Opposition. From this angle, you see, the danger consists in that the Opposition "cannot see the possibility of building socialism by the efforts of our country; it gives way to despair and is obliged to console itself with chatter about Thermidor[ian] tendencies in our party" [Ibid., p. 241].

This example of centrist confusion could be called classic if confusion could have its classics. Indeed, if to speak of the Thermidorian danger in our party is to chatter, then what is the declaration of Stalin that the victory of the right wing in the Communist Party of the Soviet Union would open the road to the restoration of capitalism? What else, if not this, would Thermidor be in a socialist revolution? To what point must one be muddled to accuse the right wing of collaborating in the restoration of capitalism and in the same breath to characterize words pointing out the Thermidorian danger in the party as "chatter"? There is your real chatter, and specifically centrist at that. For the principal trait of centrism is that it mechanically stacks up the contradictions instead of overcoming them dialectically. Centrism has always united in its beggar's purse the "reasonable" and "admissible" elements of the right and left wings—that is, of opportunism and Marxism—neutralizing the one with the other and reducing its own ideological content to zero. We know from Marx that petty-bourgeois thought, even the most radical, always consists of admitting "on the one hand" so as to deny "on the other."

In general, the whole manner of characterizing the Opposition adopted in Stalin's speech is scandalously impotent. The danger of the left deviation is supposed to be that "it overestimates the strength of our enemies, the strength of capitalism; it sees only the possibility of the restoration of capitalism, but cannot see the possibility of building socialism by the efforts of our country; it gives way to despair and is obliged to console itself with chatter about Thermidor[ian] tendencies in our party."

Understand that if you can! The Opposition "gives way to despair" because it sees only "the possibility of the restoration of capitalism" (that is, the danger of Thermidor); but it "consoles itself" (?) with Thermidorian tendencies in our party, that is, still with the same danger of the restoration of capitalism. Understand that if you can. What could really cause a person to give way to despair is this mindless centrist rigamarole. But the Opposition has not lost hope of dealing even with this pestilence—and long before the complete socialist society is built up in our country.

## B. The Conciliatory Tendency

The struggle against the right is conducted under cover of anonymity, in the sense of personalities as well as actions. Apart from the Mandelstamms, everyone votes unanimously against the right; and even the Mandelstamms are now probably voting with the others. It is natural that the workers in the ranks of the party ask: But where is this right wing? Stalin replies to them as follows: "Those comrades who in discussing the problem of the right deviation concentrate on the question of the individuals representing the right deviation are also wrong. . . . That is not the correct way of presenting the question. . . . The question is not one of individuals, but of conditions, of the situation, giving rise to the right danger in the party. Individuals can be kept out, but that does not mean that we have thereby cut the roots of the right danger in our party" [Ibid., p. 233].

Such reasoning is the consummation of the philosophy of conciliationism: it is the most striking and most solemn departure from the fundamental Leninist tradition on the field of the struggle of ideas and the education of the party. To pass over the persons representing the right deviation for the conditions which give birth to it—there is the typical argument of the conciliators. That was essentially the real error committed by the old "Trotskyism," which set it off from the methods of Lenin. Of course there are "objective conditions" that give birth to kulaks and *podkulachniki* [peasants who collaborate with the kulaks], to Mensheviks and opportunists. But from that it does not follow that the presence of such elements in the Bolshevik Party is a minor, second-rate issue. "The question is not one of individuals, but of conditions." A remarkable revelation. The old "Trotskyism" never formulated the theory of conciliation with such triviality and vulgarity. The present Stalinist philosophy is a caricature of the old "Trotskyism," all the more mischievous because it is unconscious.

Lenin invariably taught the party to hate and scorn the method of struggling against opportunism "in general," of limiting oneself to declarations, without clearly and precisely naming its most responsible representatives and their deeds. For the struggle by declarations very often serves to taint the atmosphere, to divert the dissatisfaction of the masses accumulating against the slipping toward the right; this struggle can also be utilized to frighten the right slightly, so that they will not let themselves be carried away too far and reveal their tail. Such a struggle against the right can in the end serve as a protection and concealment for them, by certain complicated and roundabout means. Centrism needs the right, not at Ishim, Barnaul, or Astrakhan [where Left Oppositionists were exiled], but in Moscow, as its main reserve, and it needs rights who submit to command, who are tamed and patient.

## C. Socialism in One Country

The theoretical crown of rightist policy is the theory of socialism in one country, that is, of national socialism. The centrists maintain this theory completely, holding up the rotting parts of the structure with new props. Even the most docile delegates to the Sixth Congress complained in the corridors: "Why are we forced to swallow this piece of fruit as part of the program?" It is not necessary to argue here about the basis of the national socialist philosophy. Let us wait for what its creators will reply to the criticism of the program. In spite of everything, they will be forced to answer; they will not succeed in evading it by silence.

Let us limit ourselves to pointing out a new prop that Stalin tried to put up at the Moscow plenum on October 19. After making the usual attacks against the opportunists "on the one hand" and the Marxists "on the other," Stalin argues that we can "achieve final victory over capitalism in our country, *if* we intensify the work of electrifying the country. . . . Hence (??) the *possibility* of the victory of socialism in our country" [Ibid., p. 238].

The speech refers to Lenin, of course, and falsely as usual. Yes, Lenin placed great hopes in electrification, as a road leading to the technical socialization of industry in general and of agriculture in particular. "Without electrification," he said, "no real socialist foundation for our economic life is possible" [Lenin's *Collected Works,* vol. 32, p. 408]. But Lenin did not separate the question of electrification from that of the world revolution, and he certainly did not oppose them to each other. This time also, it can be proved by documents, as can generally be done in all cases where the unfortunate creators of the national socialist theory try to base themselves on Lenin. In his preface to the book of the late Skvortsov-Stepanov, *The Electrification of the RSFSR [Russian Republic] and the Transitional Phase of World Economy* [Moscow, 1922], Lenin says: "Special reference must be made to the beginning of Chapter VI, where the author . . . magnificently answers the "airy" skepticism that is displayed in some quarters about the possibility of electrification" [Ibid., vol. 33, p. 245].

Now what does Skvortsov-Stepanov say at the beginning of the sixth chapter that Lenin emphasizes and recommends so warmly to the reader? Skvortsov there combats precisely the conception according to which we are supposed to believe in the realization of electrification and the construction of a socialist society within national limits. Here is what he says: "In the common conception of the realization of electrification, one generally loses sight of still another aspect: the Russian proletariat has never thought of creating an *isolated* socialist state. A self-sufficient 'socialist' state is a petty-bourgeois ideal."—Hear, hear!—"One can conceive of a certain movement in the direction of this ideal while the petty bourgeoisie predominates economically and politically; by isolating itself from the world, it seeks the means for consolidating its economic forms, which new technique and new economies transform into the most unstable forms."

It would seem that no one could express himself more clearly. It is true that after Lenin died, Skvortsov-Stepanov expressed himself differently; he began to qualify as petty bourgeois not the idea of the isolated socialist state but rather the negation of this idea. But Stalin himself has traversed the same path. Up to the end of 1924 he believed that at the basis of Leninism was the recognition of the impossibility of constructing socialism in one country, above all in a backward country; after 1924 he proclaimed the construction of socialism in one country one of the foundations of Leninism.

"A successfully conducted socialist construction"—said Skvortsov-Stepanov in the same chapter—"is only possible with the utilization of the immense industrial resources of Western Europe. . . . Should the proletariat take political power in its hands in one of the first-class industrial countries, in England or in Germany, the combination of the powerful industrial resources of that country with the immense, still intact, natural treasures of Russia, would give the possibility of driving rapidly toward the building of socialism in both countries."

It is just this elementary Marxist idea that has been denounced for the last three years in every meeting as the fundamental

heresy of Trotskyism. Now how did Skvortsov-Stepanov assess
the construction of socialism in our country before the victory of
the proletariat in the more advanced countries? Here is what he
had to say: "Naturally, if the economic region embraced by the
dictatorship of the proletariat is sufficiently vast and has a great
variety and richness of natural stores, its isolation does not
exclude the possibility of the development of the productive
forces, which is one of the premises of proletarian socialism. But
the advance toward this will be a despairingly slow one, and this
socialism will for a long time remain extremely meager, if indeed
its economic premises are not undermined, an especially likely
alternative under such circumstances" [Chapter 6, pp. 174-79].

So Skvortsov believed that without the European revolution,
the construction of socialism would inevitably have a "despairingly slow" and "meager" character; that is why he considered it
"probable" that under such circumstances the economic premises
would be undermined, that is, that the dictatorship of the
proletariat would collapse without foreign military intervention.
That is how Skvortsov-Stepanov expressed himself in the sixth
chapter of his book, as a man of little faith, they would say today.
And it is just on the subject of this so-called skeptical assessment
of our construction that Lenin wrote: "Special reference must be
made to the beginning of Chapter VI, where the author . . .
magnificently answers the 'airy' skepticism that is displayed in
some quarters about the possibility of electrification" [*Collected
Works*, vol. 33, p. 245].

Nothing goes right for the unfortunate offspring of aboriginal
centrist thought [i.e., the theory of socialism in one country].
Every attempt to present another argument in its favor invariably turns against it. Every new prop only causes this building
constructed with rotten material to totter even more.

A characteristic trait of the right wing, as is shown by the
articles and resolutions that are all patterned on the same model,
is its aspiration for a peaceful life and its fear of commotion. That
has been correctly demonstrated in—or, more exactly, copied
from—the documents of the Opposition. But that is precisely the
source of the hatred (penetrating to the very innards) against the
idea of permanent revolution. Of course it is not a question here
of the old differences, which can interest only historians and
specialists now, but rather of the perspectives for tomorrow.
There are only two possible courses: one toward the international
revolution, the other toward reconciliation with the native bourgeoisie. The right wing was consolidated in the work of defaming

"permanent revolution." Under cover of the theory of national socialism, it is marching toward reconciliation with the native bourgeoisie so as to guard itself against any convulsions.

So long as the campaign against the right is conducted under the sign of the theory of socialism in one country, we have before us a struggle going on *within the limits of revisionism itself.* This must not be forgotten for a single moment.

## D. Vital Practical Questions

If we pass to the vital political questions, the balance of centrism is almost equally unfavorable.

a. The right is opposed to the "present" rate of industrialization. But what is the "present" rate? It is the arithmetical result of tail-endism, the pressure of the market, and the lashes of the Opposition. It accumulates contradictions instead of diminishing them. It does not contain a single idea thought out to the end. It furnishes no guarantee for the future. Tomorrow, the "present rate" can be something else. The hysterical cries about "superindustrialization" signify that the doors are left open for a retreat.

b. The right denies the "expediency" of allocating credits for the collectives and the state farms. And the centrists? What are their plans, what is the span of their activity? To proceed in a revolutionary manner one must begin with the agricultural laborers and the poor peasants. Audacious and resolute measures are necessary (wages, spirit of organization, culture) *so that the agricultural workers feel that they are a part of the ruling class of the country. A league of poor peasants* is necessary. It is only if these two levers are present, and *if industry really has a leading role* that one can speak seriously of collectives and state farms.

c. The right is for "relaxing the monopoly of foreign trade." This is an accusation that is a little more concrete. (Yesterday it was still called slander to point out the existence of such tendencies in the party.) But here also it is not specified *who* proposes the relaxation and *within what limits:* is it within those fixed by Sokolnikov and Stalin in 1922 in trying to effect this "relaxation," or have these limits been extended further?

d. Finally, the right denies "the expediency of fighting against bureaucratism by means of self-criticism." It is futile to speak seriously of this difference of opinion. There exists a precise decision of the Stalin faction saying that for the purpose of maintaining a "firm leadership," *self-criticism must not touch the Central Committee, but must be limited to its subordinates.* Stalin and Molotov have explained this decision in scarcely concealed form in speeches and articles. It is clear that this reduces self-criticism in the party to zero. At bottom we have a monarchist-Bonapartist principle which is a slap in the face to all the traditions of the party. It is natural that the "subordinates" should also want to avail themselves of a little bit of the supreme inviolability. There is only a hierarchical and not a principled difference.

The present extension of "self-criticism" pursues temporary factional aims, among others. We simply have here a repetition, only on a larger scale, of the "self-criticism" that the Stalinist faction organized after the Fourteenth Party Congress, when the Stalinists "implacably" accused the Zinovievists of practicing bureaucratic oppression. It is superfluous to explain what regime the Stalinists themselves established in Leningrad after their victory.

## E. The Question of Wages

But the manner in which the centrists characterize the right wing is especially remarkable for what it leaves unsaid. We hear about their underestimation of capital investments, of collectivization, and of "self-criticism." But not a word is said about the material, cultural, and political situation of the proletariat in its daily and political life. It appears that on this field there are no differences between the center and the right. But a correct appreciation of the differences between the factions can be obtained only from the point of view of the interests and the needs of the proletariat as a class and of every individual worker (see chapter two of the Platform of the Bolshevik-Leninists, "The Situation of the Working Class and the Trade Unions" [in *Challenge 1926-27,* pp. 311-21]).

The articles and resolutions against the right clamor a good deal, but without precision, about capital investments in industry, but they do not contain a single word on wages. This question, however, must become the main criterion for measuring the success of socialist development; and consequently, also the criterion to apply to differences. A socialist advance ceases to be such if it does not uninterruptedly, openly, and tangibly improve the material position of the working class in its daily life. The proletariat is the basic productive force in the construction of socialism. Of all the investments, that which is put into the proletariat is the most "profitable." To consider the increase of wages as a premium for the increase of the intensity of labor is to be guided by the methods and criteria of the period of the primitive accumulation of capitalism. Even the progressive capitalists in the epoch of capitalist prosperity and their theoreticians (the Brentano school, for example), put forward the amelioration of the material situation of the workers as a premise for the increase of labor productivity. The workers' state must generalize and socialize at least this viewpoint of progressive capitalism, insofar as the poverty of the country and the national limitation of our revolution does not permit us and will not permit us for a long time to be guided by a real socialist criterion. That is to say, the purpose of production is to meet human needs. We will not come to such really socialist relations between production and consumption for a number of years yet, under conditions of victorious revolution in the advanced capitalist countries, when our country is included in a common economic system. But since we have socialized the capitalist means of production, we must at least socialize also, so far as wages are concerned, the tendencies of progressive capitalism and not those of primitive or declining capitalism. And for this purpose we must crush and throw to the winds the tendencies that imbue the last joint resolution of the Russian trade unions and the Supreme Council of the National Economy relating to wages projected for 1929. It is a decree of the Stalinist Political Bureau. It announces that with a few exceptions, amounting to nearly 35 million rubles, there must be no mechanical (remarkable word!) increases in wages. Innumerable newspaper articles explain that the task for 1929 is *to fight for the maintenance of the present scale of real wages.* And at the same time all the noisemakers are clattering away to announce the mighty rise of socialist construction. At the same time manufactured goods are being rushed out to the villages. Unemployment is growing. Budget appropriations for the protection of labor are insignificant. Alcoholism is on the increase. And as a perspective we have for the coming year the struggle to *maintain* the present wage of the workers. This means that the economic rise of the country is being accomplished at the price of decreasing the proletariat's share in the national income as compared to that of the other classes. No statistics can refute this fact, which is in equal parts the result of the policy of the right and the center.

In the reconstruction period, work followed the old roads blazed by capitalism. This period barely brought the reestablishment of prewar wages to the main cadres of the proletariat. In the work of reconstruction we utilized the experiences acquired by Russian capitalism, which we had overthrown. Basically, it is only now that the epoch of independent socialist development is beginning. The first steps taken along this road have already shown very clearly that in order to succeed we must have, on an absolutely new scale, initiative, ingenuity, perspicacity, creative will, and all this not only from the upper leading circles but also from the main proletarian cadres and the working masses in general. The Shakhty affair is eloquent not only of the incompetence and the bureaucratic spirit of the leadership, but also of the weak cultural and technical level of the workers of Shakhty, as well as their lack of socialist interest. Has anyone ever calculated what "socialist construction" at Shakhty cost? Neither the right nor the center has done it, so as not to burn their fingers. Nevertheless, one can boldly assert that if half, or even a third of the criminally despoiled millions had been employed at the right time to raise the material and cultural level of the Shakhty workers, to interest them more and more in their work from the socialist viewpoint, production would be at a far higher stage today. But the Shakhty affair is not an exceptional one. It is only the most flagrant expression of bureaucratic irresponsibility above, and material and cultural backwardness and passivity below.

If we speak seriously of independent socialist construction, proceeding from the miserable economic basis we have inherited, we must be fully and wholly imbued with the idea that of all the economic investments, the most undeniable, expedient, and lucrative is that which is put into the proletariat by systematically and opportunely increasing real wages.

They do not even dream of understanding this. The myopic conceptions of the petty-bourgeois manager is the most important criterion. Whipped by the lash of the Opposition, the "masters" of the center have only dimly understood, ten years after October, that without making investments in heavy industry at the proper time, we are preparing for the future a sharpening of the existing contradictions and undermining the basis of light industry; on the other hand, these sorry-looking "masters," with all their underlings, have not understood to this day that unless they make timely investments aimed at developing a skilled workforce— skilled in all respects: social, political, technical, and cultural— they are surely paving the way for the collapse of the whole social system.

The stereotyped reply—Where will we get the means?—is only a bureaucratic subterfuge. It is enough to compare the state budget, reaching almost 8 billion in 1929; the gross production of state industry, amounting to 13 billion; capital investments of more than 1.5 billion; with the miserable 35 million constituting the annual fund for wage increases. No one disputes that bricks and iron, as well as their transportation, must be paid for. The necessity of calculating the costs of production is admitted at least in principle. But the expenditures necessary for the extended reproduction of socialist labor power and the expenditures necessary to render it more qualified are considered last in all calculations, and it is at the expense of these "reserve funds" that all the contradictions of our economy, which is managed in a miserable manner, are evened up. It is not the centrists who will put an end to this state of affairs.

## VII. Possible Consequences of the Struggle

When we speak of the possible consequences of the present campaign, the question can and must be approached first of all from the aims and plans pursued by the centrist leading group, and then from the viewpoint of the objective results that can and must develop in spite of all the schemes of the centrist staff.

The refrain one hears in this whole campaign is the entirely absurd affirmation that "basically" the right and left wings are one and the same thing. This is not simply nonsense that rests on nothing and is impossible to formulate in a clear manner. This nonsense has a definite purpose, it serves a well-determined task: at a certain stage of the struggle, at the moment when the right has been sufficently terrified, fire will be abruptly opened again against the left wing. It is true that even without this the fire does not cease for a single moment. Behind the scenes of the anonymous struggle against the right, an unrestrained struggle is conducted against the left. And here the "masters" don't simply make vague references to "objective conditions." Determined long ago to stop at nothing, they wage a furious baiting campaign against specifically named individuals. Since the "remnants" are not content merely to live, but "raise their heads," the main task dominating the whole policy of the centrist staff is to bring the struggle against the left wing around to a new stage, a "higher" one, that is, to renounce definitely all attempts to convince them (in which they are obviously powerless) and to make use of stronger methods. Article 58 must be replaced with one that is still more effective. It is not necessary to explain that it is precisely on this road that the leadership condemned by history will break its neck. But the centrist bankrupts, armed with the power of the apparatus, have no other road before them. To apply these more decisive measures, the centrist leadership must settle accounts with the remnants of the "conciliatory tendency" inside the apparatus itself and around it. It is not a question here of conciliation with the right wing: that conciliation is the very soul of Stalinist centrism. No, we speak of the *tendency of conciliation toward the Bolshevik-Leninists*. The campaign against the right serves only as a springboard for a new "monolithic" attack upon the left. Whoever has not understood this has understood nothing.

But the plans of centrism are only one of the factors, even though still a very important one, in the process of the development of the inner-party struggle. That is why it is necessary to examine the consequences, "unforeseen" by the strategists of the center, that follow from the crisis of the ruling bloc.

It is evidently impossible to predict now at what point the present campaign of the center will be brought to a halt, what regroupings will immediately take place, and so forth. But the general character of the results of the crisis of the center-right bloc can be clearly perceived. The abrupt zigzags that centrism is forced to describe give no guarantee for the coming day. On the other hand, centrism can never make its zigzags with impunity. More often than not these zigzags form the point of departure for a differentiation within centrism, for the separation of one of its layers, of a section of its adherents, for the appearance within the centrist leadership of various groupings, which, in turn, facilitates the work of Bolshevik agitation and recruiting. Centrism is the strongest force in the party for the moment. Whoever sees centrism as something completely finished, and neglects the real processes taking place within and behind it, will either remain forever the oracle of some radical literary club or else will himself roll toward centrism or even further to the right. A Bolshevik-Leninist must clearly understand that even if the right-center crisis does not immediately set broader masses into motion (and that depends upon us to a certain degree), it leaves behind it seriously increasing cleavages that penetrate the masses, and around which will grow new, deeper, mass-based groupings. It goes without saying that this approach to the internal processes of the party has nothing in common with the impatient striving to grab at the tail of centrism, no matter where or how, so as not to arrive too late with one's Opposition baggage for the departure of the next special train.

The reinforcement of centrism from the left, that is, by the proletarian core of the party, even if this happens as a result of the struggle against the right, will doubtless be neither very serious nor lasting. In fighting the Opposition, the centrists are forced to weed out with the right hand what they sow with the left.

The victory of the centrists will not bring any real and tangible change either in the material situation of the workers or in the party regime, unless the workers led by the Bolshevik-Leninists exercise a strong pressure. The alert mass will continue to think in its own way about the questions of the right danger. In this the Leninists will help them. On the left flank of centrism there is an open wound which does not heal, but, on the contrary, goes deeper, keeps centrism in a feverish agitation, and does not leave it in peace.

At the same time, centrism will also weaken to the right. The proprietor and the bureaucrat saw the center-right bloc as a whole; they saw in it not only the "lesser evil" but also the embryo of an internal evolution; that is why they supported it. Now they are beginning to distinguish between the centrists and the right. They are evidently dissatisfied with the weakness of the right and its lack of character. But these are "their own people," who have momentarily gone astray. The centrists, on the other hand, are now strangers, almost enemies. By its victory on both fronts, centrism has betrayed itself. Its social basis contracts in the same proportion as its power in the apparatus increases. The equilibrium of centrism more and more approaches that of a tight-rope walker; there can be no talk of its stability.

A serious regroupment will be effected within the right wing as well. It is not absolutely impossible that a certain part of the right elements—elements who seriously believed in the existence of "Trotskyism" and who were educated in the struggle against it—will begin to reexamine their ideological baggage seriously under the impact of the shock they have just received and then turn abruptly toward the left, even as far as the Opposition. But it goes without saying that only a very small, sincere minority will take this path. The main movement of the right wing will be in the opposite direction. The lower sections will be dissatisfied with the capitulatory spirit of the upper circles. The proprietor will press hard. The Ustryalovists will whisper finished formulas. Numerous bureaucratic elements of the right will submit, of course; that is, they will mask themselves as centrists, take their place at the order of their superiors, and vote against the right deviation. The number of careerists, people who live only to save their hides, will grow in the apparatus. But the more stable and vigorous right elements will mature rapidly, will think out their tasks to the end, will formulate clear slogans, and will seek to establish more serious connections with the Thermidorian forces outside the party. So far as the group of "leaders" is concerned, predictions are especially difficult. In any case, for the work that the right has before it, the Voroshilovs and the Uglanovs are much more important than the Bukharins and the Rykovs. In citing these names we are not thinking so much of specific persons as of political types. As a result of the regroupings, the "annihilated" right wing will become stronger and more conscious.

It is true that the right wants to be at peace. Nevertheless one must not think that the right wing is entirely and absolutely "pacifist." In fighting for order, the exasperated petty bourgeoisie is capable of causing the greatest disorder. For example: Italian fascism. In fighting against crises, against commotions and dangers, the right wing at some subsequent stage can help the new proprietors and all the discontented in general to shake Soviet power so as to drive out the dictatorship of the proletariat. We must remember that the instincts of the petty bourgeoisie, when they are confined and repressed for a long time, contain in themselves an enormous explosive force. Nowhere and never in the course of history have the instincts and aspirations of preservation and property been so long and so pitilessly curbed as under the Soviet regime. There are many Thermidorian and fascist elements in the country. They have become very strong. The confidence they feel in themselves, from a political point of view, grew in the process of annihilating the Opposition. With good reason did they consider that the fight against the Opposition was *their* fight. The policy of zigzags consolidates them, tortures them, and spurs them on. In contrast to centrism, the right wing has great reserves of growth which, from the political point of view, have as yet scarcely broken through.

The final result is therefore the following: the strengthening and clearer demarcation of the wings at the expense of centrism, despite the growing concentration of power in its hands. This means a growing differentiation within the party; the false monolithism thus has to pay very dearly. There is no doubt that for the dictatorship of the proletariat this not only involves heavy costs in general, but even presents direct dangers. This is the curse of centrism. Consistent Marxist policy made the party more compact by giving it revolutionary homogeneity. Centrism, on the contrary, appears like an ideologically shapeless axis around which right and left elements turn for a certain period. In the last five years the party swelled beyond measure, losing in precision what it won in numbers. The centrist policy is on the way to being repaid now in full: first from the left side, now from the right. A centrist leadership in the last analysis always involves the crumbling of the party. To attempt now to get out of the process of differentiation in the party and the definite formation of factions by means of tearful supplication or else by conferences behind the scenes would simply be stupidity. Without a general delimitation according to lines of principle, we will only have the crumbling of the party into molecules, followed by the catastrophic crash of the usurpatory apparatus, pulling the conquests of October down with it.

Despite their great scope, the two campaigns of the centrists against the wings (against the Bolshevik-Leninists and against the Thermidorians of the right) have only a preliminary, preparatory, preventive character. The real struggles still lie in the future. The classes will decide. The question of the power of October, with which the centrist dancers are playing as they balance on the rope, will be decided by millions and tens of millions of people. Whether sooner or later, in installments or at one blow, by the direct use of violence or within the limits of the restored constitution of the party and of the soviets, will depend on the tempo of the internal processes and the changes in the international situation. Only one thing is clear: the Bolshevik-Leninists have no other path to follow than to mobilize the living elements and those capable of living for their party, to weld together the proletarian core of the party, and to mobilize the working class as a whole, efforts inseparably connected with the struggle for a Leninist line in the Communist International. The present centrist campaign against the right must show every proletarian revolutionist the need and duty of multiplying tenfold his efforts to follow an independent political line, forged by the whole history of Bolshevism and proved correct in the colossal test of events of recent years.

# ON THE TOPICS OF THE DAY

## December 1928

*NOTE: This memorandum is in reply to criticisms leveled at Trotsky for a few lines in his "Heart-to-Heart Talk with a Well-meaning Party Member," September 12, in which he offered to make an agreement with the right wing against the Stalin faction to restore inner-party democracy.*

*Krokodil (mentioned in the last paragraph) is the Soviet satirical magazine.*

*From the roman numeral at the beginning of this article, it seems that Trotsky intended to write about other "topics of the day" after writing about the "bloc" with the rights. He did not do that, for reasons that are uncertain (perhaps the intensified apparatus pressure forced him to turn to other projects).*

*By permission of the Harvard College Library. Translated from the Russian for this volume by Tom Twiss.*

### I. A "Bloc" with the Rights and Nonsense in General

The final lines of my discussion with a "well-meaning party member" quite unexpectedly provoked confusion and almost even indignation in some comrades, living, it is true, in one and the same colony. It seemed to them that the final lines of the discussion could be understood as laying the basis for a "bloc" with the rights. No more and no less. These comrades even began to send telegrams of appeal to other colonies.

At first it seemed to me—I beg forgiveness—that here we were confronted with certain indications that comrades were imagining things. This kind of disorder is caused, as everyone knows, by monotony in nature and monolithism in human life.

Our declaration to the Sixth Congress, written long before the struggle of the centrists with the rights came into the open, states: "Can the Opposition support the rights against the centrists, who formally hold power—in order to help overthrow them, to 'avenge ourselves' on them for the odious persecution, the rudeness and disloyalty, the 'Wrangel officer,' Article 58, and other deliberately vicious deeds? There have been such combinations between the left and the right in [past] revolutions. Such combinations have also ruined revolutions. In our party the right represents the link which the bourgeois classes secretly hold onto, to drag the revolution onto the path of Thermidor. *At the present moment,* the center is trying to resist, or half-resist. It is clear: the Opposition cannot have anything in common with such combinationist adventurism, counting on the aid of the right to overthrow the center" [see "Declaration to the Sixth Comintern Congress" in this volume, page 142].

Even now our declaration retains all its force in spite of certain hasty voices which pronounced the declaration "obsolete" after the July plenum and thought the situation was saved only by the postscript ["The July Plenum and the Right Danger"]. The incorrectness of such an evaluation is quite clear. The postscript reacted to a definite, very significant episode in the struggle of the centrists with the rights, and it reacted correctly. It, together with other documents and statements of our cothinkers, undoubtedly accelerated the crisis of the right-centrist bloc, explaining to rather wide circles exactly what the situation was. It is possible to say—and this will not at all be conceit on the part of the Opposition—that documents of this sort facilitated the "victory" of the centrists over the right (while not taking upon ourselves even a shade of responsibility for the centrists), for we called people and things by their right names, which is quite inadmissible to the tongue-tied centrist. Whereas the postscript dealt with a *certain moment* in the reciprocal relations of the centrists and the rights, the declaration was intended for a *more extended period.* This is why it retains all its force even now, when the campaign against the rights has taken an open form and a broad apparatus scale. Read through it now and compare it with the exercise drills of the Democratic Centralists. The comparison is not even worth discussing. It goes without saying that the passage cited above which rejects *in advance* "combinationist adventurism" which would try to "overthrow the center with the help of the rights" also retains its significance.

In some letters comrades have asked, "Are there really any such people?" I had no one in our circles in mind personally. But the logic of struggle can create such attitudes in certain elements. The warning was especially necessary because, in regard to the Zinovievists at any rate, we were never able to be sure of them, and we can't be now. It was not by chance that Bukharin, on behalf of the trio [Rykov, Tomsky, Bukharin], entered into official negotiations with Kamenev. And it was not accidental that Kamenev and Company did not inform the party about these discussions, leaving this other road open for themselves. Here, then, a clear and distinct dividing line had to be drawn in advance, and that was done in the declaration. Perhaps some valiant Democratic Centralist will ask, "Do you really have to answer for the Zinovievists?" No, we aren't answering for them. But we live the life of the party and actively intervene in all its internal relations.

The postscript cites the words of Rykov: "The main task of the Trotskyists is to prevent the triumph of the right wing." How remarkable those words sound now when Rykov and Uglanov cast their votes "monolithically" for resolutions which declare that their, Rykov's and Uglanov's, "main task is to prevent the triumph of the right wing." This "Trotskyism" has really come a long way. Quite a career it's made for itself in such a short time. Here the November plenum has monolithically adopted "the main task of the Trotskyists." Nevertheless, we are not flattering ourselves. Our heads are not spinning. We remember the German saying: "when two different people say the same thing, it is not at all the same thing." These words apply even more to different political groups. However, there is a benefit. Now even the backward party member will have to use his brains: How is it that from July to November Rykov managed to become a Trotskyist, i.e., an ardent "fighter" against the right deviation?

In full accordance with the declaration to the Sixth Congress, the postscript confirmed Rykov's threatening accusation: "Precisely correct. The victory of the right wing would be the last step leading to Thermidor. Rykov is right. Our main task now is to prevent the triumph of the right wing" [see "The July Plenum and the Right Danger"].

Thus, we took a quite timely, clear, and distinct position on this question, leaving no room for any false interpretations. What, then, is the source of the sudden alarm felt by some comrades, who, according to the French expression of Leo Tolstoy, in the heat of the moment even "made the telegraph dance." The alarm arose from the last few lines of the "Heart-to-Heart Talk." We take this opportunity to consider the question in the more concrete light in which it stands before us at the present, more developed stage.

The comrades mentioned above do not try to deny that the whole "Talk" was directed against the right wing's banal philistinism (one of its central features). In that case what do the final lines mean? Do they really stand in such flagrant contradiction not only to the declaration and the postcript but also to the rest of the "Heart-to-Heart Talk"? No, there is not even a trace of a contradiction. These lines only need to be approached with a living and vital political attitude, free from pedantry.

The fact is that the "Heart-to-Heart Talk" reduces all questions to questions of the party regime, i.e., "the regime of the Yaroslavskys," who have "great resources in their hands, not in the domain of ideas, of course, but resources that in their own way are also effective, at least for now. They will try to strangle you [the rights], while in essence carrying out your policies, although only by installments," and so on. My correspondent whined about everything that is going on in the party and plaintively urged me to return to the fold. That means that right-wing Communists of this type exist. In general we must keep in mind—let me note in passing—the extreme diversity of the internal composition of both the right and the centrist groups as a result of the underground-apparatus forms of party life. There will still be all sorts of migrations and realignments. That, in the final analysis, is, of course, what our politics in relation to the party are based on. That is why the clear and essentially finished characterization of the rights and centrists must be supplemented in practice, i.e., in agitation and propaganda, with great flexibility in addressing the living human material constituting these groups. One language with Rykov or Uglanov, another with the type of rank-and-file member or even cadre element who appeals to us with a letter on his own initiative and tearfully implores the Oppositionists to return to the party.

Another tone, another language—but of course the line has to be one. And I did not violate this line of ours to even the slightest degree. I only developed it, concretized it, and pushed it slightly further. I say to this well-meaning and confused Rykovist: You weep over the state of the party? You are afraid of a split? You are right [to be concerned]. The dangers are terribly great. It is impossible to speak frankly and honestly in the party. Self-criticism means simply that everyone is now ordered to "self-criticize" Uglanov. Most dangerous, because it is the most immediate of all dangers, is the party regime. What is the way out? To bring the party out of this underground, illegal situation [in regard to its political life]. Decrease to one-twentieth of its present size, i.e., reduce to five or six million rubles, the party budget, which has become the basis of bureaucratic arbitrariness.

Give party members the chance to vote secretly. Prepare the Sixteenth Congress honestly, i.e., so that the whole party can listen to representatives of all three tendencies with full freedom. Of course, for this it would be necessary to return the Opposition to the party. After enumerating these demands, the "Heart-to-Heart Talk" concludes: "These are strictly practical proposals. On the basis of these proposals we would even be willing to negotiate with the rights, because the implementation of these elementary preconditions of party principle would give the proletarian core the opportunity to really call to account not only the rights but also the centrists, i.e., the main support and protection for opportunism in the party."

These are the lines, then, that provoked the confusion. This is what, I am told, could be interpreted as a bloc with the rights against the center. No, dear comrades, you did not think this question through to the end. You did not try to conceive of the currently developing situation in a concrete way. And apparently you did not think enough about what a bloc is. We had a bloc with the Zinovievists. For the sake of this bloc we made isolated, partial concessions. Most often these were concessions to some of our closest cothinkers who gravitated toward the Zinovievists politically or tactically. In isolated cases these concessions obviously went too far and temporarily produced negative results which we firmly kept in mind for the future. But in all fundamental respects the bloc was formed on the basis of the ideas of the proletarian left, i.e., on *our* ground.

What kind of bloc could there be with the rights? On what ground? Is such a bloc conceivable? Is it possible in general, even for one minute, to speak or think seriously about a common platform with them? In the negotiations with Kamenev, Bukharin put matters this way: "We will conclude a bloc against Stalin and afterwards we will write a positive platform together" [see appendix to this volume]. Literally! But only died-in-the-wool horse traders or totally confused, lost, and bankrupt Balabolkins could pose the question this way. What can we have in common with these two "categories" (to use the philosophical language of the "theoretician" Stalin)?

In that case what does the phrase mean which says "on the basis of these proposals we would even be willing to negotiate with the rights"? It means precisely what it says. Concretely speaking, it responds to the well-meaning party member this way: Instead of whining and whimpering, demand as a first step the return of the Opposition from exile. We will have complete "agreement" with you on this. Demand further the honest convening of a party congress. And what do I promise the rights as compensation? The answer is given in these very lines: "to really call to account not only the rights but also the centrists, i.e., the main support and protection for opportunism in the party." Where is the bloc in this? Where is the hint of a bloc? Where is the shade of a hint? Or even the shade of a shade? No, without hallucinating you couldn't have come up with this. The final passage of the "Heart-to-Heart Talk" resounds with the bitterest mockery toward the rights: You have come to grief, you say, dear friends. You're in trouble. The apparatus is pressing you too hard. Wouldn't you like to feast on a little democracy? Try some, try some. And we will support you—as a rope supports a hanging man. There you have the meaning of the final lines. Only perhaps the malicious glee in them is veiled slightly, because after all this is a talk with a *well-meaning* party member.

But besides the taunting of the rights, these lines contain a more serious meaning intended for our cothinkers in the party. Is the possibility excluded that the rights are going to fall into opposition to the apparatus on questions of the party regime and repeat our elementary demands on this score? No, such a possibility is not excluded. It is very likely, and, given the development of the struggle, it is even inevitable. Even at the November plenum, with all its monolithism, we heard some voices of protest against the fact that the Moscow secretaries were replaced through the system of "self-criticism," that is, without a conference and without the masses (see the newspaper report on Stalin's speech [in Stalin's *Works,* vol. 11, pp. 299-300]). Just what should our cothinkers do in these cases as members of party cells? Should they expose the usurpationist system of elections? Should they demand that conferences be correctly prepared and convened? Yes, they should. But here they will "coincide" with the rights, won't they? Actually, it is not they who will coincide with the rights, but the rights who in this area will sometimes "coincide" with us, shamefacedly renouncing their theory and practices of yesterday and thus helping us to expose both themselves and the entire party regime. What is so terrible about such a "coincidence" as long as we don't make even the smallest concession in the process, but continue to develop our principled line with redoubled force? The above-quoted final lines of my "Heart-to-Heart Talk" were written precisely with the foreknowledge that this sort of "coincidence" or "half-coincidence" of votes or statements on questions of party legality is possible, even inevitable.*

If a comparison is permitted from a sphere which is entirely different and completely alien to us, I would take the example of a duel. This example is a very useful way of elucidating the question we are concerned with. A duel is a barbarous, "knightly," and extremely vile form of resolving personal conflicts: here the aim of each participant is simply to cut the other's throat. However, before every duel the "civilized" adversaries enter into an "agreement" with each other, directly or through seconds, concerning such details as the distance between them, the type of revolver each will use to fire on the other, etc. Can one say in reference to this "agreement" that the opponents concluded a bloc? It would seem not. How the devil can there be a bloc when the aim is mutual destruction? But in "civilized" society even mutual destruction is carried out not from ambush but according to certain norms which require preliminary "agreement."

The party statutes represent certain fixed norms for discussion and collective decision and action, as well as for internal ideological battle. Inasmuch as we, the Opposition, want to return to the party and since most of us actually belong to it (see Stalin's speech [ibid., p. 289]), we also recognize the statutes as the regulator of party life. But this also means the regulator of our struggle with the rights and centrists. The statutes constitute a ready-made [duelists'] agreement. But they have been trampled on, crushed, and destroyed. We are prepared to conclude an "agreement" with any section of the party in any place, on any particular matter, for even a partial restoration of the party statutes. In relation to the rights and centrists as political factions, this means that we are ready to conclude an agreement with them about the conditions for an irreconcilable struggle. That's all.

---

*It is necessary to note that a certain honest section of the rights, who have simply been deceived, may even turn back toward us, after carrying their "anti-Trotskyism" to its logical conclusion, i.e., to Ustryalovism. But this will be, of course, only a small minority. The general line of the rights leads in the opposite direction. We must expect to grow at the expense mainly of the centrist ranks, or, more accurately, at the expense of that undifferentiated mass of worker–party members who constitute the automatic support of centrism.

In his poor excuse for a speech [at the] November [plenum], which we will have to discuss separately [see "Crisis in the Right-Center Bloc"], Stalin already talks about a bloc of the lefts with the rights—either as a fact or as a possibility [*Works,* vol. 11, pp. 291-93]. On the one hand, he is obviously alluding here to Bukharin's discussions with Kamenev (even here we are helping the centrists struggle against the rights, exposing what the centrists are afraid to call by name); on the other hand, he is giving the apparatchiks "the line" in the event of possible coincidences in the statements or votes of the rights and lefts on questions of elementary party rights. Stalin wants to scare both us and the rights by this. But we are not afraid. This is also the more serious meaning of the final lines of my "Heart-to-Heart Talk." Let the rights expose the usurpation which they helped to create and even today totally support. From us they will receive only principled blows which are far more serious than the organizational pinching practiced by the Stalinists. And let the centrists, "monolithically" sitting with the leaders of the rights in a monolithic Politburo, accuse us of being in a bloc with the rights—on the grounds, don't you see, that we so generously allow the rights to demand the abolition of Article 58. Truly, this is a scene fit to amuse the gods on Olympus or to appear in *Krokodil,* if that beast with the threatening name had even one tooth left in its mouth.

# TOO CONCILIATORY A LINE?

## December 1928

*NOTE: A letter to one of the "intransigents" in the Opposition. By permission of the Harvard College Library. Translated from the Russian for this volume by Michael Sosa.*

Like several other comrades, you ask whether we are taking too conciliatory a line in advancing such demands as the honest convening of the Sixteenth Congress, a reduction in the party budget to one-twentieth of its present size, publication of suppressed works by Lenin, and so on. It is of course clear to you that we are talking about the most immediate slogans on the internal party level. These are intended to be only first steps, the implementation of which would surely show the party that a serious change had been made in the regime. The question of how likely the slogans are to be realized under the present leadership by no means decides the fate of the slogans themselves. For all of us it is absolutely clear that (a) the present leadership is bankrupt, and (b) the above-mentioned minimal slogans of an internal party nature are not realizable so long as they depend upon the goodwill of the leadership. What we are talking about is the mobilization of the proletarian core of the party—the Bolshevik faction of the AUCP, so to speak—around certain very simple, indisputable, transitional demands. The resistance of the leadership to these demands will open the eyes of the party to the character of the leadership, and will augment the Bolshevik faction of the AUCP. In other words, the significance of the proposed demands in internal party life is the same as the significance of transitional demands in the Communist program in general.

But are these demands correct, even as transitional ones? It is possible to dispute their correctness only if one proceeds from the viewpoint that "the party is a corpse" (V. Smirnov), that is, if one denies the presence of the Bolshevik faction within the AUCP and the possibility of its growing very significantly. This question is decisive at the present stage. In order to evaluate the correctness and expediency of any transitional demand, it is necessary to place oneself mentally in the position of the worker-Oppositionist speaking at a cell meeting or a general factory meeting where party questions such as "self-criticism" are discussed. If the worker-Oppositionist wants to destroy himself and his cause, he will say: "The party is a corpse, and we can expect nothing from it." Such a position would be purely reactionary. Sectarianism, in attempting to come out into the broad arena, has often played and often will play a reactionary role. The sensible Oppositionist will say: "In order for 'self-criticism' to cease being half-comedy and half-provocation, it is necessary to provide for the implementation of the most elementary prerequisites of party democracy," and he will present the demands we have mentioned. He may, and even should, add openly: "I have no confidence at all that the present leadership will willingly implement these demands, and therefore I have not one bit of confidence in 'self-criticism.' But you, comrades, believe in 'self-criticism' or wish to believe it it. So let's test it out in the case of the demands I have proposed, which nobody could argue with." That is how a serious Oppositionist, seeking ways to reach the proletarian core of the party and the masses in general, will act. Our correctness alone will not suffice. Correctness which does not strive to become a mass force is totally worthless. Far be it from us to chase around trying to out-Smirnov Smirnov. At party meetings the followers of V. Smirnov simply will not know how to behave, or they will have to devote their speaking time to trying to prove that they never actually considered the party a corpse, etc.

One must not forget, of course, that partial slogans cover only a part of the problem. But the Platform remains, as do all our other documents. The system of demands elaborated there touches upon all the major problems of the activity of the AUCP and the Comintern. In this area we have not moderated anything. On the contrary, we have sharpened and deepened our position (in particular, in our documents sent to the [Sixth Comintern] Congress). But it is necessary to present our irreconcilable criticism and "unabridged" slogans to the party in such a way that the working class core feels that we wish to and are able to speak to them in language they can understand.

The working class core and the masses in general are not yet with us. We can't forget this. This is major and fundamental. The masses are dissatisfied, as is the working class core of the party, but they express their dissatisfaction in the conventional and false language which the bureaucratic apparatus has imposed on them, and a very important part of that is hostility to the Opposition, or simply fear of it. Without giving up anything essential, we must approach the party ranks in such a way as to help them find their way to genuine party principles, starting from their present positions. These are the aims which the above-mentioned slogans partially serve.

# MARXISM AND THE RELATION BETWEEN PROLETARIAN AND PEASANT REVOLUTION

## December 1928

*NOTE: The concluding section of some unfinished materials, probably written in December 1928. Another excerpt from the materials is in the appendix to this volume. In this excerpt Trotsky explains the history of Marx's thinking about permanent revolution and clarifies the importance of considering the democratic revolution as an inseparable part of the dictatorship of the proletariat, rather than as a separate, preliminary stage, as the Stalinists did.*

*By permission of the Harvard College Library. Translated from the Russian for this volume by George Saunders.*

In 1881 Vera Zasulich asked Marx what the Russian Marxists should do until capitalism had prepared the conditions in Russia for a proletarian revolution. This is what Zasulich wrote:

"If on the other hand the village commune (the Russian *mir*) is doomed to destruction then the only thing that remains for a socialist as such is to seek more or less well-grounded measuring sticks for determining roughly for how many decades the land of the Russian peasant will pass into the hands of the bourgeoisie and how many hundreds of years will elapse before capitalism in Russia attains the same level of development as Western Europe. In that case the socialist should carry on propaganda only among urban workers, who would constantly be swamped by the mass of peasants thrown onto the streets of the large cities in search of a wage, driven there by the disintegration of the village commune" (excerpt from Zasulich's letter to Marx of February 16, 1881, from the Russian book *Emancipation of Labor Group*, second collection of writings, p. 222).

What is most remarkable in this quotation is that the socialist revolution is separated from the democratic transformation by

347

several *centuries.* To representatives of the post-October generation this will seem monstrous. But in fact that point of view
unquestionably predominated among Russian Marxists until
1905 and to a significant extent until 1917 as well. Of course, not
everyone measured the distance to the socialist revolution in
centuries. Here Zasulich was simply looking at the history of
England as though it were a mirror for the more backward
nations. But the main idea, that first there must be a bourgeois-
democratic revolution, then the productive forces must develop
for a period of unspecified length on capitalist foundations, and
only after that would come the age of socialist revolution in its
own right—that idea was the prevailing one, as the proceedings
of the Bolshevik Party conference of March 1917 show. All of its
participants, without exception, viewed things from the angle
that the democratic revolution must be completed, not that the
socialist revolution must be prepared. Those who after October
tried in any way to make a critical assessment of their attitude
toward the February revolution openly admitted that they were
heading for one door but ended up at another. Here, for example,
is what Olminsky wrote on this subject in 1921. "The coming
revolution must be only a bourgeois revolution. . . . That was an
obligatory premise for every member of the party, the official
opinion of the party, its continual and unchanging slogan right
up to the February revolution of 1917, and even some time after."

What was involved was not at all that the revolution must first
carry out the democratic tasks and only on that basis could it
grow over into a socialist revolution. None of the participants in
the March conference had the slightest inkling of such an idea
before Lenin's arrival. At that time not only did Stalin never refer
to Lenin's article of 1915 but he warned against frightening off
the bourgeoisie in exactly the same spirit as Zhordania. The
conviction that history dare not leap over a stage dictated by
some philistine prescription was already firmly implanted in his
skull. There were three stages: first the democratic revolution,
carried through to the end; then a period of the development of
capitalist productive forces; and finally the period of socialist
revolution. The second stage was conceived as quite a prolonged
one, measured, if not in centuries as Zasulich did, then certainly
in multiple decades. It was assumed that a victorious proletarian
revolution in Europe might shorten the second stage, but in the
best of cases this factor was included only as a theoretical
possibility. According to this stereotyped theory held by Stalin
and prevailing [in the party] almost totally, the position of

permanent revolution, which united the democratic and socialist revolutions within the framework of a single stage, was absolutely inadmissible, anti-Marxist, monstrous.

And yet in the general sense the idea of permanent revolution was one of the most important ideas of Marx and Engels. The *Communist Manifesto* was written in 1847, several months before the revolution of 1848, which has gone down in history as a partial, unfinished, bourgeois revolution. Germany at that time was a very backward country, thoroughly fettered by the chains of feudalism and serfdom. Nevertheless Marx and Engels did not by any means develop a perspective involving three stages. They regarded the coming revolution as a transitional one; that is, it would begin by carrying out a bourgeois-democratic program but would be transformed by the inner mechanics of the forces involved and grow over into a socialist revolution. Here is what the *Communist Manifesto* says on this point: "The Communists turn their attention chiefly to Germany, because that country is on the eve of a bourgeois revolution that is bound to be carried out under more advanced conditions of European civilization, and with a much more developed proletariat, than that of England was in the seventeenth, and of France in the eighteenth century, and because the bourgeois revolution in Germany will be but the prelude to an immediately following proletarian revolution" [*The Communist Manifesto*, New York: Pathfinder, 1970, p. 44].

This idea was not at all accidental. In the *Neue Rheinische Zeitung,* in the thick of the 1848 revolution itself, Marx and Engels put forward the program of permanent revolution and Marx even wrote an article with that phrase as the title.

The revolution of 1848 did not grow over into a socialist revolution. But it was not completed as a democratic revolution either. For an understanding of historical dynamics the second fact is no less important than the first. 1848 showed that if conditions were not yet ripe for a dictatorship of the proletariat, there was no room either for a genuine completion of the democratic revolution. The first and third stages turned out to be inseparably connected. In this fundamental sense the *Communist Manifesto* was absolutely right.

Did Marx ignore the peasant question and the task of eliminating all the feudal rubbish in general? It's absurd even to ask the question. Marx had nothing in common with the idealist metaphysic of Lassalle, who thought that the peasantry in general embodied reactionary principles. Of course, Marx did not consider

the peasantry a socialist class. He evaluated the historical role of
the peasantry dialectically. Marxist theory as a whole not only
speaks with full eloquence on this score but also and in particular
the *Neue Rheinische Zeitung* of 1848.

After the victory of the counterrevolution Marx had to make
several adjustments, postponing the day when the revolution
could be expected to come again. But did Marx admit an error?
Did he come to the realization that you can't leap over stages?
Did he at last grasp that there were precisely three such stages?
No, Marx proved to be incorrigible. At a time of victorious
counterrevolution he outlined the prospects for a new revolutionary upturn and once again tied the democratic, above all the
agrarian, revolution together with the dictatorship of the proletariat, using the knot of permanency. This is what Marx wrote in
1856: "The whole thing in Germany will depend on the possibility
of backing the proletarian revolution by some second edition of
the Peasant War. Then the affair will be splendid" [Marx and
Engels, *Selected Works,* vol. 1, Moscow, 1969, p. 529].

These words have been quoted frequently but, as the disputes
and writings of the past few years have shown, their fundamental meaning remains totally misunderstood. To back up the
dictatorship of the proletariat with a peasant war means that the
agrarian revolution is carried out, not *before* the dictatorship of
the proletariat, but *through* that dictatorship. Despite the lesson
of 1848 Marx did not adopt the pedantic philosophy of three
stages, a philosophy that in fact represents the immortalization
of a poorly digested understanding of the experience of England
and France. Marx held that the coming revolution would bring
the proletariat to power before the democratic revolution had
been carried through to completion. Marx made the victory of the
peasant war dependent on the coming to power of the proletariat.
He made the durability of the dictatorship of the proletariat
dependent on whether it rose and developed in parallel with, and
simultaneously with, the development of the peasant war.

Was Marx's orientation correct? In answering this question
today, we have much richer experience than Marx did. He was
relying on the experience of the classical bourgeois revolutions,
above all the French revolution, and made his prognosis of
permanent revolution on the basis of the changing relationship of
forces between the bourgeoisie and the proletariat. Engels in his
*Peasant War in Germany* demonstrated that the peasant war of
the sixteenth century was always led by some urban faction, that
is, by one wing of the bourgeoisie or another. Proceeding from the

fact that the bourgeoisie as a whole was no longer fit for a revolutionary role, Marx and Engels came to the conclusion that the leadership of, a peasant war must be taken over by the proletariat, which would draw new strength from the peasant war, and that the dictatorship of the proletariat could during its first and most difficult stage find a strong base of support in the peasant war, that is, in the democratic agrarian revolution.

1848 provided an incomplete and solely negative confirmation of this view. The agrarian revolution did not lead to victory and the proletariat did not develop in full or come to power. Since then, however, we have had the experience of the Russian revolutions of 1905 and 1917 and the experience of the Chinese revolution. Now Marx's conception has been decisively, indestructibly confirmed: a positive confirmation in the Russian revolution and a negative confirmation in the Chinese.

The dictatorship of the proletariat proved possible in backward Russia precisely because it was backed up by a peasant war. In other words, the dictatorship of the proletariat proved to be possible and durable only because none of the factions of bourgeois society proved capable of assuming the leadership in resolving the agrarian question. Or to put it more briefly and precisely, the proletarian dictatorship proved possible for the very reason that the democratic dictatorship proved impossible.

In China, on the other hand, an attempt to solve the agrarian problem through a special democratic dictatorship backed up by the authority of the Comintern, the Soviet Communist Party, and the USSR, led only to the defeat of the revolution. Thus Marx's fundamental historical blueprint stands totally and completely confirmed. Revolutions in the new historical era will either combine the first phase with the third or they will roll back from the first phase itself.

# WHAT IS THE 'SMYCHKA'?

## December 1928

*NOTE: A fragment, probably written in December 1928. Smychka (bond or link) was Lenin's term for the relations necessary between the peasants and the workers' state, one of two preconditions for the construction of socialism in an overwhelmingly peasant country (the other precondition was revolution in the advanced industrial countries). Trotsky takes as his jumping-off point in this essay the distortion of this idea by Bukharin and Stalin, after Lenin's death, until it became part of a mechanistic schema that guaranteed the building of socialism in one country. He also returns to the theme of the relations between the democratic and proletarian revolutions.*

*By permission of the Harvard College Library. Translated from the Russian for this volume by George Saunders.*

This word has entered into circulation internationally. Nothing was discussed so much after Lenin's death as the *smychka*. And there was perhaps no area in which so many errors were made as in this one. In fact the whole theory of socialism in one country was derived from the *smychka*. The line of thinking was this: since the *smychka* consists in correctly balanced relations between state industry and peasant agriculture, or relations that are becoming more and more correctly balanced, isn't it obvious that a gradual, even if slow, development of the productive forces, resting on the foundation of the *smychka*, will automatically lead to socialism (if foreign military intervention does not prevent it)?

This whole line of argument rests upon a string of schoolboy errors. Its premises are, first, that the *smychka* has already come into being. The grain collections crisis is decisive empirical refutation of this idea, which we subjected to a thoroughgoing theoretical critique long before this crisis. Second, even if a sturdy bond between industry and peasant agriculture had actually come into being, it would not constitute the foundation for a future socialist economy within a national framework, but only a foundation on which to build a properly balanced and stable relationship between the proletariat and peasantry within a single isolated country for the entire period of the "breathing spell," i.e., until either a new war or new revolutions in other countries. For us, proletarian victory in the advanced countries would mean a radical restructuring of the economic foundations themselves to conform to a more productive international division of labor, which is the only means by which the true foundations for a socialist system can be built.

The third and final error is that there is no guarantee that even the *smychka* that has to one extent or another been achieved today will remain stable in the future throughout the transitional period.

We aspire to make a transition from the disharmonious and therefore crisis-ridden capitalist economy to a harmonious socialist economy. But the transitional period by no means implies the gradual dying out of the contradictions or the easing of economic crises. On the contrary even a theoretical analysis should tell us in advance that the coexistence of two systems, the socialist economy and the capitalist economy, simultaneously in conflict with one another and nourishing one another, must from time to time produce crises of unparalleled severity. The planning principle tends to weaken, if not paralyze, the market mechanism, which has its own way of overcoming the contradictions of capitalism. In its very essence the planning principle during the transitional period to a certain extent is bound to be the instrument of generalized crises. This is by no means a paradox. The planning principle in the conditions of the transitional era— applied for the first time in a backward country and in a situation, moreover, of unstable world economic relations— contains within itself a tremendous risk of miscalculation.

Laplace said that we could predict the future in all fields if we had minds capable of taking into account all the processes within the universe, understanding them in their interactions and projecting their future lines of development. Laplace didn't have that kind of mind himself. And we won't go into the question of the number of Laplaces in the present leadership. The need for an a priori solution to economic problems, which takes the form of an equation with an enormous number of unknowns, inevitably has the result that in some cases through planned regulation some partial or particular difficulties are gotten out of the way by being driven inward, being swept under the rug, thus accumulating problems and laying the basis for generalized crises, crises which send sky high certain economic relationships which had seemed to be solidly established.

If we add to this the leadership's low theoretical level and practical short-sightedness, it's easy to understand how planning can become a self-destructive instrument, bringing crises to a point of extreme tension that threatens the system as a whole.

A classic example is the grain collections crisis itself, for it occurs along the line of the relationship between state industry and peasant agriculture; that is, along the very line of the supposedly solid and secure *smychka*.

It was at the same seventh plenum of the ECCI where the Left Opposition was condemned, and Marxism along with it, that Bukharin—as we know—chose this question of the grain collections as the "factor" assuring the automatic strengthening of the *smychka* and hence of socialism.

"What was the most powerful argument that our Opposition used against the Central Committee of the party (I have in mind here the autumn of 1925)? They said then: the contradictions are growing monstrously, and the CC of the party fails to understand this. They said: the kulaks, in whose hands almost the entire grain surplus is concentrated, have organized 'the grain strike' against us. That is why grain is coming in so poorly. We all heard this. . . . The Opposition estimated that all the rest was only the political expression of this fundamental phenomenon. Subsequently the same comrades intervened to state: the kulak has entrenched himself still further, the danger has still further increased. Comrades, if the first and second affirmations had been correct, we would have even a stronger 'kulaks' strike' against the proletariat this year. . . . The Opposition slanders us by stating that we are contributing to the growth of the kulaks, that we are continually making concessions, that we are helping the kulaks to organize the grain strike; the real results are proof of just the contrary" (December 9, 1926, seventh plenum of the ECCI).

This attack on us, which was so cruelly discredited by the subsequent course of economic events, follows entirely from the mechanistic conception of the economics of the transition period as the economics of contradictions that are dying out. The most abstract expression of this view and the most consummate in its scholastic lifelessness was the article by Bukharin motivating the resolution of the seventh plenum of the ECCI about our alleged Social Democratic deviation. That article proceeded deductively from the abstract scholastic conception of the *smychka,* to the abstraction of socialism in one country. And made the demand upon us that we demonstrate that point or boundary line where the steady process of the strengthening of the *smychka* and its growing over into a single integrated planned economy could be interrupted by any internal factor whatsoever.

In this schema of growing harmonization of the relations between town and country and of the economy as a whole Bukharin managed to include without any difficulty all practical questions. The peasants were enriching themselves. The kulaks were growing over into socialism. It goes without saying, of course, that from year to year the grain collections were getting better and better. (We are talking about Bukharin's schema of course, not the reality.) In his speech at the seventh ECCI plenum Bukharin chose precisely this question to illustrate the conflict between the "Trotskyist conception" and the correct "party conception" of economic problems.

At the July plenum in 1928 Rykov was obliged to admit that he had given a falsely optimistic picture of the economy at the Fifteenth Congress and had not foreseen the grain collections crisis or its severity. Yet that crisis had been predicted with absolute accuracy in a number of documents of the Opposition, and even earlier in our report on industry at the Twelfth Congress (1923!), in which the problem of the scissors was formulated for the first time.

The warning, despite all its urgency, was neither assimilated nor even understood. On the contrary, it was used as the basis for the charge of "superindustrializing," a concept which, in the light of our whole economic experience, cannot be called anything but idiotic.

What percentage of the grain collections crisis is attributable to the difficulties or contradictions embodied in the planning principle in a backward peasant country, and what percentage derives from the petty-bourgeois, passive, wait-and-see, tail-ending attitude toward the problem of the *smychka?* Of course an exact mathematical answer cannot be given to that question. But there can be no doubt that the extreme aggravation of the crisis was the result of theoretical scholasticism and practical short-sightedness.

The positive question of the *smychka* since 1923 has taken the negative form of the scissors. The administrative regulation of prices, in the context of the wrong polices followed in the distribution of the national income and in regard to the "disproportion," for a certain length of time drove the contradictions inward, hiding them from view and feeding the Bukharinist illusion that the contradictions were dying out.

From Mikoyan, in charge of domestic trade, we have heard that although it is difficult to make the government trusts in state industry submit to regulation, the task has been accomplished 100 percent in regard to rural economic operations.

Thus, theoretical scholasticism about the transitional period is supplemented by wishful thinking in the practical management of domestic trade. The grain collections crisis of 1928 was the wholesale payoff for the illusions and errors of the preceding years—or more accurately, the beginning of the payoff.

The problem of the scissors was an expression of the problem of the transition from the democratic revolution to the socialist revolution in a very precise, numerical way in terms of the market. The overthrow of the monarchical landlord regime benefited the peasants in the amount of about 500 million rubles saved on land rent and taxes annually. The scissors—that is, the change in the ratio of agricultural to industrial prices—cost the peasantry about 1.5 billion a year. Those are the basic indices of the *smychka*. What the peasantry gained in terms of land rent is a definitive statement of the favorable results of the democratic revolution. What the peasants lost through the scissors is the nondefinitive, still current statement for them of the negative results of the socialist revolution. State industry has exchanged its products for the products of peasant labor with a loss for the peasant of a billion rubles a year by comparison with the prewar period. When these illuminating figures were first cited by us at a Central Committee plenum there was of course an attempt to challenge them. Yakovlev, a well-known minimizer of statistics, tried to reduce the price deficit suffered by peasant agriculture from a billion to three or four hundred million rubles. The grain strike by the upper layers of the peasantry shows that it is harder to deal with the objective economic reality than with its reflection in statistics. Even Yakovlev, this tamer of wild Arabic numerals, could not bring himself to deny that for the peasantry the balance sheet of the two revolutions, socialist and democratic, has thus far, after the positive and negative sums are figured in, come out with a deficit of several hundred million rubles.

Of course when I speak of the democratic revolution I don't mean the February revolution, which gave the peasantry nothing, but the October Revolution, which solved the agrarian question in a radical way. The peasantry made a very clear and precise distinction between the two stages of the revolution by stating that they were for the Bolsheviks but against the Communists. The NEP retreat was the direct result of the peasants' calculation of its gains and losses from the democratic and socialist revolutions respectively.

In practical terms the tasks of the *smychka*, on the basis of NEP, were formulated as follows: to achieve a situation in which state industry and commerce could exchange the products of "socialist labor" for those of the fragmented peasant economy at least as cheaply as prewar capitalism had done, and after that in the same ratio at least as the world capitalist market. The timely narrowing of the scissors back to the prewar level would have meant that the problem of the *smychka* was solved not for all time but for a certain period of time. The same would be true concerning the problem of achieving parity with prices on the world capitalist market.

There are no calendars telling us the deadline by which we had to solve these problems. But we could not drag the process out indefinitely. The chronic grain collections crisis is evidence that things have been dragged out too long. And the farther this goes, the more will be required in order to get out of the crisis.

"In [agriculture in] the West there is disintegration and decay. That is entirely natural. Not so in Russia. In our country the development of agriculture cannot proceed along that line if for no other reason than that we have Soviet power here and the instruments of production are nationalized and therefore such a development would not be allowed." According to that logic the danger of restoration was greater before capitalism.

The democratic revolution and the socialist revolution in the villages have not yet grown together. Not in the sense that the village has not yet begun to engage in socialist production. (That would mean that the village is no longer the village. Carrying out that kind of task still remains a long-term perspective for the future.) Not even in the sense that socialist industry has shown the peasants in practice that it is increasingly advantageous for the peasants as compared to capitalism. We have in mind a much more modest stage of development. Socialist industry has not yet achieved parity, not by a long shot, with prewar capitalism's capacity to serve the needs of the villages. The price scissors constantly reopens the gap between the democratic and socialist revolutions, giving this disparity a very sharp political character. Until this wound is closed and healed over, we cannot say that the foundation has been laid—not the foundation of independent, self-sufficient socialism, but the foundation for correct relations between the proletariat and the peasantry during the period that separates us from the victorious revolution of the proletariat in the advanced capitalist countries.

Let us now approach this contradictory economic process using the criteria presented at the seventh ECCI plenum. What is our revolution in and of itself? In the light of the fundamental economic processes and realities this question must be answered as follows: Our revolution has a contradictory, dual character. Even if we leave aside for the moment how the revolution is coping in its twelfth year with the problem of the material conditions of the industrial workers, the indisputable fact remains that the socialist aspect of the October Revolution thus far represents a burdensome deficit in the budget of the peasantry—that is, the overwhelming bulk of the population. The only ones who would gloss over this fact would be cowards of the reactionary national-socialist breed or Americanized wheeler-dealers who have for the most part learned only one thing from American technology, the art of pulling the wool over people's eyes.

The peasants tried to counterpose the Bolshevik to the Communist, that is, the revolutionary democrat to the socialist reorganizer of the economy. If two really different political species were involved the choice between them would not represent any difficulty for the peasants. They would support the Bolshevik, who gave them the land, against the Communist, who buys their grain cheaply and sells them manufactured goods at high prices and in insufficient quantities. But the heart of the matter is that the Bolshevik and the Communist are one and the same. This is the result of the fact that the democratic revolution was only the introductory stage of the socialist revolution.

Here we come back again to Marx's formula of the proletarian revolution backed up by a peasant war. If the peasants had gotten the land from a democratic dictatorship and not a proletarian dictatorship, the Soviet regime, given the present price ratio, would probably not be able to last even one year. But the problem is that in that event it would never have been established in the first place. (We have discussed that amply in another chapter [see "Marxism and the Relation Between Proletarian and Peasant Revolution"].) Here we see what weighty content there still is today in the question of the political methods by which the democratic revolution grows over into the socialist revolution. Only because the agrarian question as a revolutionary-democratic question was resolved not by a petty-bourgeois, that is, a *democratic,* dictatorship but by a proletarian one—owing solely to that fact—the peasants not only supported Soviet power during a bloody, three-year civil war but are still reconciled to Soviet power in spite of the prolonged losses that state industry has meant for them.

From our analysis the apologists of capitalism and the petty-bourgeois reactionaries, above all, the Mensheviks, deduce the necessity for a return to capitalism. The semiofficial slanderers give those apologists back-handed support when they say that no other conclusion can be drawn from my analysis. But since my analysis cannot be refuted, since it rests on the indisputable facts and processes which it properly explains, the end result of the semi-official criticism is to encourage people to think along Menshevik lines, although approaching from the opposite direction. And yet what follows from my analysis is not the economic inevitability of a return to capitalism but the *political danger* of capitalist restoration. They are not at all the same thing. To say that socialist industry today is less advantageous for the peasantry than prewar capitalism was, is not the same as to say that a return to capitalism under present conditions would be more advantageous for the peasant than the existing state of affairs. No, a return to capitalism now would mean, first of all, a fierce and intense battle within the world imperialist camp for the right to control this second edition of "Old Russia." It would mean that Russia would again become part of the chain of imperialism, having the clearly understood status of a subordinate link—that is, on a semicolonial basis. It would mean turning the peasant into a payer of tribute to imperialism, while the development of the productive forces in our country would be retarded in the extreme. In other words, Russia would not take its place alongside the United States, France, and Italy but would fall into the same category as India and China.

These considerations do not all belong in the sphere of historical prediction. The reactionary character of Menshevism and the Otto Bauer school is that they think of Russia in terms of "capitalism in one country" rather than examine the question of the fate of a capitalist Russia in the light of international processes.

It is hard to ask or to expect that the peasants would be guided in their attitudes toward Soviet power by a complex historical prognosis, no matter how clear and indisputable it might be to any serious Marxist. Even the proletarian, never mind the peasant, proceeds from his own life experience. Colonial bondage is a historical perspective and at the same time a bitter past reality. That is why the present situation, which is characterized by the absence of a firm foundation for the *smychka,* gives rise not to the economic necessity, but to the *political danger* of a return to capitalism.

# REPLY TO AN ULTIMATUM

## December 16, 1928

*NOTE: In early December, Trotsky protested to the GPU about the postal blockade that had cut him off from the outside world for more than a month. On December 16, a GPU official arrived from Moscow and delivered an ultimatum: cease his "counterrevolutionary" activity at once or be completely isolated from political life and compelled to change his "place of residence." To this threat Trotsky wrote this reply.*
*From the* Militant, *April 1, 1929.*

To the Central Committee of the AUCP:

To the Executive Committee of the Communist International:

Today, December 16, the representative of the Collegium of the GPU, Volinsky, transmitted the following ultimatum to me orally: "The work of your cothinkers throughout the country"—he declared almost literally—"has lately assumed an open counterrevolutionary character. The conditions under which you live in Alma-Ata give you full opportunity to direct this work. On this ground the Collegium of the GPU has decided to demand from you a categorical promise to discontinue this work, or else the Collegium will be obliged to change the conditions of your existence to the extent of completely isolating you from political life. In this connection the question of changing your place of residence is also raised."

I informed the representative of the GPU that I would give him a written reply only if I received a written statement of the GPU's ultimatum. My refusal to give an oral reply to the GPU was called forth by previous experiences convincing me that my words would be maliciously distorted in order to mislead the working masses of the USSR and the whole world.

Nevertheless, irrespective of the further steps to be undertaken by the GPU—which after all plays no independent role in this matter but only technically carries out the old decision of Stalin's narrow faction which I have known for some time—I consider it

361

necessary to submit the following to the Central Committee of the Communist Party of the Soviet Union and the Executive Committee of the Comintern:

To demand that I renounce my political activity is to demand that I renounce the struggle for the interests of the international proletariat, a struggle I have been conducting without interruption for thirty-two years, that is, throughout my whole conscious life. The attempt to represent this activity as "counterrevolutionary" comes from those whom I accuse before the international proletariat of trampling underfoot the basic teachings of Marx and Lenin, of infringing upon the historical interests of the world revolution, of breaking with the traditions and the heritage of October, and of unconsciously—but therefore the more dangerously—preparing the way for Thermidor.

To renounce political activity would mean to give up the struggle against the blindness of the present leadership, which heaps upon the objective difficulties of socialist construction ever greater political difficulties that arise out of its opportunist inability to conduct a proletarian policy on a large historical scale.

It would mean renouncing the struggle against the stifling party regime, which reflects the growing pressure of the enemy classes upon the proletarian vanguard.

It would mean passively acquiescing in the economic policy of opportunism, a policy which is undermining and destroying the foundations of the proletarian dictatorship, hampering the material and cultural growth of this dictatorship, and at the same time dealing heavy blows to the alliance of workers and working peasants, the basis of Soviet power.

To renounce political activity would mean to cover up with silence for the disastrous policy of the Comintern leadership, which in Germany in 1923 led to the surrender of tremendously favorable revolutionary positions without a fight; a policy which attempted to cover up for its opportunist mistakes with adventures in Estonia and Bulgaria; which falsely estimated the international situation at the Fifth Congress and gave the parties directives that only weakened and split them; a policy which, through the Anglo-Russian Committee, supported the British General Council, the bulwark of imperialist reaction, in the most difficult months for the reformist traitors; which in Poland, at the height of an abrupt turn in the country's domestic politics, transformed the proletarian vanguard into a rearguard for Pilsudski; which in China carried to its ultimate conclusions the historical line of Menshevism and thereby helped the bourgeoisie to demolish, to bleed, and to behead the revolutionary proletariat; which weakened the Comintern everywhere and squandered its ideological capital.

To cease political activity would mean to submit passively to the blunting and the direct falsification of our most important tool: the Marxist method, and the strategic lessons we have acquired, using this method, in the struggle led by Lenin.

It would mean to acquiesce passively—by accepting the responsibility for them—to the theory of the kulak's growing into socialism; to the myth about the revolutionary mission of the colonial bourgeoisie; to the slogan of the "combined workers' and peasants' parties" for the East—a slogan which breaks with the foundations of class theory; and finally to the crowning point of all these reactionary fables and many others, the theory of socialism in one country, the greatest crime against revolutionary internationalism.

The Leninist wing of the party has endured blows since 1923, that is, since the shocking defeat of the German revolution. The force of these blows has increased with every successive defeat of the international and the Soviet proletariat as a result of opportunist leadership.

Theoretical understanding and political experience teach us that a period of retreat, of retrogression, that is, of reaction, can take place not only after bourgeois revolutions, but also after proletarian revolutions. For six years we have lived in the USSR under conditions of a growing reaction against October, and with it a clearing of the way for Thermidor. The most open and consummate expression of this reaction within the party is the savage persecution and the organized smashing of the left wing.

In its latest attempts to resist the open Thermidorians, the Stalin faction had to borrow fragments and "remnants" of the ideas of the Opposition. Creatively, it is impotent. The struggle against the left deprives it of all stability. Its practical policy is unbalanced, false, contradictory, and unreliable.

The campaign against the right danger, undertaken with such clamor, remains three-quarters sham and serves above all to conceal from the masses the real war of annihilation against the Bolshevik-Leninists. The world bourgeoisie and international Menshevism have both blessed this war: these judges have long ago awarded "historical rightness" to Stalin.

If this blind, cowardly, incompetent policy of adaptation to the bureaucracy and the petty bourgeoisie had not been followed, the situation of the working masses in the twelfth year of the dictatorship would be far more favorable; our military defense would be far stronger and more reliable; the Comintern would be in quite a different position, and would not have to retreat step by step before the treacherous and venal Social Democracy.

The incurable weakness of the reaction headed by the party apparatus, despite all its apparent power, lies in the fact that it does not know what it is doing. It is carrying out the command of the enemy classes. There can be no greater historical curse on a faction that arose out of the revolution and is now undermining it.

The great historical strength of the Opposition, despite its apparent weakness, lies in the fact that it keeps its fingers on the pulse of the world historical process, that it clearly perceives the dynamics of class forces, that it foresees the future and consciously prepares for it. To renounce political activity would be to renounce the preparations for tomorrow.

The threat to change the conditions of my existence and to isolate me from political activity sounds as though I were not already separated from Moscow by 2,500 miles and from the nearest railroad by 150 miles, and by approximately the same distance from the border of the desolate western provinces of China, as though I were not confined to a place where the fiercest malaria shares its dominion with leprosy and plague. As though the Stalin faction, whose direct instrument the GPU is, had not done everything in its power to isolate me not only from political life, but from any other form of life as well. The Moscow newspapers arrive here only after a delay of ten days to a month, sometimes more. Letters get to me only in exceptional cases, after they have lain around for two or three months in the files of the GPU and the Secretariat of the Central Committee.

Two of my closest co-workers from the time of the civil war, Comrades Sermuks and Poznansky, who accompanied me voluntarily to my place of exile, were arrested immediately upon their arrival, thrown into a cellar with common criminals, and then sent away to the remotest corners of the North. A letter from my hopelessly ill daughter, whom you expelled from the party and kept from all work, took seventy-three days to get to me from the hospital, so that my answer found her no longer alive. Another letter, about the serious illness of my other daughter, whom you also expelled from the party and drove from all work, I received a month ago from Moscow, forty-three days after it was mailed. Telegraphic inquiries about health hardly ever reach their destination. Thousands of the best Bolshevik-Leninists, whose services to the October Revolution and to the international proletariat are infinitely greater than the services of those who exiled or imprisoned them, are in a similar or far worse position.

In preparing still more cruel repression against the Opposition, the narrow faction of Stalin—whom Lenin characterized in his Testament as rude and disloyal (at a time when these characteristics had not yet reached one hundredth of their present development)—is attempting with the help of the GPU to lay at the door of the Opposition some kind of "connection" with the enemies of the dictatorship. Among themselves the present leaders say: "We have to do this for the masses." And very often even more cynically: "That is for the simpletons." My close co-worker, Georgy Vasilevich Butov, secretary of the Revolutionary Military Council during all the years of the civil war, was arrested and detained under unheard-of conditions. From this upright, modest, and irreproachable party comrade they tried to extort confirmation of their deliberately concocted and false accusations in the Thermidorian spirit. Butov answered with a heroic hunger strike, which lasted fifty days and brought his death in prison in September of this year. Violence, blows, torture—both physical and moral—are applied to the best worker-Bolsheviks for their loyalty to the principles of October.

These are the general conditions which, according to the Collegium of the GPU, "offer no obstacle at all" to the political activity of the Opposition in general and myself in particular.

The miserable threat to change these conditions in the direction of a stricter isolation simply means that the Stalin faction has decided to replace exile by imprisonment. This decision, as I have already said above, is nothing new to me. Adopted as a perspective as early as 1924, this decision has been gradually carried out in a series of stages, in order to gradually accustom the oppressed and deceived party to the methods of Stalin, whose rudeness and disloyalty have now matured into the most venomous bureaucratic dishonesty.

In the declaration we submitted to the Sixth Congress of the Comintern, where we refuted the slanders which besmirch only their authors, we made known our unshakable readiness to fight—within the framework of the party, with all the methods of party democracy—for the ideas of Marx and Lenin, without which the party suffocates, ossifies, and crumbles. Once more we made known our unflinching readiness to help the proletarian core of the party in both word and deed to change its political course, to restore the health of the party and the Soviet state with united forces—without convulsions or catastrophes. We will stand firmly by these words. We answered the accusation of factional work with the statement that it could be ended only if Article 58, treacherously directed at us, were revoked and if we ourselves were reinstated in the party, not as repentant sinners but as revolutionary fighters who do not betray their banner. And as if in foreknowledge of the ultimatum handed me today, we wrote the following, word for word: "Only completely corrupted bureaucrats could demand such a renunciation from revolutionaries" (renunciation of political activity, i.e., of serving the party and the international proletariat). "Only contemptible renegades could give such a promise."

There is nothing I can change in those words. I submit them again to the Central Committee of the AUCP, which bears full responsibility for the work of the GPU.

To each his own. You wish to continue to conduct affairs under the prompting of class forces hostile to the proletariat. We know our duty and will do it to the end.

# REPLY TO TWO CONCILIATORS

## January 10, 1929

*NOTE: The manuscript of this letter identifies the two concilia-*
*tors as supporters of Aleksandr Ishchenko, a conciliator who was*
*moving toward capitulation. Stalin's postal blockade was selec-*
*tive: occasional letters were able to penetrate it, if they were of a*
*pro-conciliationist nature, like the one Trotsky replies to here.*

*Throughout 1928, the only figure publicly identified as part of*
*the "right deviation" was Moshe Frumkin, a deputy commissar of*
*finance whose outspoken Bukharinist leanings made him an easy*
*target for the centrists' campaign.*

*Pyatakov had become head of the State Bank after his capitu-*
*lation.*

*By permission of the Harvard College Library. Translated from*
*the Russian for this volume by Sonja Franeta. The date of this*
*letter was supplied by the version in the French journal* Contre le
courant, *April 12, 1929.*

Dear Comrades:

At this time I am surrounded by a nearly total postal blockade.

Your letter—unlike the other letters—was delivered to me by the
post office, and in a very short time: fifteen days.

In essence your letter is the temporary, brief platform of a new
grouping with the aim of moving away from the Opposition. It is
very likely that you are not aware of this, but those who foisted
this "platform" on you are apparently very well aware of where
they are taking you.

I will answer you briefly, for the ideas you bring up are old and
have long since been refuted by our entire experience in the battle
of ideas.

1. You write that the "coming struggles for revolution in the
West" are *near at hand*. That is possible, though it hasn't been
proved. But what is to be done with the resolutions and reports of
the Sixth Congress, which are incorrect to the core? And the

eclectic program—a mixture of Marxism and social-nationalism? Perhaps you've been promised that this would be changed in the near future. Or, at least, that the pages of the press would be opened to you for a discussion of these questions. Meanwhile, the fate of the Comintern depends on these very questions.

2. You write: "The party of Lenin has shifted from the retreat to the taking of defensive positions and has partly assumed the offensive against the opportunist threat."

This is stated a little too grandly and exaggeratedly, but there has been a shift. Not the least important reason for this shift, however, is that we did not yield to the conciliators, the Zinovievists, the half-Zinovievists, and the quarter-Zinovievists. The centrists have stirred *under the blows of our whip*. Conclusion: shouldn't we now put away the whip? No, we should spur them on even more—with three whips.

3. You write that the Platform correctly indicated the dividing line between the rights (Rykovists) and the centrists (Stalinists). "The right is working in the direction of counterrevolution," you say, "and the Stalinists today (!) are working in the direction of revolution. It is impossible not to understand this." Severely put. "Today." But what about tomorrow? Or doesn't that concern you? Furthermore, if the Rykovists are working toward counterrevolution and the Stalinists toward revolution, how can they work together in the most decisive places (the Politburo, the Council of People's Commissars)? And why do they swear to the party that they have no differences with one another? And jointly thunder away at us?

4. Not only do you sidestep, in a cowardly way, the intensifying drive to smash the Bolshevik-Leninists; you yourselves are beginning to help the Stalinists with this work "in the direction of revolution." You yourselves are beginning to denounce such actions as "the pasting up of leaflets, the strike, and the secret ballot in the trade unions and soviets" (apparently you're against the demand for a secret ballot in general).

What do you propose instead of "pasting up"? Distribution by hand? A mailing? Or perhaps the pages of *Pravda* have been opened to you? You praise the Platform. Perhaps it has been legalized? You should say openly what you think—that our views are correct, but we should stop fighting for them. That's how the Zinovievists started out. And look how they ended up.

5. Or perhaps our goals have already been achieved? Perhaps at least today's zigzag to the left is guaranteed? By what? Stalin's "principled" position? Or by the individual make-up of

the leadership he dominates? Whoever thinks that should cross over openly to the Stalinists.

6. And that in fact is what you have come to. You write: "Already (?) the left wing, consisting of the former (?) centrists, is conducting a fight against the right."

If a left wing has indeed taken shape from the former (!!) centrists, they must not have any serious differences with us. Why then are they attempting to destroy us? Without any basis in principle. Is it merely out of personal rivalry? But that would mean political gangsterism. Is that what you want to say about Stalin's faction? Then you have a worse opinion of it than does the Opposition, from which you are breaking.

You ramble on without rhyme or reason about whether the main danger is from the rights or the Stalinists. The main danger is the world bourgeoisie. After that, the domestic bourgeosie. The right wing is the hook in our flesh which the bourgeoisie is tugging on. We have been calling the party's attention to this hook for several years now. The Stalinists shouted "slander!" Later they made the ever so slight admission that yes, there is a right danger. Rykov? Kalinin? Bukharin? Voroshilov? No, that is slander. Who then? Frumkin! Indeed, a gruesome, menacing hundred-headed monster. This is not fighting the rights; it is buffoonery and fraud against the party. It is concealment of the true right-wing leaders from the party. Who is doing the concealing? The centrists. Therefore, *within the party,* the chief danger is centrism. It is covering up for the right wing and trying to destroy the left.

8. The working class party member who is now moving from a right-centrist position to a left-centrist one is coming closer to the Bolshevik line. You, on the other hand, in moving away from the Opposition toward the left-centrist point of view, are taking your distance from Bolshevism. Farther along, we will meet up with the centrist worker moving to the left. But not with you, I'm afraid.

9. You say that by attacking the centrists, we are "helping the right." These words only show how completely you have slipped back toward the centrists—because you are repeating the main argument of the centrists against the left, their only argument and a thoroughly rotten one. This is what liberals have always said to Social Democrats, what Social Democrats have always said to Communists, and what centrists always say to genuine Bolsheviks.

With our relentless criticism we are helping the working class

core of the party to free itself from the half-heartedness and
falsity of centrism, thereby creating a real proletarian bulwark
against the right danger. That is the way Bolsheviks have
always acted, in big things and in small.

10. There is only one central point in the brief platform that
you have signed: "It would be good to return to the party and
establish peace and harmony." But return through which door?
There are two doors: Zinoviev's, that of capitulation; and the
Bolshevik way, through the continuation and expansion of the
ideological battle. There is no third door; there hasn't been and
there won't be. Pyatakov tried [to find one], Safarov tried, Sarkis
tried. What are they now? Political corpses. Who will trust them?
No one. They don't trust themselves. True, the door was opened to
Pyatakov—but not into the party. Into the State Bank.

We of the Opposition are in the party now much more than that
entire brotherhood of capitulators.

11. You propose that we "decisively dissociate ourselves from
Democratic Centralist moods." My goodness, you surprise me.
This was done as long ago as my theses in the fall of 1926. We
dissociated ourselves not only from their "moods" but also from
their ideas and methods. To the extent that deviations toward
Democratic Centralism become evident we have corrected them
and will correct them. As for your capitulationist line, there is
absolutely nothing we can do with that.

12. You have not only drawn up a new platform (a temporary
one, not meant to last long because it is just a short bridge to
capitulation); you have also jotted down a rough list of "leaders."
Besides myself, you name Smilga, Preobrazhensky, Radek, and—
Ishchenko. A sternly made selection. Very sternly made! To the
best of my knowledge, however, Comrade Ishchenko did not even
sign our common declaration to the Sixth Congress. Politically
this means he left the Opposition. Before November 7 [1927]
Ishchenko was on the far left. Then he suddenly swung to the
right. During the Fifteenth Congress he held the view that
without the Zinovievists we would perish. He made every kind of
bloc—with Pyatakov, with Sarkis, with Safarov—constantly
blazing new paths "to the party." But all of his allies betrayed
the Opposition, and themselves. After February, Ishchenko again
began bringing up all sorts of profound arguments. After July he
fell silent. Now again he is opening new roads. There is not two
cents' worth of principle in this position. Only confusion and
vacillation. Ishchenko keeps trying to find a special door for
himself into the party. He won't find it. There is either Zinoviev's

door (to the Centrosoyuz, the State Bank, and political death) or the other way—to march with the Opposition on the high road of principled, ideologically unyielding, Bolshevik struggle.

This road will not be a fraud.

That is the best reply I can give you in a few words.

With anticapitulationist greetings,

L. Trotsky

P.S.—I almost forgot your most farfetched argument. Since the Stalinists have severed the left wing from the party, according to you, they themselves must now perform the role of left wing. This is truly the most pure and most holy nonsense. You evidently are using the terms "left wing" and "center" in a parliamentary sense, that is, the positioning of seats in an assembly hall, not in a class sense. Otherwise, one would have to conclude that the more the opportunists hammer away at the Bolsheviks, the more they themselves become Bolshevized. The fact is that even if the centrists drove all of the proletarian revolutionaries out of the party (which cannot be done) and constituted themselves as a "left wing," that "left wing" would remain centrist. That's all there is to it.

On the other hand, you think that the centrists' fight against the right is a fight to the death. But that would mean that in driving out and smashing the rights, the centrists would themselves have to become—the right wing.

There is a grain of truth in all this. As the fight against the right and the left goes on, centrism will extrude from its own midst both right-centrist and left-centrist elements, that is, it will undergo a political differentiation and fall apart. The bureaucrats will go to the right and the workers to the left. That is what we need and want. The stronger, the more daring and principled our position is, the more quickly and healthily this differentiation process will take place. That and only that will bring the downfall of the right wing.

The conciliators and capitulators have long threatened us that we will end up totally "outside the party." Stalin was forced to admit at the November plenum that in addition to the 10,000 Bolshevik-Leninists who have been expelled, about twice as many remain in the party, that is, 20,000 [Stalin's *Works,* vol. 11, pp. 288-89]. If Stalin gives this figure, that means it must be doubled at least. There you have the left wing in a Marxist, not a topographical, sense. It is no longer possible to sever this portion of the party, because in place of every head cut off, two new ones will grow. And farther along there will come the moment when the best working class party members, shifting in their broad mass from the center to the left, will merge with us, so that the dividing line between us and them will be washed away. There you have the genuine road to the unity of the party on a Leninist basis.

All the rest is Zinoviev-itis and Safarov-itis, that is, nonsense, vanities, petty intrigue, and trifles.

L.T.

# PROTEST AGAINST DEPORTATION

## February 7-8, 1929

*NOTE: It took a full month for the Political Bureau to vote to expel Trotsky from the country. On January 20, 1929, a GPU agent handed him an order of deportation; and within twenty-four hours he and his family were being escorted through a blizzard toward the railway, their destination unknown to them. Only after they were on the train was Trotsky informed that his destination was Constantinople, later known as Istanbul, which had become a haven for White Guards and other anti-Soviet emigrés. Trotsky protested and demanded an entry permit to Germany. While the GPU agents waited for instructions from Moscow the train was diverted from the main tracks. After twelve days came the news: the German Social Democratic government, under Hermann Müller, had denied Trotsky's request. The train brought the exiles to Odessa, where they were put aboard a ship bound for Turkey, ruled by Kemal Ataturk (later Kemal Pasha).*

*Trotsky wrote this memorandum before arriving in Constantinople. A note in his handwriting on the manuscript said that points 3-5 were deleted from the version handed to the press upon their arrival.*

*By permission of the Harvard College Library. Translated from the Russian for this volume by Martin Koppel.*

1. The GPU representative has reported that the German Social Democratic government has refused me a visa. That means Müller and Stalin concur in their evaluation of the Opposition.

2. The GPU representative has reported that I will be handed over to Kemal against my will. That means Stalin has arranged with Kemal, the suppressor of Communists, for reprisals against the Opposition, as against a common enemy.

3. The GPU representative has refused to discuss minimal guarantees against White Guards—whether Russian, Turkish, or other—in the event of my forced deportation to Turkey. What is behind that is that Stalin is counting directly on assistance from

the White Guards, which is fundamentally no different from the assistance provided by Kemal.

4. The failure to keep the promise already made to me to deliver books I need from Moscow is a particular illustration of the general rudeness and disloyalty in matters large and small.

5. The statement by the GPU representative that a "written guarantee" was given by Kemal in regard to my belongings, "with the exception of weapons," i.e., my revolvers, means that in fact I will be disarmed at the outset in the face of the White Guards, and a deliberately lying excuse is given by attributing this to the Turkish government.

I report the above so that responsibility can be appropriately assigned and in order to lay the basis for the steps I consider it necessary to take against this utterly Thermidorian treachery.

# MESSAGE ON ARRIVING IN CONSTANTINOPLE

## February 12, 1929

*NOTE: A message to Kemal Ataturk, the president of Turkey. From* International Press Correspondence, *March 22, 1929.*

To His Excellency the President of the Turkish Republic
Dear Sir:

At the gateway to Constantinople, I have the honor to inform you that I have arrived at the Turkish frontier not of my own choice and that the only reason I may cross this frontier will be through the use of force upon me. I request you, Mr. President, to accept from me the sentiments that are fitting on this occasion.

Trotsky

# Appendix A
# BUKHARIN-KAMENEV MEETING

## July 11, 1928

*NOTE: In July 1928, while the plenum of the Central Committee was in progress, Nikolai Bukharin arranged through CC member Grigory Sokolnikov a secret meeting with Kamenev in order to try to win Kamenev's and Zinoviev's support for a struggle against Stalin. This was the plenum that marked a temporary end to the "left turn," through cancellation of the extraordinary measures and concessions to the wealthy peasants. Nevertheless, Bukharin took alarm at the defection of his supporters on the Central Committee as well as at the disclosure of the full extent of the extraordinary measures that had been used to collect grain from unwilling peasants. This document is Kamenev's account of the July 11 meeting, written for Zinoviev's benefit. It is not a literal rendering of the conversation but a summary. On September 22, Kamenev met with some Moscow Trotskyists. He may have given them a copy of this account at that time. Trotsky writes about it for the first time in "The Danger of Bonapartism and the Opposition's Role" (October 21, 1928).*

*The translator has tried to reproduce Kamenev's choppy, abbreviated style to preserve the drama of that historical moment. At the same time, some minimal concessions have been made to render the text more comprehensible to the reader. Abbreviations have been spelled out and some material has been inserted in brackets. (All parentheses were in the original.) Headings, based on those of Kamenev, have been given to the five main sections. Part III is preceded in the original by the words "What is underlined is verbatim" and "Copy of a copy." These comments and the underlining (or rendering in italics) have been omitted. Paragraphing and quotation marks have been made somewhat more consistent, but with no effort to alter the document's often sloppy and repetitive character. Because of the allusive and elliptical style, the annotation by Stephen F. Cohen has been retained for the convenience of the reader.*

*Reprinted by permission from* Dissent, Winter 1979, *in a translation from the Russian by George Saunders.*

### I. Letter from Sokolnikov to Kamenev
### Moscow, July 9, 1928

Dear L. B. [Kamenev],

It has been several days since we returned to Moscow—just in time for the plenum.[1] I thought I would find you here, but it seems you are still sitting quietly out in Kaluga. Will you be here anytime soon? I very much need to talk some things over with you and get your advice. Wouldn't it be possible for you to come here for a short while *during the next few days? It would be extremely important.* The plenum, apparently, will end tomorrow. Today discussion is still going on, on Mikoyan's report, and "battles" are breaking out. If possible, answer by telephone (3-49-24). Hoping to see you soon.

Best wishes

G. Sokolnikov

### II. Kamenev's Account of His
### Conversation with Sokolnikov
### Wednesday, July 11, 9 a.m.

Summary: (1) Things have gone much farther; Bukharin has made a final break with Stalin. The question of removal [of Stalin] was posed concretely. *Kalinin and Voroshilov betrayed us.*[2] They are taking a more lenient attitude now, in view of his [Stalin's] concessions. (2) Bukharin said twice: *Don't you understand that I would now give up Stalin for Kamenev and Zinoviev?* Bukharin's position is tragic: he fears most of all that you [Kamenev and Zinoviev] will say Stalin's line is correct. (3) There was no group of "Four" or "Five" in the Politburo—he swears it.[3] (4) Stalin's speech at the plenum: Two streams of Trotskyism, the genuine one—for restorative prices[4]—and the Bukharinist-Trotskyists. In order to develop industry, "tribute from the peasantry is necessary." Likewise Mikoyan: "The scissors will be with us for a long time; the scissors cannot be closed." (They claim that Trotsky too wanted to close the scissors.)[5] Sokolnikov is smuggling in Trotskyism. Molotov: "The middle peasants have become strong; that is why they have begun to clash with us." (5) Bukharin's reply: The tribute theory does not differ in any way from Preobrazhensky's "law of primitive socialist accumulation.[6] Reply by Tomsky: "If

Molotov is right, what is the perspective? You want NEP without NEPmen, kulaks,[7] or concession-holders; it won't work." Rykov cut Kaganovich to pieces. Conclusion: Stalin's line will be defeated. Bukharin is in a tragic situation. Don't praise Stalin. A positive program can be drawn up jointly with you [Kamenev and Zinoviev]. Bukharin himself wants to have a talk. A bloc to remove Stalin.

Kamenev: Why haven't they done anything?

Sokolnikov: To him [Bukharin] you are $x$ and $y$, unknown quantities. Stalin is circulating rumors that he has you in his pocket.

### III. Kamenev's Account of His Conversation with Bukharin

An hour had passed since my arrival when (at 10 a.m., July 11) without warning or ringing Bukharin and Sokolnikov came in, Sokolnikov leaving toward the end. His [Bukharin's] look was extremely troubled and tormented. With great agitation, talking for an hour without any interruption on my part, he recounted the following. (This record is as accurate as possible.)

"Before coming to the main point of our discussion I should clear up two rumors: (1) There was no vote of 4 to 5 on [your] assignment; there was no discussion of this question at all. (2) The note on Zinoviev's article was dictated by Stalin over my objection, as a compromise with Molotov, who was strenuously opposed to printing Zinoviev's article.[8] Now to the main point.

"1. Things have gone so far in the Central Committee and in the party that you (and probably the Trotskyists too) will inevitably be drawn in and play an important role in deciding the outcome.

"2. When this will happen I do not know. Perhaps it won't happen that quickly, because both sides are still leery of appealing to you. But at any rate within a couple of months it is inevitable.

"3. I therefore want you to know the situation. I know (or assume) that the Stalinists will approach you also. You of course, as political people, will take advantage of the situation to 'up the ante.' But I do not fear that. What will be decisive is the political line and I want you to know what the struggle is about."

4. I [Kamenev]: "Is this really a serious struggle?"

Bukharin: "That is what I wanted to talk with you about. We consider Stalin's line disastrous for the revolution as a whole. This line could bring our downfall. The differences between us and Stalin are many times more serious than all the differences we had with you. Rykov, Tomsky, and I unanimously agree on the formulation that 'It would be much better if we had Zinoviev and Kamenev in the Politburo now, instead of Stalin.' I have discussed this with Rykov and Tomsky quite openly. And for several weeks I have not spoken with Stalin. He is an unprincipled intriguer who subordinates everything to the preservation of his own power. He changes his theories depending on whom he wants to get rid of at the moment. In the Politburo group of 'Seven,'[9] we argued with him to the point of saying 'You lie!' 'You're talking nonsense!' and so on. He has made concessions now, so that later he can cut our throats. We understand this, but he maneuvers in such a way as to make us look like the splitters. The resolution was adopted unanimously because he disavowed Molotov—announcing that he accepted nine-tenths of my declaration, which I read to the 'Seven' without letting it out of my hands. (You can't trust him with even the smallest document.) His aim now is to take the Moscow *Pravda* and *Leningrad Pravda* away from us and replace Uglanov (with Kaganovich). Uglanov is with us completely. As for Stalin's line, it is as follows (as he expressed it at the plenum): (1) Capitalism grew either at the expense of colonies or through loans or through the exploitation of the workers. We have no colonies, they won't give us loans, and therefore our base has to be tribute from the peasantry. (You understand that this is the same as Preobrazhensky's theory.) (2) The farther socialism advances, the greater will be the resistance (see the sentence in the resolution). This is idiotic illiteracy. (3) Since tribute is necessary and resistance is bound to grow, a strong leadership is necessary. Self-criticism should not touch the leaders but only those who carry out the policies. But in fact, self-criticism has been directed against Tomsky and Uglanov. The result of this will be a police state. It isn't some question of 'Who fouled the nest?' In reality, the fate of the revolution is at stake. With this theory everything can be destroyed. At the same time, in foreign policy, Stalin is following a right-wing line: he had the Comintern removed from the Kremlin; it was he who proposed that no one be shot in the Shakhty affair (we voted against);[10] and in all negotiations he is inclined to make concessions. Tomsky formulated it this way: I (Tomsky) am 30 kilometers to the right of you (Bukharin) in international questions, but I (Tomsky) am 100 kilometers to the left of Stalin. His line is disastrous, but he does not give anyone a chance to discuss it. He sets traps and accuses people of deviations. There is a sentence in his speech where he says that only 'big landowners' can think this way, and refers word for word to a passage in a speech by Uglanov. He will cut our throats."

5. I: "What are your forces?"

Bukharin: "Rykov plus Tomsky plus Uglanov (absolutely) plus myself. The Petrograders are generally with us, but they got frightened when the possibility of replacing Stalin came up, because Komarov disavowed Stetsky's speech; but in the evening Ugarov went out of his way to apologize to me for Komarov.[11] Andreev is for us. He is being removed from the North Caucasus.[12] Stalin has bought the support of the Ukrainians by taking Kaganovich out of the Ukraine.[13] Our potential forces are enormous, but (1) the average Central Committee member still doesn't understand the depth of the differences, and (2) such members are terribly afraid of a split.[14] That was why I had yielded to Stalin on the question of the extraordinary measures, and that made our offensive against him more difficult. We don't want to appear as splitters, because then they would cut our throats. But Tomsky in his last speech at the plenum showed plainly that Stalin was the splitter. Yagoda and Trilisser are ours. There have been small-scale [peasant] revolts in 150 cases. Voroshilov and Kalinin betrayed us at the last moment. I think Stalin has some special hold on them. Our task is to gradually explain Stalin's disastrous role and to persuade the average Central Committee member of the necessity for his removal. The Orgburo is ours."

6. I: "But so far he is removing you."

Bukharin: "What can we do? At this time [his] removal will not go through the Central Committee. Sometimes at night I think to myself, Do we have the right to remain silent? Isn't this lack of courage? But careful reflection tells us to act cautiously. Rykov's report will be given on Friday. There we will dot all the *i*'s. I am going to print a series of articles in *Pravda*. It may be that another blow is needed for the party to understand where he is leading it."

7. As supplements to all this, and in between these supplements [Bukharin presented] a great heap of "revelations" about the "Seven," etc. The tone was of absolute hatred for Stalin and a complete break with him. At the same time there was wavering over whether to come out openly or not to come out. "If we do, they'll cut our throats with the no-splitting clause.[15] If we don't, they'll cut us down by petty chess maneuvers; besides this, they'll dump all the blame on us if there is no grain in October."

I: "But what are they counting on, to get grain?"

Bukharin: "That's the whole problem. On reviving the extraordinary measures if difficulties reappear. But that's war communism,[16] and sure death."

I: "And you?"

Bukharin: "Perhaps it will be necessary to try an even more far-reaching maneuver in order to make peace with the middle peasant. You can hound the kulak as much as you want, but you have to make peace with the middle peasant. But under Stalin, and that blockhead Molotov (who presumes to instruct me in Marxism—we call him 'stone bottom'), nothing can be done."

8. I: "What do you want us to do?"

Bukharin: "Stalin boasts that he has you in his pocket. Everywhere your people (Zhuk., for an individual example) are being lined up to support Stalin. That would be terrible. You will of course decide your own line, but I would beg you not to help Stalin cut our throats by giving him your approval. Stalin will very likely seek to contact you. I want you to know what it's all about.

9. "There is no reason anyone should know of our meeting. Don't talk with me by phone, because my phones are tapped. The GPU follows me and the GPU is watching you. I would like us to keep each other informed, but not through secretaries or intermediaries. Only Rykov and Tomsky know that I have talked with you. You too should tell no one. But tell your people not to attack us."

10. I: "Did Stalin show you Zinoviev's memorandum?"

Bukharin: "No. First I've heard."

I: "What will they do with us?"

Bukharin: "I don't know. They don't discuss that with us. Either Stalin will try to 'buy you off' with high appointments or he'll appoint you to such posts in order to commit you in advance; we don't know anything for sure. Goodbye. In the next few days I'll be very busy with the Comintern congress and won't be able to see you. In general we have to observe strict secrecy."

I had arranged for Sokolnikov to come by again before my departure.

I gave [Bukharin] your (personal) letter. He read it and said he is afraid of having things on paper. He is afraid a written article would bring trouble. It would be better to talk about the program in person.

Bukharin: "Stalin spoiled the [Comintern draft] program for me in many places."[17] "He himself wanted to give the report on the program at the plenum. (!!!) I had great difficulty fighting him off. He is driven by a desire for recognition as a theorist. He thinks that is the only thing he doesn't yet have."

Other than that, a mass of trifles, details. He [Bukharin] is extremely upset. At times his lips twitch from nervousness. Sometimes he gives the impression of a man who knows he is doomed. My thinking is that, any day now, signals will come from the other camp. We have to wait for them calmly. This is sure to be! Therefore, you should not come here now. We will see what they say. Call me with your answer tomorrow at eight.

### July 11, 6 p.m.

Marginal note: All this was fawning. I can find no other word for it; politically speaking, of course.

## IV. Kamenev's Additions to the Account of Bukharin's Remarks
## Night of July 11-12

1. General impression, more than anything, a sense of doom. His phrase: I wonder if all our "fuss" is just masturbation. Sometimes I say to Yefim,[18] Aren't things hopeless for us? (1) If the country perishes, we perish. (2) If the country pulls through, Stalin will make a quick about-face and we will still perish. What to do? What can you do when you are dealing with such an opponent: a Genghis Khan; the low cultural level of the Central Committee.

2. Molotov and Stalin on withdrawing from the Wuhan government.[19]

3. Stalin tells the Young Communists: The way the question of youth employment will be decided depends on whether Bukharin puts an end to his bad policies.[20]

4. If we begin a discussion, they will cut our throats. The Central Committee fears a discussion.

5. But what if we jointly submit our resignations—Rykov, Tomsky, and I?

6. If I am not removed for a while—two months—I shouldn't get entangled in day-to-day politics. But when a crisis comes, I should speak out plainly and completely openly.

7. We cannot start a discussion because it will immediately turn into armed conflict. For what will be the charges? We would say, Here is the man who has brought the country to ruin and starvation. And he would say, They are defending the kulaks and NEPmen.

8. The party and the state have completely merged—that is the whole trouble.

9. Stalin is interested in nothing but holding on to power. In making concessions to us, he kept the key to the leadership, and having kept it, he will cut our throats at a later time. What can we do? Because the subjective conditions within the Central Committee for removing Stalin, while they are maturing, have not yet matured.

10. Sokolnikov: Assume a more active policy; demand at least the removal of Molotov.

11. Stalin knows only one method—revenge, and he does it with the stab in the back. Let us remember the theory of "sweet revenge."[21]

12. Sergo [Ordzhonikidze] is no knight in shining armor.[22] He used to come to see me and curse Stalin roundly, but at the decisive moment he betrayed us.

13. A history of the plenum resolution and the fight [within the Politburo]. (1) I called for a general discussion of overall policy. Stalin demurred, saying an industrial-financial plan was necessary, etc. (2) I write Stalin a letter and demand a general discussion. He comes to see me: "Bukharin, my friend, you could strain the nerves of an elephant." But he would not agree to a discussion. (3) I write a second letter—he calls me into his office. He begins by saying, "You and I are the Himalayas; the others are nobodies." (4) We go to the "Seven." An ugly scene. He starts shouting at me. I quote his remarks about the Himalayas. He yells, "Liar! You made it up to turn the Politburo against me." We part ways. (5) I read a twenty-page declaration, without letting it out of my hands. Molotov pronounces it anti-Leninist and an antiparty document. Stalin: nine-tenths of it I can accept. Molotov leaves. This is taken as a basis. I go out to write a resolution. They do too. Unexpectedly they bring in a resolution stolen from my declaration. I make three corrections; Rykov makes one. It's all accepted unanimously. Stalin's reasoning is this: I got grain by using extraordinary measures; I did a turnabout in the nick of time and wrote the resolution myself. If measures become necessary again, I can carry them out alone. But the fact is he will bring us to ruin.

14. Varga will give a report,[23] because Stalin doesn't want Rykov to give it. What to do with this report I still don't know. Varga will argue that famine is inevitable during industrialization!

15. On the Comintern. Sémard is for Stalin, Thälmann is for

Stalin. Ewert is not a right-wing Communist but they are forcing him to become one.[24]

16. Stalin violated the decision of the Politburo (the Seven?). The decision was to send Frumkin's letter to all members of the Politburo and draft a reply.[25] Without waiting for that, Stalin wrote a reply and sent it himself. We passed a resolution reprimanding him for violating the decision. Stalin: "The reply was acknowledged to be correct, though not complete. I can't keep dragging things out."

17. On this occasion or on another one, [Bukharin] said to Stalin, "Don't think that the Politburo is just a consultative body under the general secretary."

18. Stalin's policy is leading to civil war. He will have to drown the revolts in blood.

Sokolnikov (taking up Bukharin's remarks): At one drinking bout, Tomsky, completely loaded, leaned over to Stalin and said, "Soon our workers will be shooting at you."

## V. Sokolnikov Related the Following:
### [Kamenev's Account]
### July 12, 11 a.m.

From the debates on collective farms only the following is of interest. Stalin gave a rude and vituperative speech against Tomsky. "I listened to Tomsky's speech with great surprise. Tomsky thinks that we have nothing at all to fall back on except concessions to the peasants. That is capitulationism and lack of faith in the building of socialism. And what if the middle peasants demand concessions on the monopoly of foreign trade. Or a peasant union? Concessions there too? That is capitulationism. What we have to fall back on are the state farms and our work among the poor peasants." Swarthy, sour, vindictive, and wrathful. A forbidding sight. Now everyone has understood that not only Bukharin, but Stalin too is on the offensive. The rudeness of it was astonishing.

Sokolnikov's understanding of the mechanics of the plenum is as follows: Rykov opened the offensive; Stalin replied. The Petrograders wavered and disavowed Stetsky. Then Bukharin dug in and made himself a trench, but failed to fire a single shot. Molotov got nasty and fired a volley at *Pravda* (hitting at Astrov in particular, the "one-sidedness" of *Pravda* in general, the footnote to Kritsman, etc.)[26] Then Tomsky attacked Molotov, but in a mild fashion. Finally Stalin attacked Tomsky openly and crudely.

## Notes to Bukharin-Kamenev Meeting

1. Plenum of the Central Committee of the Soviet Communist Party, July 4-12, 1928.

2. Both Mikhail Kalinin and Voroshilov were full members of the nine-member Politburo. The rightist views of Kalinin, titular president of the Soviet Union, were well known. Voroshilov, commissar of war, was a long-time crony of Stalin, but the Bukharin group apparently assumed that unrest in the peasant army would incline him to their side.

3. A reference to informal caucuses of Politburo members during the earlier factional struggles led by Bukharin and Stalin against Trotsky, Zinoviev, and Kamenev.

4. Earlier in the 1920s, "restorative prices" meant state industrial prices sufficient to cover the cost of production and to return a profit to state industry. Here, at the July 1928 plenum, Stalin accused the Bukharinists of advocating "restorative prices" for agricultural goods—that is, higher prices for grain to coax peasant surpluses back onto the market.

5. A reference to a diagram portraying the discrepancy between high industrial and low agricultural prices as the open blades of a pair of scissors.

6. Yevgeny Preobrazhensky had been the leading economist of the Trotskyist Opposition. His "law," set out in 1924, argued that Soviet state industry could expand rapidly only by exploiting, or obtaining surplus value from, the private peasant sector. The rhetoric of Preobrazhensky's argument was ferocious and caused a major political dispute, but his actual proposal merely called for "nonequivalent exchange" through relatively high industrial prices in market relations between the two sectors.

7. That is, private merchants and better-off peasants.

8. These two points refer to Politburo discussions about restoring Zinoviev and Kamenev to some official position. Part of the price seems to have been a repentant article by Zinoviev, to be published in *Pravda,* of which Bukharin was editor.

9. A reference suggesting that the seven senior members of the Politburo—Bukharin, Rykov, Tomsky, Stalin, Molotov, Kalinin, and Voroshilov—met or voted at this time without the two other full members, Valerian Kuibyshev and Yan Rudzutak.

10. In March 1928, the security police announced the uncovering of a counterrevolutionary plot involving technical specialists and foreign governments at the Shakhty mines in the Donbass industrial complex; fifty-five people were accused of sabotage and treason; many confessed. The whole Shakhty affair, and the trial that followed, remains murky. But Stalin used it to discredit Bukharin's conciliatory class policies, Rykov's

management of the state apparatus, and Tomsky's leadership of the trade unions. It became an important part of Stalin's subsequent assault on the nonparty intelligentsia in 1929-30. Though Bukharin, Rykov, and Tomsky seem not to have doubted the original criminal charges, they fought hard in the Politburo to limit the ramifications of the affair.

11. The Leningrad (formerly called Petrograd) delegation to the Central Committee plenum included Nikolai Komarov, the Bukharinist Aleksei Stetsky, and Tomsky's trade union colleague Fyodor Ugarov.

12. Andrei Andreev, party boss of the North Caucasus region, actually sided with Stalin and was not removed.

13. Kaganovich was probably the ablest and most despised of Stalin's lieutenants; his three-year tyranny, when he was general secretary of the Ukrainian party, had outraged native Ukrainian leaders.

14. The expression "average Central Committee member" is ambiguous here. It could mean average, middle-ranking, or uncommitted member.

15. The ban on intraparty factions adopted in 1921 and the basis on which earlier oppositionists had been castigated and even expelled from the party.

16. A reference to the grain requisitioning measures during the Russian civil war of 1918-21.

17. Bukharin was preparing a draft program of the Comintern for the upcoming congress.

18. As noted in the original document, Yefim Tseitlin, Bukharin's secretary.

19. After the Kuomintang led by Chiang Kai-shek had suddenly massacred its Communist allies in Shanghai in April 1927, a separatist left-Kuomintang regime had been set up in Wuhan (Hankow) with Comintern support. Comintern policy in the Chinese civil war had been a major subject of contention between the Bukharin-Stalin leadership and the Left Opposition in 1927.

20. Stalin was seeking support among Young Communists (Komsomols) by arguing that the industrial and trade union policies of Bukharin and Tomsky deprived young people of job opportunities.

21. Chatting over wine with Kamenev and Feliks Dzerzhinsky in 1923, Stalin had described what he loved most in life as follows: "The greatest delight is to mark one's enemy, prepare everything, avenge oneself thoroughly, and then go to sleep." See Robert C. Tucker, *Stalin as Revolutionary* (New York: W. W. Norton, 1973), p. 211.

22. Grigory Ordzhonikidze, head of the Central Control Commission, the party's disciplinary body.

23. Eugene Varga, a prominent economist and Comintern official.

24. Pierre Sémard, leader of the French Communist Party, and Ernst Thälmann and Arthur Ewert, leaders of the German party.

25. On June 15, 1928, Moshe Frumkin, Deputy Commissar of Finance, sent the Politburo a letter bleakly evaluating the consequences of Stalin's policy in the countryside and urging Bukharinist remedies.

26. Valentin Astrov was a young follower of Bukharin and one of his deputy editors at *Pravda*. A critical editorial note had been attached to an article by the economist Lev Kritsman praising Stalin's coercive measures in the countryside.

# Appendix B
# PHILOSOPHICAL TENDENCIES
# OF BUREAUCRATISM

## December 1928

*NOTE: The following fragments constitute a portion of an unfinished work remaining in Trotsky's archives. Its concluding section, essentially complete, appears elsewhere in this book ("Marxism and the Relation Between Proletarian and Peasant Revolution").*

*In October 1928, in the first chapter of his* Permanent Revolution, *Trotsky described a work he had been planning to write for some time, but which he had repeatedly postponed because of the press of current political issues. The planned book was to be a "historico-polemical work" aimed primarily against Stalin's* Problems of Leninism *and Zinoviev's* Leninism. *Trotsky was about to start on this polemical work in October, he explains, when once again he was compelled to set it aside in order to answer Radek's attack on permanent revolution—an answer that became the book* Permanent Revolution. *Much of the material Trotsky had assembled, he states, had to remain unused until later, "pending the writing of my contemplated book against the epigones, that is, against the official ideology of the era of reaction" (*Permanent Revolution, p. 164).

*In 1929, shortly after being deported to Turkey, Trotsky published in French a book entitled* La Révolution Défigurée, *which can be described as a "book against the epigones," although not necessarily exactly the one Trotsky had in mind in October 1928. (*La Révolution Défigurée *was issued, with a few changes, in Russian (1932) and English (1937) as* The Stalin School of Falsification.*) He did not publish any other book corresponding to his 1928 plan, and never put the incomplete materials of "Philosophical Tendencies of Bureaucratism" into a finished form.*

*Some material in these fragments was published in other forms, or was the basis of later writing on the same subject. Thus, three paragraphs (which have been omitted from this appendix) are a part of "Crisis in the Right-Center Bloc" elsewhere in this volume; and in Chapter VI of* My Life, *Trotsky was describing how, in the evolution of his own thinking, he had conquered the "multiple-factor theory" (p. 119) at the same time (the second half of 1928) that he was writing here about the monist view of Marxism as against the concept of multiple causality.*

*The opening section of this piece contains an analysis, not to be found elsewhere in Trotsky's writings, of the multiple-factor theory as the typical outlook of the bureaucracy. This is an example of his fighting to reaffirm a dialectical materialist view in the face of the general tendency (in a period of reaction) to slide back and lose what had been gained. The same is true of his masterful explanation of the dialectical relation between theory and practice—theory as the generalization of all preceding practice, as a whole, and therefore the key to fully conscious and maximally effective practice (that is, a reaffirmation of Marxism against pragmatism and narrow empiricism).*

*Trotsky focuses on the tendency of the bureaucrats to claim that "Leninism" is somehow different from Marxism—and to use the distinction between "Leninism" and Marxism as a screen for the actual revision of Marxism (particularly with the theory of "socialism in one country"). In refuting this view, Trotsky examines in detail the parallels and contrasts in the respective historical eras and in Marx's life and work in comparison with Lenin's. Here he expands on points he had touched on in earlier years (for example, in his 1924 book* Lenin *[New York: Putnam, 1973], especially pp. 145-147.). But nowhere else does he focus so clearly on the false dichotomy between Leninism and Marxism as a cover for the revision of Marxism—which remains a little-recognized but crucial aspect of official Soviet ideology even today.*

*Because this is an unfinished manuscript, it is impossible to know how Trotsky would have changed it if he had decided to finish it; he would probably have rewritten some parts of it and would have changed the emphasis or the implications of other parts. While he of course always remained bitterly opposed to the cult of Lenin that Stalin created to ease his takeover of the party, for example, in later years Trotsky did not put his major emphasis on Lenin's role as a continuator of Marx, but instead stressed Lenin's special and numerous contributions to Marxist theory and practice.*

*As few editorial liberties have been taken with this manuscript as possible. Of the sixty-page manuscript in Russian at the Harvard College Library, half was not used here because of its excessively fragmentary character. Generally, the fragments have been kept in the same order they are in at Harvard. However, in a few cases a passage has been moved to fit better into the argumentation. Because of the lack of transitions between passages dealing with particular themes, the editors have added a few sentences in brackets to introduce the theme of the segment in question or to serve as a bridge between segments.*

*By permission of the Harvard College Library. Translated from the Russian for this volume by George Saunders.*

We now have for ourselves favorable conditions for examining the question of the philosophical tendencies of bureaucratism. Of course the bureaucracy was never an independent class. In the last analysis it always served one or the other of the fundamental classes in society—but only in the last analysis and in its own special way—that is, allowing as little injury to itself as possible. If it is true that fairly often one sector or layer of a class will wage a bitter struggle for its share of the income and power, how much truer this is of the bureaucracy, which constitutes the most organized and centralized sector of civil society and which at the same time towers over and above society, including the class which it serves.

The labor bureaucracy does not constitute an exception to this general definition of that social grouping which rules and administers and is therefore privileged. The methods and habits of administration, which is of course the main social function of bureaucracy and the source of its preeminence, inevitably leave a very powerful imprint on its entire way of thinking. It is no accident that such terms as bureaucratic and formalistic apply not only to a system of management or administration but also to a definite mode of human thought. The characteristics of this type of thinking extend far beyond government departments alone. They are to be found in philosophy as well. It would be a highly gratifying task to trace the strand of bureaucratic thought down through the history of philosophy, beginning with the rise of the monarchical police state, which gathered around itself the intellectual forces of the country in which it arose. But that is a separate topic. What interests us here is a partial question, but one of great current importance—the tendency toward bureaucratic degeneration in the realm of theory, just as much as in the party, the trade unions, and the state. We can already say in an a priori way that since being determines consciousness, bureaucratism was bound to make devastating gains in the realm of theory as it has in all others.

The most appropriate system of thought for a bureaucracy is the theory of multiple causality, a multiplicity of "factors." This theory arises on the broadest basis out of the social division of labor itself, in particular the separation of mental from manual labor. It is only by this route that humanity emerges from the chaos of primitive monism. But the perfected form of multiple-factor theory, which transforms human society, and in its wake the entire world, into the product of the interplay (or what we might call the interdepartmental relations) of various factors or administrative forces, each of which is assigned its own special province or area of jurisdiction—this kind of system can be elevated to the status of "pearl of creation" only if there is present a bureaucratic hierarchy which, with all its ministries and departments, has raised itself over and above society.

A bureaucratic system, as experience has shown, needs a single individual to crown the system. Bureaucracy originally arises under monarchy and therefore has its historically inherited point of support at the top. But even in republican countries bureaucratism has more than once given rise to Caesarism, Bonapartism, or the personal dictatorship of fascism, whenever the balance of forces between the fundamental classes has opened up the possibility of a single individual gaining supreme power, or establishing himself as the crown of the system.

The theory of self-contained factors both in society and in nature ultimately needs to be crowned by one-man rule just as an oligarchy of powerful ministers does. In practical matters there arises an unavoidable question: Who in the final analysis will guide and coordinate the activity of the various more or less autonomous, nonresponsible ministers if there is no superminister or superbureaucrat? By the same token, on the theoretical plane, the same kind of question arises in regard to the theory of factors both for society and for nature. Who after all put these factors in their places? And entrusted them with the necessary powers of jurisdiction? In a word, if in politics bureaucratism requires a tsar or dictator, however poor in quality, then in theory the pluralism of factors requires a god, however lightweight that divinity may be. The French royalists, not without a touch of wit, accused the bureaucratic system of the Third Republic of having a "hole at the top." Things developed in such a way that for more than half a century bourgeois France was necessarily ruled by a bureaucracy concealed behind a parliamentary system, that is, with a hole at the top. The same thing holds true for philosophy, especially social and historical philosophy. Philosophy by no means always finds within itself the courage to fill the hole at the top with the superfactor of divinity. Instead it grants the world the opportunity of being ruled by the methods of enlightened oligarchy.

In essence the multiple-factor theory cannot get along without a deity. It simply disperses the divine omnipotence among the various lesser rulers with more or less equal powers—economics, politics, law, morality, science, religion, aesthetics, etc. Each of these factors has its own subagents, whose number increases or decreases depending on what is convenient for the administrative authority—that is to say, for the given level of theoretical cognition. At any rate power and authority proceed from the top down, from the "factors" to the facts. That is what gives this theoretical system its idealist character. Each factor, which in essence is nothing but a generalized term for a group of similar or homogeneous facts, is granted special *immanent* powers—powers supposedly inherent to said factor—to govern the body of facts under its imagined jurisdiction. Exactly like some governing bureaucrat, including one of the republican type, each factor partakes of the necessary grace, even if secularized, to administer the affairs of the department entrusted to it. Carried to its ultimate conclusion, the factor theory is a particular variety, and a very widespread one, of immanent idealism.

The breakdown of nature into subsidiary factors was a necessary rung in the ladder by which human consciousness rose from primitive chaos. Actually, however, the question of the interplay of factors, their jurisdictions, and their origins only raises the most fundamental questions of philosophy [without answering them]. The road must either ascend toward the act of Creation and a Creator or descend toward the earth's crust, of which human beings are a product—that is, to nature and to matter. Materialism does not simply reject factors, just as dialectics does not simply reject logic. Materialism makes use of factors as a system of classification of phenomena which have arisen historically—no matter how specifically their spiritual essence may have been "delimited"—out of the underlying productive forces and relations of society and from the natural, historical, i.e., *material,* foundations of nature.

[The following is an example of how the immanent-idealist outlook of the bureaucrats is expressed on the particular question of the dictatorship of the proletariat.]

What is the dictatorship of the proletariat? It is an organized correlation between classes in a certain form. These classes, however, do not remain immobile but change materially and psychologically, consequently changing the relationship of forces between them, that is, strengthening or weakening the dictatorship of the proletariat. That is what the dictatorship is for a Marxist. But for a bureaucrat the dictatorship is an autonomous, self-sufficient factor, or metaphysical category, that stands over and above actual class relations and bears within itself all the necessary guarantees. On top of that, every bureaucrat is inclined to see the dictatorship as a guardian angel hovering over his desk.

Erected upon this metaphysical conception of the dictatorship are all the arguments to the effect that since we have a dictatorship of the proletariat, the peasantry could not be experiencing a differentiation, the kulaks could not be growing stronger, and if the kulaks are growing stronger, that means they will grow over into socialism. In a word the dictatorship is transformed from a class relationship into a self-sufficient principle in relation to which economic phenomena are merely some sort of emanation. Of course none of the bureaucrats carry this system of theirs through to the end. They are too empirical for that and too closely tied to their own past. But their thinking moves along these exact lines and the theoretical sources of their errors must be sought along this path.

Marxism transcended the theory of factors to arrive at historical monism. The process that we now observe is regressive in character, because it represents a movement away from Marxism toward a metaphysical oligarchy of factors.

[The movement away from Marxism in the realm of theory was especially clearly expressed in Stalin's writings. For example, the following excerpt from Stalin's *Problems of Leninism,* written in 1924 and reissued in 1928.]

"The importance of theory. Some think that Leninism is the primacy of practice before theory in the sense that it is merely the translation of Marxist theses into deeds, their 'execution.' As for theory, it is alleged that Leninism is rather unconcerned about it." ["Foundations of Leninism," in the 1928 Russian ed., p. 89; the translation in Stalin's English-language *Works* is much more polished than the Russian original, its grammar in particular—Trans.]

This passage is a veritable Stalin microcosm. It represents equally his theoretical depth, his polemical sharpness, and his honesty toward his opponents. When Stalin said "some think," he was talking about me at a time when he had not yet decided to name me by name. All the professors, journalists, and reviewers had not yet been hand-picked sufficiently and Stalin had not yet assured himself the last word or in many cases the only word. He needed to attribute to me the absurd statement that Leninism was unconcerned about theory. How could he do that? By saying "some think" that Leninism is *only* "the translation of Marxist theses into deeds," only "execution." This is Stalin's translation of my words: "Leninism is Marxism in action." As he would have it, my formulation implied that Leninism was "unconcerned" about Marxism. But how is it possible for someone to *translate Marxist theory into deeds* while remaining "unconcerned" about Marxist theory? Stalin's own attitude toward theory cannot be called "unconcerned" for the sole reason that it is the indifference of the maneuverer. But for that very reason it never occurs to anyone to say that Stalin translates theory into deeds. What Stalin translates into deeds are the promptings of the party bureaucracy, which in turn refract subterranean impulses from class forces. Leninism is Marxism in action—that is, theory that has taken on flesh and blood. That formulation could be described as lack of concern with theory only by someone who was choking on his own spite. For Stalin that is the normal situation. The outer appearance of bureaucratic colorlessness in his articles and speeches barely conceals the all-consuming hatred that he feels for anything that surpasses his own level. By the same token, Stalin's so-called thought, like a scorpion, often strikes its own head with its poisoned tail.

What is meant by the assertion "Leninism is the primacy of practice before theory"? Here even the grammar is wrong. One should say, "primacy *over* theory . . ." or "in relation to theory." The issue of course is not grammar, which in general leads a very hand-to-mouth existence in the pages of Stalin's *Problems of Leninism*. What interests us is the philosophical content of the sentence. The author argues against the idea that Leninism proceeds from the primacy of practice over theory. But after all, that is the essence of materialism. Even if we use the antiquated philosophical term *primacy,* it must be said that practice has the same indisputable primacy over theory as being over consciousness, matter over spirit, and the whole over the part. For theory arises out of practice, engendered by practical needs, and constitutes a more or less incomplete or imperfect generalization upon practice.

In that case, are the empiricists not right—they who guide

themselves by "direct" practice as the highest court of authority? Are they not, then, the most consistent materialists? No, they represent a caricature of materialism. To be guided by theory is to be guided by generalizations based on all the preceding practical experience of humanity in order to cope as successfully as possible with one or another practical problem of the present day. Thus, through theory we discover precisely the primacy of practice-as-a-whole over particular aspects of practice.

Asserting the primacy of economics over politics, Bakunin rejected the political struggle. He did not understand that politics is generalized [or concentrated] economics and that consequently it is impossible to resolve the most important—that is, the most general—economic problems while avoiding generalization through politics.

Now we can appraise Stalin's philosophical thesis [given above] on the importance of theory. He stands the true relation between theory and practice on its head. He equates the practical implementation of theory with disregard for theory, he attributes an obviously absurd idea to his opponent and does so with the worst intentions, speculating on the worst instincts of the poorly informed reader. This totally contradictory, self-devouring thesis finds itself, on top of everything else, in total disarray grammatically. It is for these reasons that we call it a microcosm.

What sort of definition of Leninism does Stalin counterpose to mine? Here is the definition that unites Stalin with Zinoviev and Bukharin and which has found its way into every [official Soviet] textbook: [This is from Stalin's *Problems of Leninism,* page 74.] "Leninism is the Marxism of the age of imperialism and proletarian revolution. More exactly Leninism is the theory and tactics of proletarian revolution in general and the theory and tactics of the dictatorship of the proletariat in particular."

The lack of substance of that definition and at the same time its contradictory nature betray themselves if we simply ask ourselves, what is Marxism? Let us review once again its main elements.

First of all, the dialectical method. Marx was not its originator and of course never pretended to be. Engels felt that it was the merit of Marx that he revived and defended dialectics at a time of epigonism in philosophy and of narrow empiricism in the positive sciences. Engels in the "Old Preface" to *Anti-Dühring* said the following: "It is the merit of Marx that, in contrast to the 'peevish, arrogant, mediocre *epigonoi* (epigones) who now talk large in cultured Germany,' he was the first to have brought to the fore again the forgotten dialectical method" [See Marx and Engels, *Selected Works in Three Volumes* (Moscow: Progress Publishers), vol. 3, p. 64]. Marx was able to accomplish this only by freeing dialectics from idealist captivity. Here there is an enigma: How is it possible to separate dialectics from idealism in such a mechanical way? The answer to the enigma in turn lies in the dialectics of the cognitive process itself. Whenever primitive religion or magic acquired new knowledge about some force of natural law, it immediately numbered that law or force among its own powers. In the same way cognitive thought, having extracted the laws of dialectics from the material process, attributed dialectics to itself; at the same time, through Hegelian philosophy, it assumed absolute omnipotence for itself. The shaman rightly noted the widespread belief that rain falls from the clouds. But he was wrong to think that by imitating one or another characteristic of a cloud, he could cause the rain to fall. Hegel erred in making dialectics an immanent attribute of absolute Spirit. But he was right that dialectics holds sway in all processes of the universe, including human society.

Basing himself on all preceding materialist philosophy and on the unconscious materialism of the natural sciences, Marx led dialectics out of the barren wastelands of idealism and turned its face toward matter, its mother.

It is in this sense that dialectics, restored to its rights by Marx and materialized by him, constitutes the foundation of the Marxist view of the world, the fundamental method of Marxist analysis.

The second most important component of Marxism is historical materialism, that is, the application of materialist dialectics to the structure of human society and its historical development. It would be wrong to dissolve historical materialism into dialectical materialism, of which it is an application. For historical materialism to be applied to human history, a very great creative act by cognitive thought was necessary. That act opened up a new epoch in the history of humanity itself, the class dynamics of which it reflected in itself.

It can be said with full justification that Darwinism is a brilliant application—though one that, philosophically, was not thoroughly thought out—of materialist dialectics to the question of the development of the organic world in all its multiplicity and variety. Historical materialism falls into the same category. It is an application of materialist dialectics to a distinct, although enormous, part of the universe. The immediate practical importance of historical materialism is at this time immeasurably greater, since for the first time it provides the vanguard class with the opportunity of approaching the question of human destiny in a fully conscious way. Only the full victory of historical materialism in practice—that is, the establishment of a technically and scientifically powerful socialist society—will open up the practical possibility of a thorough application of the laws of Darwinism to the human species itself, with the aim of modifying or overcoming the biological contradictions lodged in human beings.

The third component part of Marxism is its systemization of the laws of capitalist economy. Marx's *Capital* is an application of historical materialism to the realm of human economics at a particular stage of its development, just as historical materialism as a whole is an application of materialist dialectics to the realm of human history.

The Russian subjectivists—that is, the empiricists of the idealist school and their epigones—fully acknowledged the competence and authority of Marxism in the field of capitalist economics, but they denied that it could be properly applied to other spheres of human endeavor. This kind of disjunction is based on a crude fetishization of the distinct, homogeneous historical factors (economics, politics, law, science, art, religion) which weave the fabric of history through their interaction and combination, just as chemical compounds are formed by the combination of distinct, homogeneous elements. But even aside from the fact that materialist dialectics also triumphed in chemistry over the empirical conservatism of Mendeleyev by demonstrating the transmutability of elements—even leaving that aside, historical factors have nothing in common with elements so far as stability and homogeneity are concerned. The capitalist economy of the present day rests upon a foundation of technology which has assimilated to itself the fruits of all preceding scientific thought. Capitalist commodity circulation is conceivable only within a framework of definite legal norms. In Europe these were established through the assimilation of Roman law and its subsequent adaptation to the needs of the capitalist economy. The historical and theoretical economics of Marx shows that the development of the productive forces at a definite, exactly describable phase destroys certain economic forms with other forms and in the process disrupts law, morals, views, beliefs; it shows also that the introduction of a system of productive forces of a new and higher type creates for its own needs—always through people, through the agency of human beings—new social, legal, political, and all other norms, in the framework of which this stage provides itself with the dynamic equilibrium it requires. Thus, pure economics is a fiction. Throughout the length and breadth of Marx's study [of capital] he points out with full clarity the connecting belts, gearwheels, and other transmitting mechanisms leading downward from the economic relations to the productive forces and to nature itself, to the earth's crust, of which human beings are a product; but also leading upward, toward the so-called superstructural apparatuses and ideological forms which have always drawn their nourishment from economics. All people eat bread; most prefer it with butter. In other words there is constant interaction between the economy and the superstructure.

Thus only a talentless eclecticism is capable of making a false distinction between Darwinism and historical materialism. But at the same time it would be absolutely wrong to simply dissolve the economic system of Marx into his sociological—or, to use the old terminology, his historico-philosophical—theory. In relation to historical materialism Marx and Engels established the fundamental methods for sociological research and provided models on a high scientific level, though they were only episodic in scope and of pamphlet size: works primarily devoted to revolutionary crises or revolutionary periods in history—for example, Engels's essay on the peasant war in Germany, the writings of both men on the period 1848-51 in France, the Paris Commune, and so on. These writings are brilliant illustrations rather than exhaustive applications of the doctrine of historical materialism. Only in the field of economic relations did Marx provide a more thorough application of his method in theoretical respects, although it is still technically deficient. He did this in a book that is one of the most accomplished products of cognitive thought in human history—*Capital*. That is why Marxist economics must be singled out as a separate, third component of Marxism.

Nowadays one can often read references to Marxist psychology, Marxist natural science, and so on. All this represents wish rather than reality, as do the various speeches about proletarian culture and proletarian literature. More often than not these conceal pretensions based on nothing solid whatsoever. It would make no sense at all to include Darwinism or Mendeleyev's table of elements as part of Marxism, despite the connection that exists between them. There can be no doubt that a conscious application of materialist dialectics to natural science, with a scientific understanding of the influence of class society upon the aims, methods, and objectives of scientific research, would enrich natural science and restructure it in many respects, revealing new links and connections and giving natural science a place of new importance in our understanding of the world. When such epoch-making works in scientific fields appear, it will perhaps be possible to speak, for example, of Marxist biology, Marxist psychology, etc. Although it is most likely that such a new system will have a new name. Marxism does not pretend to be an absolute system. It is aware of its own historically transitory significance. Only a conscious application of materialist dialectics to all fields of science can and will prepare the elements necessary for the transcending of Marxism, which dialectically will at the same time be the triumph of Marxism. From the seed grain grows a stalk upon which a new head of wheat grows at the cost of the death of the seed grain.

In itself Marxism is a historical product and it must be grasped that way. This historical Marxism includes within itself the three basic components we have mentioned: materialist dialectics, historical materialism, and the theoretical and critical analysis of capitalist economics. We have these three elements in mind when we speak of Marxism, that is, when we speak of it in a valid way.

Perhaps the system of historical materialism has changed? If so, where does this change find its expression? In the eclectic system of Bukharin, which is offered up in the guise of historical materialism? No, certainly not that. Although Bukharin revises Marxism in practice, he does not have the courage to openly admit the attempt at creating a new historico-philosophical theory adequately suited to the new epoch, the age of imperialism. In the final analysis Bukharin's scholasticism is adequate only to its own creator. Lukács made a more audacious attempt in principle to go beyond historical materialism. He ventured to announce that beginning with the October Revolution, which represented the leap from the kingdom of necessity to the kingdom of freedom, historical materialism had outlived itself and had ceased to be adequate to the age of proletarian revolutions. However, together with Lenin we had a good laugh over this new discovery, which was, to say the least, premature.

But if Stalin, Zinoviev, and Bukharin have not taken up Lukács's theory—which incidentally, its author has long since repudiated—what exactly do they have in mind?

It remains to be said that the third element of Marxism, its economic system, is the only area in which historical development since the time of Marx and Engels has introduced not only new factual material but also some qualitatively new forms. We have in mind the new stage of concentration and centralization of production, circulation, and credit, the new relations between banks and industry, and the new role of finance capital and the monopolistic organizations of finance capital. But we cannot speak in this connection of some special Marxism of the age of imperialism. The only thing that can be said here—and with full justification—is that Marx's *Capital* has need of a supplementary chapter, or an entire supplementary volume, that would fit the new formations of the imperialist epoch into the overall system. It should not be forgotten that a substantial part of this work has been done—for example, by Hilferding in his book on finance capital, written incidentally not without the influence of that salutary nudge provided by the 1905 revolution to Marxist thought in the West. However, it would never occur to anyone to include Hilferding's *Finance Capital* as a part of Leninism, even if the ever-so-poisonous elements of pseudo-Marxism in Hilferding's work were removed from it—those pseudo-Marxist elements which out of geographic politeness are called "Austro-Marxism." It of course never entered Lenin's head that his superb pamphlet on imperialism constituted any kind of theoretical expression of Leninism as a special type of Marxism of the imperialist epoch. One can only imagine the juicy epithets with which Lenin would have awarded the authors of such an assertion.

If, then, we find no new materialist dialectics, no new historical materialism, and no new theory of value for the "age of imperialism and proletarian revolution," what content should we invest in the Stalinist definition of Leninism, which has been canonized as an official definition? The canonization of this idea, incidentally, proves nothing, for the canonization of theoretical statements is usually necessary only when, as Thomas Aquinas said, one must have faith precisely because of the absurdity of things.

Backward movements within the framework of Marxism have already occurred dozens of times. All regressions to pre-Marxist theoretical views to this very day have in fact been served up in the guise of criticism, renewal, and augmentation—regressions to views that were conscientiously overcome in battle by Marxism. But revisionism is by no means always so open. And even open revisionism must be prepared by preliminary sapping, carried out most often under the pressure of empirical needs, not of theoretically grounded aims.

In essence the singling out of Leninism as a special kind of Marxism peculiar to the age of imperialism was necessary for the revision of Marxism, something Lenin in fact fought against throughout his life. Inasmuch as the central idea of this latest revision of Marxism was the reactionary idea of national socialism (the theory of building socialism in one country), it was necessary to demonstrate or at least proclaim that Leninism had taken a new position on this central question of Marxist theory and politics in opposition to the Marxism of the preimperialist era. We have already heard that Lenin supposedly discovered the law of uneven development, that there could have been no question of such a thing in the time of Marx and Engels. That is precisely the absurdity that the Thomas Aquinases of our day call on us to have faith in. What remains absolutely unexplained however is why Lenin nowhere and in no way demarcated himself on this central question from Marx and Engels and never counterposed his own "Marxism of the imperialist era" to "Marxism plain and simple." Incidentally, Lenin had a much more solid knowledge of Marx than any of the epigones have—as well as an organic intolerance for inadequate statements or lack of clarity on questions of theory. A higher honesty of theoretical conscientiousness, which in isolated cases might have seemed pedantic to an insufficiently thoughtful person, was typical of Lenin. He kept his ideological accounts current with Marx with the same meticulous care evident in his own powerful thinking and in his gratitude as a pupil. And yet on the central question of the international character of the socialist revolution Lenin supposedly never noticed his own break with the preimperialist form of Marxism or, still worse, noticed it but kept it to himself—apparently in the hope that Stalin would explain this secret to a grateful humanity in good time. And Stalin did so, creating in a few unimpressive-sounding lines the Marxism of the age of imperialism, lines which became the screening for the helter-skelter revision of Marx and Lenin of which we have been the witnesses during the past six years.

One must go back to the Middle Ages to find analogous examples of the rise of an entire new ideological system on the basis of a few lines of text which have been misinterpreted or incorrectly copied. Thus the Old Believers let themselves be burned alive for the sake of some miscopied lines from the Bible.

In the history of nineteenth-century Russian social thought we find the case of a group of progressive intellectuals who erroneously interpreted Hegel's words "All that is real is rational" to mean that everything that exists is rational and who, therefore, adopted an extremely conservative point of view. But these examples pale into insignificance—the first because of its antiquity, the second because of the very small number of people involved—in comparison with the present case, in which an organization that has a following of millions uses the hoisting machinery of the apparatus to bring in a totally new point of view, which in fact is based on a childish misinterpretation of two quotations [from Lenin; see *Challenge 1926-27,* p. 57].

But if things were actually determined by wrongly copied texts or illiterate reading of texts it might be appropriate to fall into total despair about the future of humanity. Actually however the real causal forces behind the examples we have cited go much deeper. The Old Believers had solid enough material reasons for breaking with the official church and the monarchical police state. In the case of the radical intelligentsia of the 1840s, it didn't have enough strength to fight the tsarist regime and therefore before it reached the point where it decided to arm itself with terrorist bombs—which was done no earlier than the following generation—it tried to reconcile its newly awakened political conscience with the existing realities, if only by means of some poorly digested Hegelianism.

Lastly the urge, somehow or other, to cut the umbilical cord binding the Soviet republic to the international revolution—that urge arose out of the existing conditions and developments, out of the defeats of the international revolution and the domestic pressure from native proprietary tendencies. The bureaucratic theoreticians selected the quotations in the same way that priests of all religions select holy texts applicable to existing circumstances. If in relation to texts bureaucratism is forced to make falsifications that would put most priests to shame, the fault again lies with the circumstances.

But as we have already seen from the quotation cited above, our theoretician has another definition of Leninism as well which he considers "more precise"—that is, "Leninism is the theory and tactics of proletarian revolution in general, and the theory and tactics of the dictatorship of the proletariat in particular." However, this more precisely phrased definition still further compromises a definition that was hopeless already.

If Leninism is a "theory of the proletarian revolution in

general," then what is Marxism? Marx and Engels announced themselves to the world in full voice in 1847, in the *Communist Manifesto*. What else is that immortal document if not the manifesto of "the proletarian revolution in general"? One might say with full justification that the entire subsequent theoretical activity of these two great friends was merely a commentary on the manifesto. Using the slogan of "objectivism," the academic Marxists attempted to separate Marxism's theoretical contribution to science from its revolutionary conclusions. The epigones of the Second International tried to transform Marx into a garden-variety evolutionist. Throughout his life Lenin fought against both these types in the name of genuine Marxism, that is, "the theory of proletarian revolution in general, and the theory of the dictatorship of the proletariat in particular." What in the world is meant, then, by the counterposing of Leninist theory to Marxism?

In search of grounds for counterposing Leninism to Marxism— of course with all sorts of meaningless qualifying phrases and reservations, Stalin turns to a historical criterion:

"Marx and Engels trod the boards in a prerevolutionary period (we have in mind the proletarian revolution), when there was not yet a developed imperialism, in the period of the preparation of the proletariat for the revolution, in the period when the proletarian revolution was not yet a direct practical inevitability. On the other hand, Lenin, the disciple of Marx and Engels, trod the boards in the period of fully developed imperialism, in the period of unfolding proletarian revolution" ("Foundations of Leninism," Russian ed., 1928, p. 74).

Even if we leave aside the dazzling style of these lines—with Marx and Lenin "treading the boards" like some provincial actors—still it must be acknowledged that this excursion into history is extremely unintelligible in general. That Marx was active in the nineteenth century and not the twentieth is true. But surely the essence of all of Marx and Engels's activity was that they theoretically anticipated and prepared the way for the age of proletarian revolution. If this is set aside, we end up with nothing but academic Marxism, that is, the most repulsive caricature. The full importance of Marx's work becomes evident from the fact that the age of proletarian revolution, which arrived later than he and Engels had expected, did not require any revision of Marxism but on the contrary required its purification from the rust of epigonism which had developed in the meantime. But Stalin would have it that Marxism, unlike Leninism, was the theoretical reflection of a nonrevolutionary period.

It is not accidental that we find this conception in Stalin. It follows from the entire psychology of the empiricist who lives off the land. For him theory only "reflects" the age and serves the tasks of the day. In the chapter of "Foundations of Leninism" especially devoted to theory—and what a chapter!—Stalin treads the boards this way:

"Theory *can be* transformed into a tremendous power of the working class movement *if it takes shape* in inseparable connection with revolutionary practice" (from the 1928 Russian ed., p. 89; emphasis added).

Obviously the theory of Marx, which took shape "in inseparable connection" with the practice of a "prerevolutionary age," is bound to seem outdated in relation to Stalin's "revolutionary practice." He absolutely fails to understand that theory—genuine theory or theory on a large scale—does not at all take shape in *direct* connection with the practical tasks of the day. Rather it is the consolidation and generalization of all human practical activity and experience, embracing different historical periods in their materially determined sequence. It is only because theory is not inseparably linked with the practical tasks contemporary to it, but rises above them, that it has the gift of seeing ahead, that is, is able to prepare to link itself with future practical activity and to train people who will be equal to future practical tasks. The theory of Marx raised itself like a giant watchtower above the revolutionary practical work of the Lassalleans contemporary to Marx, just as it did above the practical activity of all the organizations of the First International. The Second International assimilated only a few elements of Marxism for its own practical needs, by no means always the most essential. Only the age of historical catastrophes extending throughout the capitalist system opened up the possibility of putting into practice the fundamental conclusions of Marxism. It was only this point that made people more receptive—and not all people, not by far—to an understanding of Marxism as a whole.

The Stalinist history of Marxism and Leninism belongs to the same "school of history" of which Marx said, in the words of the Old Testament, that it always sees only the hind part of everything that is accomplished. Stalin's suggestion concerning a prerevolutionary theory of Marxism and a revolutionary theory of Leninism is in fact a philosophy of history adopted by theoretical tail-endism, which simply runs errands for the practical tasks of the day.

When Stalin speaks of "theories," he has in mind those which are created by order of the Secretariat "in inseparable connection with" the "practice," the practical needs and tasks, of the centrist apparatus leadership in a period of political backsliding.

Circling in every way around this porridge, which is too hot for him and which he did not cook himself—truly the best word for this theoretical slop is that favorite word of Lenin's, *porridge*—by zigzags and circumventions Stalin makes his stealthy approach to the idea that Leninism is "more revolutionary" than Marxism. Proceeding with his attempt to counterpose Leninism to Marxism, Stalin writes: "The exceptionally combative and exceptionally revolutionary character of Leninism is usually noted." Who has noted it? That remains unclear. Stalin simply says that it is "usually" noted. This kind of prudence passes over into cowardice. What does "exceptionally revolutionary" mean? Who knows? But what does Stalin himself "note" on this point? He says: "This is absolutely correct. *But* (!) this particular quality (a small 'particularity' in comparison to Marxism) is explained by two causes": the struggle against the opportunism of the Second International, and the proletarian revolution (Ibid. p. 74).

This is how Stalin attached himself—not very courageously, perhaps; nevertheless, he did it—to the conclusion that the "special feature" of Leninism is its "exceptionally" revolutionary character in comparison to Marxism. If this were true, then one should openly abandon Marxism as an obsolete theory, just as science in due course rejected the phlogiston theory, vitalism, and so forth, leaving them as nothing more than material for the history of human thought. But in fact the idea that Leninism is "more revolutionary" than Marxism is an out-and-out travesty against Leninism, Marxism, and the concept of what is revolutionary.

In our analysis of Stalin's second and "more precise" definition of Leninism we have until now left aside the word *tactics*. The full formula, as the reader will recall, goes like this: "Leninism is the Marxism of the age of imperialism and proletarian revolution. More precisely, Leninism is the theory and *tactics* of proletarian revolution in general, the theory and *tactics* of the dictatorship of the proletariat in particular." Tactics are the practical application of theory to the specific conditions of class struggle. The link between theory and current practice is made through tactics. Theory, despite what Stalin says, does not take shape in inseparable connection with current practice. Not at all. It rises above it and only because of that has the capacity to direct tactics by indicating, in addition to the present tasks, points of orientation in the past and perspectives for the future. The complex line of tactics in the present—Marxist tactics, that is; not tail-endist ones—is determined not by a single point [in the present] but by a multiplicity of points in both past and future.

If Marxism, which arose in a prerevolutionary period, was by no means "prerevolutionary" theory but, on the contrary, rose above its own age to become the theory of proletarian revolution, then *tactics*—that is, the application of Marxism to specific combat conditions—by its very essence could not rise above its own age, that is, the ripeness of objective conditions. From the point of view of tactics—it would be more accurate to say, from the point of view of revolutionary strategy*—the activity of Lenin differs in a colossal way from the activity of Marx and Marx's earlier disciples, just as the age of Lenin differs from that of Marx. The revolutionary leader Marx lived and died as theoretical adviser to the young parties of the proletariat and as the herald of its future decisive battles. Lenin led the proletariat to the conquest of power, made that victory secure through his leadership, and provided leadership to the first workers' state in the history of humanity and to an International whose immediate task is to bring about the worldwide dictatorship of the proletariat. The titanic work of this supreme revolutionary strategist can with full justification be placed on the same high level as the work of the supreme titan of proletarian theory.

The attempt to weigh and compare mechanically the theoretical and practical elements in the work of Marx and Lenin is pitiful, sterile, and ultimately stupid. Marx created not only theory but also an International. Lenin not only led a great revolution but did important theoretical work. So it would seem that the difference between them was simply that they "trod the boards" in different eras, as a result of which Marxism is simply revolutionary, whereas Leninism is "exceptionally revolutionary." All this we have heard already.

Marx accomplished a good deal as a leader of the First International. But that was not the main achievement of his life.

---

*See our definition of the political meaning of these terms in the *Criticism of the Draft Program of the Communist International,* a work which preserves all of its relevance as a critique of the program itself, not just the draft.

Marx would have remained Marx even without the Communist League and the First International. His theoretical feat is not coincidental in any sense with his revolutionary practical activity. He rises immeasurably higher than that by having created the theoretical basis for all the subsequent practical activity of Lenin and a number of generations yet to come.

Lenin's theoretical work had an essentially auxiliary character in relation to his own revolutionary practical activity. The scope of his theoretical work corresponded to the world-historical importance of his practice. But Lenin did not create a theory of Leninism. He applied the theory of Marxism to the revolutionary tasks of the new historical era. As early as the Third Party Congress [1905], where the first building blocks of the Bolshevik Party were laid, Lenin himself said that he considered it most justified that he be called a publicist, rather than a theoretician, of Social Democracy. This is something more than the "modesty" of a young leader who had already produced a number of extremely valuable works. If we remember that there are all kinds of "publicists," Lenin correctly defined his historical significance in these words. The work of a publicist, in his conception, is the theoretical and political application of the already existing theory to pave the way for a particular living revolutionary movement.

Even Lenin's most "abstract" work, whose theme was farthest from the issues of the day—his work on empirio-criticism—was stimulated by the immediate needs of internal party struggle. This book may be placed on the shelf next to Engels's *Anti-Dühring* as an application of the same method and the same critical techniques to partly new material from the natural sciences, aimed against new opponents. No less, but also no more than that. Here there is neither a new system nor a new method. It is totally and completely the system and method of Marxism.

The bureaucrats of pseudo-Leninism, the sycophants and slanderers, once again start howling that we are "belittling" Lenin's accomplishment. These types shout the louder about the precepts of the mentor, the more brazenly they trample them into the mud of eclecticism and opportunism. Letting the slanderers go on with their slander, we will defend Leninism, we will explain it, and we will continue Lenin's work.

Leninist theoretical work, as we have said, had an auxiliary character in relation to his own practical work. But his practical work was on a scale that for the first time required the application of Marxist theory in its full dimensions.

Theory is the generalization of all preceding practice and has an auxiliary character in relation to all subsequent practice. We have already clarified the point that theory does not take shape in direct dependence upon current practical activity, nor is it of auxiliary importance in relation to any or all practical activity. "It all depends." For the Stalinist practice of unprincipled zigzags, what is "necessary and sufficient" is an eclectic mixture of poorly digested fragments of Marxism, Menshevism, and Narodism. Leninist practice made full use of all of Marx's theory for the first time in history. It is along this line that the two great historical figures should be weighed. Stalin's comment to the effect that each of them successfully "trod the boards" of theory and practice in their respective periods, one in a revolutionary way and the other in an "exceptionally" revolutionary way, will forever remain an ugly anecdote from the history of ideological epigonism. Both Marx and Lenin joined the ranks of the immortals without a permission slip from Stalin.

However, unless these two great figures were counterposed, it would have been impossible for Stalin to single Leninism out as an independent theory. Such counterposition is the basis of all classification. We have already said that the only serious justification for such a counterpositioning—a justification which is at the same time a most devastating condemnation—is the national-socialist revision of the Marxist "theory of proletarian revolution in general and theory of the dictatorship of the proletariat in particular." The one who expressed himself most daringly about the obsoleteness of Marxism was Stalin—at least during the first few "honeymoon" months of his new theory, when the Opposition had not yet pricked this overblown cow's bladder with the sharp needle of its criticism.

# Appendix C
# SUMMARY OF CHARGES
# AGAINST TROTSKY

## January 18, 1929

*NOTE: By permission of the Library of Social History.*

HEARING: The case of citizen Trotsky, Lev Davidovich, covered by Article 58/10 of the Criminal Code regarding the accusation of counterrevolutionary activity expressing itself through the organization of an illegal anti-Soviet party, activity which during the last period was directed toward the provocation of anti-Soviet demonstrations and toward the preparation of armed struggle against Soviet power.

DECISION: To exile citizen Trotsky, Lev Davidovich, beyond the borders of the USSR.

CERTIFIED: Director of the Alma-Ata Division of the GPU, Alma-Ata, January 20, 1929.

# GLOSSARY

The persons, organizations, terms, and events in this glossary are Soviet, unless otherwise specified.

**Adler, V.** (1852-1918): Founder and leader of the Social Democratic Party of Austria.

**Alexinsky, G.** (b. 1979): A Bolshevik in 1905, thereafter moving to the right and opposing the October Revolution.

**Amsterdam:** Home of the International Federation of Trade Unions, the Social Democratic–dominated trade union federation.

**Anglo-Russian Committee:** Formed by the British Trades Union Congress and Soviet trade unions (May 1925); the Soviet unions remained in the ARC even while the British reformist leaders sabotaged the General Strike (May 1926); the British members walked out (September 1927).

**Anti-Imperialist League:** A Comintern project that held congresses (1927-1929).

**Antonov-Ovseenko, V.** (1884-1938): A leader of the Petrograd Soviet's Military Revolutionary Committee in October 1917; an early member of the Left Opposition; held various diplomatic posts; capitulated in early 1928.

**Artemovsk:** The Soviet city whose party organization was charged with corruption in a celebrated scapegoat case of March 1928.

**Article 58** (of Soviet Penal Code): Provided for punishment of those engaged in counterrevolutionary activity against the Soviet state; Stalin used it to exile and imprison Oppositionists and other dissidents.

**Article 107** (of Soviet Penal Code): Permitted repressive measures to be taken against peasants who withheld grain from state collectors.

**Ashkinazi, S.:** A Democratic Centralist exiled to Samarkand in 1928 who signed Trotsky's statement to the Sixth Comintern Congress.

**AUCP:** All-Union Communist Party.

**Balabolkin, Kolya** or **Kolechka:** Derived from the Russian word for "blabbermouth," Trotsky's name for Bukharin after he learned that Bukharin had met with Kamenev to denounce Stalin.

**Bauer, O.** (1881-1938): A leader of the Austrian Social Democracy after World War I and the chief theoretician of Austro-Marxism.

**Bebel, A.** (1840-1913): A founder and leader of the German Social Democracy.

**Beloborodov, A.** (1891-1938): A Central Committee member and Left Oppositionist; expelled at the Fifteenth Congress and deported to Ust-Kulom; capitulated in 1929.

**Benes, E.** (1884-1948): Foreign minister of Czechoslovakia (1918-35); later became Czech president.

**Bernstein, E.** (1850-1932): Leading theoretician of the German Social Democracy and Engels's literary executor; from 1899 he predicted that capitalism would gradually be transformed into socialism and rejected the prospect of socialist revolution as a guide to practical politics.

**Black Hundreds:** Violent right-wing and anti-Semitic gangs in Russia who led pogroms against Jews and left-wing workers and were supported by the tsarist government.

**Blanqui, L.** (1805-1881): French revolutionist whose name is associated with the theory of armed insurrection by small groups of conspirators.

**Blum, L.** (1872-1950): A leader of the French Socialist Party after World War I; premier of the first People's Front government in 1936.

**Bolsheviks:** Majority faction of the Russian Social Democratic Labor Party after split with Mensheviks (1903); led by Lenin, became a separate party in 1912; led the October Revolution in 1917; became the Russian CP (Bolshevik) in 1918, AUCP(B) in 1925, CPSU in 1952.

**Bonaparte, Napoleon I** (1769-1821): Emperor of France, 1804-15; suppressed discontent following the French Revolution and led campaigns of military conquest.

**Bonaparte, Napoleon III** (1808-1873): Nephew of Napoleon I and emperor, 1852-70.

**Bonapartism:** The Marxist term for a political regime basing itself primarily on the military, police, and state bureaucracy rather than on parliamentary parties or mass movements.

**Bordiga, A.** (1889-1970): A leader of the Italian CP; imprisoned by Mussolini, 1926-30; expelled from the Comintern in 1930.

**Borodai:** A Democratic Centralist exiled in Tyumen in 1928.

**Borodin, M.** (1884-1953): Stalin's chief representative in China (1923-27); his main assignment was to prevent the Communists from withdrawing from the Kuomintang and conducting an independent policy against Chiang Kai-shek.

**Brandler, H.** (1881-1967): Head of the German CP when it let the revolutionary crisis of 1923 slip; was made a scapegoat and removed from the leadership in 1924; expelled in 1929 for Bukharinist sympathies.

**Brentano school of political economy:** A reference to the German economist Lujo Brentano (1844-1931), who advocated a "class truce" and thought that the contradictions of capitalism could be overcome through reformist trade unions which would permit the capitalists and the workers to reconcile their differences.

**Brest-Litovsk treaty:** Signed March 3, 1918, ending hostilities between Germany and Russia; its harsh terms occasioned bitter controversy in the Bolshevik Party; Trotsky uses it as a metaphor for the Oppositionists who capitulated to Stalin, issuing pro forma recantations while secretly swearing revenge.

**British Labour Party:** Founded 1906, affiliated to the Second International.

**Bubnov, A.** (1883-1940): Old Bolshevik, was on the Military Revolutionary Committee that organized the October insurrection; in 1923 he lined up with Stalin.

**Budenny, S.** (1883-1973): Civil war hero and cavalry commander; became a leading military figure.

**Bukharin, N.** (1888-1938): Old Bolshevik; became the major spokesman after 1923 for right-wing prokulak policies outlined in September 1928 in "Notes of an Economist"; editor of *Pravda* (1918-29); succeeded Zinoviev as head of the Comintern (1926-29); formed the Right Opposition in 1928 and was expelled in 1929.

**Bund** (General Jewish Workers Union of Lithuania, Poland, and Russia): Part of the RSDLP until 1903, when it lost its demand for a federated party structure; allied with the Mensheviks in 1906; in 1920, a portion joined the Bolsheviks.

**Butov, G.:** Had been in charge of Trotsky's secretariat on the Revolutionary Military Council during the civil war; arrested for refusing to sign false charges against Trotsky; went on a hunger strike and died in prison, September 1928.

**Cadets** (Constitutional Democrats): Liberal bourgeois party founded 1905; led by Milyukov; initially favored a constitutional monarchy, then a republic; after the civil war existed only in emigration.

**Canton uprising** (December 1927): A putsch instigated by Stalin so he would be able to "refute" the charge of the Left Opposition that his policy had produced defeats in China; since the Chinese CP was isolated and the uprising unprepared, it was crushed in less than three days with a loss of several thousand lives.

**Centrism:** Trotsky's term for a tendency in the radical movement that stands or wavers between reformism and Marxism; since a centrist tendency has no independent social base, it must be evaluated in terms of its origins, internal dynamic, and the direction it is taking or being pushed toward by events; until 1935, Trotsky saw Stalinism as a special type of centrism: bureaucratic centrism.

**Centrosoyuz:** The Central Union of Consumer Cooperative Societies.

**Chamberlain, A.** (1863-1937): British Conservative foreign secretary (1924-29).

**Chernov, M.** (1891-1938): A leading Social Revolutionary; commissar of agriculture in the Provisional Government in 1917; sided with the counterrevolution in the civil war; emigrated in 1921.

**Chervonets:** Currency unit introduced in the monetary reform of 1922-24; equal to U.S.$5, or ten prerevolutionary gold rubles.

**Chiang Kai-shek** (1887-1975): Principal military leader of the Kuomintang from March 1925; Stalin made him an honorary member of the Comintern; staged a coup in Canton (March 1926) and a bloody massacre of Shanghai workers and Communists (April 1927).

**Chubar, V.** (1891-1941): Formerly Ukrainian head of state; was a CC member in the late twenties.

**Clemenceau thesis:** An analogy that Trotsky used in 1927 to explain why the Opposition should not renounce the struggle to change the line of the AUCP in time of war or war danger. G. Clemenceau (1841-1929) had sharply criticized the ineffectual policies of the French bourgeois government during World War I, becoming its leader in 1917 when it became apparent that he was its best defender.

**Comintern** (Communist International): Founded 1919 under Lenin's leadership as the revolutionary successor to the Second International, which had supported bourgeois governments in World War I; the theses of its first four congresses (1919-22) were the programmatic cornerstone of the Left Opposition and later of the Fourth International; after Lenin's death and with the Stalinization of the AUCP, the Comintern became an instrument of Soviet foreign policy and was finally dissolved in 1943 as a gesture to Stalin's imperialist allies in World War II.

**Contre le courant** (Against the stream): French Left Opposition journal published in Paris, November 1927 to October 1929.

**Democratic Centralist group:** Dissident Bolsheviks who held semi-syndicalist views and argued at the Ninth Congress (March 1920) that the party was run by a bureaucratic clique and that party elections were not democratically conducted; some of them adhered to the United Opposition in 1926 although Trotsky disclaimed their call for a new party; expelled in late 1927 and deported along with the Trotskyists; led by V. Smirnov and T. Sapronov.

**Dneprostroi:** The Dnepr Construction Project.

**Dzerzhinsky, F.** (1877-1926): A founder of the Social Democratic Party of Poland and Lithuania, active in Poland and Russia; member of the Soviet CP's Central Committee and first chairman of the Cheka, later called the GPU; in 1921 he was commissar of transport.

**Eastman, M.** (1883-1969): An American and an early sympathizer of the Left Opposition; a translator of several of Trotsky's books into English; the first to acquaint the American public with the issues of the Trotsky-Stalin struggle; he later renounced socialism.

**Economism:** A Russian variant of syndicalism, holding that the economic struggle of the workers was sufficient to develop a mass movement, political consciousness, and an active leadership; downplayed the revolutionary party and evaded political issues.

**Ekonomicheskaya Zhizn** (Economic Life): A Soviet periodical devoted to economic questions.

**Eltsin, B.** (1875-1937?): An Old Bolshevik; directed a group of Oppositionists in Moscow who were still at liberty in 1928; arrested in 1929 and disappeared in labor camps.

**Eltsin, V.:** An Oppositionist, son of B. Eltsin; exiled to Ust-Vym in 1928.

**Emancipation of Labour:** Founded 1883 by Plekhanov in Switzerland; its founding marks the beginning of a Russian Marxist movement; dissolved when the RSDLP was formed in 1898.

**Engels, F.** (1820-1895): The lifelong collaborator of Marx and coauthor with him of *The Communist Manifesto* and many of the basic works of

Marxism; in his last years he was the outstanding figure of the young Second International.

**Ercoli:** Pseudonym of Palmiro Togliatti (1893-1964), the Stalinist leader of the Italian CP.

**February revolution** (1917): Fed by the demands of workers' struggles and dissatisfaction with tsarist war policy, it toppled the tsarist system and instituted the bourgeois Provisional Government.

**Fischer, R.** (1895-1961): With Maslow, a central leader of the German CP after Brandler's disgrace in 1924; expelled in 1926 for supporting the Soviet United Opposition; with Maslow and Urbahns, a founder of the Leninbund, which collaborated with the Left Opposition until 1930.

**Frumkin, M.** (1878-1939): An Old Bolshevik and a Bukharinist; on June 15, 1928, as deputy commissar of finance, he sent the Politburo a letter bleakly evaluating the consequences of Stalin's policies in the countryside and urging right-wing remedies.

**Frunze, M.** (1885-1925): Old Bolshevik and a civil war commander; in 1925 he replaced Trotsky as chairman of the Military Revolutionary Council of the Republic.

**General Council:** Leadership body of the British Trades Union Congress; called off General Strike of May 1926 after nine days, abandoning the coalminers in their prolonged strike.

**Girault, S.:** A leader of one of the French Opposition groups of the mid-twenties.

**Glazman, M.:** Had been the head of Trotsky's secretariat during the civil war; hounded out of the party by the Stalinists because of his adherence to the Left Opposition, he committed suicide in 1924.

**Gosizdat:** The State Publishing House.

**Jacobins:** The most radical faction in the French Revolution (1789); dominated the revolutionary government from the overthrow of the Gironde (1791) until Thermidor (1794).

**Jacquemotte, J.** (1883-1936): The leader of the Belgian CP after a majority of its leading committee was expelled for "Trotskyism" in 1928.

**Jaurès, J.** (1859-1914): An outstanding French Socialist leader; formed a bloc with the bourgeois Radicals; assassinated at the start of World War I.

**Kaganovich, L.** (1893-    ): A CC member from 1924 and an undeviating Stalinist; he had been extremely unpopular during his three-year tenure as head of the Ukrainian party.

**Kalinin, M.** (1875-1946): President of the Soviet Central Executive Committee from 1919 and an ally of Rykov on the CC.

**Kamenev, L.** (1883-1936): Old Bolshevik CC member; in 1917 he initially opposed the October insurrection; after Lenin's death he blocked with Stalin against Trotsky until late 1925; in 1926 he and Zinoviev joined with Trotsky to form the United Opposition; appointed Soviet representative to Rome (January 1927); capitulated after his expulsion from the AUCP in December 1927 and was readmitted to the party in 1928.

**Karolyi, Count M.** (1875-1955): Hungarian prime minister after World War I and then president of the new Hungarian Republic (1918-19); overthrown by the Hungarian soviet uprising.

**Katayama, S.** (1859-1933): A member of the ECCI and its presidium from 1922, and a Comintern functionary.

**Kautsky, K.** (1854-1938): A leader of the German Social Democracy and a founder of the Second International; adopted a centrist and pacifist stand in World War I and opposed the Bolshevik revolution of 1917.

**Kerensky, A.** (1882-1970): Prime minister of the Provisional Government produced by the February 1917 revolution; deposed by the Bolsheviks in October.

**Kirov, S.** (1886-1934): CC member from 1923 and Stalinist Leningrad party secretary from 1926, when he replaced Zinoviev.

**Klim:** See **Voroshilov.**

**Kolarov, V.** (1877-1950): Former Socialist and founding leader of the Bulgarian Communist Party (1919); elected to the ECCI and its presidium (1922); after the abortive September 1923 insurrection he fled to Russia and became a Comintern functionary.

**Kornilov, L.** (1870-1918): Kerensky's commander in chief after the February revolution; later led a counterrevolutionary putsch against the Provisional Government.

**Korsch, K.** (1886-1961): Member of the German CP until 1926, when he was expelled for opposing ratification of the Soviet-German treaty of April 1926; also opposed the united front tactic.

**Kramar, K.** (1860-1937): First prime minister of Czechoslovakia (1918-19).

**Krestinsky, N.** (1883-1938): Old Bolshevik and Soviet ambassador to Berlin (1921-27); renounced the Opposition immediately after the Fifteenth Congress (December 1927).

**Krestintern:** The Peasants International, an auxiliary organization of the Comintern founded October 1923; its purpose was to "coordinate peasant organizations and the efforts of the peasants to achieve workers' and peasants' governments"; it held one further conference in November 1927 and was officially dissolved in 1939.

**Krzhizhanovsky, G.** (1872-1959): Old Bolshevik and Stalinist; head of the State Planning Commission (1921-30).

**Kulak:** Wealthy peasant who owned and rented out land or hired others to work it.

**Kun, B.** (1886-1939): Leader of the defeated 1919 Hungarian Soviet Republic; moved to Moscow and became a Comintern functionary.

**Kuomintang** (KMT): Nationalist Party of China, a bourgeois party founded by Sun Yat-sen in 1912; in 1915 it began a campaign to defeat the warlords of North China; under Chiang Kai-shek it became the ruling bourgeois party in China.

**Kuusinen, O.** (1881-1964): Finnish Stalinist and Comintern secretary (1922-31).

**La Follette party** (Progressive Party, U.S.): In 1924, Robert La

Follette (1855-1925), Republican senator from Wisconsin, ran for president on the Progressive ticket; the CP had captured a convention of the Farmer-Labor Party in 1923, and its leadership sought to link it to La Follette's third-party campaign for the presidency; the ECCI declared this policy opportunist and the CP pulled back from the La Follette candidacy.

**Lapinsky, S.** (1879-1937): A Polish Communist who worked in Berlin as an official of the commissariat for foreign affairs.

**Laplace, P.** (1749-1827): French astronomer and mathematician.

**Larin, Yu.** (1882-1932): An economist and former Menshevik who joined the Bolsheviks in August 1917.

**Lashevich, M.** (1884-1928): Old Bolshevik and former Left Opposition-ist; he recanted and was made assistant to the president of the board of the Chinese Eastern Railroad.

**Lassalle, F.** (1825-1864): A major figure in the German working class movement and founder of the German Workers' Union; his followers joined the early Marxists in founding the German Social Democracy.

**Lenin, V. I.** (1870-1924): Founder of the Bolshevik faction, leader of the October Revolution, head of the first Soviet government, founder of the Comintern.

**Leninbund:** Founded by Maslow, Fischer, and Urbahns in 1928, after their expulsions from the German CP; it took positions close to the Left Opposition until 1930.

**Lenin's Testament:** Written in December 1922 and January 1923, it gave his final evaluation of the other Soviet leaders; since it called for Stalin's removal from the post of general secretary it was suppressed in the Soviet Union until after Stalin's death; it is included now in volume 36 of Lenin's *Collected Works*.

**Levi, P.** (1883-1929): A German lawyer and leader of the German CP, expelled for his public criticism of the March 1921 uprising.

**Livshits, B.** (1896-1949): A Left Oppositionist who would capitulate in 1929.

**Longuetism:** After Jean Longuet (1876-1938), Marx's grandson and a right-wing French Socialist who voted for government war credits in World War I.

**Loriot, F.** (1870-1932): A French Socialist who helped found the CP, became an Oppositionist in 1925 and a member of the editorial board of *Contre le courant* at the end of 1927; a year later he abandoned communism for syndicalism.

**Lozovsky, S.** (1878-1952): A Stalinist and head of the Red Interna-tional of Labor Unions (1921-37); also active in Comintern and diplomatic work.

**Luxemburg, R.** (1871-1919): Leader of the left wing of the German Social Democracy and an outstanding Marxist theoretician; imprisoned for opposing World War I; assassinated by soldiers of the Social Demo-cratic government after the Spartacus uprising.

**Lyadov, M.** (1872-1947): A leading Bolshevik (1903-08); became an ultraleft and a conciliator (1909-11); joined the Mensheviks (1917);

rejoined the Bolsheviks after the consolidation of Soviet power (1920); became rector of Sverdlov Communist University in Moscow (1923) and was given prominence as a party historian; contributed to the rewriting of history and debasement of theory in the era of bureaucratic reaction; removed from leading posts after 1928 as a "Right Oppositionist."

**Lyova:** See **Sedov, L.**

**MacDonald, R.** (1866-1937): Prime minister of the first and second British Labour governments (1924, 1929-31).

**Mandelstamm, N.:** A member of the Moscow party committee and head of its Agitprop department; a supporter of the Bukharin-Rykov group.

**Manuilsky, D.** (1883-1959): Former otzovist who became a CC member in 1923 and a Comintern functionary in 1922; from 1924 on he served as Comintern representative at German CP congresses; a member of the ECCI's Secretariat (1926-43).

**Maretsky, G.:** Disciple of Bukharin in the Institute of Red Professors; in summer 1927 he published an article in *Pravda* denouncing Trotsky's "slanderous accusations" about Thermidor.

**Martynov, A.** (1865-1935): Right-wing Menshevik and opponent of the October Revolution; principal Menshevik theorist of "two-stage" revolution; joined Soviet CP in 1923 as a Stalin supporter; architect of the "bloc of four classes" in China; Comintern functionary.

**Marx, K.** (1818-1883): With Engels, the founder of scientific socialism and a leader of the First International (1864-76).

**Maslow, A.** (1891-1941): One of the central leaders of the German CP after Brandler's demotion in 1924; a member of the ECCI; supported the Soviet United Opposition and was expelled in 1926.

**Maxton, J.** (1885-1946): The principal leader of the British Independent Labour Party (1926-31) and its spokesman against right-wing Labour Party leaders.

**Mekhlis, L.** (1889-1953): A personal secretary to Stalin in the late twenties; in 1930 he would become a member of the editorial board of *Pravda.*

**Mensheviks:** Minority faction of the Russian Social Democratic Labor Party after the split with the Bolsheviks (1903); led by Martov and Dan, they were moderate socialists who believed that the working class must combine with the liberal bourgeoisie to overthrow tsarism and establish a democratic bourgeois republic; after 1921 they existed only in emigration.

**Molotov, V.** (1890-    ): Old Bolshevik and Stalin supporter; member of the CC from 1920 and of the Politburo from 1926.

**Monatte, P.** (1881-1960): French syndicalist; became a leader of the CP, which he joined in 1923, only to leave a year later; in 1926 he founded the Syndicalist League.

**Mrachkovsky, S.** (1883-1936): Old Bolshevik and famous civil war commander; expelled from the party in 1927 and arrested by the GPU for helping to publish the Platform of the Opposition; exiled to Veliky Ustyug.

**Napoleon:** See **Bonaparte.**

**Narodniks** (Populists): Movement of Russian intellectuals who saw the liberation of the peasantry as the key to the country's development; after a split in 1879, one wing led by Plekhanov became Marxist while another evolved into the Social Revolutionary Party.

**NEP** (New Economic Policy): Adopted at the Tenth Congress of the Russian Communist Party in March 1921 as a temporary measure to replace war communism; allowed a limited growth of free trade inside the Soviet Union and foreign concessions alongside the nationalized and state-controlled sectors of the economy; the NEPmen—petty traders, merchants, and swindlers, who benefited from this policy—were viewed as a potential base for capitalist restoration.

**Neumann, H.** (1902-1937?): German Stalinist on the Comintern staff (from 1925); Stalin's representative in China (1927-28); chief organizer of the Canton Commune (December 1927).

**Neurath, A.** (1886-1952): A leader of the Czechoslovakian CP and a member of the ECCI when he was expelled in 1929 as a "Trotskyist."

**Nevelson, M.:** A Left Oppositionist and Trotsky's son-in-law.

**1905 revolution:** Grew out of discontent with the Russo-Japanese war and lasted from January 9 (when police fired on workers marching peacefully to the tsar's palace) until the crushing of the December uprising in Moscow; severe repression followed this unsuccessful revolution.

**October Revolution** (1917): A revolutionary upsurge, led by the Bolsheviks, overthrew the bourgeois Provisional Government backed by the Mensheviks and SRs and instituted a workers' state with a government based on soviets (councils).

**Ordzhonikidze, G.** (1886-1937): Old Bolshevik and organizer of the Stalin faction; later put in charge of heavy industry; became head of the CCC in the autumn of 1926.

**Osinsky, V.** (1887-1938): A leader of the Democratic Centralists until 1923, then a member of the Left Opposition for a few years, and finally a supporter of the Bukharin-Rykov group.

**Otzovists** (recallists): Dissident group of Bolsheviks after the 1905 revolution who advocated the recall or withdrawal of the Social Democratic deputies elected to the Duma (parliament) on the grounds of the Duma's extremely reactionary character.

**Overstraeten, E. van** (1891-    ): A founder of the Belgian CP; expelled in 1928 and helped found the Left Opposition; he later developed differences with Trotsky and the rest of the Opposition and split in 1930.

**Paris Commune:** The first example of a workers' government, in power March 18 to May 28, 1871; overthrown in a series of bloody battles.

**Pepper, J.** (1886-1937): Member of Bela Kun's short-lived Hungarian Soviet Republic in 1919, which declared the outright nationalization of the land, alienating the peasantry and hastening the government's downfall; he went to the U.S. as Comintern representative to the American CP; in 1923 he masterminded the CP's takeover of the

Federated Farmer-Labor Party and its endorsement of Progressive Republican Robert La Follette's presidential candidacy; he later returned to Moscow.

**Petlyura, S.** (1877-1926): A right-wing Social Democrat and head of the central Ukrainian bourgeois government that opposed Soviet power in the Ukraine during the civil war; during the Russo-Polish war he fought on the side of the Poles under Pilsudski.

**Petrovsky, D.** ("Bennet"): Former member of the Bund who sided with the Mensheviks in the split in the RSDLP; he joined the Bolshevik Party after the October Revolution and in the 1920s joined the Comintern central apparatus as a specialist in British affairs.

**Pilsudski, J.** (1867-1935): Led the Polish army against Soviet forces in the Ukraine (1920); in May 1926 he led a coup that returned him to power and was dictator of Poland until his death.

**Plekhanov, G.** (1856-1918): Founder of the first Russian Marxist organization, the Emancipation of Labor, in 1883; after collaborating with Lenin on *Iskra* in emigration, he became a Menshevik and supported the Russian bourgeois government in World War I; opposed the October Revolution.

**Pravda** (Truth): Official paper of the CC of the AUCP.

**Preobrazhensky, Ye.** (1886-1937): Old Bolshevik and leading economist; produced theory of "primitive socialist accumulation" (see *Challenge 1926-27*, p. 56); author of *The New Economics* (1926); expelled in 1927 as an Oppositionist and exiled to Uralsk; capitulated in 1929.

**Proudhon, P.** (1809-1865): One of the first theoreticians of anarchism and an opponent of Marx and Engels; had important influence on the French syndicalist movement.

**Provisional Government** (1917): Set up by the February revolution; supported by the Mensheviks and SRs, it governed until the October Bolshevik Revolution.

**Purcell, A.** (1872-1935): British left Labourite and MP; a leader of the TUC General Council during the General Strike.

**Pyatakov, Yu.** (1890-1937): Old Bolshevik and an Oppositionist from 1923 to 1928; deputy chairman of the Supreme Council of the National Economy; expelled in 1927; capitulated quickly and was assigned to work in the State Bank.

**Pyatnitsky, O.** (1882-1939): An Old Bolshevik who held various posts before becoming a member of the presidium of the ECCI in 1921 and later a member of its Secretariat; he was a member of the CC and the CCC of the Soviet party as well.

**Radek, K.** (1885-1939): Prominent revolutionist in the Polish, German, and Russian Social Democratic parties before 1917; became secretary of the Comintern (March 1920) with particular responsibility for Germany and China; supported the Opposition in 1923 and was subsequently dropped from all leading Comintern bodies; expelled from the party at the Fifteenth Congress and deported to Ishim; capitulated in 1929.

**Radić, S.** (1871-1928): Leader of the Croatian Peasants Party; was suddenly hailed by Moscow as a "real leader of the people" because he attended a congress of the Peasants International in 1924.

**Rafail:** A veteran CC member of the Ukrainian CP who was a member of the Democratic Centralists.

**Rafes, M.** (1883-1942): Member of the Bund Central Committee (1912-19); participated in the anti-Communist Petlyura government in the Ukraine (1917-18); joined the CP in 1919; worked in the Comintern directing the Chinese CP in the late twenties.

**Rakovsky, Kh.** (1873-1941): Leading revolutionary in the Balkans before World War I; prime minister of the Ukrainian government (1919-23); later Soviet ambassador to Paris (1925-27); an early leader of the Left Opposition; expelled from the AUCP in 1927 and exiled to Astrakhan; capitulated in 1934.

**Raskolnikov, F.** (1892-1939): Joined the Bolsheviks in 1910; held various literary and military positions; first Soviet representative to Afghanistan (1921); active in the central apparatus of the Comintern, becoming a member of the ECCI Secretariat (1926) and a secretary of the Chinese commission.

**Reed, J.** (1887-1920): An American journalist sympathetic to the Russian revolution; author of *Ten Days That Shook the World*.

**Red International of Labor Unions** (RILU): Organized in 1920 as a Communist-led rival to the reformist Amsterdam International.

**Renner, K.** (1870-1950): Right-wing leader of the Austrian Social Democracy; supported World War I; was chancellor of Austria (1918-20).

**Rosmer, A.** (1877-1964): Revolutionary syndicalist who was a leader of the French CP and the Comintern until his expulsion as an Oppositionist in 1924.

**Roy, M. N.** (1887-1954): An Indian nationalist recruited to communism by Borodin (1919); elected to the ECCI (1921); became Comintern representative in China (May 1927); criticized for "rightist deviation" at the Sixth Congress (1928); expelled from the Comintern (November 1929).

**Rudzutak, Ya.** (1887-1938): Old Bolshevik, member of the CC from 1920 and of the Secretariat from 1923; a specialist on the trade unions and later in the economic apparatus; commissar for communications (1924-30); a member of the Politburo after the Fifteenth Congress.

**Ryazanov, D.** (1870-193?): Historian and philosopher; became a Bolshevik in 1917 and organized the Institute of Marx and Engels; withdrew from political activity after the rise of Stalinism.

**Rykov, A.** (1881-1938): Old Bolshevik, succeeded Lenin as head of state (1924-30); head of Supreme Council of the National Economy; with Bukharin, ideological leader of the right wing in the party under NEP and until his capitulation to Stalin in 1929.

**Ryutin, M.:** A leading Soviet propagandist and a member of the Bukharin-Rykov faction.

**Safarov, G.** (1891-1941): Old Bolshevik; headed Comintern section for Middle and Far East (1921-24); as a Zinovievist and a leader of the

Communist Youth, he supported the United Opposition (1926-27); expelled from the party at the Fifteenth Congress, he did not capitulate with the Zinovievist leaders and was deported; he capitulated in early 1928.

**Saltykov, M.** ("Shchedrin") (1826-1889): A novelist best known for satirical sketches of the life of the upper classes in provincial Russia, among them *The Golovlyov Family* (1875-80).

**Sapronov, T.** (1887-1939): A leader of the Democratic Centralists and a member of the United Opposition in 1926; expelled from the AUCP (1927); capitulated (1928); later developed state capitalist views.

**Second International:** Founded 1889, the first mass international workers' organization, uniting both revolutionary and reformist elements; in World War I most sections supported their own imperialist governments; revived after the war as the Labor and Socialist International.

**Sedov, L.** ("Lyova") (1906-1938): Trotsky's elder son and a Left Oppositionist; accompanied his parents in their exile (1928); Trotsky's closest collaborator.

**Sedov, S.** (1908-1937?): Trotsky's younger son and the only one of his children who had no interest in politics; he remained in Moscow when Trotsky was exiled to Alma-Ata, except for a brief visit to his parents.

**Sedova, N.** (1882-1962): Trotsky's second wife; worked for several years in the Commissariat of Education.

**Sémard, P.** (1887-1942): A former revolutionary syndicalist; became general secretary of the French CP (1924-29).

**Septemvirate:** The six members of the Politburo after Lenin's final withdrawal (excluding Trotsky) plus Kuibyshev, who was chairman of the CCC; the six others were Zinoviev, Kamenev, Stalin, Bukharin, Rykov, and Tomsky; this secret faction met and made all the major decisions for the party without its knowledge or consent; it functioned from 1923 until Zinoviev and Kamenev broke with the others in 1925.

**Serebryakov, L.** (1890-1937): Old Bolshevik and former member of the party Secretariat (1919-20); deputy commissar for communications in the mid-twenties; a supporter of the United Opposition; expelled October 1927; recanted 1929.

**Shakhty affair** (1928): The first in a series of frame-up trials against specialists associated with the Bukharin faction; it served as a safety valve to vent public indigation over corruption and bureaucratism and as a way the Stalinists could strike against the right wing.

**Shatskin, L.** (1901-1937): Member of the "Young Stalinist Left," a group of anti-Bukharinist party and Communist League of Youth leaders.

**Shlyapnikov, A.** (1883-1937): Old Bolshevik and CC member from 1915 on; chairman of the Metal Workers Union and first Soviet commissar of labor; a leader of the Workers Opposition (1921-23); expelled, readmitted, and expelled again in 1927.

**Shvarts:** Chairman of the All-Russian Miners Union and a member of the party Central Committee.

**Skvortsov-Stepanov, I.** (1870-1928): Old Bolshevik and former editor of *Izvestia;* assistant editor of *Pravda* (1924); replaced a Zinovievist as editor of *Leningradskaya Pravda* (1925); director of the Lenin Institute (1926); translated Marx and wrote on political and economic topics.

**Slepkov, A.:** Young historian and protégé of Bukharin in the Institute of Red Professors; one of the foremost elaborators of Bukharin's ideas in the official press.

**Smeral, B.** (1880-1941): Right-wing Social Democrat who became a leader of the Czechoslovak CP from its founding (1921); elected to the ECCI and its presidium (1922).

**Smerdyakov:** The fourth, illegitimate brother in Dostoyevsky's *The Brothers Karamazov,* the one who actually murders the father; he is a repellent character, always whining, fawning, and servile; literally, the name means "Stinker."

**Smilga, I.** (1892-1938): Old Bolshevik and a civil war hero; later a member of the Supreme Council of the National Economy and the State Planning Commission; CC member (1917-20, 1925-27); an Oppositionist leader; expelled in 1927; deported to Narym in 1928; capitulated in 1929.

**Smirnov, A.** (1877-1938): Commissar for agriculture and a rightist ally of Bukharin.

**Smirnov, I.** (1881-1936): Old Bolshevik and civil war hero; CC member from 1920 and commissar of posts and telegraph; an Oppositionist, expelled in 1927 and deported to Novo-Bayazet in Armenia; capitulated in 1929.

**Smirnov, V.** (1887-1937): Old Bolshevik and a leader of the Democratic Centralists; a member of the first staff of the Supreme Council of the National Economy; joined the United Opposition in 1926, although he called for a new party; expelled from the AUCP December 1927.

**Smolensk case:** A scandal, discovered in May 1928, implicating leaders of the local party apparatus in corruption and abuse of power.

**Smychka:** This Russian term has two meanings in this book: (1) the "bond" or link between the workers and peasants that the workers' state had to maintain to be able to build socialism in a predominantly peasant country; (2) Trotsky also uses it to refer to the clandestine meetings of Oppositionists held in the autumn of 1927 and subsequently.

**Social Revolutionaries** (SRs): Major radical-intellectual and peasant current in Russia from 1900 until the revolution; in 1917 the party split and the left wing supported the Soviet government until it signed the Brest-Litovsk peace with Germany.

**Sokolnikov, G.** (1888-1939): Old Bolshevik and a CC member from 1917; played an important part in the civil war; commissar of finance (1922-26); before the formation of the Leningrad Opposition, of which he was a member, he was the leading spokesman for the financial policies of the majority, including its rejection of economic planning and its reliance on currency manipulation.

**Sokolovskaya, A.:** Trotsky's first wife and the mother of his two daughters, Zinaida and Nina Bronstein; an Oppositionist from 1923 on.

**Sosnovsky, L.** (1886-1937): An outstanding Soviet journalist and one of the first Left Oppositionists; deported to Barnaul in 1928.

**Souvarine, B.** (1893-    ): A founder of the French CP, expelled in 1924 as a Trotskyist; in 1929 he broke with Trotsky and shortly thereafter turned against Marxism.

**Sten, I.** (d. 1937): A CCC member and a member of the Young Stalinist Left, an anti-Bukharinist youth group.

**Stetsky, A.** (1896-1938): Old Bolshevik and a Bukharin disciple; responsible for the Agitprop department of the CC.

**Sun Yat-sen** (1866-1925): Bourgeois nationalist leader of the Chinese revolution of 1911 and founder of the Kuomintang.

**Supreme Council of the National Economy:** Set up in December 1917, became the main instrument for centralizing and administering industry; in the early days of the revolution, it had the power to operate all branches of industry and commerce and to direct economic planning.

**Syrtsov, S.** (1893-1938): Old Bolshevik and career functionary; from 1927, member of the CC; in 1930 he became president of the council of people's commissars of the Russian Republic.

**T'an P'ing-shan** (1887-1956): Chinese Communist leader who headed the Kuomintang organization department (1924-26); minister of agriculture in the Wuhan Kuomintang government (March-June 1927), acting to suppress peasant land seizures; made a scapegoat and expelled (November 1927).

**Ter-Vaganyan, V.** (1873-1936): Old Bolshevik and civil war veteran, wrote numerous works on the national question; Left Oppositionist; expelled (1927); capitulated (1929).

**Thälmann, E.** (1886-1944): Elected to the ECCI in 1924; a faithful Stalinist, he became the unchallenged leader of the German party after the expulsion of Maslow, Fischer, and Urbahns.

**Thermidor:** By analogy with the period of reaction in the French Revolution, Trotsky used this term to mean capitalist counterrevolution; the extent to which this was being accomplished was the subject of some debate in the Opposition and in the party as a whole (see *Challenge 1926-27*, p. 17).

**Tomsky, M.** (1880-1936): Old Bolshevik, head of the Soviet trade unions and a Politburo member; he was associated with Bukharin's right-wing policies.

**Treint, A.** (1889-1972): Formerly a central leader of the French CP, he supported the Russian Leningrad Opposition and was expelled in 1927; he belonged to several Oppositionist groups before leaving the Opposition in 1932.

**Trilisser, M.:** Old Bolshevik and a GPU official.

**Tseretelli, I.** (1882-1959): Russian Menshevik who held posts in the Provisional Government but emigrated in 1919.

**Uglanov, N.** (1886-193?): Old Bolshevik and civil war veteran; secretary of the Moscow party organization and a member of the CC Secretariat from 1924; he supported Bukharin in 1928-29 and was eliminated from the leadership in 1930.

**Ustryalov, N.** (1890-    ?): Member of the Cadet Party who fought on the White side in the civil war; after the victory of the Bolsheviks he went to work for the Soviet government as an economist because he believed it would inevitably be compelled to restore capitalism.

**Vaganyan:** See **Ter-Vaganyan.**

**Valentinov, G.:** Former editor in chief of *Trud,* the trade union publication; Oppositionist, exiled in 1928 to Ust-Kulom.

**Vardin, I.** (1890-1943): Old Bolshevik and leader of the Saratov party and soviets in 1917; a Zinovievist; capitulated shortly after his expulsion from the party in December 1927.

**Varga, E.** (1879-1964): A Hungarian Social Democrat and economist who joined the CP in 1920 and became a Comintern functionary.

**Voroshilov, K.** ("Klim") (1881-1969): Old Bolshevik and Stalin supporter; member of the Politburo from 1926; commissar of war (1925-30).

**Vujović, V.** (1895-    ?): Yugoslav Communist; a founder of the Communist Youth International (1919) and its general secretary (1922-26); elected to the ECCI as a youth representative (1924); a supporter of Zinoviev and a participant in the United Opposition; expelled from the Comintern (September 1927); capitulated in 1929.

**Walecki, H.** (1877-1937): Leader of the left wing within the Polish Socialist Party, then a leading member of the new Polish CP in 1918; PCP representative to the Comintern from 1921; a Comintern functionary from then until his death; removed from the leadership of the PCP in 1924; became editor of *Communist International* (1925); from 1928 to 1935 he worked in the Balkan Secretariat under Bela Kun.

**War communism:** Harsh economic policies that prevailed during the civil war, including requisitioning needed supplies and nationalizations, required to win the military struggle; replaced by the NEP in 1921.

**Warski, A.** (1868-1937): A founder of the Polish Social Democracy and a member of the Russian party's CC from 1906; helped found the Polish CP (1918); active in the work of the ECCI (1921-24); supported the Stalin faction, but was removed from his posts in 1924; elected Communist deputy to the Polish parliament (1926); took refuge in the USSR in 1929.

**Wrangel officer:** A GPU agent introduced into the Left Opposition at the end of 1927 in an attempt to discredit the Opposition through its alleged association with White forces; so named because he was masquerading as an officer of Pyotr Wrangel (1878-1928), White Guard general who was the last commander in chief of the counterrevolutionary forces in the civil war; defeated in autumn 1920 by the Red Army.

**Yakovlev, V.:** A Moscow party committee member and a Bukharinist.

**Yakovlev, Ya.** (1896-1939): A right-winger in the Ukrainian CP after the revolution; became an ardent supporter of Stalin against the Left Opposition and was made commissar of agriculture; he was also deputy president of the Workers and Peasants Inspection.

**Yaroslavsky, E.** (1878-1943): Old Bolshevik and Stalinist; member of the presidium of the CCC and coauthor of the official charges brought against Trotsky in July 1927.

**Zetkin, K.** (1857-1933): Veteran of the German labor movement and a founder, theoretician, and activist of the women's movement; a Communist deputy in the Reichstag from 1920; served as a member of the ECCI and lived in Russia after the left wing took over the German CP leadership in 1924; she took part in enlarged ECCI plenums in 1925, 1926, and 1927.

**Zimmerwald-Kienthal:** Swiss villages, the sites of two antiwar conferences in 1915 and 1916; most of the participants were centrists and pacifists; Lenin led a minority that constituted the Zimmerwald Left, a step toward the Third International.

**Zinoviev, G.** (1883-1936): Old Bolshevik CC member, initially opposed to the October insurrection; head of the Comintern (1919-26); after Lenin's death blocked with Stalin against Trotsky until late 1925; formed the Leningrad Opposition (1925); in 1926, he and Kamenev joined with Trotsky to form the United Opposition; expelled in 1927; recanted almost at once and was readmitted to the party in mid-1928.

# Further Reading

The following works contain materials by Trotsky written during the fourteen months covered by this volume, relating directly or indirectly to the Left Opposition's activities or positions (all are published or distributed by Pathfinder Press unless otherwise indicated):

*The Stalin School of Falsification.* 1971. "On the Origins of the Legend of 'Trotskyism' " (January 3, 1928).

*Leon Trotsky on China.* 1976. "Three Letters to Preobrazhensky" (March-April); "Summary and Perspectives of the Chinese Revolution (June); "Democratic Slogans in China" (October); "The Chinese Question After the Sixth Congress" (October 4); "China and the Constituent Assembly" (December).

*Leon Trotsky on Britain.* 1973. "A Balance Sheet of the Anglo-Russian Committee" (June).

*The Third International After Lenin.* 1972. "The Draft Program of the Communist International—A Criticism of Fundamentals" (June 28); "What Now?" (July 12).

*My Life.* 1970. A letter to several comrades (August).

*The Permanent Revolution.* 1969. The key part of the book was written in October 1928; the rest was finished in 1929.

Among the works Trotsky wrote after he was forced to leave the USSR which contain important material about 1928 are the following:

*The Case of Leon Trotsky.* 1969.

*Diary in Exile 1935.* Harvard University Press, 1976.

*My Life.* 1970.

*Portraits, Political and Personal.* 1977.

*The Revolution Betrayed.* 1972.

*Stalin: An Appraisal of the Man and His Influence.* 2 vols., London: Panther, 1969.

*Writings of Leon Trotsky (1929-40).* 12 vols. plus 2-part supplement. 1969-79.

# INDEX

*(Page references in italics indicate glossary entries.)*

Adler, V., 256, *411g*

Agrarian question, 215, 349-51, 352-60

Alexinsky, G., 186, *411g*

Alfonso (Indonesian delegate to the Sixth Congress), 213

Alsky, M., 37, 102

Amsterdam International, 257, 313, *411g*

Anarchism, 41, 280, 302-03, 316

Andreev, A., 381, 387

Anglo-American antagonism, 48-49, 52

Anglo-Russian Committee, 41, 61, 62, 63, 89, 133, 145, 362, *411g*

Anti-Imperialist League, 212, 215, *411g*

Antonov-Ovseenko, V., 76, 91, 96, 108, 114, *411g*

"April Theses" (Lenin), 61

Army, 275

Artemovsk case, 110, 115, 141, 149, 218, *411g*

Article 58 (Soviet Penal Code), 30, 142, 143, 149, 150, 154, 159, 161, 246, 249, 331, 337, 343, 366, *411g*

Article 107 (Soviet Penal Code), 169, 171, 172, 239, 307, *411g*

Ashkinazi, S., 179, *411g*

Astrov, V., 385, 388

AUCP (All-Union Communist Party), 135-36, 219-20, 310-11, 314, 317, 319, 334, 368, 384, *411g*; Tenth Congress (Mar. 1921), 144; Eleventh Congress (Mar. 1922), 279; Twelfth Congress (Apr. 1923), 137, 355; Fourteenth Congress (Dec. 1925), 245, 328; Fifteenth Congress (Dec. 1927), 29, 31, 35, 94, 148, 230, 355, 370; Sixteenth Congress (June 1930), 151, 153, 161, 249, 340, 344; regime in, 30, 144-45, 153, 182-83, 246, 292-300

Austria, 32, 33, 255, 313

Bakunin, M., 396

"Balabolkin" (Bukharin), 270, 272, 277, 340, *411g*

Bauer, O., 190, 359, *411g*

Bauman, K., 123

Bebel, A., 211, 256, *411g*

Belgium, 38-39, 41, 254

Beloborodov, A., 37, 68, 87, 102, 121, 164, 245, *411g*

Benes, E., 189, *411g*

Bernstein, E., 231, *412g*

Black Hundreds, 273, *412g*

Blanqui, L., 58, *412g*

Bleskov-Zatonsky case, 88, 99-100, 102-03, 128

"Bloc of four classes," 196

Blum, L., 78, *412g*

Bolshevik-Leninists. *See* Left Opposition

Bolshevik Party, 90; in 1917, 60, 348, *412g*. *See also* AUCP

Bonaparte, Napoleon I, 270, 315, *412g*

Bonaparte, Napoleon III, 275, *412g*

Bonapartism, 270, 274-75, 319, *412g*

Bordiga, A., 254, 256, *412g*

Borodai, 292, *412g*

Borodin, M., 193, *412g*

Bourgeoisie: domestic, 143, 261, 305-06, 307, 311, 320; international, 33, 117

Brandler, H., 186, 188, 189, 207,

210, 254, 256, *412g*

Brest-Litovsk Treaty (1918), 110, 113, 148, 157, 163, *412g*

Britain, 32, 33, 34, 76, 78, 89-90, 313, 348, 349, 350; CP, 90, 162; General Strike (1926), 61, 70, 89, 91, 212, 259, 260. *See also* Anglo-Russian Committee; General Council; Labour Party

Bronstein, N., 110, 117, 127, 131, 364

Bronstein, Z., 118, 364

Bubnov, A., 271, 276, *412-13g*

Budenny, S., 271, 275, *413g*

Bukharin, N., 121, 151, 164, 175, 209, 226, 270-71, 294, 334, 352, 369, 396, 400, *413g*; and Comintern, 92, 93, 166, 181, 202-04, 213-14, 252, 253, 254-55, 262, 264, 273, 354-55, 382; vs. Stalin, 122, 123, 125, 308-09, 315, 377-88; meeting with Kamenev, 167, 270, 272, 337-38, 340, 343, 377-88

Bulgaria, 32, 34, 76, 91, 190, 362

Bureaucracy, 305, 308, 311-15, 320, 391-94

Bureaucratic apparatus, 240, 244, 251, 271, 272-73, 275, 277, 278, 288, 293-94, 307, 308, 310-11, 314, 319, 364; violence of, 35, 138, 282

Butov, G., 118, 365, *413g*

Cadets (Constitutional Democrats), 194, *413g*

Canton uprising (Dec. 1927, China), 33, 58-59, 76-77, 113, 154, 164, *412g*

*Capital* (Marx), 398-401

Capitalism, stabilization of, 32, 33, 47-48, 133, 213-14

Capitulators, 39, 64-65, 68, 104, 148, 157, 175, 177, 251, 278, 370

Central Committee (of AUCP), 132, 144; plenums: Feb. 1927, 107, 139-40; August 1927, 268-69; April 1928, 121, 123; July 1928, 166-75, 176, 179-80, 252, 268, 271, 276-77, 287, 295, 299, 303, 337, 378; Nov. 1928, 270, 271, 338, 341, 343, 371

Central Control Commission (of AUCP), 128, 244-45, 272

Centrism, 139-40, 142, 157, 160, 163, 176, 177, 211, 258, 271, 275-78, 287-88, 290, 296-99, 301-35, 336-43, 363, 364-65, 367-72, *413g. See also* Stalin faction

Centrosoyuz (Central Union of Consumer Credit Societies), 176, 177, 179, 180, 218, 245, *413g*

Chamberlain, A., 116, *413g*

Chernov, M., 307, *413g*

Chiang Kai-shek, 61, 160, 196, 206, 215, *413g*

China, 49, 237, 259; defeat in (1927), 32, 33, 34, 42, 76, 78, 89, 133, 145, 219, 260, 351, 362, 387; CP strategy in, 58-59, 61, 77, 90, 195-96, 215, 313; Ninth ECCI on (Feb. 1928), 109, 113, 161-62, 164; and Sixth Congress (July 1928), 214-15

Chubar, V., 225, 233, *413g*

*Civil War in France* (Marx), 58

Clemenceau thesis, 100, *414g*

Comintern (Communist International), 33, 41-42, 182-211, 212-20, 253, 363, *414g*; 1922 draft program, 45, 88, 90-91; 1928 draft program, 110, 119, 122, 127, 129-30, 134, 152-54, 157, 162, 213, 219, 262, 286, 367; Third Congress (1921), 185, 187, 253; Fifth Congress (1924), 48, 62, 130, 133-34, 153, 154, 161, 230, 253, 254; Sixth Congress (1928), 30, 33, 36, 45, 75-76, 110, 119, 122, 130, 132-36, 150-65, 178, 180, 191, 204, 209, 212-20, 250-64, 272-73, 297, 324, 336, 367-68; regime in, 30-31, 71, 91, 133-34, 153, 181, 313. *See also* ECCI

Communist League of Youth, 126, 253, 272, 297, 383, 387

*Communist Manifesto* (Marx and Engels), 349

Communist Party of Soviet Union. *See* AUCP

Concessions policy, 255, 232-33

Conciliationism, 39-40, 54, 87, 177-

78, 179, 252, 265, 266, 268, 271, 291, 307, 332, 344-46, 367-72
Congresses of Soviet Communist Party. *See* AUCP
*Contre le courant* (French Opposition journal), 38, 40, 44, 47, *414g*
Critical support to "left turn," 70-71, 75, 80, 177-78, 179, 180, 295, 304
Czechoslovakia, 189-90, 287, 313; Left Opposition in, 41, 255

Darwinism, 397-98, 399
Democratic Centralist group, 108, 179, 250, 261, 276, 280, 281, 283, 289, 290-91, 292-300, 337, 338, 344-45, 370, *414g*
"Democratic dictatorship" (of the proletariat and peasantry), 62, 76, 90, 130, 158, 214-15, 317
"Democratic revolution," 164-65, 268, 347-51, 352, 356, 358-59
Dialectics, 203, 260, 313, 393, 396-98
Dictatorship of the proletariat, 215, 237, 314, 347-51, 393-94
Dneprostroi, 226-29, 234, 239, *414g*
Drozdov, 68, 156
Dual power, 93, 260, 273, 282, 294-95, 316
Dzerzhinsky, F., 232, 387, *414g*

Eastman, M., 221-24, *414g*
EECI (Executive Committee of the Comintern), 133-34, 262; Seventh Plenum (Dec. 1926), 92, 199, 354, 355, 358; Ninth Plenum (Feb. 1928), 75, 93, 109, 113, 134, 154, 161, 162, 257
Economic difficulties (USSR), 34-35, 77-78, 79-80, 133, 134, 136, 137, 145, 353-55
Economism, 195, *414g*
1848 revolution, 349
Eltsin, B., 265, *414g*
Eltsin, V., 37, 68, *414g*
Emancipation of Labor group, 195, *414g*
Engels, F., 76, 207, 231, 239, 256, 349, 396-97, 399, 404, *414-15g*

England. *See* Britain
Estonia, 32, 76, 91, 154, 362
Ewert, A., 385, 387
"Extraordinary measures," 166-68, 175, 235, 236, 377, 381, 382

Faction vs. party. *See* "Second party"
February revolution (1917), 62, 76, 348, 356, *415g*
February "left turn." See "Left turn"
Finland, 190-91, 255
Fischer, R., 38, 39, 48, 50, 88, 111, 152, 154, 254, *415g*
Foreign-trade monopoly, 136, 171, 172, 173, 327, 385
France, 33, 78, 254, 313, 349, 350; Left Opposition in, 38, 40, 44, 95; spring 1928 elections in, 101, 102, 111
Frumkin, M., 226, 247, 367, 369, 385, 387, *415g*
Frunze, M., 192, *415g*

General Council (of British Trades Union Congress), 70, 90, 212, 257, 259, 362, *415g*
Germany, 33, 34, 254, 312-13, 349, 351; Left Opposition in, 38, 39, 40, 88, 95, 109, 111-12, 152; Social Democracy in, 109-12, 312-13, 314, 373; 1918 revolution, 61, 284; 1921 events, 185, 188; 1923 events, 32, 47-48, 76, 91, 133, 145, 188, 189, 207, 259, 260, 362; May 1928 elections in, 109, 111-12
Girault, S., 38, 40, 41, 254, *415g*
Glazman, M., 118, *415g*
Goethe, J., 192-93
Gosizdat (State Publishing House), 72, 73, *415g*
GPU (Soviet secret police), 30, 35, 39, 88, 225, 361, 364-65, 373, 382
Grain collections crisis, 34, 56-58, 60, 89, 92-94, 97-98, 129, 168-69, 170, 318, 352, 354, 355, 356, 357, 386. *See also* "Extraordinary measures"

Griunshtein, K. and R., 67, 179, 181, 245
Guralsky, 191, 192, 193
Gusev, S., 232, 234, 310

Habsburg monarchy, 255
Hegel, G., 397, 403
*Herr Vogt* (Marx), 50, 52, 69, 72
Hilferding, R., 401 ˙
Holland, 41
Hungary, 184-85

Immanent idealism, 314-15, 393
Independent Labour Party (Britain), 212
India, 49, 52, 76, 84, 90, 113, 200, 215
Industrialization controversy, 169-71, 234, 236, 237, 265, 271, 327, 330, 355
Institute of Red Professors, 167, 196
International Opposition, 38-45, 94-95, 105, 109-11, 154-55, 284; candidates of, competing with Communist Party candidates in Western Europe, 43, 88, 95, 111, 146. *See also* Leninbund; "Second party"
Internationalism, 32, 47-49, 76, 137-38, 216, 250, 258-62, 283, 285, 306, 313, 324-26, 353, 403
Ishchenko, A., 37, 55, 64, 68, 367, 370
*Iskra,* 195
Italy, 254

Jacobins (France), 315, 321, *415g*
Jacquemotte, J., 254, 255, *415g*
Japan, 76, 90, 113, 200-01
Jaurès, J., 256, *415g*
July plenum. *See* Central Committee, July 1928 plenum

Kaganovich, L., 120, 123, 228, 272, 309, 315, 379, 380, 381, 387, *415g*
Kalinin, M., 166, 245, 270, 271, 369, 378, 381, 386, *415g*
Kamenev, L., 39, 61, 62, 76, 95, 108, 121, 122, 125, 151, 176, 177, 245, 274, 298, *415g*; in 1917, 158, 164; meeting with Bukharin, 167, 270, 337-38, 340, 343, 377-88; meeting with Moscow Trotskyists, 270, 278, 377
Karolyi, M., 185, *416g*
Kasparova, V., 37, 46, 68, 176, 290
Katayama, S., 200, *416g*
Kautsky, K., 185, *416g*
Kavtaradze, S., 37
Kemal Ataturk, 373-74, 375
Kerensky, A., 274, *416g*
Kerzhentsev, 310
Kirov, S., 123, *416g*
Klyuchevsky, 310
Kolarov, V., 190, 202, *416g*
Komarov, N., 381, 387
Kornilov, L., 264, *416g*
Korsch, K., 111, 283, *416g*
Kramar, K., 189, *416g*
Krestinsky, N., 76, 91, 95-96, 114, 216, *416g*
Kritsman, L., 385, 388
*Krokodil* (Soviet satirical magazine), 336, 343
Krzhizhanovsky, G., 310, *416g*
Kudymkor events, 156
Kuibyshev, V., 151, 166
Kulaks, 34-35, 77-78, 79-80, 92, 140, 159, 167, 170, 275, 314, 317-18, 319, 354-55, 382, *416g*
Kun, B., 184-85, *416g*
Kuomintang, 52, 61, 62, 77, 78, 90, 113, 164, 196, 214, 307, *416g*
Kustanai events, 156
Kuusinen, O., 190-91, 197, 202, 210, 214, 234, 240, 250, 252, 255, *416g*

Labour Party (Britain), 162, *416g*
La Follette, R., 154, 185, *416-17g*
Lapinsky, S., 216, *417g*
Laplace, P., 353, *417g*
Larin, Yu., 310, *417g*
Lashevich, M., 44, *417g*
Lassalle, F. 349, 405, *417g*
Leadership: crisis of, 31, 80, 256,

260, 261; methods of, 109, 112, 114-15, 153
Left Opposition (Bolshevik-Leninists), 125; and bloc with centrists, 277, 278, 287-88; and bloc with right wing, 226, 249, 336-43; and bloc with Zinoviev and Kamenev, 50, 51, 60, 63, 87, 114, 130, 152-53, 268, 269, 277, 340; slogans, 31, 36, 90, 153, 156, 160-61, 248-49, 271, 281-82, 288-89, 304, 339-40, 344-46; strength in party, 251-52; tasks, 262-64, 179-80, 284, 296, 332, 338. *See also* International Opposition
"Left turn" (February 1928), 70, 75, 77-81, 87, 96-100, 106, 113, 114, 128, 143, 151, 154, 166, 168-69, 193, 250, 251, 257-58, 268, 286, 287, 289, 290, 295; February 15, 1928, *Pravda* editorial on, 55-58, 140, 159, 160, 169, 170, 174, 219-20, 257, 303
Lenin, V.I., 91, 190, 193, 202-03, 205-06, 232, 242, 250, 301, 323, 324-26, 390, 401, 402, 404, 407-08, *417g*; in 1917, 60, 61, 62, 158, 164-65, 348; and minority rights, 31, 253, 254-55, 256; on party leadership, 109, 114-15, 256; on permanent revolution, 287; on *smychka*, 352; on Bukharin, 203; on Kamenev, 164-65; on Kun, 185; on Lozovsky, 198; on Martynov, 193; on Pyatakov, 65; on Safarov, 105; on Smeral, 189, 255; on Stalin, 221, 365; on Zetkin, 188; on Zinoviev, 62-63; Testament of, 31, 37, 203, 221, 222-23, 308, 365, *417g*
Leninbund, 38, 88, 95, 109, 111-12, *417g*
Leningrad Opposition, 245, 328. *See also* Zinoviev group
Lentsner, 196-97
Leninism, 390, 394-95, 396, 401-09
Lesoil, L., 39
Levi, P., 188, *417g*
Livshits, B., 195, *417g*
Loriot, F., 254, 256, *417g*

Lozovsky, S., 125-26, 197-98, 202, *417g*
Lukács, G., 400
Luxemburg, R., 187, 188, *417g*
Lyadov, M., 61, 234, 310, *417-18g*
Lyova. *See* Sedov, L.

McCulloch, J.R., 72
MacDonald, R., 78, *418g*
Malakhov faction, 212, 218, 244-45
Malyuta, V., 37
Mandelstamm, N., 323, *418g*
Manuilsky, D., 186, 189, 210, 216, 234, 235, 250, 252, 253-54, *418g*
Maretsky, G., 157, 163, *418g*
Martov, L., 187
Martynov, A., 93, 164, 193-96, 197, 201, 202, 206, 210, 214, 215, 240, 255, 258, 310, *418g*
Marx, K., 50, 52, 58, 69, 72, 205, 207, 256, 322, 390, 396-98, 404, 405, 407, 408-09, *418g*; on permanent revolution, 347, 349-51, 358
Marxism, 227, 256, 390, 394-409
Maslow, A., 38, 39, 40, 48, 50, 51, 88, 154, 155, 186, 254
"Master," 88. *See* Stalin
Materialism, 393, 396, 397-99
Mekhlis, L., 270, 272, *418g*
Maxton, J., 212, 215
Mensheviks, 31, 36, 90, 193, 313, 359, 363, 409, *418g*
Mikoyan, A., 356, 378
Mill, J.S., 72
Moiseyenko, 224
Molotov, V., 121, 155, 166, 228, 229, 270, 271, 272, 297, 301, 302, 314, 328, 378-79, 380, 382, 384, *418g*
Monatte, P., 38, 40, 41, 43, 44, 254, 256, *418g*
Monism, 392, 394
Mrachkovsky, S., 51, 68, 254, *418g*
Müller, H., 373
Multiple-factor theory, 390, 391-94
Muralov, N., 32, 37, 40, 44, 46, 53, 68, 69, 221, 245

Narodniks, 85, 195, 409, *419g*

Narodolyuby (Friends of the People), 167, 169, 228
*Nashe Slovo* group, 198
Natalya. *See* Sedova, N.
*Nation* (U.S.), 116
Naumov, I., 105
Nechaev, 102
NEP (New Economic Policy), 136, 166, 173, 195, 357, 379, *419g*
Neumann, H., 189, *419g*
Neurath, A., 41, *419g*
Nevelson, M., 37, 117, 287-88, *419g*
Nikolaev, 85-86
Nina. *See* Bronstein, N.
1905 revolution, 78, 90, 194, 195, 241, 290, 351, *419g*
"Notes of an Economist" (Bukharin), 271, 273, 318

October Revolution (1917), 358, *419g*
Okudzhava, M., 104
Olminsky, M., 348
Opposition. *See* Left Opposition; International Opposition
Ordzhonikidze, G., 384, 387, *419g*
Osinsky, V., 297, *419g*
Otzovists, 290, 291
Overstraeten, E. van, 39, 254, 256, *419g*

Paris Commune, 58, 78, *419g*
Party budget, 153, 161, 339, 344
Party congresses. *See* AUCP
Party democracy, 35, 132, 143-44, 153, 160, 339
Party vs. faction. *See* "Second party"
Peasant parties, 214
"Peasant philosophers," 226, 247, 248
Peasantry, 234, 236, 247, 317, 349-51, 352-60, 382, 385
Peasants' International (Krestintern), 215, *416g*
People's Will group, 85
Pepper, J., 184-85, 186, 189, 193, 202, 206, 210, 234, *419-20g*
Permanent revolution, 187, 194, 197, 241, 266, 268, 286, 287, 326-27, 347-51, 358-59
Petersburg Union of Struggle, 195
Petlyura, S., 192, 255, *420g*
Petrovsky, D., ("Bennet"), 191-92, 193, 202, 206, 210, 215, 309, 310, *420g*
Petty bourgeoisie, 305, 311-14, 318-20, 322, 334. *See also* Peasantry
Pilsudski, J., 187, 188, 314, 362, *420g*
Poland, 33, 34, 187, 314, 362
Postnikov, 126
Poznansky, 74, 118, 364
Preobrazhensky, Ye., 37, 44, 68, 69, 79, 84, 85, 110, 121, 125, 157, 164, 176, 245, 370, 378, 380, 386, *420g*; proposal for conference, 101-03, 127, 128; appeal to Sixth Congress, 127, 129
Proudhon, P., 58, *420g*
Provisional Government (1917), 60, *420g*
Purcell, A., 78, 160, 206, 212, 215, 259, *420g*
Putilov works, 229-30, 231
Pyatakov, Yu., 38, 44, 64-65, 68, 76, 80, 89, 90, 108, 114, 121, 125, 177, 179, 180, 298, 367, 370, *420g*
Pyatnitsky, O., 212, 219, 253, 256, *420g*

Radek, K., 32, 37, 40, 44, 46, 68, 121, 125, 176-77, 202, 255, 286, 370, 389, *420g*; on China, 109, 110, 113, 161, 164, 215; on left course, 157, 268; on Opposition candidates (in Western Europe), 95, 111, 113; on Thermidor, 162-63, 268-69; theses to Sixth Congress, 157-65
Radić, S., 154, *420-21g*
Rafail, R., 299-300, *421g*
Rafes, M., 191, 192, 193, 210, 255, 310, *421g*
Rakovsky, Kh., 32, 37, 40, 44, 46, 59, 65, 67, 68-69, 84, 98, 102, 125, 128, 153, 177, 186, 245, 255, 267, *421g*; letter on bureaucracy, 114-

15, 250, 261

Raskolnikov, F., 199-200, *421g*

Reaction, period of, 304-05, 307, 310-11

Reed, J., 221, 222, *421g*

Red International of Labor Unions (RILU), 45, 121, 125, 197, 198, *421g*

Renner, K., 189, 255, *421g*

Ricardo, D., 72-73

Right-center split, 120-26, 142, 155, 161, 176, 177, 217, 219-20, 250, 265, 271-78, 287, 295-96, 301-35, 336-43, 363, 367-72

Right wing, 87-88, 98-100, 106, 139-40, 151, 166-75, 175, 211, 270-78, 288, 295

Rosengauz, 153

Rosmer, A., 38, 40, 41, 43, 254, 256, *421g*

Roy, M.N., 200, *421g*

Rozanov, 154

Rudzutak, Ya., 166, 225, 232, 239, *421g*

Ryazanov, D., 50, 72, *421g*

Rykov, A., 87, 93, 121, 122, 123, 226, 230, 271, 273, 308-09, 334, 338, 369, *421g*; in 1917, 174, 308; and July plenum, 166-75, 355, 379, 380, 381, 382, 383

Rykov faction. *See* Right wing

Ryutin, M., 123, *421g*

Safarov, G., 39, 54, 55, 104-06, 113, 125, 127, 129, 181, 248, 259, 261, 262, 297, 370, *421-22g*

Saltykov, M. ("Shchedrin"), 110, 113, 167, *421-22g*

Sapronov, T., 292, 298, *422g*

Sarkis, 370

Scissors crisis, 355-57, 378, 386

Second International, 256, 404, 405, *422g*

"Second party," 35-36, 38, 41-43, 46, 75, 79, 88, 93, 94-95, 146, 148, 219-20, 266, 269, 293, 300

Secret ballot, 271, 281-83, 368

Sedov, L. (Lyova), 47, 53, 266, *422g*

Sedov, S. (Seryozha), 102, *422g*

Sedova, N., 47, 69, 102, 117, 178, 181, *422g*

"Self-criticism," 51, 97, 99, 128, 132, 145-46, 153, 159-60, 232, 244, 252, 281, 283, 296, 301, 303, 306, 327-28, 339, 341, 345, 380

Sémard, P., 254, 255, 384, 387, *422g*

Septemvirate, 151, 153, 227, *422g*

Serebryakov, L., 37, 53, 68, 125, 266, *422g*

Sermuks, 68, 118, 364

Shakhty case, 87, 89, 96, 115, 121, 141, 149, 218, 330, 380, 386-87, *422g*

Shatskin, L., 126, *422g*

Shatunovsky, 225

Shestakov, 231

Shlyapnikov, A., 292, 300, *422g*

Shvarts, 157, 159, *422g*

Sibiryakov (Vilensky), 37, 53

Sklyansky, 192

Skvortsov-Stepanov, I., 325-26, *422-23g*

Slepkov, A., 122-23, 261, 309, *423g*

Smeral, B., 189-90, 255, *423g*

Smerdyakov, 108, *423g*

Smilga, I., 32, 37, 40, 44, 54, 68, 101, 143, 157, 370, *423g*

Smirnov, I., 37, 46, 60, 67, 121, 125, 153, 176, 245, 317, *423g*

Smirnov, V., 179, 250, 283, 289, 344, 345, *423g*; letter of, 259-62, 281, 291, 298

Smolensk case, 104, 107, 115, 141, 149, 218, 284, *423g*

*Smychka*, 172, 173, 234-36, 317, 352-60, *423g*

Social Democracy, 45, 90, 214, 303, 312-14, 316; and fascism, 116-17, 133; on Opposition, 116, 117, 257; postwar revival of, 32, 48, 217, 257, 283-84

"Social fascism," 109-10, 116-17

"Socialism in one country," 32, 133, 162, 186, 206, 216, 307, 324-27, 352, 390, 402

Socialist Revolutionaries (SRs), 36, 171, 280, *423g*

Society of Old Bolsheviks, 241

Sokolnikov, G., 98, 327, 377, 378, 382, 384, 385, *423g*

Sokolovskaya, A., 85, *423g*

Sosnovsky, L., 37, 46, 54, 60, 67, 99, 102, 110, 128, *423g*

Southern Russian Workers Union, 85, 86

Souvarine, B., 38, 41, 106, 254, 256, *424g*

Soviet Communist Party. *See* AUCP

Soviet state, class character of, 34, 38, 43, 94, 306, 314, 317

Stalin, J., 96, 151, 160, 186, 204-08, 241, 258, 270, 297, 327, 343, 352, 394-402, 404-06; in 1917, 60, 207, 310, 348; and "Trotskyism," 44, 155, 208, 322, 364-65, 369; vs. right wing, 120-22, 168, 172-73, 226, 247, 265, 271-72, 301, 302, 307, 309, 321-23, 324, 377-88

Stalin faction ("centrists"), 42-43, 240, 244, 248, 274, 297, 311, 313, 332, 364-65, 368-72, 377-88. *See also* Centrism

Sten, I., 309, *424g*

Stetsky, A., 123, 381, 385, 387, *424g*

Stolypin, P., 194, 215

Strike, right to, 279

Suhl group, 40, 112, 218

Svyatopolk-Mirsky, P., 88, 99

Syrtsov, S., 121, *424g*

Tactics, 406-07

T'an P'ing-shan, 199, *424g*

Tenth-anniversary demonstration (Nov. 1927), 31, 88, 96

Teplov, 176, 290

Ter-Vaganyan, V., 37, 55, *424g*

Tesnyaki, 190

Thälmann, E., 155, 186, 254, 255, 384, 384-85, 387, *424g*

Thermidor, 34, 36, 42, 94, 105, 116, 139-40, 146, 158, 162-63, 175, 226, 268-69, 271, 273, 274-75, 294, 297, 300, 307, 314, 316, 318-20, 320-28, 334, 337, 338, *424g*

Tilsit peace (1807), 157, 163

Timofeyev, 68

Togliatti, P., ("Ercoli"), 255, *415g*

Tomsky, M., 87, 125, 151, 226, 271, 273, 308-09, 315, 378, 380, 381, 382, 383, 385, *424g*

Transitional demands, 162, 214, 215, 282, 344-45

Treint, A., 38, 40, 41, 95, 254, *424g*

Trilisser, M., 381, *424g*

Trotsky, L.: health of, 111, 117, 156, 265, 286; deportation of, 361, 373-74

"Trotskyism," 38, 40, 44, 105, 130, 132, 153, 173, 174, 185, 187, 190, 194-95, 198, 228, 230, 234, 239, 306-07

Tseitlin, Ye., 383, 387

Tseretelli, I., 206, 264, *424g*

Two-class parties. *See* "Workers' and peasants' parties"

Two parties. *See* "Second party"

Ugarov, F., 381, 387

Uglanov, N., 123, 265, 266-67, 272, 301, 309, 320, 334, 338, 339, 380, 381, *424g*

Uneven development, law of, 170, 207, 402

United Opposition bloc (1926-27), 50, 51, 60, 63, 87, 114, 130, 152-53, 268, 269, 277, 340

United States, 48-49, 91, 133, 185, 262, 284

Urbahns, H., 38

Uspensky, G., 181

Ustryalov, N., 75, 78, 79, 93-94, 99, 106, 169, 264, 302, 303, 310, 333, *424-25g*

Vaganyan. *See* Ter-Vaganyan

Valentinov, G., 37, 68, 99, 100, 102, 250, 261, *425g*

Vardin, I., 54, 55, 127, 128, 177, 181, *425g*

Varga, E., 184-86, 216, 250, 384, 387, *425g*

Vinogradskaya, P., 83

Vitte, V., 85

Volinsky, 361

Voroshilov, K., 124-25, 126, 166,

270, 271, 275, 334, 369, 378, 381, 386, *425g*
Vrachev, 68, 111
Vujović, V., 254, *425g*

Walecki, H., 187, 202, *425g*
War communism, 166, 168, 235, 382, 387, *425g*
Warski, A., 187-88, *425g*
Workers' and Peasants' Inspection, 301, 318
"Workers' and peasants' parties," 76, 90, 154, 162, 206, 214, 220, 307, 317
Workers' Opposition, 292
Wrangel officer, 31, 142, 225, 236, 246, 337, *425g*

Yagoda, H., 381
Yakovlev, V., 91, *425g*
Yakovlev, Ya., 301, 318, 356, *425g*
Yaroslavsky, E., 122, 127, 128, 177, 232, 243, 244, 248, 278, 339, *425g*
Yudin, 104

Yudushka Golovlyov, 167, 174
Yushkin, 68

Zasulich, V., 347-48
Zetkin, K., 188-89, 200, *425-26g*
Zhordania, 348
Zimmerwald-Kienthal, 206, *426g*
Zinoviev, G., 39, 80, 96-97, 108, 121, 122, 151, 176, 177, 179, 186, 230, 245, 248, 271, 370, 396, 400, *426g*; and Bukharin, 91, 125, 272, 377-88; character of, 61-63; on China, 59, 60, 61-62; and Comintern, 130, 153, 197, 202, 253, 254; and Democratic Centralists, 94, 298; in 1917, 158; and "Trotskyism," 44, 105, 153, 174, 247, 269
Zinoviev group, 180-81; and bloc with Left Opposition, 50, 51, 60, 63, 87, 114, 130, 152-53, 268, 269, 277, 340; evolution of, 113-14, 121, 368; Jan. 1928 letter to *Pravda*, 46, 47, 50, 51, 54-55, 60. *See also* Leningrad Opposition

# Also from Pathfinder

## Imperialism's March toward Fascism and War

JACK BARNES

How the working class and its allies respond to the accelerated capitalist disorder will determine whether or not imperialism's march toward fascism and war can be stopped. In *New International* no. 10. $14.00

## To Speak the Truth

Why Washington's 'Cold War' against Cuba Doesn't End

FIDEL CASTRO AND CHE GUEVARA

In historic speeches before the United Nations and its bodies, Guevara and Castro address the workers of the world, explaining why the U.S. government is determined to destroy the example set by the socialist revolution in Cuba and why its effort will fail. $16.95

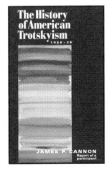

## The History of American Trotskyism

JAMES P. CANNON

"Trotskyism is not a new movement, a new doctrine," Cannon says, "but the restoration, the revival of genuine Marxism as it was expounded and practiced in the Russian revolution and in the early days of the Communist International." In this series of twelve talks given in 1942, James P. Cannon recounts an important chapter in the efforts to build a proletarian party in the United States. $18.95

## Cosmetics, Fashions, and the Exploitation of Women

JOSEPH HANSEN, EVELYN REED, AND MARY-ALICE WATERS

How big business promotes cosmetics to generate profits and perpetuate the inferior status of women. In her introduction, Mary-Alice Waters explains how the entry of millions of women into the workforce during and after World War II irreversibly changed U.S. society and laid the basis for the advances women have won through struggle over the last three decades. $12.95

## America's Revolutionary Heritage

Marxist Essays

EDITED BY GEORGE NOVACK

Essays on the struggle by Native Americans, the first American revolution, the Civil War, the rise of industrial capitalism, and the fight for women's suffrage. $21.95

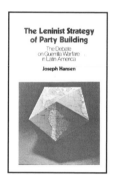

## The Leninist Strategy of Party Building

The Debate on Guerrilla Warfare in Latin America

JOSEPH HANSEN

In the 1960s and '70s, revolutionists in the Americas and throughout the world debated how to apply the lessons of the Cuban revolution to struggles elsewhere. Written with polemical clarity by a participant in that debate. $26.95

## Lenin's Final Fight

Speeches and Writings, 1922–23

V.I. LENIN

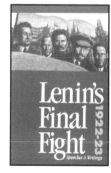

In the early 1920s Lenin waged a political battle in the leadership of the Communist Party of the USSR to maintain the course that had enabled the workers and peasants to overthrow the old tsarist empire, carry out the first successful socialist revolution, and begin building a world communist movement. The issues posed in his political fight remain at the heart of world politics today. Several items appear in English for the first time. Also available in Spanish. $19.95

# BY LEON TROTSKY

## The History of the Russian Revolution

The social, economic, and political dynamics of the first socialist revolution. The story is told by one of the revolution's principal leaders writing from exile in the early 1930s, with these historic events still fresh in his mind. Also available in Russian. Unabridged edition, 3 vols. in one. 1,358 pp. $35.95

## Trade Unions in the Epoch of Imperialist Decay

Featuring "Trade Unions: Their Past, Present, and Future" by Karl Marx "Apart from their original purposes, the trades unions must now learn to act deliberately as organizing centers of the working class in the broad interest of its complete emancipation....They must convince the world at large that their efforts, far from being narrow and selfish, aim at the emancipation of the downtrodden millions." —Karl Marx, 1866. In this book, two central leaders of the modern communist workers movement outline the fight for this revolutionary perspective. $14.95

## The Transitional Program for Socialist Revolution

Contains discussions between leaders of the U.S. Socialist Workers Party and exiled Bolshevik leader Leon Trotsky in 1938. The product of these discussions, known as the Transitional Program for socialist revolution, was first adopted at a 1938 leadership meeting of the SWP. It remains an important tool for communist workers today. $20.95

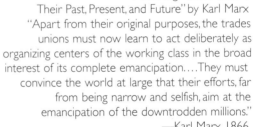

**SEE FRONT OF BOOK FOR ADDRESSES.**

# New International
### A MAGAZINE OF MARXIST POLITICS AND THEORY

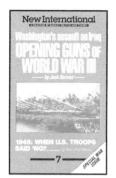

## New International no. 7
Opening Guns of World War III: Washington's Assault on Iraq *by Jack Barnes* • Communist Policy in Wartime as well as in Peacetime *by Mary-Alice Waters* • Lessons from the Iran-Iraq War *by Samad Sharif* $12.00

## New International no. 5
The Coming Revolution in South Africa *by Jack Barnes* • The Future Belongs to the Majority *by Oliver Tambo* • Why Cuban Volunteers Are in Angola *two speeches by Fidel Castro* $9.00

## New International no. 1
Their Trotsky and Ours: Communist Continuity Today *by Jack Barnes* • Lenin and the Colonial Question *by Carlos Rafael Rodríguez* • The 1916 Easter Rebellion in Ireland: Two Views *by V.I. Lenin and Leon Trotsky* $8.00

**Distributed by Pathfinder**
Many of the articles that appear in
***New International*** are also available in
Spanish in ***Nueva Internacional,*** in French
in ***Nouvelle Internationale,*** and in Swedish
in ***Ny International.***